MARK

*Images of an
Apostolic Interpreter*

Plaque depicting St. Peter dictating the Gospel to St. Mark (Negative no. 37960, by courtesy of the Board of Trustees of the Victoria & Albert Museum, London).

Mark

Images of an Apostolic Interpreter

by C. Clifton Black

University of South Carolina Press

Studies on Personalities of the New Testament
D. Moody Smith, General Editor

BS
2475
.B57
1994

Copyright © 1994 University of South Carolina

Published in Columbia, South Carolina, by the
University of South Carolina Press

Manufactured in the United States of America

Library of Congress Cataloging-in-Publication Data

Black, C. Clifton, 1955–
    Mark : images of an apostolic interpreter / C.
Clifton Black.
        p.   cm. — (Studies on personalities of the New Testament)
    Includes bibliographical references and indexes.
    ISBN 0–87249–973–1 (alk. paper)
    1. Mark, Saint. 2. Evangelists (Bible)—Biography. 3. Bible.
N.T. Mark—Criticism, interpretation, etc. 4. Fathers of the
church. I. Title. II. Series.
BS2475.B57   1994
226.3'06—dc20   93–37578
                                                              CIP

To the memory of my parents
Iris Rebecca Hill Black
(1920–1983)
and
Carl Clifton Black
(1920–1992)
ἐάν τε οὖν ζῶμεν ἐάν τε ἀποθνῄσκωμεν
τοῦ κυρίου ἐσμέν

John Mark, the cousin of St. Barnabas (Col. 4.10), a Jew, set out with St. Barnabas and St. Paul on their first missionary journey, but for reasons which failed to satisfy St. Paul turned back (Acts 12.25, 13.5, 13, 15.37f.). Afterwards he accompanied Barnabas on a mission to Cyprus (Acts 15.39), and he was in Rome with St. Paul (Col. 4.10, Philem. 24, 2 Tim. 4.11) and St. Peter (1 Pet. 5.13), whose "interpreter" (ἑρμηνευτής), acc[ording] to Papias, he was; and it was no doubt in Italy, if not at Rome itself, that he wrote his Gospel. Acc[ording] to Eusebius (*H.E.*, II.xvi.1 and xxiv.1), he afterwards went to Alexandria and was its first bishop, while in later tradition he is also associated with Venice. . . .
—*The Oxford Dictionary of the Christian Church*, 2d. ed.

Our knowledge is a little island in a great ocean of non-knowledge.
Isaac Bashevis Singer
—*The New York Times Magazine*
3 December 1978

Contents

Preface

An apt epigraph for this book could be borrowed from the French novelist Colette: "By means of an image we hold onto our lost belongings; but it is the pang of separation that forms the image, gathers the flowers of remembrance, binds the bouquet."[1] In the pages that follow I shall maintain that the personality of Mark is, in the nature of the case, irretrievable, that personage's biography impossible. This will surprise neither New Testament specialists nor patristic historians. Less predictably and more positively, I further propose that the *figure* of Mark is marvelously intricate and potentially informative for our understanding of some early Christian traditions. With the crafting of a religious image—especially the attribution of the Second Gospel to Mark—the patristic church was engaged, I suggest, in a formative process of religious memory and theological warrant, an enterprise obliquely foreshadowed in that Gospel itself. With ever widening separation, in time and culture, from their genesis in the movement begun by Jesus, early Christians found in Mark (among other figures) an image by which they could hold fast to their confessional identity and sense of religious belonging.

The investigation of these claims ramifies in different directions, inevitably leading us down several highways and byways of current biblical exegesis: historical and social scientific inquiry, narrative and epistolary analysis, the study of classical rhetoric, tradition criticism, the history of biblical and doctrinal interpretation. Latent in this methodological array is my conviction that probing early Christian images of Mark constitutes no fanciful flight from the scholarly obligation to interpret ancient texts in their historical contexts. To the contrary, our investigation will drive us straight, and sometimes uncomfortably, into the heart of that responsibility. Even so, like the other volumes in this series, this study is aimed at a general readership, interested in matters religious, which is by no means restricted to the guild of professional academicians.

While preparing this book, I have incurred many debts, impossible to repay yet gratefully acknowledged. Germinal arguments of mine were criticized, drafts of chapters were read, and bibliographical references were supplied by many friends and colleagues, notably Jouette M. Bassler, Ellen T. Charry, R. Alan Culpepper, Victor P. Furnish, Beverly R. Gaventa, and Charles M. Nielsen. William S. Babcock kindly perused a penultimate recension of the entire manuscript and offered important suggestions for the improvement of its substance and style. During the fall of 1992 an earlier version of chapter 1 was helpfully considered by two groups, the Faculty Symposium of Perkins School of Theology and the Biblical Criticism and Literary Criticism Section of the Society of Biblical Literature. Without such expert help I could scarcely have fulfilled an undertaking like this. Nevertheless, responsibility for the book's final form, and particularly for the mistakes that remain, rests squarely on my shoulders alone.

Throughout its gestation this project has received generous support from several benefactors. During an instructional leave granted by the University of Rochester in 1988 I was able to carry on substantial research, thanks to a faculty fellowship that was underwritten by the Andrew Mellon Foundation. At that time I enjoyed the academic hospitality of Colgate Rochester Divinity School / Bexley Hall / Crozer Theological Seminary, especially the ample resources of their Ambrose Swasey Library. Following a shift in my institutional affiliation to the Perkins School of Theology, Southern Methodist University, a Perkins Scholarly Outreach Award helped to sustain this project, and Dean James E. Kirby graciously granted me some unencumbered time in which to complete it. Invaluable service has been rendered to me by the able staff of Bridwell Library, above all Laura Randall and Page Thomas. The manuscript was processed, skillfully and repeatedly, by Mary Ann Marshall, who lavishes upon the work of others the meticulous care that she gives to her own. The indexes of primary references and modern authors were prepared by Harriet Black, whose labor must be categorized as beyond supererogation.

I continue to benefit immeasurably from the friendship, wise counsel, and model scholarship of the series editor, D. Moody Smith. In this, as in other academic endeavors, he encourages me more than he knows. My thanks go also to Kenneth J. Scott, director of the University of South Carolina Press, and Margaret V. Hill, managing editor of the Press, for their lively interest in this volume and its painstaking production. Of course, its completion would have been altogether impossible without the support of Harriet Fesperman Black and Caroline Elizabeth Black. Amid more than one extraordinary dislocation, my wife and daughter have created a haven in which my aspirations could flourish, charitably permitting the mysterious Mark to intrude into time and activities that rightly belonged to them. This book, nevertheless, is dedicated to two others. Harriet and Caroline, I trust, will understand the reasons—not least among which is the binding of another bouquet.

C. Clifton Black
The Feast Day of Saint Mark
23 April 1993

NOTE

1. (Sidonie-Gabrielle) Colette, *Mes Apprentissages* (1936), *Oeuvres complètes de Colette de l'Académie Goncourt* (Paris: Le Fleuron, 1949), 11:82. Here, as throughout this volume (unless otherwise indicated), my own translation is offered.

Abbreviations

AB	Anchor Bible
ABD	*Anchor Bible Dictionary*, ed. D. N. Freedman
ACNT	Augsburg Commentary on the New Testament
ANF	*The Ante-Nicene Fathers*
ANRW	*Aufstieg und Niedergang der römischen Welt*
ATR	*Anglican Theological Review*
AusBR	*Australian Biblical Review*
BAG	W. Bauer, W. F. Arndt, F. W. Gingrich, *Greek-English Lexicon of the New Testament*
BBET	Beiträge zur biblischen Exegese und Theologie
BHT	Beiträge zur historischen Theologie
Bib	*Biblica*
BJRL	*Bulletin of the John Rylands University Library of Manchester*
BNTC	Black's New Testament Commentaries
BTB	*Biblical Theology Bulletin*
BUJS	Brown University Judaic Studies
BZ	*Biblische Zeitschrift*
BZNW	Beihefte zur *Zeitschrift für die neutestamentliche Wissenschaft*
CBQ	*Catholic Biblical Quarterly*
CBQMS	Catholic Biblical Quarterly—Monograph Series
CGTC	Cambridge Greek Testament Commentary
CQR	*Church Quarterly Review*
CSRBul	*Council of Societies for the Study of Religion Bulletin*
CurTM	*Currents in Theology and Mission*
EKKNT	Evangelisch-katholischer Kommentar zum Neuen Testament
EM	Eichstätter Materialien

xvii

ETL	*Ephemerides theologicae lovanienses*
EvQ	*Evangelical Quarterly*
EvT	*Evangelische Theologie*
ExpTim	*Expository Times*
FBBS	Facet Books, Biblical Series
FFLF	Foundations and Facets: Literary Facets
FFNT	Foundations and Facets: New Testament
FRLANT	Forschungen zur Religion und Literatur des Alten und Neuen Testaments
GBSNTS	Guides to Biblical Scholarship, New Testament Series
GNTNTD	Grundrisse zum Neuen Testament, Das Neue Testament Deutsch
HNT	Handbuch zum Neuen Testament
HNTC	Harper's New Testament Commentaries
HTKNT	Herders theologischer Kommentar zum Neuen Testament
HTR	*Harvard Theological Review*
HTS	Harvard Theological Studies
HUT	Hermeneutische Untersuchungen zur Theologie
IB	*Interpreter's Bible*
IBS	*Irish Biblical Studies*
ICC	International Critical Commentary
IDB	*Interpreter's Dictionary of the Bible*, ed. G. A. Buttrick
IRT	Issues in Religion and Theology
ISBE	*International Standard Bible Encyclopedia,* rev. ed., ed. G. W. Bromiley
ITL	International Theological Library
JBL	*Journal of Biblical Literature*
JETS	*Journal of the Evangelical Theological Society*
JSNT	*Journal for the Study of the New Testament*
JSNTSup	Journal for the Study of the New Testament— Supplement Series
JTS	*Journal of Theological Studies*
LCC	Library of Christian Classics
LCL	Loeb Classical Library
LEC	Library of Early Christianity
LQ	*Lutheran Quarterly*
LSJ	Liddell-Scott-Jones, *Greek-English Lexicon*

LXX	Septuagint
MeyerK	H. A. W. Meyer, Kritisch-exegetischer Kommentar über das Neue Testament
MNTC	Moffatt New Testament Commentary
MTA	Münsteraner Theologische Abhandlungen
NCB	New Century Bible
NClB	New Clarendon Bible
NEB	New English Bible
NICNT	New International Commentary on the New Testament
NJB	New Jerusalem Bible
NovTSup	Novum Testament, Supplements
NPNF	*Nicene and Post-Nicene Fathers*
NRSV	New Revised Standard Version
NTA	*New Testament Abstracts*
NTL	New Testament Library
NTS	*New Testament Studies*
NTT	*Nederlands Theologisch Tijdschrift*
PC	Proclamation Commentaries
PG	*Patrologia graeca*, ed. J. Migne
PGC	Pelican Gospel Commentaries
PGL	*Patristic Greek Lexicon*, ed. G. W. H. Lampe
PL	*Patrologia latina*, ed. J. Migne
PRS	*Perspectives in Religious Studies*
PRSSS	Perspectives in Religious Studies—Supplement Series
PSTJ	*Perkins School of Theology Journal*
RBén	*Revue bénédictine*
RevExp	*Review and Expositor*
RNT	Regensburger Neues Testament
SAC	Studies in Antiquity and Christianity
SBLDS	Society of Biblical Literature Dissertation Series
SBLMS	Society of Biblical Literature Monograph Series
SBLSBS	Society of Biblical Literature Sources for Biblical Study
SBLSP	Society of Biblical Literature Seminar Papers
SC	Sources chrétiennes
SD	Studies and Documents

Sem	*Semeia*
SJT	*Scottish Journal of Theology*
SNTSMS	Society for New Testament Studies Monograph Series
ST	*Studia theologica*
SUNT	Studien zur Umwelt des Neuen Testaments
TDNT	*Theological Dictionary of the New Testament*, ed. G. Kittel and G. Friedrich
TS	*Theological Studies*
TU	Texte und Untersuchungen
VC	*Vigiliae christianae*
WBC	Word Biblical Commentary
WC	Westminster Commentaries
WPC	Westminster Pelican Commentaries
WUNT	Wissenschaftliche Untersuchungen zum Neuen Testament
ZB	Zürcher Bibelkommentare
ZKT	*Zeitschrift für katholische Theologie*
ZNW	*Zeitschrift für die neutestamentliche Wissenschaft*
ZTK	*Zeitschrift für Theologie und Kirche*

MARK

Images of an Apostolic Interpreter

Introduction

The Quest for the Historical Mark?

What do we know of Mark the Evangelist, the author of the Second Gospel in the New Testament?

A MAXIMAL RECONSTRUCTION

One answer, associated with popular Christian belief and some conservative biblical scholarship, runs something like this:[1]

The Second Gospel was composed by a man whose Hebrew name was John (*Ioan[n]es = Yōchānān*, or *Yechōchānān*, "Yahwch is gracious"); "but, since then, as now, there were many [persons named 'John'], he is usually known by his Latin name, Marcus"[2] ("a large hammer"). Mark was the son of a certain Mary, a rich widow of Jerusalem (see Acts 12:12), in whose house Jesus and the Twelve were accustomed to rendezvous. It was there, in a long room on the roof, that the Master and his disciples gathered for what was to be their Last Supper (cf. Mark 14:12–31). In his bedroom below, alert and sensing the danger that lurked about the house, Mark may have lain and listened to the hurried footsteps of the betrayer as he shuffled down the stairs. Soon afterward Mark heard the scuffling of more feet, as the rest of the dinner guests departed. Perhaps on sudden impulse the young lad seized a linen sheet from his bed, wrapped it around himself, and followed the band to a garden nearby. Crouching beneath some olive trees, he watched as a torch-lit posse stormed into Gethsemane and apprehended Jesus (cf. Mark 14:32–50). Suddenly, the boy felt rough hands laid upon his shoulders; terrified, he slipped out of his sheet and dashed away, naked, into the night (cf. Mark 14:51–52).

When next we meet Mark, according to this explanation, it is after Easter, possibly some fifteen years later. Still in Jerusalem, Mark had become well acquainted with Simon Peter, a friend of the family, who had fled to Mary's house following his breathless escape from prison (Acts 12:1–17). During this period, perhaps, Mark learned by heart, and precisely recorded in Aramaic, all that he was told by Peter. Since

1

Paul had conferred with Peter during one or more visits to Jerusalem (Gal 1:18–24, 2:1–10; Acts 15:1–11), Mark may have been privy to Paul's teaching as well as to the recollections of other disciples of Christ. In any event Peter left Jerusalem, possibly around the year A.D. 45 (see Acts 12:17), at which point Mark became closely associated with Paul's missionary endeavors. Mark's means of access to this entourage may have been through his kinsman, Barnabas, who was Paul's own apostolic mentor (Acts 9:27; cf. Col 4:10). After Paul and Barnabas had delivered a love offering from Antioch's Christians to the church in Jerusalem, Mark joined the missionaries in their return to Antioch (Acts 11:27–30, 12:25). Perhaps (some conjecture) it was in the Syrian capital that Peter's stories and recollections were first translated into Greek, the cosmopolitan language of the day.[3]

According to this popular reconstruction, Mark's Gospel bears a number of telltale indicators of Peter's style and influence.[4] Summoned in evidence are the vivid details in which the narrative abounds: actions and gestures of Jesus, in the course of healing and teaching, which seem to have been captured by an onlooker (see Mark 3:4–5, 5:41), as well as an intimate, candid knowledge of boats and fishing, and of Peter's deeds and thoughts, which (it is claimed) could only have come directly from the disciple himself (Mark 1:16, 4:36–38, 9:6, 14:72). Moreover, the Gospel exhibits an artless, even clumsy, grammatical style that suggests the freshness of a firsthand witness: for example, a repetitive use of the imperfect tense (see, e.g., Mark 1:21; 3:2, 30; 4:33–34; 10:32) and the striking manner in which third-person plural pronouns can be put back into lively first-person plural narration (implying virtually literal transcriptions of Peter's own oral recounting [e.g., Mark 1:29]).[5] From among the Twelve Peter receives notably separate and distinctive mention throughout the Second Gospel (see, e.g., Mark 1:36; 8:29, 32; 9:5; 10:28; 14:29, 54–72; 16:7). For one British New Testament scholar all of this, taken together, pointed to one conclusion: "In strong contrast to Matthew and Luke, Mark's Gospel may be called autobiographical. They write Lives of Christ, he records the experience of an eyewitness and companion."[6]

When Paul and Barnabas set out on their first missionary journey (ca. A.D. 47?) Mark was tapped to accompany them as both travel secretary and authorized catechist. "His occupation was to see that the converts really knew who and what the Apostles were talking about. He had to impart the Gospel history and to secure that it was accurately grasped."[7] From Antioch this missionary trio traveled by way of Seleucia to the island of Cyprus, Barnabas's homeland (Acts 4:36), and from there by sea to Perga in Pamphylia (Acts 13:1–13a).

It was in Pamphylia that Mark deserted his cohorts and returned to Jerusalem (Acts 13:13b), an action subject to speculative interpretations. Maybe his nationalistic, Jewish sympathies could not abide the universalism of Paul's mission. Maybe his faith to this point had been little more than a secondhand inheritance from his mother, Mary, who had pushed him ambitiously into missionary work. Perhaps he simply had not the stomach for the dangers and sacrifices of so strenuous a calling. Whatever the reason, "he put his hand to the plow, but he looked back and proved that at this time he was not fit for the Kingdom of God. He started but he did not finish."[8] The very qualities of terse, impulsive hastiness which would render his Gospel so memorable emerged, in the harsh light of pioneer ministry, as decided character flaws.[9] For whatever reason, Paul and Barnabas continued without their attendant (Acts 13:14).

When next the threesome was reunited it was in Antioch, following the Jerusalem conference at which the apostles determined the restrictions incumbent upon Gentile converts to Christianity (ca. 49? [Acts 15:1–35]). As Paul and Barnabas prepared to embark on a second missionary journey, Mark rejoined them, though not for long; angrily, Paul refused the company of their erstwhile defector (Acts 15:36–38). For his part, with a leniency not unexpected of a relative, "Barnabas believed that when a young man had failed once he should be given a second chance."[10] Once more there was a parting of the ways: Barnabas and Mark headed for Cyprus; Paul took Silas as his new companion and journeyed through Syria and Cilicia to Derbe and Lystra, where Timothy "signed on" to fill the position left vacant by Mark (Acts 15:39–41, 16:1–5).

The misbegotten missionary drops from sight until near life's end for his two most famous apostolic patrons. By the mid-sixties Mark had recovered his nerve and found his way to Rome in the valued service of the imprisoned Paul. Where once rancor had divided the two, now—as seemingly evidenced in the apostle's letters to the Colossians (4:10), Philemon (v. 24), and Timothy (2 Tim 4:11b)—there was reconciliation. (Had Paul, having seen a version of Mark's Gospel, at last been convinced of the committed vitality of the young Evangelist's faith?)[11] So, too, did Peter find consolation in Mark's company on the eve of that apostle's execution in Rome, as he indicated in a letter penned to Christians in northern Asia Minor (1 Pet 5:13): "Peter knew what it was to fail and to be restored, . . . [and] Mark will always stand before us as an example of a failure who made good."[12]

The Evangelist may have died in the imperial capital not long thereafter, during Nero's notorious pogrom against the Roman Christians (Tacitus, *Annals* 15.44). Perhaps Mark was completing a revised edition of his Gospel only moments before his own demise, since the narrative appears to end all too abruptly, with the women's frightened flight from the empty tomb (Mark 16:8).[13] "[It] is possible that Mark ended his writing at that point. . . . The clash of grounded spearbutts in some Roman courtyard, the harsh battering on the door, the hasty thrusting of the hurried last pages of the Gospel into concealment— and the end. . . ."[14]

A MINIMALIST RECONSIDERATION

The foregoing portrait, or at least portions of it, may seem familiar and plausible to modern Christian laity and perhaps even to some clergy.[15] Such persons may be surprised to learn that practically every aspect of that reconstruction has been challenged by biblical scholars for several decades. One Markan investigator has tactfully but candidly summarized the current critical consensus in this way: "A 'new look' at the Gospel, if we may call it that, has been emerging, one character-ized, among other things, by an open mind, or even lack of interest, in such historical questions."[16]

Critics are sometimes suspected of being overly skeptical, even cynical; in this case, however, their incredulity seems warranted.[17] If our question is framed thus—"What do we know, directly, about the author of Mark's Gospel?"—then the answer must surely be: "Nothing at all." The simple title, "According to Mark," apparently was added to the book decades later by the early church, in order to distinguish that Gospel from the others; aside from that traditional ascription, nowhere in the text of the Second Gospel does its author identify himself (or herself).[18] Stripped of its imaginative associations with other persons and events in the narrative, the oblique account of the naked young man who fled from the garden (Mark 14:51–52) remains, frankly, cryptic;[19] whatever interpretation is suggested, nowhere in that anecdote is the young lad identified. The writer of the Gospel may have been named Mark, and, in making that identification, third- and fourth-generation Christians may have been correct. If so, however, then we could say with certainty only that the Gospel's author shared with many in the Greco-Roman world a very common name.[20] In itself that name tells us nothing of the writer who may have borne it.

One might protest: What of the other references to Mark in the New Testament, in Acts and in the letters of Paul and Peter? Do they not refer to Mark the Evangelist? Possibly, but not necessarily. None of those canonical references identifies "Mark" as the author of a Gospel; nor is it clear that those passages are referring to the same "Mark." In fact, if we begin by assuming that there is no single person named Mark whom all of these writers have in mind, then our "maximal reconstruction" collapses, bereft of textual support.

Still, to take the most common equation, is it not likely that the Evangelist Mark and John Mark of Acts are one and the same? Few modern critics find much in the Second Gospel to support that identification.[21] Would John Mark, a resident of Jerusalem, have known so little of Palestinian topography that he could have penned the confused itinerary of Jesus in Mark 7:31?[22] (As one recent commentator puts it, traveling from Tyre to the Sea of Galilee by way of Sidon and the Decapolis would be like traveling from Philadelphia to Washington, D.C., by way of New York City and central Pennsylvania.)[23] Would not a first-century Judean Jew have known that Palestinian women could not legally sue their husbands for divorce (see Mark 10:11–12)?[24] Could anyone other than a Gentile author, writing for a Gentile audience, have casually made the inflammatory comment that Jesus abolished the distinction between prohibited and kosher foods (Mark 7:19b; cf. Matt 15:15–20)?

Nor is it any easier to align the content of the Second Gospel with what little we know or might infer about the preaching of Peter and Paul, the two apostles with whom Mark seems most closely associated.[25] Judged strictly on the basis of the New Testament, the affiliation of Mark with Peter is doubly problematic. On the one hand, the narrative in Acts never directly ties the two figures: Peter enjoys the patronage of Mary, the mother of John Mark (Acts 12:12), but her son does not participate in that apostle's missionary journeys.[26] On the other hand, there is little in Mark's Gospel that is demonstrably Petrine in origin. Since the sermons of Peter in Acts have been filtered through the mesh of Luke's own concerns,[27] and if (as many scholars suspect) 1 and 2 Peter were not actually written by their namesake,[28] then we have no firsthand evidence of Peter's preaching or correspondence. If that is so, then the New Testament does not permit us to clinch a theological connection between Mark and Peter. (In addition, if 1 Peter 5:13 occurs in a pseudonymous letter, then the New Testament's only explicit link between the Evangelist and the apostle is historically questionable, albeit early.) If we further allow, as seems reasonable, for a generous degree of imaginative and legendary embroidery in the recounting of stories about Jesus and the Twelve during the decades intervening Easter and the composition of the Second Gospel, then there is little in Mark that might confidently be regarded as eyewitness testimony. Moreover, Peter's role hardly looms larger in the Second

Gospel than in the others (see Matt 16:16–19; Luke 5:1–11, 22:31–34; John 6:66–69, 20:1–10, 21:15–19). In sum:

> [Mark's Gospel] does not sound like the writing of a man who was recording what a disciple had told him, for it lacks the vividness and personal character that one would expect in descriptions of events by someone who had actually taken part in them—even if reported second-hand. Rather, the author seems to have no more acquaintance with Jesus than anyone could obtain from the traditions that were circulating in the Church at that time.[29]

Not surprisingly, "a direct and uniform Petrine connection has not in practice been a basic premise of most . . . [Markan] studies appearing in the 1960's onwards."[30]

Although the connection between Mark and Paul seems firmer in Acts and in certain letters attributed to that apostle, the evidence of Pauline influence within the Gospel itself is in no way obvious. To be sure, both Markan and Pauline theologies are centered on the cross (Mark 8:34; 1 Cor 1:18–31), and the Second Gospel betrays some Gentile sympathies (7:1–30, 15:39); however, the Evangelist need not have inherited these things from Paul. Indeed, absent from Mark are many, though not necessarily all, of Paul's distinctive theological interests: the post-Easter enthronement of Jesus as Lord and Son of God (Phil 2:9–11; Rom 1:4), the justification of sinful humanity by grace through faith (Rom 1:17, 3:21–26), the contrast between life in the flesh and in the spirit (Rom 8:5–27; Gal 5:16–26). Conversely, missing from Paul's letters is the emphasis on Jesus' words and deeds which is manifest in the Second Gospel.[31]

Since the Second Gospel is anonymous, with doubt surrounding its association with Peter and Paul, what then can we say of its author? "About the best we can do is to describe [him] as an unknown first century Gentile Christian."[32] Though most scholars date the book around A.D. 70, the year in which Roman troops destroyed Jerusalem, a precise date is impossible to ascertain. Nor can we pinpoint the Gospel's place of origin: its combination of Palestinian Jewish Jesus-traditions with a Gentile missionary outlook could have been found almost anywhere in the Greco-Roman world. Galilee, Syrian Antioch, Rome, and Alexandria, Egypt, have been proposed: "All are possible, none are necessary."[33]

For all of the agnosticism evidenced in this "minimalist reconsideration" of Mark's origins, most recent scholarship displays certitude on one point: namely, that questions of the Gospel's authorship and its

Evangelist's identity are relatively unimportant.[34] The critical focus should rest on a known quantity—the Gospel itself, as a literary product—not on its author, about whom we can say nothing for sure. Paul Achtemeier's judgment is sound: "The best conclusion is to admit the uncertainty of our knowledge about the author of our Gospel, to give full weight to the traditional nature of the Markan materials, and to resist the temptation to allow imagination to provide the key for the interpretation of our Gospel, as though its intention were historical fact rather than proclamation of what it means that Jesus of Nazareth was God's anointed Son."[35]

SOME CRITICAL SHIFTS

Between our maximal reconstruction and minimalist reconsideration of the figure of Mark there is, obviously, a world of difference. Even though earlier in this century most learned commentators on the Second Gospel presupposed, to some degree, the picture of Mark with which we began this chapter,[36] the second, more skeptical, presentation has carried the day in recent biblical scholarship. It would be fatuous, however, to suggest that Markan scholars were a generally gullible lot until around 1950, at which time the scales fell from their eyes and their vision became critical. Nor is there any demonstrable, inverse correlation between criticism and confessionalism: there is no evidence that proponents of the more conservative presentation are numbered among the church's more committed sons and daughters or that those subscribing to the more liberal reconstruction are hostile to Christian faith. Rather, by the middle of the twentieth century some fundamental shifts had occurred in the way that New Testament interpreters conceived the origins of Mark and the other Gospels. These critical shifts, in turn, seemingly diminished the credibility of other, more traditional explanations. Achtemeier's comment, quoted at the end of the preceding section, nicely sums up three pronounced effects of recent, critical reflection on Mark: enhanced appreciation of the Gospel's background and character; increased uncertainty about the precise identity of the Second Evangelist; and restraint of the interpreter's imagination.

The Background and Composition of the Gospels

The single most dramatic shift in this century's understanding of the Gospels may be attributed to the impact of form and redaction criticism. Implicit in the older, maximal reconstruction of Mark's origins was the belief that the Gospels were practically verbatim transcriptions of the apostles' remembrances of Jesus. From that assumption it seemed natural to infer that the Markan narrative was based on eyewitness testimony, principally that of Simon Peter (as attested by traditions of the primitive church). That granted, the conclusion seemed irresistible: the Gospel of Mark presents a historically reliable account of Jesus' ministry, death, and resurrection. And if the Gospels were trustworthy sources of information about Jesus, then it seemed reasonable to think that the Epistles and the Book of Acts afforded dependable evidence for the identity of Mark and the other Evangelists.

Notwithstanding its internal consistency, this position founders on the evidence presented by the Gospels themselves. First, it is not at all clear that the Evangelists' expectations of "eyewitness testimony" were the same as our own: although the preface of the Third Gospel (1:2) claims such attestation, Luke, evidently employing Mark as a source,[37] proceeds to rearrange circumstantial details (cf. Luke 11:16, 29; 12:1; Mark 8:11–12, 15) and to omit whole episodes and swatches of teaching (cf. Mark 6:45–8:10, 16–26) which are presumably connected with eyewitness testimony.[38] For Luke the significance of witness has less to do with verbatim transmission than with proximity to Jesus' ministry and resurrection (Luke 24:48; Acts 1:21–22, 2:32).[39] Second, the Gospels do not appear, by and large, to be absorbed in the niceties of historical or biographical reportage: Mark's narrative, for instance, is supported by only the most slender geographical and chronological framework (see, e.g., 1:4, 9; 2:13, 23; 4:1, 35; 7:31; 8:1). Third, most of the material in Mark displays a detached and stylized character (see, e.g., 1:21–28, 4:21–25, 10:13–16, 12:13–17); narrative color, not historical veracity, seems best to account for what some scholars have regarded as Mark's "vivid detail."[40] Fourth, the unabashed purpose of the Gospels is not to report dispassionate history but, rather, to nurture Christian beliefs (Matt 1:1; Mark 1:1; Luke 1:4; John 1:1–18, 20:30–31).

It was to account for these phenomena that form criticism emerged: the hypothetical reconstruction and disciplined analysis of discrete, oral traditions about Jesus, which were presumably circulated within the early church and adapted to its liturgical and catechetical needs. Redaction criticism was designed to track the literary outcome of that traditional process—the manner in which each Evangelist, acting as a creative author, synthesized inherited traditions into a theologically coherent, narrative portrait of Jesus. In time form and redaction critical insights were applied to other Christian literature, with the result that Acts and the Epistles, no less than the Gospels, were regarded as having been accommodated to the religious beliefs and needs of primitive Christianity.[41]

The Evangelists' Uncertain Identities

With the advent of this critical reassessment of early Christian writings, the image of a particular Evangelist named Mark receded into the shadows of scholarship. Within the anonymous Second Gospel there had never been grounds for speculation about its author's identity. Now, in light of the Christian community's handling and reworking of its traditions about Jesus during the decades between Easter and the first written Gospel, there seemed even less hope of pinpointing the authorial personality behind Mark and scant confidence at all in the Gospel's Petrine pedigree. Even if one supposed that the Second Evangelist was the Mark who appeared in Acts and the Epistles, the historical reliability of those documents was now subject to the same critical suspicion attached to the Gospels: namely, that the Petrine and Pauline "character" of Acts, 1 Peter, Colossians, and 2 Timothy was an apostolic fiction, designed to mold or even fabricate history in the service of particular religious or theological ends.[42]

Thus, in pondering the personality of Mark, imaginative restraint and critical skepticism have become the order of the day. Gone, for most scholars, are the old connections, wrought among different Christian documents, which have no explicit basis in the New Testament itself: the celebration of the Last Supper at Mary's house (and Mark's overhearing of it); the young Evangelist's naked flight from Gethsemane on the night of the arrest; Barnabas's leniency toward Mark because of their blood relation; Mark's transcription, at Peter's knee, of the gospel story; a poignant reconciliation between Paul and Mark following their row in Antioch. Other arguments—Mark's service as a general assistant and catechist (cf. Acts 13:5; see chapter 1); the Gospel's quasi-autobiographical use of the imperfect tense—have lost their persuasiveness, because they depend on the presupposition of the Evangelist's apostolic associations. Since just such an assumption is made by many of the early church fathers, patristic traditions about the Evangelist behind the Second Gospel have fallen far out of critical favor. The comments of Papias (A.D. 130), Irenaeus (180), and Clement of Alexandria (180), among others, are generally regarded by modern scholarship as inferences from, and conflations of, obscure and divergent New Testament references. These patristic deductions, it is argued, were cobbled together for religious and perhaps apologetic reasons: gaps in Christians' knowledge about the origins of the Gospels were thereby filled, the authority of the church's primary religious charters was reinforced, and heretical abuse or neglect of those documents was repudiated. Liberal New Testament scholarship has tended to impute some of the same motives to more conservative, maximal reconstructions of the Second Evangelist and his Gospel: modern attempts to correlate Mark's Gospel with other New Testament and patristic traditions are sometimes viewed with suspicion, even castigated, as misbegotten attempts to validate Christian faith through the forging of a spurious historical continuity between Jesus and the church that succeeded him.[43]

THE RECONSIDERATION RECONSIDERED

If these critical shifts and their attendant minimalist judgments constitute scholarship's last word on the figure of Mark, then there would seem to be little more to say. For this reason most recent commentaries on Mark dash through the question of its authorship in a paragraph or so, and the references to Mark in Acts and in the Epistles are almost never correlated with the Second Gospel. The assured results of form and redaction criticism are cited; the overactive imagination of the church fathers is acknowledged. *Quod erat demonstrandum,* and the conversation veers to something else.

It is, or should be, a commonplace of critical scholarship that when its results appear so assured, and its consideration of any question becomes so perfunctory, then the whole matter probably invites careful rethinking. Arguably, the prevailing minimalist reconsideration of Mark itself needs to be reconsidered—not in spite of, but by reason of, the very shifts that biblical criticism has undergone.

1. *The principle of honest uncertainty cuts in both directions, not only toward the maximal reconstructions of Mark but also toward their minimalist reconsiderations.* As we shall see, patristic thinkers at times did harmonize discordant or disparate tendencies within both the New Testament and emerging church traditions, often without clear historical warrant. Thus, different figures named Mark could well have been conflated into one legendary composite, later identified with the Second Evangelist. Moreover, in any consideration of the figure of Mark the anonymity of the Second Gospel is a not inconsiderable fact. Whoever it was, the author of that work deliberately intended to remain nameless, and that anonymity must be pondered, not whisked away.

On the other hand, a high degree of uncertainty pervades current scholarly suggestions about the origin (or "provenance") of the Gospel of Mark, as we have already observed. Though most believe its author to have been Gentile, commentators are by no means unanimous on this.[44] And when the discussion turns to locating the Gospel within a particular setting in the life (*Sitz im Leben*) of primitive Christianity, confusion usually triumphs. The unvarnished truth is that twentieth-century interpreters, no less than second-century ecclesiarchs, usually presuppose in their reading of Mark an "author" or "creative community," whose precise contours are embarrassingly ill defined. This is clearly a problem for form and redaction critics: their focus, ironically, is on an author whom they confess not to know but whose methods they claim to uncover with extraordinary precision.[45] Less obviously, authorial uncertainty quietly haunts literary critics of Mark. Such interpreters typically prescind from judgments about the "real author" and historical circumstances of the Gospel; however, what is implied by an "implied author" and his narrative, if not the purposeful activity, in space and in time, of a real author?[46] In short, if uncertainty bedevils traditional claims about Mark, then the same holds true for the claims of Mark's modern critics.

2. One of the really curious paradoxes of contemporary scholarship is its insistence on ambitious speculations concerning the traditions about Jesus, prior to Mark's Gospel, and its comparative disparagement of the actual traditions that came to be attached to that book in the early history of the church. One need not be a fussy antiquarian to detect something a bit arrogant in the modern critical assumption that our hunches about the resources and concerns of the Second Evangelist are more objective and reliable than those of interpreters who were, in fact, much closer to the composition of the Gospel than we.[47] *If "full weight" is to be given to the traditions associated with Mark, a judicious examination should encompass traditions manifestly postdating the Gospel as those purportedly antedating it.*

Whatever prejudices the early church harbored for or against the Second Evangelist and his Gospel, we should not permit our own biases to blind us to the potential value of what those traditions report, or omit to say. For instance, the reason for the Second Gospel's attribution to Mark is not in the least bit clear. The Gospel never makes such a claim. Little is explained by the argument that the Gospel was so ascribed because of its presumed author's derivative prominence, through association with Peter or Paul: Why, then, did not second- and third-century Christians employ a customary expedient and simply assign the book's composition to one of the apostles? Moreover, in almost every early tradition that we know, both within and beyond the New Testament, "Mark" cuts a decidedly second- or third-rate figure. Among the fascinating characteristics of the early traditions about Mark are their proliferation and oddity: relative to their references to the other Evangelists and Gospels, patristic texts seem to discuss Mark more yet use his Gospel less. Furthermore, in their comments about the Evangelist, the majority seem noticeably awkward, apologetic, and sometimes even pejorative. Even if it proves beyond our ability to recover completely, something's afoot in all of this; compounding the mystery is the reticence of New Testament investigators to pursue it.

Beyond grappling with an intriguing riddle, Gospel exegetes might reap other benefits by reviewing the traditions about Mark. For one, we learn that many of those traditions are critical in their own right, and none is as "maximal" in its reconstruction of the figure of the Evangelist as the familiar portrait rendered at the start of this chapter.[48] In addition, for critics interested in the social description of early Christian groups, the testimony of the chuch fathers could profitably be weighed in the formulation of theories concerning the range, influence, and confluence of various streams of primitive Christianity.[49]

3. Implicit in the foregoing comments is a simple but important consideration: *Inquiry into the figure of Mark may assist in restraining the imagination of critical, New Testament scholarship*. At first blush this assertion might seem redundant, if not impertinent: Why should scholarship that is indeed critical need help in restraining its imagination? Dare one suggest that modern New Testament research, so technical and meticulously vetted within its guild of expert practitioners, could be guilty of untrammeled flights of fancy?

For all of its undeniable sophistication the study of the New Testament is not an exact science. Throughout its various subspecialties biblical criticism operates largely in the realm of intelligent hypotheses and informed conjectures. To acknowledge this is in no way to denigrate scholarship, which could scarcely function without such disciplined imagination. Yet, as its proponents well know, New Testament scholarship occasionally slips the traces of plausibility. When that happens historical research has proven to be an effective and salutary, though not infallible, bridle.

To take one example: four decades of redaction criticism have encouraged scholars to dispense with historical inquiry into the figure of Mark and to focus instead on the text attributed to him, as a known quantity with a discernible setting in the life of first-century Christianity. For that "known quantity," however, a staggering number and variety of religious and cultural settings have been propounded, each of which has been claimed essential for interpreting the Second Gospel.[50] A representative, though by no means exhaustive, sample of these suggested *Sitze im Leben* includes understanding Mark as an apocalyptic directive, addressed to Jerusalem Christians, to flee to

Pella at the onset of the Jewish War (A.D. 66);[51] as a Christian Passover recital for Roman Jews;[52] as a pro-Roman apology, written for pagans;[53] as a catechetical document, underwriting an early church's apostolic legitimacy;[54] as a consolatory exhortation to Christian faith, under siege during Roman persecution;[55] and as a polemical attack against miracle-mongering heretics.[56] All of these proposals have appealed for support to redaction criticism; in itself, however, that method has proved unable to adjudicate the validity or relative plausibility of these and other competing alternatives for understanding the background and intentions of the Second Gospel.[57] These issues cannot be completely resolved by critical reassessment of the traditions attached to the figure of Mark; nevertheless, such an exercise may provide, at most, some general constraints upon scholars' imaginative recontructions and may suggest, at least, which among them carry greater likelihood.[58] Even if many of the historical questions swirling about the Second Gospel's origins resist clear solutions, the traditions about the figure of its Evangelist may raise issues of social, religious, and theological significance for historians of early Christianity.

A WAY TO PROCEED

In general, the tides of recent research may be shifting in directions that would favor a fresh examination of the traditions attached to Mark, the Gospel and its Evangelist. Even so, such a reassessment should be structured in a way that honors the insights and orientations of modern New Testament study. Beyond touching base with pertinent areas of scholarship, the following plan has some advantage in proceeding from that which is relatively clearer and better known, to matters that are more obscure and less certain.

In part 1 the investigation proper will begin with a review of *the figure of Mark in the New Testament*. Here we shall collect and examine, within their various literary contexts, the scattered and explicit refrences to Mark in Acts, Colossians, Philemon, 2 Timothy, and 1 Peter. Although historical issues will not be ignored, the emphasis in chapters 1 and 2 will fall on the narrative or epistolary function of those references to Mark. In other words, we shall ask, "How, in each of these New Testament books, does the figure of Mark serve their authors' persuasive or rhetorical purposes?"

Next we shall turn, in part 2, to *the figure of Mark in patristic literature*. Again our task will be, first, to assemble as many as possible of the sporadic, overt references to Mark in the writings of the church fathers of the first four centuries. Second, drawing upon the recent research of church historians, we shall approach these ancient sources with such questions as these: (1) What functions are served by the figure of Mark in early Christian, noncanonical documents? In the light of the Greek and Roman fathers' own theological concerns, to what degree are their references to Mark historically reliable? How did the traditions about Mark evolve in early Christianity? Was there one line of traditional thought about Mark, from which all of the church fathers drew? Were there several, divergent lines or "trajectories" of tradition surrounding that figure?

Then, in part 3, we shall consider *the relationship between the Gospel of Mark and Markan traditions,* within and beyond the New Testament. Drawing upon the firmest results of modern criticism, these chapters will ponder the salient features of the patristic "portrait" of Mark the Evangelist, in the light of the evidence presented by the Second Gospel itself. Here a cluster of questions should come into focus: Just how secure does the Second Gospel's association with first-century Roman, Petrine, or Pauline Christianity appear to be? Is the early fathers' identification of the Second Evangelist subject to historical confirmation? Is the figure of Mark to be identified with the author of that Gospel? If not, do the social and religious tendencies of the Second Gospel comport, in a measurable way, with patristic attribution of that Gospel to Mark, as the figure of the Evangelist was styled?

For theological students or nonspecialists who may approach this book with Christian confessional commitments, perhaps we should be clear, from the start, what a study like this can and cannot do. Occasionally, some adherents of conservative scholarship have correlated the historical reconstruction of a figure named Mark with the truth-claims of that Gospel attributed to him.[59] As I noted earlier, more liberal interpreters have tended to challenge that correlation as being both historically and theologically suspect. When so much is invested, religiously, in the fullness and determinacy of a particular historical reconstruction, there is a genuine risk that the interpretation of available evidence will be skewed in an apologetic direction. Furthermore, it can be argued that the integrity of faith is jeopardized when it is rendered dependent on a scholarly retrieval of "the historical Mark."

These, I think, are valid objections. Whatever truth may be enshrined in the Gospel of Mark is both logically and theologically independent of the question of its authorship. The results of our investigation must be allowed to fall out however they will. In any case, they are not *central* to understanding the message of the Second Gospel or in assessing the religious validity of Christianity as presented by Mark.[60]

On the other hand, for both Christians and non-Christians, inquiry into the shadowy "personality" of Mark, and what that figuration has meant to the church, is not an entirely irrelevant exercise. Beyond responding to normal curiosity about the beginnings of Christianity, this kind of study may serve to remind us of the complex dynamics by which religious traditions are sustained as well as of the peculiar interplay that has always existed in Christianity between historical circumstances and theology, the disciplined reflection on faith. Such interactions are at work within the Second Gospel itself: creatively melding earlier traditions, Mark's Gospel ties faith in the risen Christ to remembrance of the historical Jesus.[61] If the figure of Mark informed, in some sense and to some degree, the church's "apostolic tradition,"[62] then the reclamation of that figure's contribution is not religiously irrelevant, even if, for Christians, it is not religiously essential.[63]

If a "life of Jesus," in the modern sense of that term, lies beyond our evidence and competence to write,[64] then all the more hopeless would be "a quest for the Mark of history." Nevertheless, we can say some things with relative confidence about the *figure* of Mark in early Christianity: its components and their development; its persistence and mutability; its significance for the context within which the early church read the Gospel attributed to that figure. That sort of quest is possible and potentially fruitful. To that enterprise, in all of its perplexity and fascination, the balance of this book is devoted.

NOTES

1. The "maximal reconstruction" that follows is a composite of the following scholars' synthetic presentations: Theodor Zahn, *Introduction to the New Testament* (Edinburgh: T & T Clark, 1909), 2:386–46; M.-J. Lagrange, *Évangile selon Saint Marc*, Études Bibliques (Paris: J. Gabalda, 1911), esp. xvii–cli; George Edmundson, *The Church in Rome in the First Century: An Examination of Various Controverted Questions relating to Its History, Chronology, Literature and Traditions* (London: Longmans, Green, 1913), esp. 64–122; Willoughby Charles Allen, *The Gospel according to Saint Mark with Introduction and Notes,* Oxford Church Bible Commentary (New York: Macmillan, 1915), 5–6; C. H. Turner, "The Gospel according to St. Mark," in *A New Commentary on Holy Scripture Including the Apocrypha,* ed. C. Gore, H. L. Goudge, and A. Guillaunu (New York: Macmillan, 1928), pt. 3, 42–124; R. O. P. Taylor, *The Groundwork of the Gospels, with Some Collected Papers* (Oxford: Basil Blackwell, 1946), 20–41; Holmes Rolston, *Personalities around Paul: Men and Women Who Helped or Hindered the Apostle Paul,* 2d. ed. (Richmond: John Knox, 1955), 43–47; T. W. Manson, "The Foundation of the Synoptic Tradition: The Gospel of Mark," in *Studies in the Gospels and Epistles,* ed. M. Black (Philadelphia: Westminster, 1962), 28–45; Edward

Musgrave Blaiklock, *The Young Man Mark: Studies in Some Aspects of Mark and His Gospel* (Exeter: Paternoster, 1965), 9–20; and Donald Guthrie, *New Testament Introduction* (Downers Grove, Ill.: Inter-Varsity, 1970), 68–76.

2. Archibald M. Hunter, *The Gospel according to Saint Mark,* Torch Bible Commentaries (London: SCM, 1948), 17.

3. The allusion here is to a hypothetical document that, in earlier scholarship, was referred to as *Urmarkus,* or "Proto-Mark."

4. Such matters are the preoccupation of Cecil S. Emden, "St. Mark's Debt to St. Peter," *CQR* 154 (1953): 61–71.

5. Though not the first to suggest it, C. H. Turner is best known for this theory of "autobiographical pronominal retroversion" ("Gospel according to St. Mark," 48–49; "Marcan Usage: Notes, Critical and Exegetical, on the Second Gospel," *JTS* n.s. 26 [1925]: 225–40).

6. Turner, "Gospel according to St. Mark," 48; Manson, "Foundation," 40–41.

7. Taylor, *Groundwork,* 25; see also "The Ministry of Mark," *ExpTim* 54 (1942–43): 136–38.

8. Rolston, *Personalities,* 44. Note also H. Dermott McDonald's dramatic paraphrase of Mark's defection: "Recant, said the devil; you lost your *sindon* [linen cloth] for Christ; will you lose your life?" (*Commentary on Colossians and Philemon,* Theta Books [Waco, Tex.: Word Books, 1980], 141).

9. Thus, see Blaiklock, *Young Man Mark,* 12.

10. J. B. Phillips, *Peter's Portrait of Jesus: A Commentary on the Gospel of Mark and the Letters of Peter* (London: Collins & World, 1976), 13.

11. As conjectured by Blaiklock, *Young Man Mark,* 14.

12. Rolston, *Personalities,* 46.

13. Later Greek manuscripts add various endings to the text of the Second Gospel, some of which appear in modern translations (e.g., Mark 16:9–20). Whether the Gospel was unfinished or its original ending was lost or Mark intended such a provocatively open finale remains an issue of considerable debate. For a useful assessment of the problem, see Andrew T. Lincoln, "The Promise and the Failure: Mark 16:7, 8," *JBL* 108 (1989): 283–300.

14. Blaiklock, *Young Man Mark,* 20.

15. Nor, in several quarters, is some such reconstruction passé: see, for instance, the recent presentation of "The Story of Mark" by Warren Dicharry, *Human Authors of the New Testament,* vol. 1: *Mark, Matthew, and Luke* (Collegeville, Minn.: Liturgical, 1990), 17–33.

16. William Telford, "Introduction: The Gospel of Mark," in *The Interpretation of Mark,* ed. W. Telford, IRT 7 (Philadelphia and London: Fortress/ SPCK, 1985), 2.

17. The following critique reflects the tendencies evident in the standard New Testament introductions and commentaries on Mark: among others, Reginald H. Fuller, *A Critical Introduction to the New Testament* (London: Duckworth, 1971), 104–7; Werner Georg Kümmel, *Introduction to the New Testament,* rev. ed. (Nashville: Abingdon, 1973), 95–98; Norman Perrin and

Dennis C. Duling, *The New Testament, An Introduction: Proclamation and Paranesis, Myth and History*, 2d. ed. (New York: Harcourt Brace Jovanovich, 1982), 257; James L. Price, *The New Testament: Its History and Theology* (New York and London: Macmillan/Collier, 1987), 123–24; Hans Conzelmann and Andreas Lindemann, *Interpreting the New Testament: An Introduction to the Principles and Methods of N.T. Exegesis* (Peabody, Mass.: Hendrickson, 1988), 218–19; Dennis Eric Nineham, *The Gospel of St. Mark*, PGC (Baltimore: Penguin, 1963), 38–43; Eduard Schweizer, *The Good News according to Mark* (Richmond, Va.: John Knox, 1970), 24–26; Hugh Anderson, *The Gospel of Mark*, NCB (Grand Rapids, Mich., and London: Eerdmans / Marshall, Morgan & Scott, 1976), 24–32; Rudolf Pesch, *Das Markusevangelium*, HTKNT (Freiburg: Herder, 1976), 1:3–11; Joachim Gnilka, *Das Evangelium nach Markus*, EKKNT (Zurich and Neukirchener-Vluyn: Benzinger/Neukirchener, 1978), 1:32–34; Paul J. Achtemeier, *Mark*, 2d. rev. ed. (Philadelphia: Fortress, 1986), 125–32; Dieter Lührmann, *Das Markusevangelium*, HNT 3 (Tübingen: Mohr [Siebeck], 1987), 3–7; and Morna D. Hooker, *A Commentary on the Gospel according to St. Mark*, BNTC (London: A & C Black, 1991), 5–8.

18. It is not impossible that the author of the Second Gospel could have been female. As Paul's letters attest (Rom 16:3–16; 1 Cor 1:11; Phil 4:2–3), women assumed positions of authority in early Christianity. Women also play important roles in Mark's Gospel (7:24–30, 12:41–44, 14:3–9, 15:40–41, 16:1–8). Mary Ann Tolbert notes an upturn in literacy among women, beginning in the third to second centuries B.C. (*Sowing the Gospel: Mark's World in Literary-Historical Perspective* [Minneapolis: Fortress, 1989], 27 n. 10). On balance, however, I agree with Tolbert that the probability of female authorship of the Second Gospel is low; accordingly, I shall use the traditional masculine pronouns in referring to the Second Evangelist. At present the most extensive treatment of women in Mark's Gospel is Monika Fander's *Die Stellung der Frau im Markusevangelium: Unter besonderer Berücksichtigung kultur- und religionsgeschichtlicher Hintergründe*, MTA 8 (Altenberge: Telos, 1989). In English, note the helpful study by Elizabeth Struthers Malbon, "Fallible Followers: Women and Men in the Gospel of Mark," *Sem* (1983): 29–48.

19. Various interpretations of this mysterious incident have been proposed, including allusions to the young man in Mark 16:5, the linen cloth in 15:46, and naked flight in Genesis 39:12 (Amos 2:16). Although Jesus' equanimity during his arrest and a follower's abject desertion may be contrasted, the passage defies clarification.

20. Thus, the provincial administrator, Marcus Junius Brutus; Marcus Antonius, the general; the orator, Marcus Tullius Cicero; and Marcus Aurelius, the philosopher-emperor. Some of the inscriptional evidence for the Roman praenomen "Marcus" is listed in Henry Barclay Swete, *The Gospel according to St. Mark: The Greek Text with Introduction, Notes, and Indices*, 3d. ed. (London: Macmillan, 1927), xiii–xiv. The widespread use of "Mark" makes it improbable that the name was used to distinguish its bearer (see Hunter, *Gospel*, 17).

21. See Kurt Niederwimmer, "Johannes Markus und die Frage nach dem Verfasser des zweiten Evangeliums," *ZNW* 58 (1967): 172–88.

22. More will be said, in chapter 8, regarding the Second Gospel's geographical obscurities.

23. Paul J. Achtemeier, *Invitation to Mark: A Commentary on the Gospel of Mark with Complete Text from the Jerusalem Bible* (Garden City, N.Y.: Image Books / Doubleday, 1978), 27.

24. The problems associated with Mark 10:10–12 will be considered further in chapter 8.

25. A familial relation between Mark and Barnabas is suggested by the term *cousin* (*ho anepsios*) in Colossians 4:10; however, neither this nor any passage in the New Testament develops Mark's relationship with that apostle. See chapter 2.

26. Though the matter will be considered further in chapter 1, I assume for the moment that Acts 3:1, 11, and 4:13 refer to John, the brother of James and son of Zebedee (see Acts 1:13).

27. Martin Dibelius, "The Speeches in Acts and Ancient Historiography," in *Studies in the Acts of the Apostles* (New York and London: Charles Scribner's Sons / SCM, 1956), 138–85; Eduard Schweizer, "Concerning the Speeches in Acts," in *Studies in Luke-Acts*, ed. Leander E. Keck and J. Louis Martyn (Philadelphia: Fortress, 1980), 208–16. The problem of correlating Mark with the preaching of Peter in Acts will be explored further in chapter 7.

28. John Norman Davidson Kelly, *A Commentary on the Epistles of Peter and Jude* (1969; reprint, Grand Rapids, Mich.: Baker Book House, 1981), 30–33, 235–37; F. W. Beare, *The First Epistle of Peter: The Greek Text with Introduction and Notes*, 3d. rev. ed. (Oxford: Basil Blackwell, 1970), 43–50; Ernest Best, *1 Peter*, NCB (Grand Rapids, Mich., and London: Eerdmans / Marshall, Morgan & Scott, 1971), 49–63.

29. Curtis Beach, *The Gospel of Mark: Its Making and Meaning* (New York: Harper & Brothers, 1959), 12. Notice the flat contradiction between Beach's assessment of Markan "vividness" and that of Turner ("Gospel according to St. Mark," 48–49) and Manson ("Foundation," 40–41).

30. Telford, "Introduction," 1.

31. Nevertheless, the scholarly assumption that Paul knew practically nothing of Jesus' teaching has been forcefully challenged by Dale C. Allison, Jr., "The Pauline Epistles and the Synoptic Gospels: The Pattern of the Parallels," *NTS* 28 (1982): 1–32.

32. Keith F. Nickle, *The Synoptic Gospels, An Introduction: Conflict and Consensus* (Atlanta: John Knox, 1980), 75.

33. Nickle, *Synoptic Gospels*, 75. For further reflections on the Gospel's provenance, see chapter 8 of the present study.

34. Thus, see Nineham, *St. Mark*, 39; Perrin and Duling, *New Testament*, 257.

35. Achtemeier, *Mark*, 128.

36. Prior to the middle of this century most English-speaking scholars

accepted such a reconstruction: E. P. Gould, *A Critical and Exegetical Commentary on the Gospel according to St. Mark*, ICC (New York: Charles Scribner's Sons, 1896), xii–xvii(n); S. J. Case, "John Mark," *ExpTim* 26 (1914–15): 372–76; Swete, *Gospel according to St. Mark*, xiii–xxviii; Vincent Taylor, *The Gospel according to St. Mark*, 2d. ed., Thornapple Commentaries (1946; reprint, Grand Rapids, Mich.: Baker Book House, 1981), esp. 1–131. More recently, one might also include in this company C. E. B. Cranfield, *The Gospel according to Saint Mark*, CGTC (Cambridge: Cambridge University Press, 1959), esp. 5–20; Josef Schmid, *The Gospel according to Mark*, ed. A. Wikenhauser and O. Kuss, RNT (Staten Island, N.Y.: Alba House / Mercie, 1968), 7–15n; William L. Lane, *The Gospel according to Mark*, NICNT (Grand Rapids, Mich.: Eerdmans, 1974), esp. 7–23; and Ralph P. Martin, "Mark, John," *ISBE* 3 (1986): 259–60. On the other hand, critics who acknowledge the dearth of positive information about the Second Evangelist occasionally suggest fanciful portraits of their own: witness F. C. Grant, who imagined that Marcus was a young warehouse clerk, of small education and social prominence, who by day checked long bills of lading and by night edited the Gospel for which his church had commissioned him (*The Earliest Gospel: Studies of the Evangelic Tradition at Its Point of Crystallization in Writing* [New York: Abingdon, 1943], 53–57).

37. Implied in this observation is the customary resolution of "the Synoptic Problem," which of late has been formidably challenged though not overturned. Most scholars consider Mark to have been the earliest of the New Testament Gospels and a source for Matthew and Luke, both of which are thought to have been written toward the end of the first century.

38. Dennis Eric Nineham, "Eye-Witness Testimony and the Gospel Tradition. I, II, III," *JTS* n.s. 9 (1958): 13–25, 243–52; 11 (1960): 253–64; B. Harvie Branscomb, *The Gospel of Mark*, MNTC (London: Hodder & Stoughton, 1937), xxii.

39. Neither does the presence of eyewitnesses necessarily guarantee the accurate interpretation of something supposed to have actually happened (see John 12:28–29).

40. As against Gould, *St. Mark*, xii; also *pace* Taylor, *St. Mark*, 135–40, who accepts form-critical principles but tends to minimize the degree to which they might impugn Mark's historical authenticity. Nevertheless, scholars are not of one mind on the degree of fictionalization inherent in the Gospel narratives: contrast the different conclusions of Mary Ann Tolbert (*Sowing the Gospel*, 29–34); and Eugene E. Lemcio (*The Past of Jesus in the Gospels*, SNTSMS 68 [Cambridge: Cambridge University Press, 1991]).

41. A classic statement of the form- and redaction-critical perspective is R. H. Lightfoot's *History and Interpretation in the Gospels* (London: Hodder & Stoughton, 1935). More recent, and equally lucid, is the presentation by Christopher M. Tuckett, *Reading the New Testament: Methods of Interpretation* (Philadelphia: Westminster, 1987), 95–135. The most recent, ambitious attempt to reconstruct a history of the Synoptic tradition, and its crystallization

in the Synoptic Gospels, is Gerd Theissen, *The Gospels in Context: Social and Political History in the Synoptic Tradition* (Minneapolis: Fortress, 1991).

42. For a standard assessment of these issues, see Kümmel, *Introduction*, 160–73, 340–46, 370–84, 421–24. (In disagreement with some scholars, Kümmel upholds the Pauline authenticity of Colossians.) Questions regarding the authorship of various Epistles will be taken up in chapter 2.

43. Thus, see Howard Clark Kee, *Jesus in History: An Approach to the Study of the Gospels*, 2d. ed. (New York: Harcourt Brace Jovanovich, 1977), 137–38; Werner H. Kelber, *The Oral and the Written Gospel: The Hermeneutics of Speaking and Writing in the Synoptic Tradition, Mark, Paul, and Q* (Philadelphia: Fortress, 1983), 212–14.

44. Among others, Branscomb (*Gospel of Mark*, xxxi–xxxviii) and Gnilka (*Markus*, 1.33) hold that the Second Evangelist was a Jewish Christian.

45. I have discussed this in "The Quest of Mark the Redactor: Why Has It Been Pursued, and What Has It Taught Us?" *JSNT* 33 (1988): 19–39.

46. Thus, see, for example, David Rhoads and Donald Michie, *Mark as Story: An Introduction to the Narrative of a Gospel* (Philadelphia: Fortress, 1982), 35–44, employing the now standard distinctions suggested by Wayne C. Booth, *The Rhetoric of Fiction* (Chicago and London: University of Chicago Press, 1961). On literary-critical distinctions among the "real author," "implied author," and "narrator," see chapter 1 of the present study.

47. As Martin Hengel has argued, "[Early Christian history] did not get lost in an anonymous, unbounded, and imaginary setting" (*Acts and the History of Earliest Christianity* [Philadelphia: Fortress, 1980], 27). Accordingly, Hengel has mounted detailed arguments for the positive historical value of early Christian tradition; see his book *Studies in the Gospel of Mark* (Philadelphia: Fortress, 1985).

48. For instance, believing that the Second Gospel was not written by an eyewitness of Jesus, the earliest church fathers did not identify its author with the youthful fugitive in Mark 14:51–52.

49. Much recent research has followed the lead suggested by E. A. Judge's *The Social Pattern of the Christian Groups in the First Century* (London: Tyndale, 1960). Within this critical framework an important contribution to Markan studies is Howard Clark Kee, *Community of the New Age: Studies in Mark's Gospel* (Philadelphia: Westminster, 1977). Two important analyses of the theologies characteristic of various streams of primitive Christianity are James D. G. Dunn, *Unity and Diversity in the New Testament: An Inquiry into the Character of Earliest Christianity* (London: SCM, 1977); and Raymond E. Brown and John P. Meier, *Antioch and Rome: New Testament Cradles of Catholic Christianity* (New York and Ramsey, N.J.: Paulist, 1983). Some reflections from this critical standpoint will be offered in chapter 8 of the present volume.

50. For a concise survey of recent redaction-critical proposals, consult Seán P. Kealy, *Mark's Gospel: A History of Its Interpretation from the Beginning until 1979* (New York and Ramsey, N.J.: Paulist, 1982), 159–237.

51. Willi Marxsen, *Mark the Evangelist: Studies on the Redaction History of the Gospel* (New York and Nashville: Abingdon, 1968 [German original, 1956]).

52. John Bowman, *The Gospel of Mark: The New Christian Jewish Passover Haggadah*, Studia postbiblica 8 (Leiden: E. J. Brill, 1965).

53. S. G. F. Brandon, *Jesus and the Zealots: A Study of the Political Factor in Primitive Christianity* (New York: Charles Scribner's Sons, 1967).

54. Robert P. Meye, *Jesus and the Twelve: Discipleship and Revelation in Mark's Gospel* (Grand Rapids, Mich.: Eerdmans, 1968).

55. Ernest Best, *Following Jesus: Discipleship in the Gospel of Mark*, JSNTSup 4 (Sheffield: JSOT, 1981).

56. Theodore J. Weeden, Sr., *Mark—Traditions in Conflict* (Philadelphia: Fortress, 1971).

57. I have explored this phenomenon at length in *The Disciples according to Mark: Markan Redaction in Current Debate*, JSNTSup 27 (Sheffield: Sheffield Academic Press, 1989).

58. For example, if the supposed consanguinity between the Second Evangelist and Petrine traditions has some basis in fact, then shadows of doubt would be cast upon recent suggestions that Peter in Mark's Gospel is aligned with christological heresy (among others, U. B. Müller, "Die christologische Absicht des Markusevangeliums und die Verklärungsgeschichte," *ZNW* 64 [1973]: 159–93). For a balanced estimate of the corrective potential of historical investigation into the figure of Mark, see Reginald H. Fuller, "Classics and the Gospels: The Seminar," in *The Relationships among the Gospels: An Interdisciplinary Dialogue*, ed. William O. Walker, Jr. (San Antonio: Texas University Press, 1978), 173–92.

59. Even in the work of a careful scholar such as Vincent Taylor the urgent tone of special pleading can be heard: "If we deny this relationship [between John Mark and Peter], we lose our right to say anything of value concerning personal contacts in the earliest community" (*Gospel according to St. Mark*, 30).

60. Thus, see F. C. Grant:

> It adds nothing to our knowledge of John Mark—of whom we know practically nothing—to attribute this Gospel to him; it adds nothing to our understanding of the Gospel to call him its author, since he is too shadowy a figure; and it adds nothing to our knowledge of the Gospel's content, or to our knowledge of the historical Jesus, to make this attribution. To all intents and purposes we must study the Gospel as if it were anonymous, like most of the books of the Bible—a "traditional book," that is, a book based on a common tradition, not a product of personal literary authorship. ("Gospel according to St. Mark," *IB* 7 [1951]: 632)

For a helpful consideration of the irrelevance of a document's authorship for its truth or authenticity, see John Knox, *Criticism and Faith* (New York and Nashville: Abingdon—Cokesbury, 1952), 101–4.

61. William L. Lane, "From Historian to Theologian: Milestones in Markan Scholarship," *RevExp* 75 (1978): 601–17. It is doubtless true to say, with Achtemeier *(Mark,* 128), that Mark's Gospel intends to proclaim not historical fact but, instead, Jesus of Nazareth as God's anointed Son. This is, however, liable to misunderstanding if one concludes (as Achtemeier himself would not) that Mark is therefore totally uninterested in the Jesus of history. Some of the questions concerning the question of faith and history, raised by this study, will be taken up in the conclusion.

62. As we shall note in part 2, patristic commentators distinguished the supposed authorship of the Second Gospel from the character of the tradition that it preserves, and they displayed rather more interest in the latter than in the former. Modern Christians also might find this a distinction worth preserving.

63. Here I am indebted to a distinction drawn, in a different context, by Marcus J. Borg *(Jesus, A New Vision: Spirit, Culture, and the Life of Discipleship* [San Francisco: Harper & Row, 1987], 13–14).

64. The classic treatment of the problem is Albert Schweitzer, *The Quest of the Historical Jesus: A Critical Study of Its Progress from Reimarus to Wrede* (New York: Macmillan, 1968 [German original, 1906]). A more recent, important attempt at historical reconstruction of Jesus is E. P. Sanders, *Jesus and Judaism* (Philadelphia: Fortress, 1985).

Part I

Glimpses of Mark
in the New Testament

Chapter One

The Wayward Attaché
Mark in the Acts of the Apostles

In this and the following chapter we begin our investigation of Mark by attending to the appearance of that shadowy figure within some of primitive Christianity's "charter documents": Acts, Paul's letter to Philemon, the Epistle to the Colossians, 2 Timothy, and 1 Peter. In accordance with the comments and cautions expressed in the preceding chapter, at least two working assumptions are imperative and should be clearly stated at the outset.

First, phrased negatively, we cannot presuppose that more than one, much less all, of the New Testament references to someone named Mark refer to one and the same person. Compared with the standard procedure of an earlier era of scholarship, it is precisely here that the present study diverges, guided by an appropriate recognition of the luxuriant diversity of New Testament Christianity and its manifold literary outcroppings.[1] Our investigation may lead us to conclude that two or more of these scriptural strands, and their acknowledgments of Mark, are entwined. Contrariwise, our study may direct us away from such a conclusion. However our results fall out, a prior prejudice toward harmonization is not permissible. To frame the matter more positively: before rendering any literary or historical judgments on the relationship of various ancient testimonies to Mark, or the lack thereof, we should attend to the nature of each reference within a specific document.

This leads directly to the second working assumption on which the following analysis is based: before any judgments can be reasonably ventured concerning the historicity of the New Testament traditions about Mark, we first must observe how those references function within the documents in which they occur. This is neither to presume nor to preclude the possibility that any or all references to Mark within the New Testament are fundamentally ahistorical or intentionally fictional. Rather, it is to acknowledge that no mention of Mark within the

Christian canon appears to be motivated *purely* or *primarily* by historical concerns. The notion that "Mark was a historical personage whose reality is important for believers to accept" is neither asserted nor intimated by any of the authors whose works shall be considered in this chapter or the one that follows. The references to Mark in these documents serve purposes that are essentially literary or, one might say, rhetorical: they assist the writers in making or in supporting certain persuasive points that, while not of necessity historically irrelevant, are not coterminous with strictly historical preoccupations.[2] Therefore, before considering whatever historical questions may be of interest to us, we should begin by honoring, and attempting to understand, the rather different reasons for which certain early Christian authors may have made mention of Mark. Whatever may be its outcome for historical investigation, tracing the figure or figures of Mark in the New Testament is surely the place for us to start.

THE PORTRAYAL OF MARK IN ACTS

Although a character named "Marcus" is explicitly identified in chapter 12 of the Book of Acts, a scholarly minority has argued for the earlier appearance of that figure in Acts 3:1–11 and 4:13–22. According to this interpretation, the "John" in attendance with Peter at the healing of the lame man at the Beautiful Gate, and at the ensuing sermon and arrest at Solomon's portico, is the John whose other name was Mark (Acts 12:12, 25). The supposed advantage of this suggestion is that it lends support to the postulation of a source, originating in some primitive Christian center, which connected the Second Gospel (whose best manuscripts end abruptly and equivocally at 16:8) with Acts, the second volume of the Third Evangelist's two-volume history (whose opening chapters seem to overlap redundantly with Luke 24:36–53).[3] In other words, the identification of John in Acts 3 with John Mark seemed to build a bridge between two anomalous documents: one Gospel (Mark) whose narrative lacked final resolution and another (Luke) whose narrative contained more resolution than was needed.

For several reasons the majority of interpreters have not been persuaded by this hypothesis. First, and most obviously, in Acts 3:1, 11, 4:13, and 19, Luke does not identify Peter's associate with John, surnamed Mark (cf. Acts 12:12, 25). Second, within the Lukan narrative (cf. Luke 6:14, 9:28, 22:8 [perhaps]; Acts 1:13), Peter is usually associated with John, the son of Zebedee.[4] Related to both of these points is a third that has not always received due consideration: as a stylist, Luke is characteristically (though not consistently) careful to distinguish between characters in the Third Gospel and Acts who share a common name: thus Simon, whom Jesus called Peter, is differentiated proximately both from Simon, who was called (*ton kaloumenon*) the Zealot (Luke 6:14–15), as well as from Simon, the tanner in whose lakeshore house Peter was staying when Cornelius received an angelic vision (Acts 10:5, 18, 11:13, all of which contain various forms of the verb *epikaleō*; cf. also 13:1 with 15:14). Likewise, the fact that, at Acts 12:12 and 25, John is identified as the one whose other name was Mark (*tou epikaloumenou Markou / ton epiklēthenta Markon*) suggests that Luke wishes to discriminate between that character and the other John, James's brother, who has theretofore played a supporting role in the narrative (cf. Acts 1:13; 3:1, 11; 4:13, 19; 8:14; 12:2). Fourth, in critical retrospect the theory of some preliterary bridge between Mark and Acts probably creates more problems than it dispels: though jarring at first blush, both the elliptical ending of Mark 16:8 and the double ascension tradition in Luke–Acts are by no means exegetically inexplicable.[5] Moreover, a lingering ambiguity attends the assignment of a provenance to the presumed bridging source, as evidenced by the plethora of suggestions ventured for the sources underlying Acts in general (Galilee, Jerusalem, Samaria).[6] The force of these observations lends credence to the majority interpretation: Peter's colleague in Acts 3–4 is most likely John, the son of Zebedee, not John Mark, who is introduced in Acts 12.

Acts 12:12

Thus, we turn to Acts 12:12, in which, in passing, Luke mentions "John, whose other name was Mark," as the son of a certain Mary, to whose house in Jerusalem Peter repaired after his miraculous release from prison (Acts 12:6–12). Beyond the familial connection, in 12:12 we learn nothing directly about John Mark.[7] Indirectly, we learn that his mother is a Jerusalemite woman of substance: Mary is served by a maid (*hē paidiskē* [12:13]) and owns a house, access to which was gained by a gateway, or porch (*to pylon* [12:13]), and large enough to accommodate a congregation of believers who had gathered to pray, presumably for Peter's welfare (12:5, 12).[8] Interestingly, in Luke's narrative John Mark is introduced in order to identify his mother, Mary; it is not the other way around, as we might have anticipated. Equally intriguing and contrary to our expectations is the fact that neither here nor anywhere in Acts is John Mark explicitly associated with Peter: when, after being comically detained at the door (12:13–16), Peter finally gains entry to Mary's house, he stays only long enough to describe his miraculous jailbreak and to ask that the report be relayed to James and the other believers in Jerusalem (12:17). Luke does not state or even intimate what has sometimes been assumed: "Presumably Mark was at home in those days, and so found himself in association with early representatives of the new religious movement,"[9] Peter in particular. In fact, the narrator of Acts[10] whisks Peter off the premises almost as quickly as he arrives: "Then [Peter] left and went to another place" (12:17). In Acts 12:12–17 the name of John Mark is tangentially employed to identify Peter's influential patron, Mary, not to establish a connection between her son and that apostle. On a first reading of Acts, oblivious to other early Christian traditions or literature, a reader would have no reason to expect that John Mark would reappear at all.

Acts 12:25

Therefore, at Acts 12:25 it is rather surprising to learn that John Mark has been tapped into an apostolic entourage: "Then Barnabas and Saul returned [to Antioch: see 13:1], after completing their mission at Jerusalem, taking along with them John, whose other name was Mark."[11] The reader's expectations are given a new twist: perhaps, one might suppose, this John Mark will emerge as a major player in the drama of Acts. After all, he is traveling in the company of Barnabas and Saul, who by now have emerged as key missionary delegates, operating at the behest of the significant Christian centers at Jerusalem and Antioch (9:26–30, 11:19–30). Moreover, both of those leading characters were themselves introduced as minor figures who first appeared then quickly disappeared (cf. 4:36–37, 8:1a), in a manner that contributes to the narrative unification of Acts and seems characteristic of its implied author.[12] On the other hand, one cannot be certain of John Mark's potential influence, since he does not appear to be the fully equal partner of those whom he accompanies: rather than collocating John Mark with Barnabas and Saul, Luke completes his update on the latter with a subordinate clause to the effect that the former "was taken along with [them]" (symparalabontes).[13] John Mark is the junior member of the team; his character and fortunes await further disclosure.

From among all the Christian faithful in Jerusalem, why was John Mark selected to accompany Barnabas and Saul? Intriguingly, Luke never explains. Henry Barclay Swete gave voice to what is probably the most common suggestion: "It was for Barnabas to seek fresh associates in his work, and John was a near relative of Barnabas,"[14] which in turn rests upon the coordination of John Mark in Acts 12–13 with the reference to Mark in Colossians 4:10. Yet, while Luke identi-

fies Mary as John Mark's mother—as though the latter would have
been more widely known than the former—he never identifies Barnabas and John Mark as cousins. If Luke's intention, in Acts 12:12, was
to relate Mary to someone with whom his readers might be better
acquainted, and, if Luke had known of the cousinship of Mark and
Barnabas, why would he not have identified Mary as Barnabas's
kinswoman? Equally lacking in narrative foundation is the proposal
that Barnabas and Paul lodged with Mark's mother during their stay in
Jerusalem,[15] or that "Mark was taken on Paul's first missionary journey
because his eye-witness reminiscences supplied an element in the
Gospel-preaching that neither Paul nor Barnabas could supply."[16]

So the question remains: Why is John Mark suddenly aligned with
Barnabas and Saul in Acts 12:25? In the absence of clear narrative
clues any response is necessarily conjectural. One possibility, which
responds at the level of tradition criticism, is that Luke learned of this
association from one of his sources and simply reported it, either
without knowing its rationale or without interest in explaining it. (As
such, the historicity of this datum would not be subject to verification;
in its favor, however, would be the unlikelihood of Luke's fabrication
of the embarrassments in which Mark is later implicated [Acts 13:13b,
15:37–40].) Another possibility, attempting to engage with the narrative logic of Acts, might inquire into the allusive resonances between
John Mark and the characters and events with which, in 12:25, he is
related. For example, through his mother Mark is indirectly associated
with both wealth and piety (as typified by the Christians gathered at
Mary's house, in fervent prayer [12:12]). This, in turn, seems reminiscent of the terms with which Luke has introduced and sketched Joseph
Barnabas: the "son of encouragement,"[17] who laid the proceeds for
the sale of certain real estate at the apostles' feet (4:36–37) and, as a
leading delegate of both the Jerusalem and Antiochene churches
(11:22, 30),[18] manifested goodness, fidelity, and fullness of the Holy
Spirit (11:24a). Similarly, John Mark is identified by Luke as a Jerusalemite (12:12, 13:13): his presence at the start of Paul's first major
missionary journey into Gentile territory (13:4–14:28) effectively, albeit tacitly, may be intended to represent the reach of Jerusalemite
Christianity, whose general influence is maintained in Acts yet harmonized with other potent spheres of Christianity beyond Judean boundaries.[19] (Earlier, at 4:35–36, Barnabas, a Cypriot, has subjugated himself to the apostles in Jerusalem, who bestow on him a new name;[20]
somewhat later, at 9:26–30, Saul, a Cilician [see 21:39, 22:3, 23:34], is
accredited by Barnabas before the Jerusalem apostolate.) Furthermore, in the light of certain events to come it may not be complete

happenstance that the beginning of John Mark's travels with Barnabas and Saul coincide with very different narratives of divine intervention and rectification in the midst of human thickheadedness or outright hubris (12:14–16 [Rhoda and the Jerusalemite congregation]; 12:18–23 [Herod Agrippa]). While I do not think these narrative and theological interrelations are intrinsically farfetched, particularly in discussing a sophisticated literary stylist like Luke, their elusiveness must be conceded nevertheless. Luke simply asserts that, on the threshold of a significant missionary expedition, Barnabas and Saul took John Mark with them. It is left for the reader to ponder why.

Acts 13:5b

When next we meet John Mark in Acts it is during the mission of Barnabas and Saul (now referred to as Paul [13:9]) in Cyprus, Barnabas's homeland (4:36). "When they arrived at Salamis, they proclaimed the word of God in the synagogues of the Jews; and they had John as a *hypēretēs*" (13:5). With respect to the characterization of Mark in this verse at least two problems exist. Of the two the minor question involves Luke's mention of "John" and the potential ambiguity of that reference. As there has been no mention of anyone else named John in the few verses intervening between 13:5 and 12:25, containing Luke's last mention of "John, whose other name was Mark," surely we are meant to construe John Mark as the referent in 13:5b. The fact that the character is denoted as John, here and at 13:13b, may be suggestive of Luke's own preference for Mark's Hebrew name or of his assumption that it was by that name that this figure was better known among the readership of Acts. Perhaps both were contributing factors in the author's decision.

The more difficult problem, and the one that has exercised various commentators, concerns Luke's intention in describing John (Mark) as a *hypēretēs* and, therefore, how that appositive should best be translated. In classical Greek the root meaning of *hypēretēs* is that of a galley slave, one who pulled the oars in the lower tier of a trireme (a ship with three rows or banks of oars on each side).[21] Already in Herodotus (*Persian Wars* 3.635.111) and Plato (*Politicus* 289c) the term is used to refer more generally to an underling, a servant or attendant. Rather quickly, the word comes to be employed for all sorts of subordinate relations in domestic, political, or religious spheres, and this general and varied usage persists in the writings of Hellenistic Judaism (thus, the Septuagint translations of Prov 14:35, Wis 6:4, Isa 32:5; similarly in the *Epistle of Aristeas* 111, Philo, and Josephus). More technically, in the works of the later Attic historians, Thucydides

(*Peloponnesian War* 3.17) and Pseudo-Xenophon (*Cynegeticus* 2.4.4, 6.2.13), *hypēretēs* is used in military contexts to designate an armed foot soldier's attendant (who carried the warrior's baggage, rations, and shield) or any adjutant, staff officer, or aide-de-camp.

The preceding stroll into Greek etymology could be prolonged, but for our purposes this may serve as sufficient background for interpreting not only Luke's usage of the term in his Gospel and Acts but also the sometimes sweeping claims, made by certain scholars, regarding John Mark's "service." Occurring six times in Luke-Acts, *hypēretēs* is employed in no single and consistent way; rather, Luke's usage captures different nuances within the term's semantic field:

1. The more general sense of subordinate service, albeit within a religious framework, is suggested in the preface to the Third Gospel (Luke 1:2: "those who from the beginning were eyewitnesses and servants of the word") and in Paul's description, before Agrippa, of his appointment by the Lord as Jesus' "servant and witness" (Acts 26:16). The same connotation appears to be present in Luke's use of the verbal cognate *hypēreteō* (Acts 13:36, 20:34, 24:23).

2. The more specific nuance of a cultic functionary is present in Luke 4:20, in reference to the liturgical assistant to a synagogue's president.

3. The more specific use of the term, denoting military "officers" who answered to the high priest and Sanhedrin, appears in Acts 5:22 and 26.

Which, if any, of these connotations is predominant with reference to John Mark in Acts 13:5, the only remaining occurrence of *hypēretēs* in Luke-Acts? In the recent history of scholarship, variations and elaborations of possibilities (1) and (2) have been propounded:

1. Among others, Hans Conzelmann and Ernst Haenchen opine that only the most general sense of "assistance" is appropriate to Acts 13:5.[22] In overall agreement are other scholars, like Swete, who nevertheless attempt to define that assistance more precisely: "Mark may have been required to baptize converts . . . , but his work would include all those minor details which could safely be delegated to a younger man, such as arrangements for travel, the provision of food and lodging, conveying messages, negotiating interviews, and the like."[23]

2. Wide currency has also been given to a more technical interpretation of Mark as *hypēretēs* in Acts 13:5. In an oft-cited article (1935), B. T. Holmes argued that the term probably entailed the

function of looking after documents: "Mark handled a written memorandum about Jesus in the course of the first Gentile mission in
Cyprus."[24] Similarly, though with a greater attempt at etymological
precision, R. O. P. Taylor proposed that *hypēretēs* in Acts 13:5 was
functionally equivalent to the *chazzan*, the priestly assistant in the
cult of Palestinian and later rabbinic Judaism.[25] Thus, for Taylor,
John Mark was "the schoolmaster—the person whose duty was to
impart elementary education[, which] consisted in teaching the
actual wording of the sacred records, the exact and precise statements of the facts and dicta on which their religion was based."[26] It
is this kind of image that various scholars presuppose of Acts 13:5
when they speak of Mark as the teacher, or catechist, authorized by
Paul and Barnabas.[27]

How shall we adjudicate among these alternately bland and intriguing possibilities? If, as we have observed, Luke does not employ the
word *hypēretēs* in a single and constant sense, then clearly we must
allow the context of Acts 13:5b to lead us to the more probable
conclusion.

The first thing to be noted is the commissioning scene in Acts 13:1–
3. Gathered at Antioch, worshiping and fasting, are various prophets
(*prophētai*) and teachers (*didaskaloi*): Barnabas, Symeon Niger, Lu-
cius of Cyrene, Manaean, and Saul. John Mark is not mentioned as
one such prophet or teacher, even though we have just been informed
that he had been accompanying Barnabas and Saul (12:25). Similarly,
John Mark is not explicitly singled out, as are Barnabas and Saul, as
one set apart for the particular work to which they have been called by
the Holy Spirit (13:2). Nor is it even clear, in 13:3, that Mark is among
those who, after fasting and prayer, either laid hands upon the Spirit's
delegates or had others' hands laid upon him. If the reader of Acts is
intended to regard John Mark as an emissary with prerogatives for
teaching, or catechesis, then Luke has certainly left unexploited a
fitting juncture in the narrative at which that point might have been
clearly communicated.[28]

Dispatched by the Holy Spirit, the delegates proceed to Seleucia,
the ancient port city of Antioch, and from there sail to Salamis,
Cyprus, where they proclaim the word of God in Jewish synagogues
(13:4–5a). In a dependent clause Luke adds (13:5b) that they had John
Mark as a *hypēretēs*. While proclamation could be included in this
hypēresia, the wording and syntax of Acts 13:4–5 mitigate against
construing Mark's role in especially exalted terms. First, since John is
distinguished from those whom he assists, the subject pronoun in 13:5b

must refer to Barnabas and Saul, which in turn suggests that it is these apostles whom Luke has had most prominently in mind in the statement of itinerary at 13:4–5a. Second, almost as an afterthought, Luke informs the reader that Barnabas and Saul are still accompanied by John Mark (13:5b), a datum that, on a first reading of Acts, we would have had no reason whatever to presume. As in 12:25, John still appears in a subordinate position: to judge by Luke's phraseology, neither here nor soon afterward (in 13:7) does John appear to stand on equal footing with his patrons, who are very much the focal missionaries in the narrative. (This remains so throughout the story, immediately following, of the confrontation between the missionaries and Elymas the magician [13:6–12]: John Mark again drops from sight, and Saul, in particular, steps into the spotlight.) Third, and perhaps most tellingly, Acts 13:5b explicitly says that John was present as an assistant, neither to the Holy Spirit (cf. 13:2, 4) nor to the Lord (cf. Acts 26:16) nor to the word (cf. Luke 1:2) but, instead, to Barnabas and Saul. John Mark's status is not overtly denigrated but, rather, significantly qualified: he is indeed a *servus*, but a *servus servorum Dei*.

The thrust of the narrative, therefore, argues in favor of interpreting *hypēretēs* in the most neutral terms possible: John Mark was simply at the disposal of Barnabas and Saul.[29] Within that context all speculation about the kinds of service that he rendered, whether sanctified (preaching or teaching) or mundane (handling baggage or booking passage), probably veers away from Luke's intentions. Of all references to a *hypēretēs* in Luke-Acts John Mark's attribution as such in Acts 13:5b is arguably the most colorless.

Acts 13:13b

At Acts 13:13 we encounter Luke's next, and doubtless most tantalizing, reference to John (Mark). Having worked their way from Salamis, on the east coast of Cyprus, through the whole of the island to the western port at Paphos, Paul and his companions (literally, *hoi peri Paulon*, "those around Paul") set sail northwest for Perga, the principal seaport of Pamphylia, in southern Asia Minor. "John, however, withdrew from them and returned to Jerusalem" (13:13b).

In translating this verse, a few details may be worth mentioning. In both classical and Hellenistic Greek, the verb *apochōrein* ("to withdraw from") means, generally, "to go away from" or "to depart," though it can carry the connotation of retirement or withdrawal after a defeat (such as an army might do in battle [Thucydides, *Peloponnesian*

War 2.89]). Beyond Acts 13:13 this verb appears only twice in the New Testament. At Luke 9:39, with reference to a demonic spirit, it may, though need not, carry this nuance of capitulation (and probably does not do so in Matthew 7:23). The other verb in Acts 13:13b, *hypostrephein*, may simply be translated as "to return," its most common connotation in Luke-Acts (see, e.g., Luke 1:56; Acts 1:12), or it can convey the more negative nuance of retreat under fire (Homer, *Iliad* 5.581, 12.71; Herodotus, *Persian Wars* 7.211, 9.14; Thucydides, *Peloponnesian War* 3.24; cf. Luke 11:24 and 23:48). (It is perhaps coincidental but no less interesting that both of these verbs in Acts 13:13b, as well as *hypēretēs* in 13:5b, were used by classical historians to portray military circumstances.) Finally, it should be noted that the precise timing of John Mark's separation from Paul and company is rather vague. Later, at Acts 15:38, we shall learn that John accompanied Paul and Barnabas as far as Pamphylia; without that clarification in Acts 13 the wording of the Greek (in 13:13b) could have suggested that John withdrew from the others at Paphos, the point of their Asian embarkation. Somewhat clearer, at 13:13b, is the probably adversative connotation of the connective particle *de*: at the outset of their mission to Asia the apostles headed in one direction; John, however, went in the other. Similarly, if *de* is taken as an adversative at the beginning of 13:14, we are helped in geographically positioning all of the principals: at Perga (not Paphos) John Mark withdrew, but Paul and Barnabas passed on to Antioch of Pisidia.

No less than that of the average reader, the curiosity of scholars has been piqued by John Mark's conduct. Why did he turn away from Paul's company and return to Jerusalem? Suggested explanations have ranged all over the exegetical map: from his missionary commitment, limited from the start, up to but not beyond Syrian Antioch[30] or Cyprus;[31] to his overall unwillingness to participate in Paul's mission to the Gentiles[32] or his resentment at his cousin Barnabas's falling into second place behind Paul;[33] to his consternation at the prospect of crossing the formidable Taurus Mountains of northern Pamphylia;[34] to his sense of responsibility to his mother back in Jerusalem;[35] and even to his preference for Mary's home cooking![36] Not surprisingly, other interpreters have judged it futile to speculate on reasons left undisclosed by the narrator.[37]

One may sympathize with those who refuse to engage in uncontrollable speculation about John Mark's intentions at Acts 13:13. Yet we ought not succumb to the temptation of dropping the matter too quickly, without pondering Luke's intentions in presenting the story as he has. John Mark's unexplained return to Jerusalem is not unlike the Philippian magistrates' unexplained about-face regarding the arrest of Paul and Silas (Acts 16:35), the ambiguity surrounding the condition of Eutychus and the degree of symbolism, if any, that pervades the story of his resuscitation (Acts 20:7–12), and the contradiction between Governor Felix's promise to render a verdict on Paul's case and his subsequent failure to do so (Acts 24:22–27). In all of these cases the narrator withholds information from the reader, which permits multiple interpretations. In his study of Hebrew narrative Meir Sternberg distinguishes between "gaps," either temporary or permanent omissions of material that are relevant to interpretation, and "blanks," omissions judged by the narrator to be unimportant or irrelevant.[38] With what kind of omission are we dealing at Acts 13:13b?

The briefest and best answer is that, at this stage, we cannot tell. Not only does Luke withhold from the reader any explanation for John's activity; on a first or naive reading of Acts it is not even clear that John's return to Jerusalem is inherently problematic. After all, John is a Jerusalemite (12:12), and throughout the narrative the Jerusalem church functions as the principal base and collective arbiter of early Christianity's operations (Acts 1:4, 12; 9:26–30; 11:1–18, 27–30; 15:1–35; 16:4; 21:15–26). That John should withdraw to Jerusalem at this juncture is mysterious but not intrinsically sinister.

On the other hand, the implied author has left some clues in the narrative that, while not decisive, could support a negative assessment of John Mark's conduct. First, there is the fact, already observed, that John's standing does not appear equal to that of Barnabas and Saul. To this point he has been a passive figure, taken along by the other two missionaries; because we as readers have not witnessed his assertion of positive Christian values or behavior, we cannot be certain of his character. (Although relations among believers tend to be portrayed in Acts as remarkably harmonious [for example, 2:43–47, 4:32–37], Luke by no means suppresses all Christian malfeasance [see 5:1–11, 8:9–24].) Second, we may recall, and now wonder, that John Mark was neither explicitly set apart and dispatched by the Holy Spirit nor confirmed by the Antiochene church for the missionary journey (13:1–4). Third, immediately preceding the notice of John's separation from his patrons, the reader is told of a Roman proconsul's conversion and Paul's ensuing confrontation with Elymas the magician (13:6–12). From this story emerge at least three points, which might be suggestive for interpreting the character of Mark.

First, the story of Elymas involves an example of human obstinance and corruption, which must be overcome by divine intervention. Interestingly, Luke's first references to John Mark (12:12, 25) bracketed different stories (Peter's reception at Mary's house [12:12–17]; Herod's atrocities [12:18–23]) which also convey these themes.

Second, the two references to John in Acts 13 (his assistance of Barnabas and Saul [v. 5b]; his departure from them [v. 13b]) frame a story whose outcome is the conversion to Christianity of a prominent Gentile. While we cannot know John's response to this, we do know that the Jerusalemite has been most directly associated with missionary activity within Jewish synagogues (v. 5a), and we shall quickly learn (in Acts 15) that all qualms attaching to Jewish and Gentile relations were not allayed at the Jerusalem conference described in Acts 11:1–18.

We might note a third point, even though we cannot know how or if it be related to John Mark. It is with the story of Elymas and Sergius Paulus that the erstwhile relationship between Barnabas and Saul is reversed (cf. 9:26–30; 11:19–30; 12:25; 13:1–2, 7), and Paul becomes the "senior member" of the missionary team: from here onward Paul's name is usually mentioned first or representatively (13:13, 43, 45, 46, 50; 14:9, 11; 15:2, 35; though cf. 14:14; 15:12, 25),[39] and Paul's authority, preaching, and fortunes markedly assume center stage (13:9–12, 16–41; 14:9–11, 19–20; 15:36). Indeed, although Paul and Barnabas are described as jointly acting or preaching (13:43, 46–47, 50–52; 14:1–7, 14–18, 21–28; 15:2–4, 12, 22, 30–35), no specific action or sermon of Barnabas alone is portrayed throughout the first missionary journey, the Jerusalem conference, or its immediate aftermath (Acts 13:1–15:35). Again, we cannot be sure of its significance, but it remains the case that John Mark enters the narrative of Acts at precisely the point at which Paul moves into ascendance and the role of Barnabas recedes.[40]

It must be emphasized, however, that these associations, tensions, and reversals attending John Mark's entrance and exit into the narrative of Acts are exceedingly subtle. By no means do they amount to any demonstrative explanation for that character's movement "offstage" at 13:13b. At most, they are suggestive; at least, irrelevant. At this point in the narrative we simply cannot decide whether John's disappearance is an inconsequential blank or a significant gap or, if the latter, whether the omission is temporary or permanent. In the face of apostolic triumph amid adversity (13:42–52, 14:1–28, 15:30–35) the cryptic statement of John Mark's withdrawal might plant in the reader's mind a seed of suspense, or (equally plausibly) it could pass unnoticed. Having read no farther than 13:13b, the reader could easily think that John Mark has made his last appearance in Acts.

Acts 15:36–40

The narrative continues, however, with Acts 13–14 offering a representative portrait of Paul's missionary endeavors in a Gentile world:[41] bold preaching and miraculous deeds, favorably though not universally received (13:14–50); encounters with Gentile polytheism and predominantly Jewish persecution in Iconium, Lystra, and Derbe (13:51–14:20); and pastoral fidelity, signified by Paul and Barnabas's strengthening of their newly organized churches (14:21–25). In a progress report made to the congregation in Syrian Antioch, where they had received their commission by the Spirit, Paul and Barnabas credit God for opening a door of faith among Gentiles (14:26–28). A potentially catastrophic rupture between the congregations of Antioch and Jerusalem is obviated in Acts 15:1–35, with the consensus decision of the apostles and elders that Gentile converts to Christianity need not be circumcised but, rather, adhere only to the fundamental Mosaic requirements in Leviticus 17:1–18:30 (Acts 15:19–21, 28–29). At stake in this "apostolic decree" are several Lukan desiderata: the intrinsic legitimacy of the Gentile mission, the absolution of Gentiles from conversion to Judaism, and a *modus vivendi* between Jewish and Gentile believers in Christ. Although the church at Antioch understandably rejoices at this decision (15:30–31), significantly its initiation and authoritative endorsement are attributed by Luke to the Jerusalem church.

On the verge of a new voyage, at Acts 15:36, Paul proposes to Barnabas a return visit with the believers in every city that they have previously missionized.

> (37) Now Barnabas wanted also to take with them John, the one called Mark. (38) Paul, however, thought it best not to have along with them this one, who had deserted them at Pamphylia and had not gone with them to the work. (39) And so sharp a disagreement arose that they separated from each other: taking Mark with him, Barnabas sailed away to Cyprus. (40) And choosing Silas, Paul set out, having been commended to the grace of the Lord by the [Antiochene] brothers. (41) And he went through Syria and Cilicia, bolstering the churches. (Acts 15:37–41)

Initially, two things about this passage may be observed. First, after a lengthy absence John Mark unexpectedly returns to the narrative. Now we know that the omission of this character since Acts 13:13b has constituted a temporary gap, not an irrelevant blank. Straightaway, we also learn how John Mark's withdrawal was regarded by Paul: the latter was not favorably disposed to the former's return to Jerusalem (see Acts 13:13), thus confirming our worst fears concerning John

Mark's behavior. This assessment is supported, second, by the strikingly harsh tone of this small tableau, which is apparent from Luke's choice of tenses, words, and placement of words.

1. The two supplementary infinitives in verses 37 and 38, *symparalabein* ("to take with") and *symparalambanein* ("to have along with"), stem from the same Greek verb, which was used with reference to Mark also in Acts 12:25. The first infinitive, however, whose subject is Barnabas, is in the Greek aorist tense, which here probably implies a pointed or instantaneous action; the second, whose subject is Paul, is in the present tense, which suggests a linear or continuous action. The shift in tenses thus may signify a subtle difference between Barnabas's and Paul's points of view: the former was willing, on the spur of the moment, to take Mark along; the latter refused to have Mark with them, as it were, day after day.[42]

2. The vocabulary used to portray the characters' actions in this passage is tart. John Mark is described as the one, in Paul's judgment, who in Pamphylia had withdrawn from them: the participle *ton apostanta* stems from *aphistēmi*, a verb that typically connotes desertion, defection, or apostasy (see Luke 8:13, LXX Jer 3:14, 1 Macc 11:43, and often throughout the Septaugint with reference to falling away from God).[43] Moreover, the term used to capture Paul and Barnabas's "sharp disagreement" (v. 39) is *paroxysmos*, from which is derived the English word *paroxysm*, a sudden, violent outburst.[44]

3. By the placement of a demonstrative pronoun at the end of verse 38, John Mark is emphatically identified as the defector: a more stilted translation might be, "Him who had deserted and had not accompanied them, . . . Paul thought best not to have along this one." One might also observe the balanced contrast between the missionaries after their parting of the ways: Barnabas took Mark and sailed away to Cyprus; Paul chose Silas and went out, headed for Syria and Cilicia (vv. 39–41). Not only do the erstwhile partners separate; they head out, with new associates, in opposite directions.

Such as it is, the history of this passage's exegesis often has tended to highlight things neither stated nor reasonably suggested by Luke. For example, family feeling, expressed by an elder to a younger cousin, frequently has been proposed as the motivation for Barnabas's intervention on Mark's behalf.[45] Perhaps even more prominent has been the suggestion that the author of Acts 15:36–40 knows more than he is willing to admit of the apostolic controversy narrated in Galatians 2:11–14 and consequently shifts the cause of Barnabas and Paul's separation away from missionary substance to the less volatile issue of certain personalities (in particular, John Mark's unreliability).[46]

Doubtless, Acts 15:36–40 bears an underdeveloped quality, which might suggest Luke's discomfiture at airing this portion of early Christianity's "dirty linen" (particularly as it involves two heroic apostles). Yet Luke's concern for personalities can be misconstrued. He never mentions, and may not have known, the tradition underlying Colossians 4:10, to the effect that Barnabas and Mark were cousins; certainly, this item is never offered in explanation of Barnabas's judgment in Acts 15:37–39.[47] Nor does it seem accurate to speak of Luke's account as "neutral"[48] or to reduce it to the supposedly less consequential matters of personality: in fact, *paroxysmos* is anything but a neutral term for describing the disagreement between Paul and Barnabas, which is left quite unresolved[49] and clearly entails more than Paul's pique with a blemish in Mark's character (note "the work" [Acts 15:38]).

However subtle its presentation, Acts 15:36–40 amounts to a disturbing, if not traumatic, rift within Luke's narrative, and John Mark stands at its epicenter. The falling-out between Paul and Barnabas ruptures the common mind and concerted action within the Christian community—traits that Luke has taken great pains to establish in the narrative of Acts (see, e.g., 2:41–47, 4:32–37).[50] Even more pointedly, as Richard Cassidy points out, the reader of Acts has been encouraged to regard Barnabas with great favor: as magnanimous (4:36–37), insightfully supportive of the newly converted Saul (9:26–27, 11:25–26), and, in Luke's own words, "a noble man, full of the Holy Spirit and of faith" (11:24a). To the reader of Acts Barnabas's estrangement from Paul is both startling and distressing, especially since their breach is never healed; even though Paul functions as an agent of reconciliation elsewhere in the narrative (15:1–31, 16:3–4, 21:18–26), after Acts 15:36–40 no further contact between him and his closest colleague is ever reported.[51] The shift of the story at this point into a temporarily minor key may be further suggested by developments in the immediate aftermath of the John Mark imbroglio: although Paul and his new partner, Silas, strengthen the churches in Syria and Cilicia (15:40), Paul's efforts to extend his previous mission are frustrated by the Holy Spirit (16:6–7). Luke never suggests, nor would I, that Paul's missionary failures at this point are the direct, punitive consequence of his divorce from Barnabas and Mark. Rather, by underscoring the variable coincidence of human and divine purpose which can exist in the course of human and divine projects, Acts 16:6–10 may shed some light on Acts 15:36–40.

Within the narrative we are permitted access neither to Mark's reason for returning to Jerusalem (13:13b) nor to Barnabas's later rationale in reintegrating him into the missionary team (15:37). Not surprisingly, given his more prevalent role in Acts, we are told what Paul thinks: that it was best not to take with them one who had resigned and "had not gone with them to the work" (*mē synelthonta autois eis to ergon* [15:37]). What is "the work" that (the Lukan) Paul has in mind? The absolute use of *to ergon* occurs six times in Acts.[52] The first, employed by Rabbi Gamaliel in his cautionary speech to the Sanhedrin (5:38), is so general in its reference that it is variously translated as "undertaking" (NRSV), "movement" (NJB), or "[an idea's] execution" (NEB). Often translated as "deed," the singular term also appears twice in 13:41, in a quotation from the Septuagint (Hab 1:5). The remaining occurrences in Acts of *to ergon* are all relatively proximate to each other: 13:2, referring to that work for which Barnabas and Saul were specially set apart by the Holy Spirit; 14:26, regarding the work that those two missionaries fulfilled in Cyprus, Pamphylia, Pisidia, and Galatia; and 15:38, the work from which John Mark recoiled. Evidently, the particular work that Luke has in mind is the propagation of faith among Gentiles, the door to which God has opened (thus, the climax of Paul's first missionary journey at 14:27 [see also 10:1–11:18]). If that is the case, then it is this same work that, in Paul's (read Luke's) judgment, John Mark rebuffed.[53] And, if that is how Acts 15:38 is to be understood, then its conventional interpretation misses the point by a considerable margin: in Luke's judgment the problem with John Mark would be not that he simply "threw in the towel"; rather, Mark recalcitrantly had given up on the Christian mission to Gentiles.

Various scraps of circumstantial evidence seem to support this conclusion. First, even though Acts tells us precious little about Mark, clearly he is a Jerusalemite with undeniable sympathy for that city (12:13, 25; 13:13b). Through his civic affiliation Mark (better known by his Jewish name, John) is thus associated with the locus for the Judaizing party: those who held the position, "Unless you are circumcised according to Moses' custom, you cannot be saved" (Acts 15:1; cf. Gal 2:12). Indeed, throughout the second half of the narrative in Acts no little tension is generated by observant Jews or Jewish Christians who repeatedly oppose Paul's liberal mission among Gentiles.[54] Second, we have learned of Mark's assistance of his apostolic mentors in the context of proclamation in Jewish synagogues (Acts 13:5); precisely at the point at which a Gentile proconsul is converted, John Mark withdraws from their mission, back to Jerusalem (13:6–13). Third, immediately preceding Mark's reintroduction to the narrative is the articulation of a plan of communion between Christian Jews and

Gentiles, devised by the apostles in Jerusalem and joyously confirmed at Antioch (15:1–35). Fourth, immediately following the apostolic estrangement over John Mark in 15:36–39, Paul constitutes a new missionary team (15:40–16:5). In place of Barnabas he enlists Silas, a believer from among the leading Jerusalemites (15:22b, 27, 32). Into the position of assistance formerly occupied by John Mark steps Timothy (16:1–5), whose mixed parentage symbolizes the ethnic alliance of Jews and Gentiles which, for Luke, should be the wave of Christianity's future.

To be sure, Luke could have been much clearer; admittedly, much of the preceding is unavoidably speculative. But, if this hypothesis be accepted, then the trouble with John Mark in Acts 15:35–40 entails something far more profound than a character flaw or temporary lapse of judgment. In effect, Mark may represent in Acts an aborted future for Christianity—a religious outgrowth of Judaism that stubbornly attempted to remain within the confines of old Israel. If this be the case, then the narrative of Acts would suggest a mitigated tragedy, not only for an Israel that largely rejected a message of the fulfillment of its most cherished hopes,[55] but also for early Christianity, one of whose forms may have been stunted, being too closely wedded to an ethnically exclusivistic conceptualization of that hope.

But would Luke have us infer that Barnabas, Mark's advocate (15:37–39), supported a position so parochial and ultimately unavailing? After all, does not Luke persistently present Barnabas as a mediating figure between Jews and Gentiles, between Jerusalem and Antioch (Acts 11:19–30, 13:1–28, 15:1–35)?

This, indeed, is the case and perhaps helps us to understand the poignance of the episode in Acts 15:35–40. From the start, with his initial appearances at 4:32–36 and 9:26–27, Barnabas has been sympathetically portrayed by Luke as a "son of encouragement," the defender of underdogs, and the standard-bearer of Christian unity and generosity.[56] If, however, we have rightly construed John Mark's role in Acts, then the character of Barnabas is situated, in Acts 15:35–40, on the horns of a dilemma on which he cannot help but be impaled. If Barnabas cast his lot with Paul (another Jew with missionary proclivities toward Gentiles) and split with John Mark, whose sympathies were narrower, then the Christian enterprise would be internally fractured. If he broke with Paul and sided with Mark (as, for probably different reasons, he had once stood beside Paul [9:26–30]), the result would be precisely the same. Luke may not have known Paul's account, similar though not identical, about the apostolic dispute at Antioch over the question of Jewish relations with Gentiles (Gal 2:11–14); however, Acts

15:35–40 whispers something of the same painful and perhaps unresolved controversy, dramatized in terms of Barnabas's effective ensnarement in a tactically divisive, and unavoidable, Catch-22. Perhaps it is precisely for this reason that Luke handles the split between Paul and Barnabas over John Mark with such a light touch: in 15:35–40, as in 15:1–5, we encounter one of the few instances in Acts in which opposition to Christianity's future is expressed "in-house" by other, more traditionally observant, Jewish Christians. But unlike the Jerusalem controversy, which ended in a compromise satisfactory to all (the apostolic decree in Acts 15:22–35), here we find a fracture within the Christian movement which proved to be immediately if not indefinitely irreparable.[57]

For reasons left inexplicit, yet in a manner consistent with his character in Acts, Barnabas separates from Paul and takes Mark back to Cyprus. With the benefit of hindsight, we may now understand why the pronounced leadership of Barnabas has been subtly receding since chapter 13: that character is preparing to vanish entirely, his place in the narrative to be assumed by his colleague, Paul. As commentators regularly observe,[58] a positive outcome may be intimated by this sad state of affairs: with the division between Barnabas and Paul and their respective entourages, from Luke's point of view the Gentile mission may have been effectively doubled. Though such an ironically providential twist would cohere with his theology, evidenced elsewhere,[59] in fact Luke is not utterly clear about this either: while considered Gentile territory, Cyprus has been previously missionized (13:4–12), and no itinerary beyond that island is suggested for Barnabas and John Mark. On the contrary, these two characters fade out of the narrative, simply and completely, without ever being smoothly reconciled with the primary thrust of the evangelical mission thereafter associated with Paul.[60] The same could be said, both historically and theologically, for the narrower vision with which John Mark appears to have been associated.

CONCLUSION:
JOHN MARK IN THE LUKAN TRADITION

In the Book of Acts John Mark plays a minor but suggestive role:

1. He is patently associated with the early Christian community at Jerusalem (12:12, 13:13), perhaps latently with the piety and wealth of those among its number (12:12).

2. He is directly associated with Barnabas and Paul, at whose invitation he renders general service at the start of their first mission

to Cyprus (12:25, 13:5). He is not kin to Barnabas (cf. Col 4:10), nor is he directly or indirectly linked with Peter (though the latter takes refuge at the home of Mark's mother, Mary: 12:12).

3. He is implicitly connected with the Christian mission exercised within Jewish synagogues (13:5) and implicitly detached from the broader sweep of that mission among Gentiles (13:13, 15:38).

4. In general, John Mark is cast in an obscure (13:5, 13) or outrightly negative light (15:38–39), arguably owing (in Luke's view) to his reticence or refusal to engage in the Christian mission to Gentiles. Evidently for this reason, in Luke's account, he is the cause of the breakup between Barnabas and Paul (15:39b–40).

5. With his patron, Barnabas, John Mark disappears from the Lukan narrative after chapter 15, never to return.

If my analysis of these selected portions of Acts is defensible, then John Mark might be regarded as a foil: a typical, though individualized, character who reveals the protagonists of a narrative (and, often, the values of its implied author).[61] Admittedly, the Lukan Mark lacks sharp definition, and the reader of Acts must work hard to discern the significance of this character. Yet it can scarcely be doubted that John Mark's primary role in Acts is to provide a foil for its principal characters: through Mark's presence and behavior, the implied author subtly discloses or confirms the values and purposes of Barnabas, Paul, and even God, who through the Holy Spirit initiates and sustains their missionary program.[62]

By way of concluding this chapter, what may be said with assurance concerning the traditions underlying Luke's treatment of John Mark and the historicity of those traditions? Unfortunately, precious little. The once popular enterprise of analyzing the sources of Acts has fallen on hard times in recent scholarship, owing to the practical impossibility of differentiating Luke's style from that of his sources. This is true even of the Antiochene source and the "we-source," which once were confidently believed to provide a skeletal framwork for, respectively, Acts 6–12, 15 and Acts 16–28.[63] Even were there sufficient basis to uphold the existence of such sources, however, they would afford us virtually no help in the interpretation of John Mark, who (as we have seen) is more closely associated with Jerusalem Christianity than with any other primitive stream. Moreover, the identification of traditions would not guarantee their trustworthiness as sources for historical information. Of late, to be sure, some scholars have forcefully reasserted the essential though qualified trustworthiness of Acts as a source for early Christian history;[64] one may even admit that the portrayal of

John Mark in Acts is not historically improbable. Still, working only within the framework of Acts, we are more securely positioned to verify Luke's theological concerns, bearing on John Mark, rather than the historicity of that presentation.

NOTES

1. Perhaps the best general treatment of this complex subject is James D. G. Dunn, *Unity and Diversity in the New Testament: An Inquiry into the Character of Earliest Christianity* (London: SCM, 1977). On the specific position of Mark and Luke-Acts within pluriform primitive Christianity, see Étienne Trocmé, "The Beginnings of Christian Historiography and the History of Early Christianity," *AusBR* 31 (1983): 1–13.

2. For this reason various forms of "narrative criticism" recently have been employed in the interpretation of biblical texts. Representative of the kind of perspective that I shall adopt in this chapter are the following: Seymour Chatman, *Story and Discourse: Narrative Structure in Fiction and Film* (Ithaca and London: Cornell University Press, 1978); Wayne C. Booth, *The Rhetoric of Fiction* (Chicago and London: University of Chicago Press, 1962); and Wallace Martin, *Recent Theories of Narrative* (Ithaca and London: Cornell University Press, 1986). A major literary investigation of Luke-Acts is Robert C. Tannehill, *The Narrative Unity of Luke-Acts,* 2 vols. (Philadelphia and Minneapolis: Fortress, 1986, 1990).

3. F. J. Foakes Jackson and Kirsopp Lake, eds., *The Beginnings of Christianity,* pt. 1: *The Acts of the Apostles* (London: Macmillan, 1922), 2:146–47; cf. Foakes Jackson and Lake, *Beginnings of Christianity,* pt. 1, 4:31; A. E. Haefner, "The Bridge between Mark and Acts," *JBL* 77 (1958): 67–71.

4. Although the vagueness of Galatians 2:9 forbids certain identification, presumably Paul also numbers John, the son of Zebedee, along with Peter ("Cephas") and James, among the "pillar apostles." See Hans Dieter Betz, *Galatians: A Commentary on Paul's Letter to the Churches in Galatia,* Hermeneia (Philadelphia: Fortress, 1970), 101.

5. Thus, see Andrew T. Lincoln, "The Promise and the Failure: Mark 16:7, 8," *JBL* 108 (1989): 283–300, and the literature cited therein; Mikeal C. Parsons, *The Departure of Jesus in Luke-Acts: The Ascension Narratives in Context,* JSNTSup 21 (Sheffield: JSOT, 1987).

6. Cf. the presentations in Jacob Jervell, "Zur Frage der Traditionsgrundlage der Apostelgeschichte," *ST* 16 (1963): 25–41; Pierson Parker, "Mark, Acts, and Galilean Christianity," *NTS* 16 (1970): 295–304; Ernst Haenchen, *The Acts of the Apostles: A Commentary* (Philadelphia: Westminster, 1971), 81–90; and Werner Georg Kümmel, *Introduction to the New Testament,* 17th ed., trans. Howard Clark Kee (Nashville: Abingdon, 1973), 174–85.

7. In particular, no connection is forged between Mary's house in Acts 12 with the site of the Last Supper in Luke 22 (*contra* F. F. Bruce, *The Acts of the Apostles: The Greek Text with Introduction and Commentary* [Grand Rapids, Mich.: Eerdmans, 1951], 247 and elsewhere).

8. In *The First Urban Christians: The Social World of the Apostle Paul* (New Haven and London: Yale University Press, 1983), 75–77, Wayne A. Meeks offers cursory, social scientific reflections on the household model for the Christian *ekklēsia* in the mid-first century. The topic will be probed somewhat further in our consideration of Roman Christianity (chap. 8).

9. Shirley Jackson Case, "John Mark," *ExpTim* 26 (1914–15): 372; see also Henry Barclay Swete, *The Gospel according to St. Mark: The Greek Text with Introduction, Notes, and Indices,* 3d. ed. (London: Macmillan, 1927), xv. Even less convincing is James Moffatt's attempt to identify John Mark as the ultimate source of Acts 12:12–17, on the basis of certain linguistic peculiarities common to Acts 12:8, 10, and Mark 4:28, 6:9 (*An Introduction to the Literature of the New Testament,* ITL [Edinburgh and New York: T & T Clark / Charles Scribner's Sons, 1918, 1929], 293).

10. Literary analysts are wont to distinguish the "real [flesh-and-blood] author" from the author whose ideals and perspective are implied in a literary work. The "implied author" can be further differentiated from the "narrator" whose voice is heard to be "telling" the story (thus, see Chatman, *Story and Discourse,* 147–58). As there is arguably no difference in the values and beliefs of the implied author and the narrator of Luke-Acts, I shall employ these terms interchangeably. References to "Luke" will be used for convenience, without any particular assumptions about the real author of Luke-Acts. See also Tannehill, *Narrative Unity,* 1: 6–8.

11. Acts 12:25 contains a difficult text-critical problem: the best manuscripts preserve the reading, "And Barnabas and Saul returned to [*eis*] Jerusalem," the geography of which makes little sense in the context of Acts 11:27–30 and 13:1 (wherein the pair return to Antioch, after having been previously in Jerusalem). My translation attempts to reconcile syntax and sense, though no resolution of the problem is completely satisfying. For further discussion, consult Bruce M. Metzger, *A Textual Commentary on the Greek New Testament* (N.p.: United Bible Societies, 1971), 398–400.

12. Tannehill, *Narrative Unity,* 2:78, 99. Note also Philip's introduction and later development in Acts 6:5, 8:26–40.

13. The same verb is similarly used by Paul with reference to Titus in Galatians 2:1.

14. Swete, *Gospel according to St. Mark,* xvi.

15. F. F. Bruce, *Commentary on the Book of the Acts,* NICNT (Grand Rapids, Mich.: Eerdmans, 1954), 258.

16. G. J. Paul, *St. John's Gospel: A Commentary* (Madras: Christian Literature Society, 1965), 16 n. 1. For alerting me to this interpretation and for making the quotation available to me I am indebted to Beverly R. Gaventa.

17. *Pace* Luke (Acts 4:36), the name "Barnabas" means "son of Nebo," not "son of encouragement." Nevertheless, in Acts the characterization holds, if not its etymological association.

18. One might even say that Barnabas is the "senior member" of those delegations. Consider Paul's nominal subordination to Barnabas in Acts 9:27; 11:25–26, 30; 12:25; 13:1–2, 7; 14:14.

19. See also Howard Clark Kee, *Good News to the Ends of the Earth: The Theology of Acts* (London and Philadelphia: SCM/TPI, 1990), 54.

20. On the pivotal role played by Barnabas in Acts, see Luke Timothy Johnson, *The Literary Function of Possessions in Luke-Acts*, SBLDS 37 (N.p.: Scholars Press, 1977), 53, 203–4.

21. See LSJ, 2.1872b; James Hope Moulton and Wilbert Francis Howard, *A Grammar of New Testament Greek*, 3d. ed. (Edinburgh: T & T Clark, 1929), 2:328. This connotation of the noun may still be present in Paul's metaphor at 1 Corinthians 4:1.

22. Hans Conzelmann, *Acts of the Apostles: A Commentary on the Acts of the Apostles*, ed. E. J. Epp with C. R. Matthews, Hermeneia (Philadelphia: Fortress, 1987), 99; Haenchen, *Acts*, 397. Cf. Henry Joel Cadbury's correlation of *hypēretēs* in Acts 13:5 with the word's appearance in Luke 1:2 (Foakes Jackson and Lake, *Beginnings of Christianity*, 2:497).

23. Swete, *Gospel according to St. Mark*, xvi.

24. B. T. Holmes, "Luke's Description of John Mark," *JBL* 54 (1935): 63–72.

25. Thus, for example, "the ministers of the Temple" in the Mishnaic tractate, *Tamid*; see also *Tosefta Sukka* 4.11–12.

26. R. O. P. Taylor, "The Ministry of Mark," *ExpTim* 54 (1942–43): 136; see also *The Groundwork of the Gospels, with Some Collected Papers* (Oxford: Basil Blackwell, 1946), 25 (as quoted in the introduction to the present study); and F. H. Chase, "Mark (John)," in *Dictionary of the Bible*, ed. James Hastings (Edinburgh: T & T Clark, 1909), 3:245–46.

27. Thus, see Bruce, *Acts* (1951), 255; *Commentary* (1954), 263; E. P. Blair, "Mark, John," *IDB* 3.277–78; William Barclay, "A Comparison of Paul's Missionary Preaching and Preaching to the Church," in *Apostolic History and the Gospel: Biblical and Historical Essays Presented to F. F. Bruce on His Sixtieth Birthday*, ed. W. Ward Gasque and Ralph P. Martin (Grand Rapids, Mich.: Eerdmans, 1970), 165–75, esp. 169–70.

28. *Contra* Taylor, *Groundwork*, 24, 38. Because Mark was a "synagogue-minister," "he had often to take on the work of interpreter during the services." (At this point Taylor becomes less an exegete and more the conservator of tradition that he takes Peter and Mark to have been.) In her recent monograph, *Mark's Audience: The Literary and Social Setting of Mark 4.11–12*, JSNTSup 33 (Sheffield: Sheffield Academic Press, 1989), 63–67, Mary Ann Beavis gravitates toward a similar judgment.

29. Thus, see K. H. Rengstorf, *"hypēretēs, hypēreteō,"* TDNT 8 (1972): 541.

30. Swete, *Gospel according to St. Mark*, xvii.

31. Foakes Jackson and Lake, *Beginnings of Christianity*, 4:147.

32. R. Alan Culpepper, "Paul's Mission to the Gentile World: Acts 13–19," *RevExp* 71 (1974): 487–97, esp. 488.

33. Bruce, *Acts* (1951), 259; *Commentary* (1954), 266. Notice the argumentative presumption of Colossians 4:10.

34. Gerhard A. Krodel, *Acts*, ACNT (Minneapolis: Augsburg, 1986), 231.

35. Swete, *Gospel according to St. Mark*, xvii.

36. Krodel, *Acts*, 231, although one suspects that this possibility is proposed with tongue in cheek.

37. Haenchen, *Acts*, 407; Conzelmann, *Acts*, 105 (though Conzelmann's comment that Acts 13:13 is "explained" by 15:38 is more than somewhat mysterious).

38. Meir Sternberg, *The Poetics of Biblical Narrative: Ideological Literature and the Drama of Reading* (Bloomington: Indiana University Press, 1985), 230–40. For an insightful appropriation of Sternberg's concepts, see Tannehill, *Narrative Unity*, 2: 199–200, 248–50, 306–7. Tannehill does not explore the possibility of intentional obscurity with reference to Acts 13:13.

39. It may not be fortuitous that, within the context of happenings at Jerusalem, Barnabas's name tends to precede Paul's (Acts 15:12 and esp. 15:25).

40. *Contra* Haenchen, *Acts*, 462, who charts the emergence of Paul's dominance from Acts 15 onward.

41. See also Tannehill, *Narrative Unity*, 2:182.

42. Thus, see Moulton and Howard (*Grammar*, 1:130), who attribute this difference to the characterization of Barnabas as one "with [the] easy forgetfulness of risk."

43. See LSJ 1.291ab; BAG 126a. The transitive form of the verb is used by Herodotus (*Persian Wars* 1.76, 154), Thucydides (*Peloponnesian War* 1.81), Josephus (*Ant.* 8.198, 20.102), LXX Deut 7:4, and Luke (Acts 5:37) to describe one who misleads others or incites a revolt. In the patristic literature *aphistēmi* may be used to refer to one's withdrawal from church communion (Irenaeus, *Adv. Haer.* 3.4.2) or apostasy (Hermas, *Sim.* 8.8.2; Irenaeus, *Adv. Haer.* 1.13.7); see also Lampe, *PGL*, s.v.

44. *Paroxysmos* stems from the verb *paroxizō*, "to have a sharp smell" (LSJ 2.1342b), which in turn suggests another metaphor with reference to Acts 15:39: at Antioch Barnabas and Paul "raised a stink" with each other over John Mark's inclusion.

45. Bruce, *Acts* (1951), 306; *Commentary* (1954), 319; Krodel, *Acts*, 294.

46. Conzelmann, *Acts*, 123; Paul J. Achtemeier, *The Quest for Unity in the New Testament Church: A Study in Paul and Acts* (Philadelphia: Fortress, 1987), 41–42.

47. To assess Luke's silence as knowledgeable suppression (as does Zahn, cited in Haenchen, *Acts*, 474) is to build inordinate speculation upon hypothesis.

48. Haenchen, *Acts*, 474.

49. Equally unresolved is Galatians 2:11–14, which is by no means "neutral" either.

50. See Kee's discussion in *Good News*, 86–89.

51. Richard J. Cassidy, *Society and Politics in the Acts of the Apostles* (Maryknoll, N.Y.: Orbis, 1987), 26, 66–67, 190 n. 38. My comments here are indebted to Cassidy's sensitive reading.

52. Not including a poorly attested variant reading in 15:18, the plural, "works," appears, with various nuances of meaning, five times in Acts: 7:22, 41; 9:36; 15:18 (var.); 26:20. However, it is the singular, absolute form that is potentially significant at 15:38.

53. Thus, see Culpepper, "Paul's Mission," 488, although his assessment, unlike mine, focuses on the probable intentions of Mark, not of Luke.

54. See Lawrence M. Wills's interesting discussion, "The Depiction of the Jews in Acts," *JBL* 110 (1991): 631–54, esp. 640–43.

55. Robert C. Tannehill, "Israel in Luke-Acts: A Tragic Story," *JBL* 104 (1985): 69–85. Luke's perception of the Jews is a highly controversial issue in current interpretation of Acts. Consider the range of exegetical possibilities collected by Joseph B. Tyson, ed., *Luke-Acts and the Jewish People: Eight Critical Perspectives* (Minneapolis: Augsburg, 1988).

56. Although some scholars have proceeded incautiously by psychologizing Barnabas's actions at Acts 15:36–39, doubtless they have correctly intuited the intention of Luke's narrative rhetoric.

57. In private correspondence (6 March 1991) Beverly Gaventa has pointed out to me a cognate contrast between the antagonists in Acts 15 and those in Acts 5:1–11 and 8:9–24: "Perhaps Luke treats Mark (and Barnabas) with such care because they are not villains in the blatant sense [that Ananias, Sapphira, and Simon Magus are]. [Mark and Barnabas] are reputable members of the community, whose position (on the Gentile mission) Luke will not endorse."

58. Among others, see Bruce, *Acts* (1951), 306; *Commentary* (1954), 319; Haenchen, *Acts,* 474; Krodel, *Acts,* 295; Achtemeier, *Quest for Unity,* 42.

59. See also Acts 8:1 and 26:32, where persecution and imprisonment become vehicles for the dispersion of the gospel.

60. In this connection it is odd that Conzelmann would speculate on Luke's knowledge of the tradition of Mark's later reunion with Paul, inasmuch as that commentator believes that Luke had no direct knowledge of a Pauline letter like Galatians (*Acts,* 123–24).

61. Among some literary critics such a character is called a "ficelle." Consult, for instance, the discussion in W. J. Harvey, *Character and the Novel* (London: Chatto & Windus, 1965), 58, 62–68.

62. On the calculated passivity of the protagonists in Acts, Luke's emphasis on their role in reacting and verifying, see the discussion by Tannehill in *Narrative Unity,* 2:102–5.

63. Helmut Koester, *Introduction to the New Testament,* vol. 2: *History and Literature of Early Christianity* (Philadelphia, Berlin, and New York: Fortress / Walter de Gruyter, 1982), 49–52.

64. Thus, see Martin Hengel, *Acts and the History of Earliest Christianity,* trans. John Bowden (Philadelphia: Fortress, 1985); Gerd Lüdemann, "Acts of the Apostles as a Historical Source," in *The Social World of Formative Christianity and Judaism: Essays in Tribute to Howard Clark Kee,* ed. Jacob Neusner, Peder Borgen, Ernest S. Frerichs, Richard Horsley (Philadelphia:

Fortress, 1988), 109–25; Gerd Lüdemann, *Early Christianity according to the Traditions in Acts: A Commentary* (Philadelphia: Fortress, 1989); Colin J. Hemer, *The Book of Acts in the Setting of Hellenistic History,* WUNT 49 (Tübingen: Mohr [Siebeck], 1989).

Chapter Two

A Beloved Junior Partner
Mark in New Testament Letters

As our inquiry into the New Testament's depiction of Mark continues, our primary assumptions from the preceding chapter remain in force. First, in the absence of clear evidence to the contrary, we shall not assume that the *same* figure of Mark is necessarily envisioned by all of the New Testament writers who refer to that figure. Second, our investigation will not be concentrated on the historicity of New Testament images of Mark (about which very little can be said). Rather, our focus will be on how the figure of Mark *functions* in certain New Testament Epistles.

There are four references to someone named Mark in letters of the New Testament: they occur in 1 Peter and three Epistles associated with the apostle Paul (Philemon, Colossians, and 2 Timothy). Although none offers even the cursory amount of information about Mark presented by Luke in Acts, each of these documents warrants consideration. We shall begin with the Pauline corpus, moving in the most probable chronological sequence.

THE PAULINE TRADITION

Philemon

Of all the Pauline Epistles Philemon is the briefest and most like the many "nonliterary," or documentary, letters that have survived from antiquity.[1] Though its Pauline authenticity is virtually undisputed, its time and place of origin are uncertain. Most of the letter's *dramatis personae* seem to be associated with Asian Christianity in the Phrygian city of Colossae, which was situated in the upper Lycus Valley (thus, see Archippus: Philem 2/Col 4:17; Onesimus: Philem 10/Col 4:9; Epaphras: Philem 23/Col 1:7; 4:12). In turn, this likely destination may favor an Ephesian, rather than a Roman, setting for Paul's imprisonment at the time of the letter's composition (Philem 1, 9–10, 13, 23; see also 1 Cor 15:32; 2 Cor 11:23), inasmuch as Paul anticipates an imminent release and visit to Philemon (v. 22).[2] Depending on the provenance assigned to the letter, it can be dated from the early fifties (if from Ephesus) to the early sixties (if from Rome).

From among the various types of letters in antiquity,[3] Philemon most closely resembles a letter of petition: Paul requests of its recipient the concilatory acceptance of Onesimus, an erstwhile fugitive slave (v. 17). Yet this Epistle also resembles a letter of recommendation, insofar as Philemon is introduced to his slave's new status as a Christian (vv. 10–17).[4] And, because Paul adopts familial metaphors in relating himself to Philemon and "the church in [his] house" (v. 2; cf. vv. 1, 7, 16 ["brother"]; v. 2 ["sister"]; v. 10 ["child" and "father"]), the tenor of this Epistle is also reminiscent of ancient family letters. Thus, as with Paul's other letters, in Philemon we observe the apostle's creative compounding and modification of the epistolary genres that were customary for him and his readers.

Particularly characteristic of ancient family letters is the expression of an extended interest in the correspondents' welfare, correlative to which are extensive salutations, often to or from third parties, in the closing of the letter.[5] It is within this context in Philemon that the reference to Mark occurs. Immediately prior to Paul's concluding benediction (v. 24) and following mention of Epaphras, the apostle's "fellow prisoner-of-war" (*synaichmalōtos* [v. 23], metaphorically employed), Mark is grouped with Aristarchus, Demas, and Luke as Paul's "fellow workers" (*synergoi*), who send greetings to Philemon (cf. Col 4:10–14).

Although we learn nothing further about the identity, as such, of Mark and these other figures, their attribution as Paul's "coworkers" is significant. Besides the four personages mentioned in Philemon 24, eleven others in the Pauline corpus are described as *synergoi*: Prisca and Aquila (Rom 16:3), Urbanus (Rom 16:9), Timothy (Rom 16:21; 1 Cor 16:10; 1 Thess 3:2), Apollos (1 Cor 3:6–9), Titus (2 Cor 8:23), Epaphroditus (Phil 2:25), Clement (Phil 4:3), Justus (Col 4:11), Philemon (Philem 1), and Paul himself (1 Cor 3:9). The term is also implicitly used with reference to Stephanas, Fortunatus, and Achaicus (1 Cor 16:16–18), Euodia and Syntyche (Phil 4:2–3), and Silas (1 Thess 3:2). Of a few of these figures (like Timothy) we know something; of others (like Urbanus), practically nothing. Yet, insofar as it is possible to discern, the common denominator among most if not all of these so-called *synergoi* is their active participation in Paul's ministry of preaching and congregational supervision. The term is applied less frequently to believers in general,[6] who on occasion are seemingly differentiated from the coworkers (1 Cor 3:9; 2 Cor 1:24, 8:23), and more usually as an honorific for those whose work with Paul was worthy of the community's esteem.[7] At least that much, if nothing else, may be implied of Mark in Philemon 24.

With specific reference to the Epistle to Philemon, perhaps further comment is warranted regarding the rhetorical function of this particular denotation of Paul's apostolic entourage. So seemingly straightforward is this letter that to speak of its "rhetoric" might seem audacious. Nevertheless, as F. Forrester Church has convincingly demonstrated,[8] a rather sophisticated use of the techniques of classical persuasion is displayed therein: while Paul ostensibly refrains from compelling Philemon to receive Onesimus with impunity, the letter's argument is carefully crafted to maneuver Philemon into just that course of action while permitting him to act honorably and voluntarily (see vv. 12–14). To this end one of the strategies employed by Paul is a consistent, pathetic alignment of his addressee with the larger interests of the apostle and of the church. Accordingly, the letter is addressed not only to Philemon but also to Apphia, Archippus, and the congregation meeting in Philemon's house (vv. 1–2); Philemon is lavishly commended for his ongoing love and fidelity toward the Lord, Paul, and "all the saints" (vv. 5–7); Paul hopes soon to avail himself of Philemon's notable Christian hospitality (v. 22). Within this rhetorical context the reference to Mark (along with Epaphras, Aristarchus, Demas, and Luke) is more than merely part of a conventional epistolary closing: as Mark and the others are celebrated fellow workers with Paul during his captivity for Christ (v. 23), so too is Philemon, "our beloved fellow worker" (tō agapētō kai synergō hēmōn [v. 1b]), implored to accede to his "brother" Paul's request for clemency toward Onesimus, another, once errant "brother" (vv. 7, 16–17). In other words, by drawing together himself, Mark, Philemon, and Onesimus with the rhetoric of collaboration and family relationships, Paul is gently forcing a point of honor by reminding Philemon of the larger dimensions of ecclesial unity and compassion, implied by the Onesimus affair.[9] The reference to Mark as synergos, without further (and potentially distracting) identification, subtly but pointedly contributes to Paul's rhetorical strategy and to the exemplification of the apostle's theological principle.

Colossians

From among the letters of the New Testament ascribed to Paul the authenticity of Colossians is one of the most difficult to adjudicate. The primary "sticking points" concern the Epistle's language and style, its seeming divergence from (or at least development beyond) the theology of the undoubtedly Pauline letters, and its similarity in style and thought to Ephesians (which is more generally regarded as the work of a later Pauline proponent). For two reasons the latter consideration is arguably the least decisive: first, the author of Ephesians appears to have depended upon Colossians, while the reverse does not appear to be the case;[10] second, Colossians appears to be even more closely related, at least circumstantially, to the undoubtedly authentic Philemon.[11] The arguments for and against the literary and theological consanguinity of Colossians with the undisputed letters of Paul are unusually well balanced and inconclusive;[12] as a result, on the question of Colossians' authenticity, at present there appears to be a hung jury among Pauline interpreters.

As important as it is for one's perspective on the letter, clearly the question of its authenticity is far too complex to be settled here. Accordingly, we shall first focus our attention on the rhetorical function of the reference to Mark in 4:10 within the argument of Colossians, apart from the question of authorship. Afterward, we shall reflect briefly on the difference made for our observations by the attribution to this letter of Pauline or non-Pauline authorship.

A primary purpose of Colossians is to warn the Asian Christians in the Phrygian city of Colossae against a syncretistic "philosophy" that, in the author's judgment, was aberrant, erroneous, and dangerous (2:8–23). The dimensions of this specious wisdom (2:23) are diffuse and for that reason notoriously difficult to define.[13] Nevertheless, some Hellenistic elaboration of originally Jewish rites and traditions is suggested by the general reference to nullified legal demands (2:14) and by the specific derogations of circumcision (2:11), dietary regulations (2:16, 21), and festivals of new moons and sabbaths (2:16). Following this cautionary polemic (to which also the christological doctrine preoccupying 1:15–2:7 is tacitly addressed), the author moves to a lengthy section of paraenesis, or moral exhortation (3:1–4:6), after which the letter concludes with instructions and personal greetings (4:7–18). Again, as in Philemon 23, it is in the epistolary conclusion that reference to Mark is made (4:10); similar, yet even more striking, is the reappearance in Colossians 4:9–17 of a host of figures mentioned in the Letter to Philemon: Onesimus (Col 4:9/Philem 10, 12), Aristarchus (Col 4:10/Philem 23), Epaphras (Col 1:7; 4:12/Philem 23), Luke and Demas (Col 4:14/Philem 24), Archippus (Col 4:17/Philem 2).

What role is played by the reference to Mark at the close of this letter? In one sense the rhetorical strategy here is similar to that exhibited in Philemon: in both cases Mark (among others) is mentioned as a way of cementing an ecclesial bond between the Epistle's sender and recipients. In Colossians this seems to be accomplished in three ways. First, Mark is described as one of Paul's "fellow-workers in the kingdom of God" (*synergoi eis tēn basileian tou theou*), who has been a source of comfort for him (Col 4:11), which is similar though not identical to the simpler but no less estimable characterization of Mark as a *synergos* in Philemon 24. Again, in both letters the description of a Pauline associate as *synergos* carries a subtly persuasive connotation: even as Mark and others are Paul's valued coworkers, so too, by inference, should be Philemon's household and the Colossians (through compliance with the apostle's instructions, given elsewhere in their respective communiqués).

Second, Mark, Aristarchus, and Jesus (called Justus) are identified by the letter's author as "the only ones of the circumcision" (*hoi ontes ek peritomēs houtoi monoi*) among Paul's coworkers (Col 4:11).[14] By explicitly recognizing and relaying the salutations of the apostle's Jewish colleagues, a subtle boost is given to the author's reserve toward those Jewish practices, circumcision in particular, which may have deleteriously preoccupied the church at Colossae (cf. Col 2:10–14, 16–17).[15] It may be that the references to Paul's Gentile associates—Epaphras (4:12, see also 1:7), Luke, and Demas (4:14)—serve, in part, a cognate function: to accredit the author's rejection of the more Hellenic features of the erroneous teaching and practice in Colossae (2:8–9, 15, 18–23).

Third, Colossians 4:10 refers to previous instructions about, and a potential visit from, Mark.[16] Although it is impossible to infer the content of these apostolic directives or commands (*entolas*), their very existence, conjoined with the possibility of a visit from a Pauline associate and the exhortation that he be hospitably welcomed (*dechomai* [see also Matt 10:14, 40, 41; Mark 6:11; Luke 9:5, 53; 10:8, 10; John 4:45; Heb 11:31]), forges between the writer and his letter's recipients a link that is centered on Mark. Like that of Philemon, the closing of Colossians anticipates a congregational visit that implicitly strengthens a union between the letter's sender and its recipients; in Philemon, however, the expected visitor is the apostle, whereas in Colossians it is an apostolic delegate.

The identification, in Colossians 4:10, of Mark as the *anepsios* of Barnabas is eye-catching. Although the translation of this word in the King James Version of 1611 suggests that Mark is Barnabas's "nephew" ("Marcus, sister's son to Barnabas"), the preferred rendering of the Greek term in this verse is almost certainly "cousin." From its appearance in Homer's *Iliad* (9.464, 15.554) and other classical texts (e.g., the writings of Herodotus and Aeschylus) through its infrequent occurrence in the Septuagint (Num 36:11; Tob 7:2) to its presence in Josephus (*J. W.* 1.662; *Ant* 1.290, 15.250) and Philo (*On the Embassy to Gaius* 67), *anepsios* consistently carries the connotation of "cousin," though occasionally in a figurative or comical sense (e.g., as in a work by the fifth-century B.C. writer Strattis).[17]

It is difficult to determine the precise purpose served by the identification of Mark as cousin of Barnabas. As this is the only appearance of the word in the Pauline corpus (and its only occurrence anywhere in the New Testament, generally), it is highly doubtful that here *anepsios* is intended to suggest a figurative sense of affectionate or ecclesial attachment (such as is often the case with "brother" or "sister" in Paul's letters). If, as seems more likely, the term suggests an actual relationship by blood, at the very least its use in Colossians 4:10 distinguishes this from the many "Marks" of the period, some of whom may have been known by the Colossian church and potentially confused with Barnabas's relative. As there is little reason to deny the reference in this verse as applying to the same personage whom we know from Galatians 2:13 (and Acts), a better-known figure (Barnabas) is sensibly being used to identify one less well known (Mark). Judged purely on the basis of the evidence in this single text, the historicity of the identification of Mark as the cousin of Barnabas is neither improbable nor verifiable. This much can be said: contrary to the assumption of many commentators,[18] there is nothing in Colossians that directly indicates its author's knowledge of the Lukan Acts in general, or of the particular story in Acts 12–15 that correlates Paul, Barnabas, and *John* Mark. The association among these figures *may* be assumed in Colossians 4:10;[19] that Colossians "no doubt"[20] refers to the John Mark of Acts overstates an inference drawn from very skimpy evidence.

If the Epistle to the church at Colossae was written by Paul, we have in it corroborating evidence that, during the time of his (Ephesian?) imprisonment, a certain Mark was numbered among his valued colleagues. Moreover, beyond what is said in Philemon we learn that this Mark was Jewish, was collaterally related to Barnabas, and functioned as an emissary for Paul within the sphere of Asian Christianity. If Colossians is pseudonymous (written not by Paul but by a Paulinist), then the apostle's dispatch of Mark is dubious (and probably an extrapolation from Philemon 24), though the other pieces of information (regarding Mark's ethnicity, lineage, and association with Asian Christianity) may still be accurate. (The adoption of pseudonymity does not logically entail completely imaginative fictionalizations within the document; indeed, the maintenance of verisimilitude would almost necessitate the preservation of at least some historical data.) Whatever the historical realities may have been, the author of Colossians, if not Paul, was in touch with a tradition about Mark that associated him with Jewish Christianity, a Christian community in Asia, and with the figure of Barnabas.

Does the rhetorical strategy implied by Colossians 4:7–18, in which the citation of Mark appears, incline toward or away from Pauline authorship? As noted earlier, the references to *synergoi* and a (surrogate) apostolic visit in Colossians 4:10–11 are reminiscent of Philemon 22–24; in itself, however, this is inconclusive with respect to authorship. On the one hand, Paul could have written both; on the other hand, the former could be mimicry of the latter. The tacit specification of Mark's (and others') Jewish lineage to bolster a critique of the Colossians' preoccupation with Jewish practices is more interesting, insofar as it may remind one of a similar strategy adopted by Paul in Galatians 2:1–10: there, too, Paul implicitly argues for the validity of Gentile Christian faith apart from circumcision on the basis of its accreditation by the Jewish-dominated Jerusalem church. Again, however, this cannot establish the case for Paul's authorship of Colossians: similarity of strategy does not guarantee identity of authorship. More problematic for the Pauline authenticity of Colossians is the author's more overt, rhetorical strategy of evincing responsibility for, and presuming the right to direct, a Christian community that Paul has not visited, much less founded (see Col 1:23, 2:1)—a tactic that seems to violate Paul's principle of noninterference with a church founded by someone else (Rom 15:20; cf. Col 1:7). The rather authoritarian tenor of the author of Colossians is more analogous to the flatly directive, royal letters of antiquity[21] than to the commendatory, petitionary, or family correspondence with which Philemon exhibits parallels. Moreover, the biographical details in Colossians 4:7–18—including the information about Mark—create the sort of formal, but substantively extraneous, Pauline coloration that can be witnessed in the unquestionably Pauline pseudepigrapha of later centuries (3 *Corinthians* and *The Acts of Paul and Thecla* [both A.D. 150], *The Prayer of the Apostle Paul* [150–300], and *The Apocalypse of Paul* [300–400?]).[22]

As with most of the considerations pertaining to authorship, the assessment of the evidence in the closing of Colossians is subject to debate. On balance the force of the cumulative evidence nudges me toward skepticism of Colossians as Pauline. Regardless of its authorship, however, the letter contributes some interesting features to the figures of Mark which emerge from the New Testament and its underlying traditions.

2 Timothy

Touching the question of authorship, and nothwithstanding some artic-
ulate protestations to the contrary,[23] most scholars think themselves
on firmer footing with the Pastoral Epistles (1, 2 Timothy and Titus)
than with Colossians. That is, when the relevant considerations are
taken together (their vocabulary, style, and theological attitude; their
presumed sociohistorical situation and weak attestation in the early
church), the Pastorals appear more likely to have stemmed not from
Paul but, rather, from his second-century interpreter(s), who attempted to apply the apostle's teaching to post-Pauline situations and
needs.[24] The origin and destination of these first "commentaries on
Paul" are uncertain: as in Philemon and Colossians, the apostle's
imprisonment is assumed (2 Tim 1:8, 16; 2:9), though pointedly not
located at Ephesus in the case of 2 Timothy (see 4:12). Whether this
indirectly suggests a Caesarean (Acts 24–26) or Roman (Acts 28; 2 Tim
1:17) provenance is debatable. If the intended recipients resided in the
locales with which "Timothy" and "Titus" are associated, then the
Pastorals could have addressed conditions among second- or third-
generation Christians in Asia (N.B. "Ephesus," 1 Tim 1:3; cf. 2 Tim
1:15, 4:13 ["Troas"]) or Crete (Tit 1:5, 12).

As it happens, the mention of Mark in 2 Timothy 4:11 is located in
material whose authenticity has been particularly subject to debate.
Earlier in this century, P. N. Harrison mounted a detailed argument for
the preservation, within the pseudonymous Pastoral Letters, of fragments from authentic, yet otherwise unknown, Pauline material. In
defense of this theory, Harrison claimed, was the vivid, concrete, and
theologically irrelevant character of the various "personalia" that
occur in the Pastorals, including 2 Timothy 4:9–12 (and its reference
to Mark in v. 11).[25]

Although we cannot engage this theory in its details, suffice it to say
that the majority of interpreters have not found it persuasive. Hypo-
thetically, it demands a partitioning of the Pastorals which is less than
convincing, while leaving unanswered the question of how such detached and innocuous snippets could ever have survived.[26] In the
judgment of most commentators the personalia in the Pastorals more
likely comport with the inherent need of these pseudonymous documents to maintain the fiction of their Pauline authorship, whether by
outright deception[27] or by the creative adaptation of earlier (true or
false) traditions, in accordance with the customary technique of first-
century pseudepigraphy.[28] If neither the Pauline authorship of 2 Timothy nor the historicity of the traditions underlying 4:9–21 may be

assumed, that of course does not preclude further discussion of the reference to Mark in that material. Rather, as we saw in discussing the relevant passages in Acts and Colossians, the question may simply require reformulation: What epistolary or rhetorical function is served by the reference to Mark, among others, in 2 Timothy?

First, and most perhaps most obviously, Mark again appears in the closing of a purportedly Pauline letter. Along with that of Demas and Luke, his appearance reminds one of the list of greetings in Colossians (4:10, 14) and Philemon (24), lending an air of verisimilitude to 2 Timothy.[29] A concern for verismilitude probably accounts for the mention made, in 2 Timothy 4:13, of "the books and parchments" (*ta biblia; tas membranas*). Although some interpreters have claimed that this constitutes a veiled recommendation of the Second Gospel,[30] detailed desiderata like this are common in ancient pseudepigraphical letters, and references to books and parchments would especially befit an itinerant apostle known for writing letters.[31]

Second, as with the concluding salutations and instructions elsewhere in the Pauline corpus, those in 2 Timothy 4:9–21 create the impression of personal attachment among Christians dispersed throughout the Roman world. The acknowledgment of Mark and others, interacting with the author and the letter's recipient(s), arguably creates or bolsters a social linkage with coreligionists in other Mediterranean cities (cf. Rom 16; Col 4:7–18).

Third, and even more specifically, in 2 Timothy 4:11 Mark is presented as one whose companionship with Paul is sought and whose ministry or mission to the apostle is notably useful or beneficial (*estin gar moi euchrēstos eis diakonia*).[32] This alignment of the figures of Mark and Paul may function rhetorically in at least two ways. First, it suggests that Mark, like Luke (2 Tim 4:11a) and Tychicus (4:12), serves as a positive example for the readers of the letter. Implicitly, a contrast is being established between them and Demas the deserter (4:10a) as well as Alexander the malevolent (4:14–15): unlike the latter pair, Luke, Mark, and Timothy are among the few remaining faithful who are huddling around an otherwise derelict apostle. The status of Crescens and Titus (v. 10b) is questionable: only Demas's leaving is described as defection, yet the departures of Crescens and Titus contribute to Paul's abandonment, underlined in 4:11a (see also 1:15).[33] It is not implausible, though practically impossible to confirm, that the figures of Mark and, say, Demas were implicitly associated by the author and readers of this letter with rival factions who split over competing theological positions (cf. 2 Tim 2:14–26).

Second, and related to the preceding consideration, the figure of

Mark in 2 Timothy supports that of Paul as the primary model of steadfast endurance in suffering—which, for the author of this document, is paradigmatic of the Christian life in general.[34] Repeatedly in 2 Timothy, adherents of the Lord are called to their "portion of sufferings for the gospel in the power of God" (1:8; cf. 1:12; 2:3, 8–10; 3:10–15; 4:6–8). If Mark has proved supportive of Paul (*moi euchrēstos eis diakonian* [4:11b]; cf. *emoi euchrēston*, speaking of Onesimus [Philem 11]), it would seem to follow, by implication, that it is precisely this kind of ministry, which is prepared to suffer for the ultimate "crown of righteousness," which Mark may be regarded as having performed in exemplary fashion.

Summary: Mark in the Pauline Tradition

Temporarily bracketing out the question of authorship, we may observe that, in these three letters, the figure of Mark bears some intriguingly consistent features:

1. In all three letters Mark is tacitly correlated with Asian Christianity, regarding the locale either of the intended recipients (Col 1:2; cf. Philem 2, 23–24, with Col 1:7, 10, 12, 17; 2 Tim 1:15; 4:12–13) or of the apostle's imprisonment (if an Ephesian captivity is implied by Philemon 22 and Colossians 4:10).[35] If these documents actually or imaginatively presume the imperial capital as their provenance, then possibly, though less obviously, Mark could also be associated with Roman Christianity in the captivity Epistles.

2. In all three letters Mark's apostolic association is closely, even affectionately, acknowledged. In Philemon (24) and Colossians (4:11) Mark is ranged alongside other esteemed coworkers with Paul; in 2 Timothy he is distinguished as one whose service to "the apostle" is especially beneficial. In Colossians (4:10) Mark's alignment with the leadership of the primitive church is broadened through his familial association with Barnabas.

3. References to Mark, among others, are made in all three letters to emphasize, or actually to foster, communion among Christian congregations throughout Mediterranean antiquity. This is especially conveyed by Mark's consistent appearance in the concluding sections of Philemon, Colossians, and 2 Timothy, all of which aim to create ecclesial unity between their senders and recipients. One dimension of this phenomenon is specified in Colossians 4:10–12 (also 4:13–17), which underlines the solidarity of Jewish Christians such as Mark, Aristarchus, and Justus with Gentile coreligionists like Epaphras and the Colossians themselves.

4. Qualitatively speaking, Mark plays a decidedly positive though minor role in the tradition(s) known to us through these letters. This is perhaps crystallized by his minimal attribution as Paul's coworker, an honorific that nevertheless "puts Mark in his place." Unlike Paul or Apollos in 1 Corinthians 3:9, Mark is never identified as a *synergos* of God; rather, he is always related, and tacitly subordinated, to the more "senior" apostolic figure of Paul (or Barnabas).

Given the sheer paucity of reference to Mark in the Pauline corpus, this amounts to a strikingly coherent picture of an otherwise shadowy figure. But is this an unwarranted coherence? Have we too quickly fabricated a unified figure of Mark, errantly cobbled together from divergent sources? Perhaps so—if our sources are actually divergent, if there is no literary interdependence among these three letters. That is to say, if all three, or two of these three, Epistles were written by Paul at different times, in response to different situations, it could be that he referred to different personages, all named Mark, whom we have unwittingly conflated into one figure. A different scenario seems to me more probable overall: a unified and coherent figure of Mark emerges from these Epistles in part because of their literary interdependence. Thus, Colossians was written not by Paul but, rather, by one writing in Paul's name, drawing heavily on the apostle's letter to Philemon (among other Epistles); 2 Timothy, in turn, was composed by a still later author, perhaps indebted to an even broader corpus of Pauline letters. If these or similar circumstances attended the composition of Philemon, Colossians, and 2 Timothy, then the figure of Mark in the New Testament's Pauline tradition is understandably coherent and unified: pseudonymous authors have retained and at points elaborated the personalia mentioned in their "model" Epistles. In other words, one might say that arguments against the Pauline authorship of Colossians and 2 Timothy favor, by implication, the coherence of the figure of Mark in the Pauline tradition.

THE PETRINE TRADITION

After some years of generally benign neglect 1 Peter has surfaced among New Testament investigators as the object of both interesting research and lively discussion, not all of which has yet merged into consensus.[36] Nevertheless, some interpretive trends are discernible and contextually relevant to the present study. First, although most interpreters would concede some influence of primitive Christian worship upon 1 Peter, fewer seem convinced that the document is a paschal liturgy with epistolary trappings, as once was believed.[37] More scholars now seem inclined to regard 1 Peter as an actual letter, addressed to various Christian congregations throughout northern Asia Minor (1:1).[38]

Second, though it continues to enjoy some defenders,[39] the view that this Epistle was written by the apostle Peter remains a minority position.[40] On the other hand, the bald assertion of 1 Peter's pseudonymity seems unsatisfying to an increasing number of scholars, who attempt to locate the letter's intricate blend of Jewish, Gentile, and primitive Christian traditions within a definable stream, or streams, of early Christianity which aligned themselves with Peter. Thus, while denying apostolic authorship, a leading interpreter of the Epistle has recently asserted, "1 Peter is the product of a Petrine tradition transmitted by Petrine tradents of a Petrine circle."[41] Moreover, some recent research suggests that Petrine Christianity, perhaps more so than other detectable forms, bridged and consolidated many of the diverse expressions of Christianity in the first century.[42] Such a suggestion, for example, could account for the rough similarities between the theology of 1 Peter and that of the Pauline Epistles, without presuming the former's literary dependence on the latter.[43] Interestingly, a blend of Jewish and Gentile, conservative and liberal Christianity appears to have thrived in Rome, a city that early on is associated with Peter (*1 Clem.* 5.2) and is almost certainly the intended referent of "Babylon" in 1 Peter 5:13 (see also Rev 14:8; 16:19; 17:5; 18:2, 10, 21; *2 Apoc. Bar.* 11.1, 67.7; *Sib. Or.* 5.143, 159).[44]

Third, John Elliott has recently argued that the occasion and purpose of 1 Peter may be defined less by direct imperial persecution of Christians, the contours of which have always seemed fuzzy,[45] and more by the various social estrangements—defamation, ostracism, economic oppression—experienced by Asian Christians during the middle years of the Flavian emperors' reign (ca. 73–92). From this vantage point the pseudepigraphy of 1 Peter connotes not merely literary or theological but also social implications: a significant purpose of the letter would be to strengthen social identity and cohesion within and among various groups of Asian Christians under duress as well as to establish and to enhance bonds between Roman-Petrine Christians and their dispersed counterparts.[46]

The brief reference to Mark in 1 Peter 5:13 stands, I think, at this intersection of literary, religious, and social concerns. (1) Literarily, Mark is mentioned in the letter's conclusion (5:12–14): a position at which, rhetorically speaking, the author would naturally recapitulate some aspects of the argument, presented earlier, and seek to arouse the emotions of his audience in order that certain judgments might be rendered or forms of behavior might be adopted.[47] Such concerns are manifest in 5:1–11, which emphasizes the need among believers for humble fidelity to Christ under the pressure of requisite suffering (see also, e.g., 1 Pet 2:11–25). 1 Peter 5:12 neatly summarizes these concerns as well as the writer's hortatory aim: "in a few words I have written [to you], encouraging and testifying this to be the true grace of God. Stand fast in it." The very appearance of Mark, along with "the faithful" Silvanus (5:12), suggests at least that their mention was intended to contribute to the positive, persuasive force of the author's epistolary epilogue.

(2) One may reasonably press this observation further: an overtly social function is served by the references to Mark and Silvanus and by the framework in which those references are couched. Thus, Silvanus is regarded by "Peter" as a "faithful brother" (*tou pistou adelphou* [5:12]); Mark, as "my son" (or "my child," *ho huios mou*). The latter sends greetings, along with "the co-elect in Babylon" (*hē en Babylōni syneklektē*, a feminine construction referring to the Christian community in Rome [5:13]). As in the "family letters" of antiquity, whose conclusions extend their correspondents' interest in each other's welfare,[48] so here in 1 Peter the *dramatis personae* and their characterizations as members of an ecclesial family are intended to unify various Christian congregations in Asia and Europe. In short, the appellations in 1 Peter 5:12–13 probably are not to be taken as vacuous compliments; rather, the salutations of "brother Silvanus," "sister Rome," and "son Mark" assist in consolidating dispersed coreligionists, whose dislocation in Roman society is comparable to that of "resident aliens" (*paroikoi* [1:17, 2:11]), into a socioreligious unity, "the spiritual household of God" (2:5, 4:17; see also 2:9–10 and 5:14, the latter with its injunction for communion sealed through "the kiss of love").[49]

(3) Is the reference to Mark in 1 Peter 5:13 intended to carry not only rhetorical and social but also religious import? In other words, does the conjunction of Peter, Silvanus, and Mark betoken a distinctive religious tradition within primitive Christianity, a "Petrine circle," whose tendencies the recipients of 1 Peter are being encouraged to adopt? Various interpreters seem to think so, even though there exists no scholarly consensus on the dimensions or character of that group's perspective. (a) The "traditional" view, espoused (among others) by E. G. Selwyn and W. C. van Unnik, hypothesizes that 1 Peter was essentially authored by the apostle Peter, whose accounts of the Lord were memorized and compiled by Mark, the Second Evangelist, and adapted by Silvanus to the needs of Christians in Asia Minor.[50] The

difficulties with this approach are at least threefold. First, as I have already noted, the apostolic authorship of 1 Peter is sufficiently problematic that it can no longer be assumed without argument. Second, neither may we automatically presume a correlation of the religious perspectives of 1 Peter and the Gospel of Mark, although an argument for a kind of relationship between those documents can be constructed (as we shall observe in chap. 7 of this study). Third, this traditional coordination of Peter, Mark, and Silvanus rests less on the evidence of relevant New Testament documents and more on later patristic traditions about those documents. As we shall see in part 2, the problem here is that some of the early fathers' comments about Mark may amount to inferences deduced from 1 Peter 5:13, rather than knowledge of Petrine Christianity and its exemplars which is independent of that epistolary notice.

(b) The view adopted by F. W. Beare seems to accord little religious significance, as such, to the collocation of Peter, Silvanus, and Mark in this letter, emphasizing instead the literary fiction of those names in a pseudepigraphical document. "The men who are mentioned here are prominent figures of the Apostolic Age, their names familiar to all Christians; it required no great effort of the imagination to place Marcus and Silvanus in the entourage of Peter at Rome."[51] What, however, is the evidence that Mark was so prominent and well known in primitive Christianity? If the personal references in 1 Peter 5:12–13 attempt nothing more than apostolic versimilitude, why should the author have chosen these names over those of personages more widely known (such as Paul himself)? Even on the assumption that 1 Peter is pseudonymous, the significance of the particular figures mentioned by its author remains a question that invites an answer.

(c) Between these two positions lie various attempts to coordinate the names that appear in the conclusion of 1 Peter with traditional streams that have left some residue in the literature of primitive Christianity. For example, Norbert Brox has suggested that the clause in 5:12, *dia Silouanou hymin . . . egrapsa* ("through Silvanus, to you . . . I have written") repristinates the emissarial function served by Silas (= Silvanus) in Acts 15:22–23;[52] similarly, Brox believes, the reference to Mark in 1 Peter 5:13 derives from Acts 12:12, or its underlying tradition, concerning John Mark.[53] Developing but modifying Brox's suggestions, John Elliott argues that 1 Peter originated not with the apostle but, instead, with a group of Roman Christians whose theology and concerns accurately mirrored those of Peter, as preserved and elaborated by those with whom he was most closely associated. Other than Peter himself, Silvanus and Mark would have been regarded as the chief representatives of this tradition, a possibility that Elliott finds supported by a high degree of formal and material correspondence between 1 Peter and Acts 15: for example, the connection of Peter and Silvanus (Acts 15:6–11, 22b, 30—32; see also Mark's implied presence at the apostolic council [Acts 13:13b]); their mutual association with Jerusalem Christianity;[54] their shared ecumenical tenor and theological features (such as emphasis on God's election [Acts 15:7; 1 Pet 1:1, 2:4–10, 5:13] and impartiality [Acts 15:9; 1 Pet 1:17]; salvation as the gift of grace and object of faith [Acts 15:11; 1 Pet 1:2–5, 10–13; 2:2; 3:21]; the equal standing of Jewish and Gentile believers [Acts 15:8–11; 1 Pet 2:4–10]).[55]

Some related tendencies within early Christianity, germane to the present discussion, seem incontrovertible: the second and third generations of Christians produced literature for the church under the name and in the guise of notable forebears, neither maliciously nor capriciously but, rather, in order to connect their understanding of Christian witness and practice with an emerging "apostolic tradition."[56] As this was the case, the first two options, suggested above (strict historicity or unreflective pseudepigraphy), seem to me less persuasive than some version of the third: 1 Peter probably was the product of a distinctive group, or circle, within primitive Christianity, perhaps originating in Rome, which aligned itself with the witness of the apostle Peter. The precise character of that tradition is necessarily intractable, (first) because no specimen of irrefutably authentic Petrine teaching has survived which could be regarded as a standard for judgment, and (second) because Petrine Christianity appears to have been so highly synthetic and amalgamative of other Christian forms.

Is it possible that the minor figure of Mark, cited in 1 Peter 5:13, could offer us help in understanding the traditions that informed the document and its presumed religious audience? As we have seen, an affirmative verdict has been returned by both Brox and Elliott, who have correlated the form and substance of 1 Peter with Luke's narration of the Jerusalem council in Acts 15 and have concluded that a Petrine tradition underlies both documents. Yet one may wonder if that is the only, or most convincing, way to interpret the evidence.

First, it must be conceded that, if a Petrine tradition to any degree underlies Peter's speech and its effect at the apostles' conference (Acts 15:7–29), it has been thoroughly filtered through Luke's own set of theological concerns and convictions. Like all of the discourses in Acts, those of Peter, James, and the apostles in chapter 15 (vv. 7–11, 13–21, 23–29) are *Lukan* constructions and cannot be regarded as direct evidence for the testimonies of the individuals or groups to

whom they are attributed.[57] Accordingly, many of the formal and
material similarities between Peter's address in Acts 15:7–11 and 1
Peter, delineated by Elliott,[58] are replicated in other speeches in Acts,
not all of which are delivered by Peter: the address of the hearers as
"brothers" (2:29, 3:17, 7:2, 13:26, 22:1, 23:1, 28:17); God's act of
election (2:16–21, 23; 3:20–26; 4:28; 7:3–8; 13:17–21, 48; 17:26–27a,
31; 20:32; 22:10; 26:6, 18); God's impartiality and equal acceptance of
Jews and Gentiles (2:21, 3:25, 10:43, 11:5–18, 13:46–48, 15:14–20,
17:26–31, 22:21, 26:16–23, 28:25–28); salvation as the gift of grace and
object of faith (2:28, 3:19, 4:12, 5:31, 10:43, 13:38–39, 28:28). The fact
that these and other elements recur throughout the discourses in Acts,
irrespective of the speaker on particular occasions, suggests that Luke
has exercised the license, conventional in his day, of composing
"typical Christian rhetoric" as he understood it.[59] Of course, it is not
inconceivable that Luke's compositions could have utilized some Petrine traditions; so theologically homogenized are the sermons in Acts,
however, that distinctive Petrine features have likely been effaced and
are virtually impossible to recover. In any case, to regard the theology
of 1 Peter as reflected in Acts 15 is surely to "see through a glass
darkly."

Second, although Mark could have been regarded as a notable
member of "the Petrine circle," prior to and assumed by 1 Peter, the
evidence that we have collected in this and the previous chapter points
instead toward the tendency of the first-century church to position the
figure of Mark away from Peter and toward Paul. After all, in both Acts
and the Pauline corpus, Mark is explicitly associated with the entourage not of Peter but of Paul (and sometimes of Barnabas). Indeed, it
is only at 1 Peter 5:13 that a connection is established in the New
Testament between Mark and Peter, and even there the connection
appears to have been made by way of Paul: for Silvanus (or Silas), with
whom Mark is associated in 1 Peter 5:12–13, is himself consistently
linked with Paul in both Acts and the Pauline epistolary tradition.
Moreover, both functionally and substantively, the depiction of Mark
in 1 Peter is far less reminiscent of John Mark in Acts and far more
similar to Mark in the Pauline and Deutero-Pauline letters:

1. As in the Pauline tradition, Mark in 1 Peter is associated with
Gentile Christianity of the diaspora, generally in Asia though perhaps also in Rome (unlike Acts, in which Mark appears to be aligned
with Jerusalem Christianity).[60]

2. As in the Pauline tradition, Mark in 1 Peter is regarded as a
positive though minor figure (unlike Acts, in which Mark appears to
be regarded rather pejoratively).

3. As in the Pauline tradition, the figure of Mark in 1 Peter is cited for the purpose of fostering communion between the writer and his letter's recipients (unlike Acts, which portrays Mark as representative of a more parochial strain within primitive Christianity).

Of course, the very existence of 1 Peter 5:12–13 demonstrates that Silvanus and Mark were associated early on with the figure of Peter. What seems less certain to me than to some interpreters is that the former pair was originally regarded as paradigmatic of Petrine Christianity, much less that this association is further betokened by the narrative in Acts 15. To me it appears more probable that Mark, like Silvanus, was remembered in rather minor though consistently positive association with the Pauline tradition,[61] which in both broad dimensions and particular details was in turn incorporated into a highly amalgamative Petrine Christianity, one ancient distillate of which is 1 Peter.

SOME CONCLUSIONS:
THE DIFFERENT PORTRAYALS OF MARK
IN THE NEW TESTAMENT

Insignificant though it may appear, the portrait of Mark in the New Testament has emerged as surprisingly complex. Indeed, *it seems that there is not one but at least two, and perhaps three, figures of Mark explicit in the Christian canon:*

1. The *Lukan* portrayal of John Mark, associated with Jerusalem and Christianity of the synagogue, whose antipathy toward Gentile proselytization severs his erstwhile connection with Paul (though not with Barnabas and a collateral Pauline movement);
2. The *Pauline* depiction of Mark the servant and coworker, affectionately associated with that apostle and employed by Paul and later Paulinist Christians to consolidate Gentile Christianity of the diaspora;
3. The *Petrine*, or *Roman*, representation of Mark as Peter's faithful "son," apparently appropriated from the Pauline tradition and adapted for the social and religious edification of persecuted or culturally disaffected Christians in Asia Minor.

Though it is tempting to blend these images and to fashion them into a coherent, unitary picture of Mark—the Jewish-Christian backslider who, with his cousin's help, returned to the Pauline and Petrine fold[62]—the temptation probably should be resisted. Except within the Pauline corpus, in which it appears that the Deutero-Pauline Epistles knew and employed authentic Pauline materials, the evidence is simply insufficient to establish that these depictions all refer to one and the same figure. Indeed, for all of their sketchiness, the Lukan, Pauline, and Petrine depictions of Mark manifest the superficial similarity and distinctive differences that would be expected of documents that otherwise appear to have been traditionally interrelated at some level yet literarily independent of one another.[63]

Of course, the Mark of Christian folklore and popular piety has never been derived solely from the New Testament but, rather, has evolved through the mediation of centuries of Christian tradition. How does the figure of Mark fare in ancient Christianity beyond the canon, and what is the relation of that figure to the author of the Second Gospel? These are some of the questions that await us.

NOTES

1. Handily collected by John L. White, *Light from Ancient Letters,* FFNT (Philadelphia: Fortress, 1986).

2. Thus, see Eduard Lohse, *Colossians and Philemon: A Commentary on the Epistles to the Colossians and to Philemon,* ed. Helmut Koester, Hermeneia (Philadelphia: Fortress, 1971), 188. Alternatively, consult Peter T. O'Brien, *Colossians and Philemon,* WBC 44 (Waco, Tex.: Word Books, 1982), xlix–liv, for a judicious weighing of the evidence for Rome, Caesarea, and Ephesus, concluding that the probabilities lie with Rome.

3. For discussion, see White, *Light,* 193–97; "Ancient Greek Letters," in *Greco-Roman Literature and the New Testament: Selected Forms and Genres,* ed. David E. Aune, SBLSBS 21 (Atlanta: Scholars Press, 1988), 88–105, esp. 88–95.

4. This mixed type accounts for the overt paradox of Paul's position therein: though he is bold enough to command Philemon and fully expects his reciprocation (vv. 8, 20; cf. recommendations among peers in ancient letters), Paul willingly adopts the position of an inferior (as is characteristic of petitionary epistles) in beseeching Philemon to accept Onesimus.

5. White, *Light,* 197.

6. Nevertheless, as E. Earle Ellis points out ("Paul and His Co-Workers," *NTS* 17 [1971]: 440 n. 1) this usage does occur, with qualifications: coworkers "with God" (1 Cor 3:9; 1 Thess 3:21); "in Christ" (Rom 16:3, 9; cf. 1 Thess 3:2); of Paul (Rom 16:21; Phil 2:25; Philem 24); and for the Christian community (2 Cor 8:23; cf. 1 Cor 3:9; 2 Cor 1:24).

7. Thus, see John Knox, *Philemon among the Letters of Paul* (London: Collins, 1960), 56–58; and see Ellis, "Paul and His Co-Workers," 437–52, esp. 440–41.

8. F. Forrester Church, "Rhetorical Structure and Design in Paul's Letter to Philemon," *HTR* 71 (1978): 17–33.

9. It may be, as Norman R. Petersen has suggested, that Paul's "fellow

workers" were considered (by Paul and others) to hold "a position of hierarchical superiority over those ['brothers and sisters'] who were not" (*Rediscovering Paul: Philemon and the Sociology of Paul's Narrative World* [Philadelphia: Fortress, 1985], 108 [see also 172 n. 5]). Interestingly, however, Paul's rhetoric does not clearly appeal to Philemon's superior status in interpreting Christian responsibility toward Onesimus.

10. Werner Georg Kümmel, *Introduction to the New Testament*, trans. Howard Clark Kee, 17th rev. ed. (Nashville: Abingdon, 1973), 346, 358–60; against the critically unpersuasive suggestion by J. Coutts, "The Relationship of Ephesians and Colossians," *NTS* 4 (1957–58): 201–7.

11. Thus, see C. F. D. Moule, *The Epistles of Paul the Apostle to the Colossians and to Philemon*, CGTC (Cambridge: Cambridge University Press, 1977), 14; J. L. Houlden, *Paul's Letters from Prison: Philippians, Colossians, Philemon, and Ephesians*, WPC (Philadelphia: Westminster, 1977), 138–39.

12. Cf. Kümmel, *Introduction*, 340–46, with Lohse, *Colossians and Philemon*, 84–91, 177–83. Both regard considerations of style as indecisive; Lohse judges the theology as un-Pauline, whereas Kümmel attributes the differences to the distinctive exigences of the letter.

13. For a helpful collection and evaluation of the leading proposals for the nature of the so-called Colossian heresy, consult Fred O. Francis and Wayne A. Meeks, eds., *Conflict at Colossae: A Problem in the Interpretation of Early Christianity Illustrated by Selected Modern Studies*, SBLSBS 4 (N.p.: SBL, 1973).

14. It is hard to know if this description is intended to apply as well to Barnabas (though Acts 4:36 would support such an identification). On the difficulty of translating the participial clause in Colossians 4:11, consult Moule, *Colossians*, 137.

15. For this suggestion I am indebted to George E. Cannon, *The Use of Traditional Materials in Colossians* (Macon, Ga.: Mercer University Press, 1983), 219–29.

16. Grammatically, the instructions and visit could refer to Barnabas; conjoined with the familial relationship to Barnabas, however, the instructions and visit more likely refer to Mark (thus, see Andreas Lindemann, *Der Kolosserbrief*, ZB (Zurich: Theologischer, 1983], 73).

17. Accordingly, see LSJ 1.137a; BAG 65ab; N.B. Josephus, *Ant.* 1.290, in which the familial relations are clearly articulated. Thus, Donald Guthrie's passing, and undefended, reference to Mark as Barnabas's nephew in Colossians 4:10 is a decidedly minority position (*New Testament Introduction* [Downers Grove, Ill.: Inter-Varsity, 1970], 71).

18. Joseph Barber Lightfoot, *St. Paul's Epistles to the Colossians and to Philemon*, 2d. ed. (London: Macmillan, 1876), 236–37; Lohse, *Colossians and Philemon*, 172; Ralph P. Martin, *Colossians and Philemon*, NCB (London: Oliphants, 1974), 131–32; Joachim Gnilka, *Der Kolosserbrief*, HTKNT 10 (Freiburg: Herder, 1980), 237–38; Eduard Schweizer, *The Letter to the Colossians: A Commentary* (Minneapolis: Augsburg, 1982), 238–39; O'Brien, *Colossians and Philemon*, 250.

19. Thus, see Lindemann, *Der Kolosserbrief,* 73–74, who nevertheless notes the odd disjunctions between Acts and Colossians.

20. O'Brien, *Colossians and Philemon,* 250.

21. See the discussion in White, "Ancient Greek Letters," 93–95; and cf. the representative examples in C. B. Welles, *Royal Correspondence in the Hellenistic Period: A Study in Greek Epigraphy* (New Haven and Prague: Yale University Press / Kondakov Institute, 1934).

22. See also David K. Rensberger, "As the Apostle Teaches: The Development of the Use of Paul's Letters in Second-Century Christianity" (Ph.D. diss., Yale University, 1981), 333–34.

23. For example, John Norman Davidson Kelly, *A Commentary on the Pastoral Epistles,* HNTC (New York: Harper & Row, 1963); Luke T. Johnson, *The Writings of the New Testament: An Interpretation* (Philadelphia: Fortress, 1986), 381–407.

24. The standard arguments for pseudonymity of the Pastorals are summarized by Martin Dibelius and Hans Conzelmann, *The Pastoral Epistles: A Commentary on the Pastoral Epistles,* ed. Helmut Koester, Hermeneia (Philadelphia: Fortress, 1972), 1–10; Kümmel, *Introduction,* 370–84.

25. P. N. Harrison, *The Problem of the Pastoral Epistles* (London: Oxford University Press, 1921), esp. 93.

26. For a sympathetic, yet ultimately negative, verdict on Harrison's theory, rendered by a onetime proponent, see Anthony Tyrell Hanson, *The Pastoral Epistles,* NCB (Grand Rapids, Mich., and London: Eerdmans / Marshall, Morgan & Scott, 1982), 10–11.

27. Lewis R. Donelson, *Pseudepigraphy and Ethical Argument in the Pastoral Epistles,* HUT 22 (Tübingen: Mohr [Siebeck], 1986), esp. 23–24.

28. Thus, see Dibelius and Conzelmann, *Pastoral Epistles,* 127–28; also Peter Trummer, *Die Paulustradition der Pastoralbriefe,* BBET 8 (Frankfurt am Main: Peter Lang, 1978), 132–35.

29. In this respect Donelson offers an illuminating comparison of the Pastorals with other ancient pseudepigrapha, in *Pseudepigraphy and Ethical Argument,* esp. 23–42.

30. T. C. de Kruijf, *De pastorale brieven,* Het Nieuwe Testament (Roesmond-Masseik: J. J. Romen, 1966), 107–8, known to me only through Trummer, *Die Paulustradition,* 85 n. 154; G. M. Lee, "The Books and the Parchments (Studies in Texts: 2 Tim 4:13)," *Theology* 74 (1971): 168–69.

31. Thus, see Donelson, *Pseudepigraphy and Ethical Argument,* 56–57, citing the *Epistles of Socrates and the Socratics* 28:14, in which the writer complains that he cannot write any more because of the scarcity of *biblion.* Although consonant with the Pastorals' concern for Paul as a model for Christian behavior, I found somewhat forced Peter Trummer's suggestion that the references to cloak and books amount to a coded urging of church leaders for self-sufficiency and reliance on sacred scripture (" 'Mantel und Schriften' (2 Tim 4,13). Zur Interpretation einer persönlichen Notiz in den Pastoralbriefen," *BZ* 18 [1974]: 193–207).

32. *Diakonia* in 2 Timothy 4:11 is probably not to be taken in the fully developed, technical sense of "the diaconate" (so also C. K. Barrett, *The Pastoral Epistles in the New English Bible,* NClB [Oxford: Clarendon, 1963], 120). On the other hand, the Pastoral Epistles may evince a movement toward a perception of deacons as officers, whose service for the gospel has been somehow commissioned (see John N. Collins, *Diakonia: Re-interpreting the Ancient Sources* [New York and Oxford: Oxford University Press, 1990], 237–38).

33. Thus, see also Donelson, *Pseudepigraphy and Ethical Argument,* 107.

34. Cf. Dibelius and Conzelmann, *Pastoral Epistles,* 128.

35. However, because *correlation* does not equal *provenance,* one may no more deduce that the Mark of the Pauline tradition was regarded as having originated within Asian Christianity than one should conclude that Paul's origins were in Achaia, since repeatedly he visited and corresponded with Corinth.

36. For the recent history of the document's interpretation, see John H. Elliott, "The Rehabilitation of an Exegetical Stepchild: 1 Peter in Recent Research," *JBL* 95 (1976): 243–54; Birger A. Pearson, "James, 1–2 Peter, Jude," in *The New Testament and Its Modern Interpreters,* ed. Eldon Jay Epp and George W. MacRae (Atlanta: Scholars Press, 1989), 371–406, esp. 376–82.

37. A theory popularized earlier in this century by F. L. Cross, *1 Peter: A Paschal Liturgy* (London: Mowbray, 1954).

38. C. F. D. Moule, "The Nature and Purpose of 1 Peter," *NTS* 3 (1956–57): 1–11. Cf., on the one hand, Kümmel, *Introduction,* 416–25, who expresses skepticism regarding the identity of the readers, with Colin J. Hemer, "The Address of 1 Peter," *ExpTim* 89 (1978): 239–43, who offers, on the basis of 1 Peter 1:1, a precise reconstruction of an "East Galatian" missionary route.

39. Thus, see C. Spicq, "La Iᵃ Petri et le témoignage évangélique de Saint Pierre," *ST* 20 (1966): 37–61; Robert H. Gundry, " 'Verba Christi' in I Peter: Their Implications concerning the Authorship of I Peter and the Authenticity of the Gospel Tradition," *NTS* 13 (1967): 336–50; Gundry, "Further Verba on Verba Christi in First Peter," *Bib* 55 (1974): 211–32; Kelly, *Commentary,* 30–33; J. Ramsey Michaels, *I Peter,* WBC 49 (Waco, Tex.: Word Books, 1988), lxvi–lxvii.

40. The arguments against the apostolic authorship of 1 Peter are helpfully marshaled in two studies: Ernest Best, "I Peter and the Gospel Tradition," *NTS* 16 (1970): 95–113; and Norbert Brox, "Zur pseudepigraphischen Rahmung des ersten Petrusbriefs," *BZ* 19 (1975): 78–96.

41. Elliott, "Rehabilitation," 248. Richard J. Bauckham argues (sagely, I judge) that it may be more accurate to speak of a Petrine "circle," a fluid group of working associates, rather than of a Petrine "school," employing more homogeneous theological and literary resources (*Jude, 2 Peter,* WBC 50 [Waco, Tex.: Word Books, 1983], 146, 161).

42. James D. G. Dunn, *Unity and Diversity in the New Testament: An Inquiry into the Character of Earliest Christianity* (London: SCM, 1977), 385–

86; also François Bovon, "Foi chrétienne et religion populaire dans la première epître de Pierre," *ETL* 53 (1978): 25–41. As John H. Elliott has argued, the theologically synthetic character of 1 Peter can be maintained apart from hypotheses, proposed by F. C. Baur and his successors, that the Epistle is a *Unionsdokument,* reconciling the positions of contesting Christian perspectives ("The Roman Provenance of 1 Peter and the Gospel of Mark: A Response to David Dungan," *Colloquy on New Testament Studies,* ed. Bruce C. Corley [Macon, Ga.: Mercer University Press, 1983], 181–94).

43. Against F. W. Beare, *The First Epistle of Peter: The Greek Text with Introduction and Notes,* 3d. rev. ed. (Oxford: Basil Blackwell, 1970), 44; and Brox, "Zur pseudepigraphischen Rahmung," who (among others) assume direct dependence of 1 Peter on Paul, cf. the analyses in Ernest Best, *1 Peter,* NCB (Grand Rapids, Mich., and London: Eerdmans / Marshall, Morgan & Scott, 1971), 32–36; and Raymond E. Brown and John P. Meier, *Antioch and Rome: New Testament Cradles of Catholic Christianity* (New York and Ramsey, N.J.: Paulist, 1983), 134–39. Both of the latter volumes point toward a more intricate interweaving of Petrine and Pauline Christianities in the first century.

44. The possible connection between Roman and Petrine Christianities will be explored in chapter 8.

45. Cf. the apparently more definite statements in 1 Peter 4:12, 14, 19; 5:6, 8, with the vaguer comments in 1:6; 2:20; 3:14, 17.

46. John H. Elliott, *A Home for the Homeless: A Sociological Exegesis of 1 Peter, Its Situation and Strategy* (Philadelphia: Fortress, 1981), esp. 270–82. If this approach to 1 Peter is valid, one practical consequence would be the need to rethink the supposedly timeless generality that has been attributed to the letter, both in the tradition of the church (which came to dub 1 Peter as a "Catholic Epistle") and in critical scholarship (see, e.g., White, "Ancient Greek Letters," 100–101), and to reconsider its situational specificity.

47. A useful discussion of effective conclusions (*peroratio; epilogos*) for public address in antiquity is provided by Quintilian, *Education of the Orator* 6.1–5. On the subtle interrelation of ancient rhetorical and epistolary theory, see Abraham J. Malherbe, *Ancient Epistolary Theorists,* SBLSBS 19 (Atlanta: Scholars Press, 1988).

48. White, *Light,* 196–97.

49. Here I am indebted to the treatment by John H. Elliott, "Peter, Silvanus and Mark in 1 Peter and Acts: Sociological-Exegetical Perspectives on a Petrine Group in Rome," in *Wort in der Zeit: Neutestamentliche Studien,* ed. W. Haubeck and M. Bachmann (Leiden: E. J. Brill, 1980), 250–67.

50. E. G. Selwyn, *The First Epistle of St. Peter: The Greek Text with Introduction, Notes, and Essays,* 2d. ed., Thornapple Commentaries (1946; reprint, Grand Rapids, Mich.: Baker, 1981), 17–63; see also W. C. van Unnik, who opines that the referrent in 1 Peter 5:13 "cannot be other than the [second] evangelist" ("Peter, First Letter of," *IDB* 3 [1962]: 763, cf. 762–64); and P. Gächter ("Die Dolmetscher der Apostel," *ZKT* 60 [1936]: 161–87), who

suggests that Silvanus was asked to edit 1 Peter because the apostle had never fully mastered Greek.

51. Beare, *First Epistle of Peter,* 208–9.

52. Though beyond knockdown proof, the identification of Silas in Acts with Silvanus in the Pauline corpus (2 Cor 1:19; 1 Thess 1:1; 2 Thess 1:1) is probable and accepted by most commentators. *Contra* Leonhard Goppelt, *Der erste Petrusbrief,* MeyerK 12/1 (Göttingen: Vandenhoeck & Ruprecht, 1978), 66–70, 317, 1 Peter 5:12 less likely indicates Silvanus's authorship of the letter; cf. Brox, "Zur pseudepigraphischen Rahmung," 84–90.

53. Brox, "Zur pseudepigraphischen Rahmung"; Brox, *Der erste Petrusbrief,* EKKNT 21 (Köln: Benzinger, 1979), 246–48.

54. On the presence of Palestinian tradition in 1 Peter, see esp. Goppelt, *Der Erste Petrusbrief,* 53–68, 348, and elsewhere.

55. Elliott, "Peter, Silvanus and Mark"; Elliott, *Home for the Homeless,* 267–95.

56. David G. Meade, *Pseudonymity and Canon: An Investigation of the Relationship of Authorship and Authority in Jewish and Earliest Christian Tradition* (Grand Rapids, Mich.: Eerdmans, 1986).

57. Among many others, see Eduard Schweizer, "Concerning the Speeches in Acts," in *Studies in Luke-Acts,* ed. Leander E. Keck and J. Louis Martyn (Philadelphia: Fortress, 1980), 208–16; Hans Conzelmann, *Acts of the Apostles: A Commentary on the Acts of the Apostles,* ed. Eldon Jay Epp, trans. James Limburg et al., Hermeneia (Philadelphia: Fortress, 1987), xliii–xlv. Whereas neither Brox nor Elliott would deny this phenomenon, one wonders if its implications have been fully factored into their proposals.

58. Elliott, "Peter, Silvanus and Mark," 264 n. 31; Elliott, *Home for the Homeless,* 294 n. 40.

59. Cf. Kenneth S. Sacks, "Rhetorical Approaches to Greek History Writing in the Hellenistic Period," in *Society of Biblical Literature 1984 Seminar Papers,* ed. Kent Harold Richards (Chico, Calif.: Scholars Press, 1984), 123–33.

60. Beare (*First Epistle of Peter,* 209) wonders why, if 1 Peter were authentically apostolic, no Asian Christian in Rome is found to be sending greetings back home. Ironically, that is precisely what we encounter in 1 Peter 5:13, inasmuch as the figure of Mark in the Pauline corpus is associated with Asian Christianity.

61. At least on this point I concur with Ulrich H. J. Körtner, "Markus der Mitarbeiter des Petrus," *ZNW* 71 (1980): 160–73. In part 3 I shall offer a reconstruction, different from Körtner's, of possible relationships between Petrine Christianity and the Second Gospel.

62. Thus, in recent study, note the tendencies of Pierson Parker, "The Authorship of the Second Gospel," *PRS* 5 (1978): 4–9; Clayton N. Jefford, "Mark, John," *ABD* (1992): 557–58.

63. The common denominator in all of these presentations appears to be Mark's association with Paul or a Pauline circle (including Barnabas and

Silvanus). The author of Acts, however, appears not to have known the Pauline letters (thus, see Philipp Vielhauer, "On the 'Paulinism' of Acts," in Keck and Martyn, *Studies in Luke-Acts,* 33–50); a literary connection between Acts and the Pastorals is tenuous at best (notwithstanding the spirited arguments by Jerome D. Quinn, "The Last Volume of Luke: The Relation of Luke-Acts to the Pastoral Epistles," in *Perspectives on Luke-Acts,* ed. Charles H. Talbert, PRSSS 5 [Danville and Edinburgh: Association of Baptist Professors of Religion / T & T Clark, 1978], 62–75; and S. G. Wilson, *Luke and the Pastoral Epistles* [London: SPCK, 1979]); and the relationship between 1 Peter and Pauline Christianity can be explained (as we have seen) in terms of merging currents within Roman Christianity, without resort to theories of literary dependence (thus, see Best, *1 Peter,* 32–36).

Part II

Portraits of Mark
in Patristic Christianity

Chapter Three

Lineaments of an Apostolic Author

The Figure of Mark
in the Second Century

As we move beyond the New Testament into patristic literature, we should remind ourselves anew of that for which we are probing. The purpose of this and the next three chapters is simply to observe how "Mark" emerges, shifts, and perhaps evolves as a discernible figure within early Christian tradition. As in our earlier exploration of canonical presentations of Mark, we shall not be concerned, in the first instance, with the historical reliability of the materials inspected. Such questions, of course, have their own legitimacy and will be considered more fully in part 3 of this study, at least as regards the relevance of portrayals of the Evangelist for understanding the Second Gospel's origins. On the other hand, these are not our primary questions, nor is the historical credibility of patristic citations about Mark the Evangelist something that at every stage we need feel compelled to establish or to refute.

Entailed, to some degree, in these next chapters is attention to the earliest church fathers' interpretation of some New Testament texts. Patristic exegesis will, however, prove to occupy our attention far less than might be expected for the simple if surprising reason that the earliest noncanonical traditions about Mark make relatively little use of the passages from Acts and the Epistles which we have reviewed. Similarly, and equally remarkable, that which the writers of the New Testament never attribute to someone named Mark—responsibility for the Second Gospel that came to be canonized—becomes a salient concern among those early, noncanonical witnesses that speak of Mark. This patristic preoccupation does not eventuate in detailed exegesis of the Second Gospel, however—a fact that perfects a trio of surprises. As one modern investigator has noted, "It is a curious phenomenon that for the gospel that was least read or esteemed in the early church there is more tradition relating to its date of composition than any other."[1]

SOME ORIENTATIVE OBSERVATIONS

The various puzzlements to which I have referred suggest that our expectations of the patristic materials need calibration before we plunge immediately into their citation and interpretation. First, *the interests or concerns of modern students and scholars are not necessarily shared by the fathers of the early church.* At present, for example, both specialists and novitiates in the study of the Gospels are tantalized, if not confounded, by three overarching problems: the clarification of mutual relationships that exist among Matthew, Mark, and Luke (typically referred to as "the Synoptic problem");[2] the relationship between John and the Synoptic Gospels;[3] and the relationships that exist between these Gospels, which ultimately were canonized, and the fifty or so that were not.[4] These are genuine and genuinely fascinating problems, whose modern investigation was adumbrated by patristic scholars.[5] Yet none of these issues seems to have preoccupied the fathers to the degree that they have perplexed modern scholars, and many early Christian interpreters appear to have ignored them outright. As often as not, *their* primary concern appears to have been something that modern students of the New Testament usually take for granted: the very existence of multiple Gospels as literary testimonies to a single *kerygma,* or proclamation, of "the good news concerning Jesus Christ."[6]

Analogously, and more directly pertinent to this book's concern, scholars of the nineteenth and twentieth centuries have sometimes synthesized, from disparate New Testament texts, putative profiles of Mark and of the other Evangelists. Not infrequently, they have assumed that the patristic authors did the same. As we shall see, however, such an endeavor is not universally present among Christian sources that speak of Mark or of the Gospel attributed to him. Moreover, where this interest is present, the reconstruction offered in a given patristic source is often rather different from that proposed by modern investigators.

A second presupposition is really the flip-side of the one just considered: *the early church fathers had their own special interests that motivated, and at times may have distorted, their comments about figures like Mark.* Whenever possible these tendencies or biases should be identified for the purpose not of disparaging but, rather, of better understanding their observations. For example, we shall repeatedly witness in these documents an implicit or manifest concern for the *apostolicity* of Mark's Gospel. Consequently, it is important that we try to understand the issues at stake for patristic interpreters and their particular ways of framing those issues.

Third, even if it cannot always be answered with confidence, *the question of the sources underlying patristic comments should never be far from our minds.* With respect to the Gospels and to the figures (such as Mark) with whom they were associated, our circumspection should be at least bifocal:

1. When a patristic author recalls a tradition associated with one or more of the Gospels, we cannot automatically assume that the citation refers precisely to that literature which came to be fixed within the New Testament. After decades of scrupulous research into the problem, modern scholarship has arrived at a practical consensus: stated negatively, there is little evidence for a direct, literary dependence of the earliest church fathers upon the Gospels as we know them, in their canonical form. Stated positively, the majority of patristic references or allusions to the Gospels appear to have originated from the memory of Gospel traditions that for years were transmitted orally, before and even after those traditions had crystallized into the literary forms with which we are familiar.[7] Therefore, when a second-century Christian mentions a Gospel attributed to Mark, we cannot be certain in every case that this document was identical to the Second Gospel that was preserved in the Christian canon centuries later. And, even if the putative literature were essentially replicative of Mark in the form known to us, it need not have possessed for that patristic witness the scriptural authority that was more generally accorded to Mark (as well as to Matthew, Luke, and John) many centuries later. During the era with which this chapter is concerned, at a time long before the establishment of firm canonical boundaries, fluidity in citation and appropriation of the Gospels appears to have been the rule, not the exception.[8]

2. Second, in examining some specific texts, we should bear in mind the understandable, and unabashed, tendency of the church fathers to depend on their predecessors for many of their comments about figures like Mark. A half-dozen patristic comments about Mark, the latest of which may have been derived from the earliest, obviously would not amount to independent, corroborative testimony.[9] On the contrary, we should observe the warning issued by a British investigator earlier in this century: "The historian, then, has not done his duty unless he has tested every item of patristic evidence in the light of the tendency of the Fathers to copy and improve upon the statements of their predecessors."[10]

THE APOSTOLIC FATHERS

The earliest Christian writings outside the New Testament, known since the seventeenth century as "the Apostolic Fathers," date from approximately 95 to 150 and thus are roughly contemporaneous with much of the material that was eventually canonized. Their relevance for our present purposes is at once simple and largely negative. First, nowhere in these documents are we permitted any glimpses into the emerging figure of Mark in primitive Christianity. Second, with only few exceptions, the case for dependence in the Apostolic Fathers on written Gospels is decidedly weak. That is, there are few instances of identical wording or deliberate quotation (with or without an introductory formula like "as it is written"). Third, while there are numerous allusions to Synoptic tradition in the Apostolic Fathers, such verbal echoes more frequently are reminiscent of Matthew or Luke than of Mark. The closest correspondences between Mark's Gospel and some of the Apostolic Fathers are found in discrete, pithy sayings of Jesus (such as Polycarp's *Epistle to the Philippians* 7.2/Mark 14:38; *Didache* 11.7/Mark 3:28; *Barnabas* 5.9 and *2 Clement* 2.4/Mark 2:17) and, interestingly, in some quotations from the Old Testament which seem to correspond more closely with Mark than with the Septuagint (*1 Clement* 15.2/Mark 7:6; *Didache* 1.2/Mark 12:29–31; *2 Clement* 3.4/ Mark 12:30). In these isolated instances dependence on Mark's Gospel is a possibility. Equally possible, however, is the Apostolic Fathers' reliance on oral tradition that was similar to, but separate from, a written Gospel (or, with respect to the Old Testament allusions, a translation other than the Septuagint).

The lack of dependence on Mark and the other Gospels at this stage of Christian history may be less surprising than at first we might think. For one thing, written Gospels did not immediately enjoy scriptural status, which was primarily associated with those texts that later would be categorized by Christians as "the Old Testament."[11] Another factor to bear in mind was the importance accorded to oral tradition in primitive Christianity. This bias is manifest in two comments, attributed respectively to Papias (ca. 60–155) and Irenaeus (ca. 130–200), in Eusebius's *Church History* (323):

> For unlike the many, I did not delight in those who have much to say, but in those who teach the truth, nor in those who relate the commandments of others, but in those who repeated [the commandments] given to faith by the Lord and derived from truth itself. And if ever anyone came who had been a follower of the elders [or "presbyters," *presby-*

terois], I inquired into the words of the elders, what Andrew
or what Peter had said [*eipen*], or what Philip, or what
Thomas or James, or what John or Matthew, or any other
of the Lord's disciples, and that which Ariston and the elder
John, the Lord's disciples, were saying [literally, "are saying," *legousin*]. For I was of the opinion that things out of
books do not profit me so much as what comes from a living
and abiding voice. (3.39.4)[12]

I remember better the things then than the happenings of
late (for what we learn as children grows up with the soul
and is united to it), so that I am able to speak even of the
place in which the blessed Polycarp sat and debated; and
his comings and goings and character of life and bodily
appearance; and the discourses that he made to the crowd;
and, as he reported, his life along with John and with the
rest of those who had seen the Lord; and how he remembered their words, and what were the things about the Lord
that he had heard from them, about his mighty works and
about his teaching; how, having received from eyewitnesses
the word of life, Polycarp reported all things in harmony
with the scriptures. Even then, through the mercy of God
which had been given to me, I listened earnestly to these
things, making notes of them not on paper but in my heart;
and ever since by the grace of God I ruminate on them.
(5.20.5–7)

Within such a context it was natural for a rich oral tradition to flourish
alongside, and early on to supersede, written Gospels.

Even at this early stage, however, some tendencies are evident which
would become more pronounced in later patristic literature.[13] First,
not infrequently and without differentiation, the words of Jesus, particularly those that supported ethical catechesis in the early church, were
placed alongside quotations from the Old Testament (*Didache* 5.2–6.1;
Barnabas 10.11–12; *2 Clement* 13.2; among many others).[14] Second,
the Twelve whom Jesus had appointed were quickly accorded an
apostolic authority derivative from Jesus but superior to the church
fathers' own (see *1 Clement* 42.1–2; Ignatius, *Trallians* 3.3; 12.2;
Romans 4.3; Polycarp, *Philippians* 3.2).[15] Third, these apostles were
regarded as the particular beneficiaries of a holy tradition, "the gospel," entrusted to them by Jesus for propagation to the church and in
the world (Polycarp, *Philippians* 6.3; *Barnabas* 5.9).[16] At this stage the

accent tended to fall on the presumed unity of the gospel as a whole, not on its variant presentations "according to Matthew," "according to Mark," and so forth. In time, however, the conceptual challenge posed by these alternative interpretations of Jesus' message and activity would be keenly felt.

PAPIAS OF HIERAPOLIS

Preserved within Eusebius's *Church History* are some statements attributed to Papias, who was Bishop of the Hierapolitan diocese (located in the region of Phrygia, Asia Minor, or modern-day Turkey) and a contemporary of two Apostolic Fathers, Ignatius of Antioch and Polycarp of Smyrna (*H.E.* 3.36.1). Already we have glanced at one of those fragments, concerning Papias's consideration for oral traditions (*H.E.* 3.39.4). The bishop may be even better known for his comments on "Mark, who wrote the Gospel" (3.39.15–16). These remarks appear to constitute the oldest surviving witness to the composition of a literary work associated with Mark; moreover, they appear to form much of the bedrock for patristic tradition about Mark in the decades and centuries that followed. For the study in which we are engaged Papias's testimony is undeniably one of the most important.[17]

It is also one of the most problematic and tantalizing, if not exasperating. As we shall see, Eusebius's quotations from Papias are obscure extracts, almost every aspect of which is enveloped in an interpretive controversy that may ultimately prove beyond the capacity of scholars to resolve. In the period from 1960 to 1981 alone, some three thousand five hundred monographs and two hundred scholarly articles were devoted, partially and sometimes wholly, to Papias, and the torrent of research shows no signs of abating.[18] For all of that, as noted by a respected patristics scholar who has contributed to this research, "The fragments of Papias still continue to be looked at for more than they can possibly give."[19]

During the course of the following discussion some of the nits will of necessity be picked. Three overarching questions, however, might serve in organizing our procedure:

1. One cluster of questions arises from the fact that we have no firsthand access to Papias's remarks but are dependent for them on the report of a fourth-century historian. How trustworthy is Eusebius's presentation of Papias?

2. The second question deals more directly with what Papias says: the sources of information to which he acknowledges indebtedness, the meaning of his terms, and his own persuasive intentions. In

brief, how should we interpret Papias's observations about Mark and the composition of that Gospel?

3. Finally, how might we assess the significance of Papias's comments about Mark?

Modest expectations are in order. Given our fuzzy snatches of evidence, the reader should anticipate nothing more than tentative answers to these questions. I shall try to underscore those points on which scholars appear to be converging toward interpretive consensus. On the many issues that still inspire interpretive division, I shall cast my vote with supporting reasons, while granting that the jury remains hung.

The Comments of Papias about Mark, as Reported by Eusebius

And in the same writing he [Papias] recounts other disclosures of the Lord's words [*logōn*] transmitted by the aforementioned Ariston and traditions of John the elder [or "presbyter," *presbyteros*], to which we refer the studious. Now we must append to the previous excerpts quoted of him a tradition about Mark, the one who wrote the Gospel, which he sets forth as follows: "Now this is what the elder used to say: 'Mark became Peter's interpreter [*hermē-neutēs*] and wrote accurately whatever he remembered, but not in order [*ou mentoi taxei*], of the things said or done by the Lord.['] For he had neither heard the Lord, nor had he followed him, but later on, as I said, [followed] Peter, who used to offer the teachings in anecdotal form [alternatively, "as need arose," *pros tas chreias*] but not making, as it were, a systematic arrangement [*syntaxis*] of the Lord's oracles [*logiōn*], so that Mark did not miss the mark in thus writing down individual items as he remembered them. For to one thing he gave forethought: to leave out nothing of what he had heard and to falsify nothing in them.[']" This, then, is related by Papias about Mark.

And about Matthew this was said: "Matthew systematically arranged [*synetaxato*] the oracles [*ta logia*] in the Hebrew language [*Hebraidi dialektōn*], and each interpreted them as he was able."

The same writer made use of testimonies from John's first epistle and likewise from Peter's, and has set forth another account about a woman who was accused before the Lord of many sins, which the Gospel according to the Hebrews contains. Let this suffice for us, beyond the excerpts that have been attended to. (*H.E.* 3.39.14–17)

Eusebius as Interpreter of Papias

Papias's comments originated in a five-volume work, which may have been extant in manuscript as late as 1218.[20] Since then it has entirely disappeared and is known to us only through Irenaeus (*Adv. Haer.* 5.33.4) and Eusebius (*H.E.* 3.39.1–2), the latter referring to it as *An Interpretation of the Oracles of the Lord (Logiōn Kyriakōn Exēgēsis)*. The date of these volumes is in doubt: they are unlikely to have been written later than 130, and some scholars assign them a date even earlier (anywhere from 95 to 110).[21] Equally disputed is Papias's purpose in preparing this work: whether it was intended as a commentary on the Jesus-tradition that he had inherited or as a literary Gospel in its own right or for some other reason.[22] Given our scant evidence, probably we shall never know for sure.

Our inescapable uncertainty is due also to the fact that most of what is known about Papias has been filtered through Eusebius (ca. 260–340), a fourth-century bishop of Caesarea and author of the principal history of Christianity from the apostolic period to his own day. Eusebius fashioned a history of the church which displayed chronological scope, an anthological structure, and a range of recurring themes. In these and other respects his influence on historians who came after him, and on the enterprise of early ecclesiastical historiography itself, was undeniably profound.[23]

Like any historian, however, Eusebius had his biases, which evidently colored and sometimes distorted the personages and occurrences about which he reported. Procedurally, for example, he appears to have been circumspect in his use of oral traditions, favoring written sources whose authors, titles, and even portions could be cited for indebtedness.[24] Thematically, perhaps no subject was of greater importance to Eusebius than the continuity of apostolic succession, the guarantor (in his judgment) of the church's orthodox self-identity (see *H.E.* 1.1.1–4):[25] "The brightness of the universal and only true church proceeded to increase in greatness, for it ever held to the same points in the same way" (*H.E.* 4.7.13). Consequently, for Eusebius the canonical Gospels constitute "a holy tetrad," which, like the rest of the New Testament, "according to the ecclesiastical tradition are true and genuine and recognized" (*H.E.* 3.25.1, 6). The apocryphal Gospels are irredeemably heretical, "to none of which has any who belonged to the succession of the orthodox ever thought it right to refer in his writings" (*H.E.* 3.25.6).

In this context the Book of Revelation was enormously problematic for Eusebius, who had been schooled in the tradition of Alexandrian theology and harbored extreme prejudice against apocalyptic eschatology (see *H.E.* 7.24.6). For him Christ's Ascension had consummated human history, and any speculation that he would return and reign on earth for a thousand years (the principal tenet of chiliasm, or millenarianism) was repugnant (*H.E.* 1.2–5, 13; 2.1, 13; 3.39.11–13). Accordingly, throughout his *Church History* Eusebius appears to suppress mention of chiliastic doctrine within sources that he otherwise respects (such as Justin's *Dialogue with Trypho* 80.5 and 81.4 and Irenaeus's *Against Heresies* 5.32–36).[26] Ultimately, he even reversed himself on the authorship of Revelation: whereas earlier he had concurred with Irenaeus in ascribing the Apocalypse to John, the apostle and evangelist (*H.E.* 3.18.1–3), in a later revision of his *History* Eusebius drew on another (and weaker) tradition, attributing Revelation to the fraudulence of Cerinthus, a notorious heretic (*H.E.* 3.28).[27]

All of this may seem annoyingly diverting from our task at hand. In fact, I think that first we must carefully interpret Eusebius's *use* of Papias; then, within such a framework, we might better discern and appreciate Papias's comments on their own terms. Accordingly, the following points should probably be kept in mind.

First, not only must we concede that we do not have firsthand evidence for Papias's report about Mark; we also must reckon with the possibility that neither did Eusebius. Typically, Eusebius is rather scrupulous in citing the particular book or volume from among those works on which his information is dependent. His acknowledgment of Papias, however, is unusually vague, which has led at least one scholar to wonder if Eusebius was dependent on secondary sources for all that he knew about Papias.[28]

Second, it is helpful to remember that, with respect to dubious authors or doctrines, Eusebius's standard policy was to suppress or to ignore that which he thought heretical, discomfitting, or unuseful. Thus, when he reports Irenaeus's statement that Papias was known as John's auditor—without telling us the content of what was heard (*H.E.* 3.39.1)—we should not be astonished to discover that the tradition in question was apocalyptic (according to another millenarian, Irenaeus [*Adv. Haer.* 5.33.3–4]).[29] Virtually all scholars are agreed that Eusebius's characterization of Papias as "a man of very limited intelligence" (*H.E.* 3.29.12–13) refers specifically to his unchastened chiliastic views, as the context of that slur makes clear (*H.E.* 3.29.7–13). What commentators sometimes neglect to explain is why Eusebius quoted Papias and took him so seriously, if his theology was such an embarrassment.[30]

The answer may be that Papias was simply too highly regarded by his successors, and in certain respects by Eusebius himself, to be ignored or thoroughly censored. In matters eschatological Eusebius could question the intelligence of Papias; that the latter was "well known" or "distinguished" (*egnōrizeto*, per *H.E.* 3.36.2), however, could not be denied.[31] Nor did Eusebius exaggerate this: as we shall see, Papias's perspective on Mark, for example, appears to have exercised a profound influence on many commentators who succeeded him. In fact, though it is frequently overlooked, Eusebius himself refers "the studious" (*tous philomatheis*, "lovers of learning") to Papias's *Interpretation of the Lord's Oracles* (*H.E.* 3.39.14). Indeed, there may have been much in Papias's perspective and literary practice with which Eusebius was sympathetic. Papias's discrimination of traditions, oral (*H.E.* 3.39.3–4) and written (*H.E.* 3.39.15), which were in allegedly lineal descent from the Lord squared nicely with Eusebius's own procedure and concern for apostolic succession. Interestingly, the Phrygian bishop's literary preservation, in a multivolume work, of interpretations of collected traditions anticipated the Caesarean bishop's multivolume church history; it seems unlikely that this parallel would have escaped Eusebius. And, from among the things cited in Papias's comments about Mark, is it pure happenstance that the church's first great anthologist would highlight the seemingly anthological character of that Gospel ("[things written] not indeed in order": *H.E.* 3.39.15)?

None of this, naturally, is tantamount to an assessment of Papias's reliability, on which we are not yet prepared to pass. It is, rather, a third dimension of the context in which his report about Mark arguably should be heard. However limited was Eusebius's access to primary sources on Papias, and however loathsome he found Papias's apocalypticism, we may reasonably assume that Eusebius tried "to get Papias right"—if for no other reason than to shore up some of Eusebius's own cherished beliefs and commitments.[32]

Interpreting Papias's Comments about Mark

Our exegetical reflections on *Church History* 3.39.14–17 may be conveniently subdivided into three categories: the antecedent sources acknowledged by Papias; the images of Mark and Peter which emerge from Papias's statement (which entails various problems of translation); and the overall tenor of the passage in question.

On what sources for his portrayal of Mark does Papias acknowledge dependence? Papias claims no firsthand knowledge of either of the two principals discussed in his statement, Mark and Peter; rather, he cites that which "the presbyter used to say" (3.39.15). Who is "the presbyter"? In his prefatory remarks Eusebius takes this as a reference to "John the Presbyter" (or "Elder" [3.39.14]), whom Papias elsewhere identifies as one of his principal informants about the oral traditions of Jesus (3.39.4). Scholars have long debated whether Papias regards "the presbyter John" and "the apostle John" as one and the same, and much of the uncertainty stems from what distinction, if any, Papias recognizes between "the Lord's disciples" (that is, one of the Twelve, seven of whom Papias names in 3.39.4) and "the presbyters." As used by Papias, these terms appear to be largely overlapping, suggestive of "elder authorities known for their attachment to Jesus,"[33] and it is possible to interpret *H.E.* 3.39.4 to mean that Papias was an auditor of the apostle John, the Lord's disciple.[34]

Nevertheless, three things in 3.39.4 may suggest that Papias presumes two different figures, both named John. (1) The second "John" is conjoined by Papias (and later, in 3.39.14, by Eusebius) with "Ariston," of whom nothing is known but who never appears in any listing of the twelve apostles. (2) This John is designated as the Elder, as though implicitly to distinguish him from John the member of the Twelve, who had just been mentioned. (3) Papias expresses interest in what John from among the Twelve "said" (*eipen*, past tense) and the Presbyter John (and Ariston) "are saying" (*legousin*, present tense [3.39.4]), as though Papias had outlived the former but was contemporary with the latter.[35] If Papias, who was described by Irenaeus as "one of the old ones" and a companion of Polycarp (ca. 69–155 [*Adv. Haer.* 5.33.4; cf. *H.E.* 3.39.1]), regarded a certain informant as his (and others') elder,[36] then the presbyter John may have been a transitional figure in primitive Christianity, bridging its first and second generations (the apostolic era of John and the Twelve and the subapostolic era of Papias and the Apostolic Fathers).[37]

In any case, two conclusions seem justified in the matter of Papias's acknowledged sources. First, contrary to the opinion of some scholars,[38] it is not at all clear to me that the literary connection, described by Papias as existing between Peter and Mark, was deduced by the bishop of Hierapolis from 1 Peter 5:13, even though Eusebius claims that Papias knew that Epistle (*H.E.* 3.39.17). On the one hand, this should not surprise us: whereas 1 Peter 5:13 links the figures of Peter and Mark, it says nothing of the latter's acting as the former's *literary interpreter*. On the other hand, had Papias drawn such an unwarranted inference from 1 Peter 5:13, why would he not have ascribed that

tradition to Peter himself, an esteemed apostle and the supposed author
of the letter, rather than to a comparatively superfluous middleman
like John the presbyter (*H.E.* 3.39.15)? Though conjecture is unavoidable, the scraps of available evidence may suggest that, toward the end
of the first century, more than one tradition, trickling through more
than one region of primitive Christianity (Rome [1 Peter]; Asia Minor
[the Elder John/Papias]), associated the figures of Peter and Mark.[39]

A second conclusion follows from this: the more specific collocation
of Peter and Mark, who wrote the Gospel, may be located quite early
within primitive Christianity and along a trail of tradition which, even
as early as 95–130, was remarkably circuitous, if not downright con-
voluted. Eusebius read it in Papias (or, perhaps, in a secondary source
that had quoted Papias), who in turn heard it from the Elder John (or,
perhaps, from one of the presbyter's followers [*H.E.* 3.39.4]), who in
turn either knew the tradition firsthand or got it from yet another
intermediary.[40] Although the tributaries and eddies of the tradition and
its transmission can never be mapped with precision, the Papias-
fragments quoted by Eusebius suggest a development that was complex, not simple.

How is the figure of Mark portrayed in Papias's statement? With
this deceptively simple question we step into one of the more tangled
patches of recent scholarship on Papias. To clear our way we might
briefly note several stages in the scholarly conversation.

Most scholars over the centuries have attempted to take Papias's
remarks at their supposed face value, then have weighed the cogency
of the result. One recent Markan commentator has offered a sympathetic summary of this familiar reading:

> [Papias's statement] represents Mark as closely associated
> with Peter and testifies to his accuracy, while at the same
> time drawing attention to a certain lack of order in his
> gospel (whether the reference is to chronological order or
> to systematic arrangement and comprehensiveness is not
> clear). The exact meaning of *hermēneutēs Petrou genomen-
> ous* ["became Peter's interpreter"] is problematical—per-
> haps that Mark acted as interpreter when Peter was teach-
> ing, translating his Aramaic into Greek, or perhaps that by
> writing down Peter's reminiscences he made them available
> to more people.[41]

Assuming such an interpretation of Papias's statement, critics have
diverged in their assessments. Scholars with more conservative leanings have tended to accord it plausibility.[42] Increasingly, in the light of

twentieth-century form and redaction criticism,[43] many Markan investigators have found little evidence within the Gospel itself to support
Papias's report; some have deemed it "historically worthless"[44] or
"twaddle" (*Gewäsch*).[45] A mediate position between these extremes
accepts a portion of Papias's testimony (e.g., that the author of the
Second Gospel could have been someone named Mark), while questioning or disregarding the rest (that the Gospel preserves Petrine
reminiscences).[46]

Scholarly reflection on Papias entered a rather different phase during
the 1960s and 1970s, with the appearance of a series of technical
studies by Josef Kürzinger, of the University of Eichstätt.[47] Essentially, Kürzinger argued that the traditional reading of Papias had
misunderstood his vocabulary, and thus his intentions, in speaking of
Mark (and Matthew): in defending Mark's trustworthiness, Papias had
employed the standard rhetorical terminology of his day. Viewed in
this light, Kürzinger suggested, particular words took on an altered,
arguably more intelligible meaning. Thus, when Papias spoke of Mark
as Peter's "interpreter" (*hermēneutēs*), probably he did not mean that
the former translated the latter's words from one language to another;
rather, Papias's Mark (according to Kürzinger) acted as an "intermediary," or middleman, in representing and transmitting the Petrine
preaching of dominical *logia* (not exclusively "sayings" [*logoi*] but,
rather, "what the Lord had said and done").[48] Moreover, Mark's
"remembrance" could have included the "recording" of material that
was written, not just the recollection of oral traditions.[49] The statement
that Mark's record lacked order (*ou mentoi taxei; ouch . . . syntaxis*)
refers to neither logic nor chronology[50] but, instead, reflects a rhetorical judgment: Papias's point is that, in contrast to Matthew (cf. *synetaxato*, "orderly arranged"), Mark did not prepare a book with "literary artistry." Similarly, a technical term is presumed in the claim that
Peter's presentation was *pros tas chreias* (an idiomatic prepositional
phrase, usually translated "as necessity demanded" or "as need
arose"): Petrine tradition was formulated and preserved by Mark
"anecdotally," drawing upon antiquity's widespread tradition of
chreiai (maxims or biographical illustrations, used by rhetoricians for
training elementary pupils in composition and oration).[51] Taken together, the preceding pair of reinterpretations informs Kürzinger's
exegesis of the obscure comment, "each interpreted them as he was
able": Papias suggested not that all who read Mark and Matthew
translated them as best they could but, rather, that the dominical *logia*
were conveyed *by the Evangelists* in alternative, appropriate ways
(Mark, through *chreiai*; Matthew, in a more artistic composition that

conformed *Hebraidi dialektō*, "with Semitic norms" [not "in the Hebrew language"]).[52]

If these "traditional" and "revisionist" interpretations of Papias have tried to grasp the overall sense of his portrayal of Mark, then concurrent research has attempted to distinguish some layers assumed in both reconstructions. For example, within the quotation in Eusebius's *Church History* there is an internal quotation (the Elder, as cited by Papias): thus, one problem is determining where John's comments stop and Papias's commentary begins. (In my earlier translation of Eusebius I have indicated in brackets ['] alternative points at which the presbyter's statement may have ended.) If, as Eusebius maintained, Papias agreed with everything recorded in *H.E.* 3.39.15, the resolution of this problem may be, if not forthcoming, at least relatively inconsequential.[53]

Another question, however, is more nettlesome and certainly more intriguing: When Papias speaks of Mark's record of Peter's teaching, does the bishop have in mind the document that we know as the Second Gospel? Many readers have assumed so,[54] but herein lurk some problems. For one thing, in Eusebius's excerpt Papias says nothing of the composition of Mark's *Gospel*. Interestingly enough, neither does Eusebius: that which he introduces is "a tradition [from Papias] about *Mark, the one who wrote the Gospel*" (*H.E.* 3.39.1; emphasis added.)[55] Beyond this curious silence one may wonder if Papias's description of Mark's composition actually fits the Gospel that came to be attributed to Mark: at least, that document seems to possess a kind of order (if not completeness);[56] at most, if we accept the judgment of some scholars, the Second Gospel displays a remarkably complex construction.[57]

To what *was* Papias referring, if not to the Gospel we know? Various suggestions have been offered, ranging from the hypothetical sayings-source (Q) which may underlay the Gospels of Matthew and Luke[58] to another edition of Mark's Gospel, distinct from the one that was canonized.[59] Alternatively, could Papias have been thinking of *hypomnēmata* (Latin: *commentarii*), "notes" that were taken by Mark and later polished into the Gospel that bears his name (in accordance with a procedure known to have been employed by the classical biographers, Plutarch and Suetonius)?[60] Should it turn out that such complexity were harbored by Papias's seemingly simple comments, it would be no less than scholars have long suspected of the Gospels, the process of whose composition may have been extraordinarily complicated indeed. The more complex the solutions, however, the less likely that they ever could be recovered and confirmed beyond a reasonable doubt.

From the available scraps of evidence, what kinds of claims, on balance, does Papias appear to have made about Mark? Few of the "traditional" readings have been as ham-handed as some critics seem to think, and even those favoring a traditional approach have acknowledged its insufficiency, if not inability, to resolve various questions (such as the sort of "interpretation" and "order" that Papias had in mind).[61] It may be for this reason that Kürzinger's "revisionist," or "rhetorical," construction of Papias's statement[62] has been warmly received by many investigators: it suggests a framework that (1) makes sense of the text within the oral and literary environment of antiquity (in which the practice of rhetoric was common currency)[63] and (2) coheres with the text's own concerns about Mark's literary activity.

Not all of Kürzinger's interpretations of Papias's phraseology have been found equally convincing. While many scholars agree, for instance, that *hermēneutēs* and *logia* can carry the connotations, respectively, of "intermediary" (not just "translator") and "oracular accounts" (not merely "words"),[64] few have been persuaded that by "*Hebraidi dialektōn*" Papias means, as Kürzinger argues, "Semitic style" (not "Hebrew language," surely a more natural translation).[65] In a word, Kürzinger may overwork rhetorical categories, at some points attributing to Papias a more consistently technical terminology than the bishop originally intended.[66]

Nevertheless, Kürzinger's overall perspective seems to me sound, sensible, and saddled with fewer problems than other interpretive possibilities: Papias portrays Mark as a responsible anthologist, whose disordered literary style faithfully represented and mediated dominical traditions as they were occasionally conveyed by Peter. *Thus understood, Papias's presentation of Mark may have been focused not on his work's authorship or apostolicity for its own sake but, rather, on its composition.* That is to say, Peter's authority and practice appear to have been summoned by Papias in order to explain and to justify a particular traditionist's literary style.[67] Insofar as the *Church History* permits us accurately to reconstruct it, the *direction* of Papias's apparent argument is very interesting, and perhaps just the reverse of Eusebius's interests and our own expectations. The reason that Papias chose this axe for grinding may be implicit in our next question.

What is the tone of Papias's statement about Mark? Of all questions pertaining to Papias this one probably receives the most univocal answer among investigators: even in its highly fragmentary form in Eusebius, Papias's comments seem apologetic of Mark's warrants and technique. To assert that "Mark did not miss the mark in thus writing down individual items as he remembered them" practically presupposes a criticism, prior to Papias and perhaps even prior to John the Presbyter, that Mark indeed *had* missed the mark. At least as far as Papias is concerned, Mark has been challenged for his report's incompleteness and lack of order. In both respects Mark could be acquitted: Mark had followed and faithfully interpreted not the Lord but, rather, Peter, and the latter's teaching had been piecemeal and catch-as-catch-can. Mark, on the other hand, was as comprehensive in his coverage as his primary source would permit: "[he left] nothing out of what he heard." If Mark's account seems lacking or disordered, then that actually redounds to the fidelity of his reporting and attests to a premeditated decision "to falsify nothing in [what he had heard]."

Among scholars there is considerably greater disagreement over the precise reason for Papias's apologetic concerns. With what was Mark's composition being contrasted then denigrated? Both the Gospels of Luke and John have been suggested, the former primarily because of its professed attempt to be "an orderly account" (Luke 1:3), the latter for its seemingly more encompassing portrayal of a three-year ministry of Jesus (John 2:23, 6:4, 12:1; cf. 5:1).[68] However, Papias's knowledge of either of these two Gospels is hard to sustain and probably impossible to prove. As Kürzinger thinks, the point of comparison may be Matthew, who "[did] systematically arrange the oracles." This suggestion also has its difficulties: the comparison of Mark with Matthew may owe less to Papias and more to the way that Eusebius has extracted and edited Papias's comments (see *H.E.* 3.39.16). Yet another possibility has been suggested: in preparing an *Interpretation of the Oracles of the Lord* a version of Mark may have been employed by Papias, who therefore would have been interested in ratifying its reliability. While plausible, this too floats in a sea of speculation.[69]

Of the little that we know of Papias two things seem relatively clear. First, like his contemporaries (the Apostolic Fathers), he held in esteem those oral traditions about Jesus which were believed to be reliable (*H.E.* 3.39.3–4). Second, Papias's defense of Mark attempts to justify his literary technique by appealing to its fidelity to Petrine teaching, as it was heard and remembered (*H.E.* 3.39.14–15). If these conclusions are fair to Papias and may be fairly wedded, then perhaps Papias is defending Markan literature not so much against the proposed superiority of other written documents,[70] as against the acknowledged superiority of *oral traditions* about the Lord.[71] Therefore, "Mark did not miss the mark *in writing down* individual items as he remembered them" (emphasis added). Why? Because "[Mark left] out nothing *of what he had heard*" (again, my emphasis). For Papias, Mark's very disorganization was the clearest, positive evidence that his literary endeavor had falsified nothing in an oral tradition that was equally disordered.[72] Such an interpretation, I think, plausibly construes some admittedly fragmentary evidence, though it is no more susceptible of knockdown proof than its alternatives. For whatever reason, quite early in the first century Papias comes across as decidedly defensive of Mark.

The Significance of Papias's Presentation of Mark

To assess, at this point, Papias's importance for interpreting the Second Gospel or his influence on later patristic Christianity would be premature. Such questions will be considered in due course. Here I wish only to offer a few evaluative observations about Papias's statements, taken on their own terms.

First, in my judgment Papias's comments cannot bear the weight of the sweeping claims, both approbative and pejorative, which sometimes have been made of them. The surviving evidence is too fragmentary, too ambiguous, and too highly edited to permit secure, far-reaching conclusions about either his trustworthiness or his unreliability.

Second, recent research has suggested fresh ways in which Papias's remarks can be construed. If these modest findings do not uncritically validate everything that Papias says, then neither do they support an impulsive prejudice against them. As two thoughtful commentators have recently noted, "[T]he simplistic understanding of Papias which dismisses him out of hand must be questioned if not abandoned."[73]

Third, what Papias does *not* disclose about Mark is as strikiing as that which he does. Neither he nor his informant says anything about that figure's association with Paul (if indeed they knew of it). Mark is linked with Peter, yet neither Papias nor the presbyter offers any basis whatever for that linkage. Although the existence of the Second Gospel that came to be canonized may be presumed, nothing in what Papias says of Mark's literary record could lead us confidently to conclude that. If an inference from silence may be tentatively drawn, it appears that Papias (as mediated to us by Eusebius) was interested very little in what might be called the *personality* of Mark.

Fourth, the thing, apparently, which most profoundly interests Papias is the *tradition* in which the figure of Mark stood—a tradition that, as early as the turn of the first century, had become sufficiently roundabout, proliferous, and polymorphous that its discrimination and discussion were deemed necessary by Papias and his implied interlocutors. Because so little of his observations have survived, we know practically nothing about Papias's understanding of that tradition's content; for that, however, the bishop is not to be faulted. We may be in slightly better position to say that, for Papias, the primary criterion satisfied by Mark was his *faithful recollection*, dependable remembrance and conveyance, of dominical traditions that were associated with Peter.[74] Whether or not Papias was correct in that judgment remains to be demonstrated, if in fact it can ever be shown. For now the critical point to be registered is his regard for Mark as one firm link in a chain of memory of Jesus. An early second-century concern for apostolic continuity, betokened in Papias's portrayal of Mark, is by no means coextensive with its later developments (either patristic doctrines of orthodoxy or post-Enlightenment theories of historicity); nor have we any reason to suspect that Papias held such far-flung presuppositions. Such conceptions as these may be more accurately regarded as the variegated flowering of seeds that were planted by Papias and his contemporaries.

JUSTIN MARTYR

Some of Papias's tendencies are confirmed, and just as intriguingly neglected, in the work of Justin Martyr (ca. 100–165), a schoolmaster and Christian philosopher who defended the rationality and morality of the faith against Roman and Hellenistic Jewish antagonists.[75] In connection with Gospel research Justin is probably best known for making over a dozen references to "memoirs," or "reminiscences" (Greek: *apomnēmoneumata*; Latin: *memorabilia*), of the apostles and those who followed them (*Apol.* 1.66.3, 1.67.3; *Dial.* 100.4; 101.3; 102.5; 103.6, 8; 104.1; 105.1, 5, 6; 106.1, 4; 107.1).

In antiquity what is an *apomnēmoneuma*? Though rare in early Christian writings, the term is at home in ancient literary criticism; according to the first-century rhetorician Theon, it refers to an account of a person's sayings or doings, having practical significance. It is, in essence, an elaborated *chreia*, an anecdote of that type to which Papias may have alluded. Unlike *hypomnēmata* (research notes, or *aides-mémoire* for private use), *apomnēmoneumata* usually referred to somewhat more polished pieces, intended for publication.[76]

Scholars are in broad agreement that the *apomnēmoneumata* to which Justin refers were generally circulated writings about Jesus' words and deeds.[77] To judge from his remarks Justin appears to have considered them important in at least two respects: first, their derivation from the apostles, or from apostolic adherents; second, their character as historical records (cf. *Apol.* 1.34.2, 1.35.9, 1.48.3). Although he is rather more allusive about it, Justin may have considered these memoirs useful in another related aspect: their apologetic value in rebutting both early Christian heresies and pagan charges of Christianity's irrationality.[78] According to Justin, excerpts from the apostolic *apomnēmoneumata,* along with compilations from the Old Testament prophets, were customarily read by Christians in Sunday worship (*Apol.* 1.67.3); he does not suggest, however, that these literary memoirs were considered either "scriptural" or "inspired."[79] Interestingly, only once (*Apol.* 1.66.3) does Justin apply to these "apostolic memoirs" the term *Gospel,* in the sense of a literary category.[80]

Justin represents some interesting points of contact and divergence from Papias and the Apostolic Fathers. Although it does not appear in the surviving fragments of Papias, the phrase "memoirs of the apostles" is reminiscent of Papias's emphasis on the remembrance, exhibited by certain apostolic followers, of Jesus' teaching and activity. Moreover, no less than Papias, Justin appears to have been conditioned in an environment that was heavily oral and aural: for him, scripture—that is, the Old Testament—"speaks," and his preferred citations from the tradition are, notably, Jesus' sayings.[81] On the other hand, there is some evidence to suggest that the *written* character of apostolic testimony ascends to greater prominence in Justin than in Papias.[82] This may be associated with Justin's attempt to render Christianity philosophically respectable to its cultured despisers: for when he speaks of "apostolic memoirs," Justin may have more immediately in mind not Papias (among whose extant comments that phrase does not appear) but, instead, Xenophon's *Apomnēmoneumata* about Socrates—the philosopher whom Justin implicitly considers to have been superseded by Jesus (*Apol.* 2.10.8; see also 1.5.3, 2.10.5, 2.11.2–7).[83] In any event Justin seems to assume what Papias apparently thought necessary to defend: a legitimacy for the literary character of evangelical proclamation alongside its oral delivery.

Yet nowhere does Justin seem in the least preoccupied with the hallmark of Papias's defense: the *particularity* of apostolic recollection, which can be discriminated and associated now with Mark, then with Matthew. While varying conclusions are drawn by scholars who have minutely examined Justin's use of Gospel materials, a minimal agreement holds that, instead of directly quoting the Gospels, Justin seems to have relied on a complex compound of sources, mixing oral tradition, a compilation of Jesus-sayings that are later than our Gospels, and Gospels unknown to us.[84] Justin does not clearly appeal to the Gospel of Mark as we know it, with one possible exception:

> And . . . it is said that [Jesus] changed the name of one of
> the apostles to Peter; and . . . it is written in his memoirs
> that this so happened, as well as that he changed the names
> of two other brothers, the sons of Zebedee, to Boanerges,
> which means "the sons of thunder." . . . (*Dial.* 106.3)

Among our Synoptic Gospels the translation *Boanerges* appears only
in Mark 3:17. This fact, conjoined with the assumption that Justin is
alluding to Mark's composition of "Peter's reminiscences" ("his memoirs"), suggests to some scholars that Justin knew both Mark's Gospel
and Papias's references to it.[85]

There are, however, other possibilities. In itself the reference to
Boanerges tells us nothing of where Justin found that datum, whether
from what we know as Mark's Gospel or (as easily) from another
tradition no longer known to us. Equally ambiguous is the reference to
his memoirs. *Whose* memoirs: Peter's or Jesus'? Justin does not say.
Usually, though not always, the possessive noun or pronoun with the
term, *apomnēmoneumata,* refers to the *subject* of the reminiscences,
not to their author.[86] On this reading Justin would be referring to
"memories of (or about) Jesus." If so, then the allusion to Mark, while
not precluded, does appear less obvious. On the other hand, Justin
could be suggesting "Peter's reminiscences"—as (tacitly) chronicled
by Mark. If we take this tack, then two things might be concluded.
First, Justin may have known Papias's correlation of Peter with a
document attributed to Mark. Second, Justin is so manifestly *uninterested* in this association that he does not spell it out, much less
elaborate it (by mentioning Mark's name and linkage with Peter).
Either way, both the passage in question and his literary remains in
general suggest that Justin has practically no interest in distinguishing
Gospels by identifying their apostolic pedigree, much less a concern
for the personality of Mark. To that degree Justin appears to be on a
trail that intersects with, but veers away from, that traversed by Papias.

TOWARD THE CENTURY'S END:
MARK AND HIS GOSPEL IN SYRIA, LYONS, AND ROME

By the end of the second century Mark's Gospel had joined with
Matthew, Luke, and John in achieving a perceptible prominence in
several centers of Christianity. Correlative with that status was a
certain coalescence of "traits" that were believed, in some quarters,
to describe Mark the Evangelist.

The *Diatessaron*

Some years after Justin's execution for being a Christian one of his
students produced an important literary composition in the early

church. Tatian was a Syrian Christian, schooled in Greek rhetoric and philosophy, whose best-known work, the *Diatessaron* ("through [the] four [Gospels]"), was a sophisticated interweaving of four separate Gospels into a continuous narrative. Except for a single Greek fragment, discovered as recently as 1933, our knowledge of the *Diatessaron*'s framework and contents stems from commentaries, translations, and adaptations, which were distributed in various languages throughout Eastern and Western churches.[87]

For our purposes Tatian's *Diatessaron* is, like Justin's comments, as interesting for what it does not reveal as for what it does. From what we know of this work nothing emerges about the figure of Mark, as personified by early Christians. Given the nature of the *Diatessaron,* this probably should not come as a surprise: in a project devoted to the *conflation* of different Gospels one might expect Tatian to be rather uninterested in differentiating their alleged authors and points of view. The *Diatessaron* testifies to a fluid situation in which four Gospels had ascended to a collective preeminence yet were not regarded as uniquely canonical. Tatian appears to have been preoccupied by the *contents* of these select four,[88] not by their authorship. From him we do learn that, apart from (or perhaps presuming)[89] the attempt to establish its apostolic *bona fides,* the Gospel attributed to Mark had attained by the middle of the second century a nonetheless privileged stature, comparable to that of the Gospels associated with Matthew, Luke, and John.[90] Doubtless, this eminence was given luster by the immense popularity enjoyed by Tatian's harmony, which until the fifth century was the standard presentation of the Gospels in Syriac-speaking Christianity.

The Muratorian Canon

Very late in the second century, or very early in the third, an annotated list of authoritative works for use in Christian worship was compiled, probably in the West and perhaps in Rome.[91] Named for Lodovico Muratori, the Italian historian who discovered it (in a later version, poorly translated into Latin), the Muratorian Canon stands as the oldest surviving catalog of predominantly Christian writings.

Unfortunately, part of this list has not survived; especially regrettable for our study is that all of what was probably said about Matthew, and much about Mark, is lost. The fragment begins with the words *quibus tamen interfuit et ita posuit,* "among which, however, he was present and so he set it down." Following that elliptical comment are rather detailed statements about "the third Gospel book" and its association with Luke, Paul's traveling companion, and "the fourth of the Gospels, that of John among the disciples." Before turning to Acts and the Epistles, an interesting conclusion about the Gospels is offered: "And therefore, though various rudiments are taught in the several Gospel books, yet that matters nothing for the faith of believers, since by the one guiding Spirit everything is declared in all."[92]

Given the ragged quality of the evidence, it is difficult to reach firm conclusions about the portrayal of Mark and the evaluation of the Second Gospel in the Muratorian Canon. At the start of the fragment who was present? Mark? Present where, or on what occasion(s)? What was it that was set down? Certain answers are unattainable.

Two comments, made almost offhandedly, could be significant for indirectly reconstructing something of this document's perspective on Mark. First, of Luke it is said that "neither did he himself see the Lord in the flesh," implying that yet another Evangelist was not an eyewitness of the things reported. Since the Muratorian fragment describes the Fourth Evangelist as one of the disciples, and since it is probable that the First Gospel would have been attributed to Matthew from among the Twelve, then it is arguably the author of the Second Gospel who the author has in mind. Second, and related to this, the concessive adverb *tamen* ("still," "notwithstanding," "nevertheless") seems to suggest a measure of defensiveness on behalf of the author of the Second Gospel: though lacking some qualifications, in another respect—namely, his being "present"—he was sufficiently justified in "put[ting something] down." This sort of reconstruction *might* comport with knowledge, among the framers of the Muratorian Canon, of Papias's comments about Mark. On the other hand, so indeterminate is the fragment's wording that the demonstration of such an acquaintance virtually requires its prior assumption, which is scarcely a convincing proof.[93]

Clearer, perhaps, if more general, is the fragment's rather labored defense[94] of multiple Gospels, whose diversity "makes no difference for the faith of believers": such an apologia whispers of other Christians' disturbance at divergences among the four Gospels that were gaining in prominence.[95] Whereas Tatian had resolved this problem by blending the dominant Gospels into a consecutive narrative, blurring if not eradicating their distinctive features, the Muratorian Canon adopted another approach: the admission and justification of diversity, moderated "by the one guiding Spirit." Judging from the elaborations about Luke and John in the Muratorian fragment, an important ingredient in that defense was the particularization and personalization of the Gospels' authors as accredited (or at least credible) apostolic agents. More's the pity, in this light, that so little has survived of the

Muratorian depiction of Mark; the general strategy, however, is discernible. Not for the last time would it appear among patristic considerations of a Christian canon in the making.

Irenaeus of Lyons

To this point scrappy assertions and uncorrelated points of view have bobbed to the surface then resubmerged: diverse assessments or assumptions regarding the quality and comparative merits of oral and literary traditions about Jesus; an emerging importance for the Second Gospel, among others; a rather hazy figure of Mark. Many of the pieces at last are smoothed and fitted together by Irenaeus (ca. 130–200), Lyons's bishop and catholic Christianity's first great synthetic theologian.[96]

Such an achievement is altogether appropriate for Irenaeus, whose life, in a sense, was lived at the intellectual crossroads of early catholicism. Born in Asia Minor, tutored in Smyrna and later in Rome, Irenaeus claimed firsthand acquaintance with Polycarp (Eusebius, *H.E.* 5.20.5–7) and knowledge of Papias's five-volume *Interpretation of the Lord's Oracles* (*Adv. Haer.* 5.33.4). Irenaeus's *magnum opus*, and our source for his comments about Mark, was the *Refutation and Overthrow of the Supposed but False "Knowledge"* (180–200). *Adversus Haereses* (= *Against Heresies*), as it is usually called, was designed to sum up the primary lines of second-century catholic theology and to preserve that tradition, inviolate, from what Irenaeus regarded as the specious novelty of Christian Gnosticism (an esoteric philosophy of religion, based on the radical dualism of matter and spirit). Among the acknowledged weapons in Irenaeus's antiheretical arsenal was the Gospel of Mark and a tradition about its composition. It is precisely within this context that his scattered comments about Mark should be heard.

For the purposes of our study Irenaeus makes at least three significant contributions. First, he crystallizes traditions about Mark and the Second Gospel (as well as the other Evangelists and Gospels) which heretofore have been allusive and scattered. Moreover, he focuses those traditions to underscore the Gospels' apostolic origination, which, in turn, confers on those writings canonical authority.[97]

> Now Matthew published a written Gospel among the Hebrews in their own tongue [*dialektō*], while Peter and Paul were evangelizing and founding the church in Rome. But after their departure [*exodon*] Mark, the disciple and interpreter [*hermēneutēs*] of Peter, himself also handed over to

us, in writing, the things preached by Peter. And also Luke, the follower of Paul, put down in a book the gospel preached by him. Then John, the Lord's disciple who even reclined on his breast, himself also gave out the gospel while staying in Ephesus, Asia. (*Adv. Haer.* 3.1.1 [quoted by Eusebius, *H.E.* 5.8.2–3]; see also *Adv. Haer.* 3.10.5)

In this excerpt we might note a few particulars. Irenaeus knows and quotes from 1 Peter (*Adv. Haer.* 4.9.2, 4.16.5, 5.7.2); therefore, for his comments on Mark the Evangelist, he could be drawing an imaginative inference from 1 Peter 5:13. However, the wording more likely suggests Irenaeus's dependence on Papias (whose work, as we have seen, he claimed to know).[98] Also reminiscent of Papias, though couched quite differently, is Mark's somewhat *distanced association* with Peter: according to Irenaeus, Mark's work was handed down after Peter's and Paul's "departure" (*exodon*), which could be a euphemism for their death (cf. the term's connotation in Luke 9:31, 2 Pet 1:15). That which separates evangelist and apostle in Papias's comment, and the matter that must be explained and defended, is Mark's presentation of Peter's oral testimonies. For Irenaeus, on the other hand, the literary transcription of oral tradition seems to be not only a settled issue but also an understandable and desirable development. Still, within the tradition conveyed by Irenaeus a kind of detachment of Mark from Peter persists.[99] Irenaeus arguably introduces into that tradition yet another obliquity: although one might infer from his statement that Mark's Gospel was written in Rome, the city in which Peter and Paul ceased their activities, on closer inspection it is clear that Irenaeus speaks only of the timing of Mark's composition, not of its place of origin.[100]

Second, with Irenaeus we are on firmer ground in assuming that the literary work with which Mark has been associated is the Second Gospel of our acquaintance. With Papias, Justin, and perhaps even Tatian, we cannot be altogether certain; in the Muratorian Canon the probability is strong but incapable of verification. Irenaeus, by contrast, (1) forthrightly connects Mark with a *written Gospel* (*exēnegken euangeliou . . . kai . . . engraphōs*); (2) explicitly cites Mark's Gospel for authoritative evidence (*Adv. Haer.* 3.10.5 [cf. Mark 1:1–3], 3.16.3 [cf. Mark 1:1]) or repeatedly quotes Synoptic material that is unique to the Second Gospel (1.21.2 [cf. Mark 10:38], 4.18.4 [cf. Mark 4:28], 4.37.5 [cf. Mark 9:23]); (3) interestingly defends Mark's orthodoxy against its misappropriation by certain heretics "who separate Jesus from Christ, alleging that Christ remained impassible, but that it was Jesus who suffered" (3.11.7).

Related to this last point is a third principal contribution of Irenaeus: his inclusion of Mark's presentation within a fourfold literary canon, which consists of differently inflected renditions of the gospel.

> For the cherubim have four faces, and their faces are images of the activity of the Son of God [cf. Ezek 1:4–14; Rev 4:6b–8]. For the first living creature, it says, was like a lion, signifying his active and princely and royal character; the second was like an ox, showing his sacrificial and priestly order; the third had the face of a man, indicating very clearly his coming in human guise; and the fourth was like a flying eagle, making plain the giving of the Spirit who broods over the Church. Now the Gospels, in which Christ is enthroned, are like these. For that According to John expounds his princely and mighty and glorious birth from the Father, saying, "In the beginning was the Word, and the Word was with God, and the Word was God" [John 1:1], and, "All things were made by him, and without him was nothing made" [1:3]. Therefore this Gospel is deserving of all confidence, for such indeed is his person. That According to Luke, as having a priestly character, began with the priest Zechariah offering incense to God [Luke 1:5, 9]. For a fatted calf was already being prepared, which was to be sacrificed for the finding of the younger son [cf. 15:23–24]. Matthew proclaims his human birth, saying, "The book of the generation of Jesus Christ, son of David, son of Abraham" [Matt 1:1], and, "The birth of Jesus Christ was in this manner" [1:18], for this Gospel is manlike, and so through the whole Gospel [Christ] appears as a man of a humble mind, and gentle. But Mark takes his beginning from the prophetic Spirit who comes on men from on high, saying, "The beginning of the gospel of Jesus Christ, as it is written in Isaiah the prophet" [Mark 1:1–2], showing a winged image of the Gospel. Therefore, he made his message compendious and cursory, for such is the prophetic character. Again, the Word of God himself used to speak to the patriarchs before Moses, in a divine and glorious manner, but for those under the Law he established a priestly and liturgical order; after this, becoming human, he sent out the gift of the Holy Spirit into the whole earth, guarding us by his own wings. As is the activity of the Son of God, such is the form of the living creatures; and as is the form of the

living creatures, such is also the character of the Gospel.
(*Adv. Haer.* 3.11.8)[101]

Irenaeus is well known for this allegorical justification of four Gospels, neither more nor less, as representing the normative apostolic witness to Christ. Why *four* Gospels, after all? Because, Irenaeus observes, there are four terrestial zones, four principal winds, quadriformity in living creatures, four principal covenants given to the human race, and (most emphatically in the preceding excerpt) four-faced cherubim surrounding the heavenly throne. Behind this fanciful (but, to its creator's mind [3.11.9], suggestive) explanation lurks something more than an obsession with numerology, perhaps even more than concern for the legitimacy of a multiple-Gospel canon. As suggested by the context of his argument (3.11.7, 9), Irenaeus is challenging heretics who have fastened upon only one Gospel (a book, even one with apostolic derivation), thereby missing "the true gospel" (a proclamation): trustworthy doctrine about God, whose multifaceted truth is manifested in Jesus Christ (3.5.1). Within this framework Mark's Gospel is both corrective of and liable of correction by three other, complementary shapings of the church's common evangel.[102]

If we neglect this dimension of Irenaeus's perspective, we shall likely misconstrue his statements about Mark the Evangelist. Regarding that figure and the Gospel with which he is associated, Irenaeus seems preoccupied neither with antiquity nor historicity for its own sake. For Irenaeus the importance of Mark's "prophetic personality" as "Peter's disciple and literary interpreter" resides in *Mark's particular, chastened, and derivative apostolicity*, literarily preserved and ecclesiastically interpreted. As the medium of Peter's apostolic witness, Mark communicates a truthful proclamation received from Christ and delivered, as though on eagle's wings, to the church's children throughout the world (see also *Adv. Haer.* 5.Pref.). With Irenaeus we find not so much an elaboration of the figure of Mark as a theological framework within which that emerging figure has been set and interpreted. And, not unlike the christological doctrine for which the bishop of Lyons is best known, that framework creatively recapitulates much of the tradition about Mark in his patristic predecessors.

NOTES

1. John A. T. Robinson, *Redating the New Testament* (Philadelphia: Westminster, 1976), 107.

2. A recent, comprehensive treatment of the Synoptic problem may be found in E. P. Sanders and Margaret Davies, *Studying the Synoptic Gospels* (London and Philadelphia: SCM / Trinity Press International, 1989), 49–119.

3. Consult D. Moody Smith, *John among the Gospels: The Relationship in Twentieth-Century Research* (Minneapolis: Fortress, 1992).

4. Ron Cameron, ed., *The Other Gospels: Non-Canonical Gospel Texts* (Philadelphia: Westminster, 1982), is a useful collection of primary sources. Helmut Koester, "Apocryphal and Canonical Gospels," *HTR* 73 (1980): 105–30, provides a responsible overview of this material.

5. For example, Augustine delivered a tradition that the canonical order of the Gospels replicated the order in which they were composed (*De consensu evangelistarum* 1.2.3), a passage that we shall consider in chapter 4. Two centuries earlier Clement of Alexandria attributed the difference between the Synoptics and John to the former's presentation of the "bodily facts" (*ta sōmatika*), the latter's offering of a "spiritual Gospel" (*pneumatikon euangelion*) (Eusebius, *H.E.* 6.14.7). According to Eusebius (*H.E.* 6.12.1–6), Serapion of Antioch (d. 211) approved the use of the *Gospel of Peter* in the church at Rhossus—and retracted his authorization after reading that document in its entirety.

6. Oscar Cullmann, "The Plurality of the Gospels as a Theological Problem in Antiquity," in *The Early Church: Studies in Early Christian History and Theology*, ed. A. J. B. Higgins (Philadelphia: Westminster, 1956), 37–54.

7. The basic judgments of Helmut Koester, *Synoptische Überlieferung bei den apostolischen Vätern*, TU 65 (Berlin: Akademie, 1957), have been upheld by subsequent research (and, indeed, were anticipated by earlier scholarship: cf., for example, Henry Barclay Swete, *The Gospel according to St. Mark: The Greek Text with Introduction, Notes, and Indices*, 3d. ed. [London: Macmillan, 1927], xxix–xxxiv). For a recent, concise treatment in English that summarizes the main issues and reaches comparable conclusions, see Donald A. Hagner, "The Sayings of Jesus in the Apostolic Fathers and Justin Martyr," in *Gospel Perspectives: The Jesus Tradition Outside the Gospels*, ed. David Wenham (Sheffield: JSOT, 1984), 233–68.

8. The earliest manuscript traditions of the Second Gospel support this asumption: O. Linton, "Evidences of a Second-Century Revised Edition of St. Mark's Gospel," *NTS* 14 (1968): 321–55. In fact, as Harry Y. Gamble notes, Mark's textual tradition exhibits more scribal corrections than those of the other Gospels, which may be due to its lengthier period of circulation (*The New Testament Canon: Its Making and Meaning*, GBSNTS [Philadelphia: Fortress, 1985], 27).

9. For this reason the conclusion drawn by Joseph F. Kelly ("The Patristic Biography of Mark," *Bible Today* 21 [1983]: 44) is, while accurate, neither as surprising nor as significant as one might otherwise suppose: "The patristic tradition is unanimous that Mark wrote Mark's Gospel."

10. Burnett Hillman Streeter, *The Primitive Church, Studied with Special Reference to the Origins of the Christian Ministry* (New York: Macmillan, 1929), 20.

11. Tatian and Irenaeus, writing in the last quarter of the second century, offer the earliest, clear assumption of a four-Gospel canon within patristic Christianity. The earliest Greek manuscript that preserves the four Gospels (plus Acts) is the first of the Chester Beatty biblical papyruses (usually referred to as p⁴⁵), which may be dated in the first half of the third century.

12. Although A. F. Walls ("Papias and the Oral Tradition," *VC* 21 [1967]: 137–40) has rightly argued that Papias did not so much denigrate written sources as criticize contemporary writings that lacked apostolic origin, Papias's high regard for credible oral tradition remains nonetheless clear and implied by his concern for appropriate warrants.

13. For further discussion of these issues, see Hagner, "Sayings of Jesus," 252–59.

14. A similar use of the sayings of Jesus appears already in some of Paul's letters, from the early to mid-50s of the first century: for example, 1 Corinthians (7:10–11 [cf. Mark 10:2–9], 9:14 [cf. Luke 10:7], 11:23–26 [cf. Luke 22:14–20]) and Romans (12:14 [cf. Matt 5:44], 13:8–10 [cf. Matt 22:40; Mark 12:31]). Could the dearth of Jesus-sayings in Mark, compared with their abundance in Matthew and Luke, have been one of the reasons for the Second Gospel's relative neglect in the early church?

15. Again, a similar phenomenon may be witnessed in the probably post-Pauline Epistle to the Ephesians (2:19–21, 3:4–5).

16. In the Pastoral Epistles, which may date from the late first or early second century, we can see a corollary concern for the preservation and perpetuation of "the deposit of faith," increasingly understood as sound doctrine and ethical practice (1 Tim 4:6–16, 6:2b–5; 2 Tim 2:1–2; Tit 2:1–10).

17. As patristic Christianity evolves, there flowers an anecdotal and fragmentary tradition about Papias himself, much of which centers on his audition of apostolic predecessors (see Eusebius, *H.E.* 3.39.3–4). As the present study is devoted to the early Christian figure of Mark, not of Papias, only those excerpts that involve Mark or the authorship of the Gospel will be discussed; for our purposes the rest (and bulk) of these extracts may be safely ignored. Most of the extant Papias-fragments have been collected, translated, and thoroughly annotated by William R. Schoedel, *The Apostolic Fathers*, vol. 5: *Polycarp, Martyrdom of Polycarp, Fragments of Papias* (London: Thomas Nelson & Sons, 1967), 89–123.

18. See the bibliography compiled by E. König and M. Vinzent in Josef Kürzinger, *Papias von Hierapolis und die Evangelien des Neuen Testaments: Gesammelte Aufsätze, Neuausgabe und Übersetzung der Fragmente, Kommentierte Bibliographie*, EM 4 (Regensburg: Friedrich Pustet, 1983), 139–250. To date the most recent and comprehensive investigation of the Papias-fragments is Ulrich H. J. Körtner, *Papias von Hierapolis: Ein Beitrag zur Geschichte des frühen Christentums*, FRLANT 133 (Göttingen: Vandenhoeck & Ruprecht, 1983).

19. William R. Schoedel, "The Apostolic Fathers," in *The New Testament and Its Modern Interpreters,* ed. Eldon Jay Epp and George W. MacRae (Atlanta: Scholars Press, 1989), 472. For this reason a measure of caution is probably warranted in evaluating the more detailed constructions that have been proposed by both Papias's scholarly advocates (e.g., A. C. Perumalil, "Are Not Papias and Irenaeus Competent to Report on the Gospels?" *ExpTim* 91 [1980]: 332–37) and detractors (e.g., S. G. Papadopoulos, "*Hoi presbyteroi kai hē paradosis tou Papias,*" *Deltion Biblikon Meleton* 2 [1974]: 218–29, an article, unavailable to me, for whose argument I am dependent on *NTA* 19 [1975]: 253).

20. Benjamin Wisner Bacon, "Papias," in *The New Schaff-Herzog Encyclopedia of Religious Knowledge,* ed. S. M. Jackson (New York and London: Funk & Wagnalls, 1910), 8:336.

21. The majority of scholars has tended toward a later dating (see, e.g., Joachim Gnilka, *Das Evangelium nach Markus,* EKKNT (Zürich and Neukirchener Vluyn: Benzinger/Neukirchener, 1978), 1:32–34. Körtner, however, has made a persuasive case for a relatively early date for Papias (ca. 110 C.E.; *Papias von Hierapolis,* esp. 225–31); and Schoedel suggests that a date in the late first or early second century may now be preferable ("The Apostolic Fathers," in Epp and MacRae, *New Testament and Its Modern Interpreters,* 474). On this question of date, see also Engelbert Gutwenger, "Papias: Eine chronologische Studie," *ZKT* 69 (1947): 385–416; Rupert Annand, "Papias and the Four Gospels," *SJT* 9 (1956): 46–62; R. W. Yarbrough, "The Date of Papias: A Reassessment," *JETS* 26 (1983): 181–91.

22. Full consideration of the question is given by Körtner (*Papias von Hierapolis,* 151–72), whose own suspicion is that Papias's work was intended as an interpretive presentation of the Lord's sayings and doings, not unlike those of the Synoptic Evangelists (163–64).

23. Consult the seminal study by Arnaldo Momigliano, "Pagan and Christian Historiography in the Fourth Century A.D.," in *The Conflict between Paganism and Christianity in the Fourth Century,* ed. A. Momigliano (Oxford: Clarendon, 1963), 79–99; see also R. A. Markus, "Church History and Early Church Historians," in *The Materials, Sources and Methods of Ecclesiastical History,* ed. D. Baker, Studies in Church History 11 (Oxford: Basil Blackwell, 1975), 1–17.

24. Copious examples are cited in Robert M. Grant, *Eusebius as Church Historian* (Oxford: Clarendon, 1980), 63–72. See also B. Gustafsson, "Eusebius' Principles in Handling His Sources, as Found in His Church History, Books I–VII," *Studia Patristica* 4, TU 79 (Berlin: Akademie, 1961), 429–41; and Momigliano, "Pagan and Christian Historiography," 89–92.

25. For consideration of Eusebius's views on orthodoxy, see Markus, "Church History and Early Church Historians," 5–6; on heretics, see Grant, *Eusebius as Church Historian,* 84–96.

26. This has been persuasively demonstrated by Robert M. Grant, "Eusebius and His Church History," in *Understanding the Sacred Text: Essays in*

Honor of Morton S. Enslin on the Hebrew Bible and Christian Beginnings, ed. John Reumann (Valley Forge, Pa.: Judson, 1972), 235–47 (esp. 235–40).

27. For discussion of this interesting shift, consult Gustafsson, "Eusebius' Principles," 439–40; Grant, *Eusebius as Church Historian,* 130–36.

28. Gustafsson, "Eusebius' Principles," 429–33. Eusebius's knowledge of Papias's treatises in five volumes could have been derived from Irenaeus (*Adv. Haer.* 5.33.4), whom Eusebius cites (*H.E.* 3.39.1).

29. For this point I am indebted to Grant, "Eusebius and His Church History," 236–37, 246 n. 2.

30. Robert M. Grant has raised this question and suggested an answer: Eusebius quoted Papias "out of reverence for Irenaeus, who as he knew relied upon what Papias taught" ("Papias in Eusebius' *Church History,*" in *Mélanges d'histoire des religions offerts à Henri-Charles Puech sous le patronage et avec le concours du Collège de France et de la section des sciences religieuses de l'Ecole pratique des hautes études* (Paris: Universitaires de France, 1974), 212 (see also 209–13). While doubtless true, Grant's suggestion may not be entirely satisfying, insofar as Eusebius nevertheless felt forced to apologize for the deleterious effect of Papias's eschatology upon Irenaeus and "whoever else appears to have held the same views" (*H.E.* 3.39.13).

31. In this connection one might note Grant's interesting exercise in redaction criticism of the *Church History* ("Papias," esp. 212–13). Grant argues that, as Eusebius's tolerance for the Johannine Apocalypse waned, to the same degree his disgruntlement toward Papias appears to have waxed (see also *Eusebius as Church Historian,* 130–36).

32. In my opinion this aspect of Eusebius's tendentiousness has not received as much attention as have his other biases. Though not to be pressed too far, such an interpretation seems to me *prima facie* more satisfying than the claim that "Eusebius . . . could find nothing in Papias worth preserving" (Wilfred Lawrence Knox, *The Sources of the Synoptic Gospels,* vol. 1: *St. Mark* [Cambridge: Cambridge University Press, 1952], 73).

33. Johannes Munck, "Presbyters and Disciples of the Lord in Papias," *HTR* 52 (1959): 223–43; G. M. Lee, "Presbyters and Apostles," *ZNW* 62 (1971): 122.

34. Thus, see Grant, "Papias in Eusebius' *Church History,*" in *Mélanges d'histoire des religions,* 210; Bo Reicke, *The Roots of the Synoptic Gospels* (Philadelphia: Fortress, n.d.), 161–62.

35. As pointed out by A. C. Perumalil, "Papias," *ExpTim* 85 (1974): 363.

36. I take the term *presbyteros* in its basic sense, referring to one of venerable age. In the case of John the Presbyter it could also refer to one who held a position of recognized, even quasi-official, responsibility in early Christianity (cf. 1 Tim 5:17–22; Tit 2:2–10; 2 John 1; 3 John 1).

37. See Körtner, *Papias von Hierapolis,* 114–32; *pace* K. Beyschlag, "Herkunft und Eigenart der Papiasfragmente," *Studia Patristica* 4, TU 79 (Berlin: Akademie, 1961), 268–80. A differentiation between these two personalities, both named John, was certainly attributed to Papias by Eusebius (*H.E.*

3.39.5–7) and Jerome (*De viris illustribus* 18). Conceivably, however, these later patristic writers could have had their own apologetic motives for drawing such a conclusion.

38. Among others, Jürgen Regul, *Die antimarcionitischen Evangelienprologe*, Vetus Latina 6 (Freiburg: Herder, 1969), 96; cf. 113–60; Kümmel, *Introduction*, 97; Gnilka, *Das Evangelium nach Markus*, 1: 33.

39. So also Hengel, *Studies in the Gospel of Mark*, 47. Hengel may partially overstate the case by claiming that these two traditions, while independent, "provide reciprocal confirmation" (150 n. 56). 1 Peter and Papias reciprocally confirm only the association of Peter and Mark, not their *literary* association.

40. The traditional succession in which Papias purports to stand could have been deliberately fabricated in an ambiguous way (thus, see Schoedel, "Apostolic Fathers," 474). On the other hand, would one so defensive about Mark's credibility construct a rationalization so obscure?

41. C. E. B. Cranfield, *The Gospel according to Saint Mark*, CGNT (Cambridge: Cambridge University Press, 1959), 3–4.

42. Among many others, see Vincent Taylor, *The Gospel according to St. Mark*, 2d. ed., Thornapple Commentaries (1946; reprint, Grand Rapids, Mich.: Baker Book House, 1981), 1–3; Cranfield, *Gospel according to Saint Mark*, 5; William L. Lane, *The Gospel according to Mark*, NICNT (Grand Rapids, Mich.: Eerdmans, 1974), 7–9.

43. See my comments in the introduction to the present study.

44. Willi Marxsen, *Introduction to the New Testament: An Approach to Its Problems* (Philadelphia: Fortress, 1968), 143.

45. Hans Conzelmann, *History of Primitive Christianity* (Nashville: Abingdon, 1973), 153. (In the book's German edition Conzelmann's comment is, "Aber was Papias schreibt, ist Gewäsch" [*Geschichte des Urchristentums*, 4th ed., GNTNTD 5 (Göttingen: Vandenhoeck & Ruprecht, 1978), 134].) Comparable though more moderate in tone is the same author's assessment in his volume, written with Andreas Lindemann, *Interpreting the New Testament*, 218–19. A good statement of reservations, attached to the Papias-notice on this point, is found in Petr Pokorný, "Das Markusevangelium: Literarische und theologische Einleitung mit Forschungsbericht," *ANRW* 2.25.3 (1985): 1969–2035, esp. 1974–75, 2019–20.

46. Pesch, *Das Markusevangelium*, 1: 9–11; Lührmann, *Das Markusevangelium*, 5; Robert A. Guelich, *Mark 1–8:26*, WBC 34A (Dallas: Waco, 1989), xxvii–xxviii.

47. Conveniently collected in Kürzinger, *Papias von Hierapolis*.

48. Josef Kürzinger, "Das Papiaszeugnis und die Erstgestalt des Matthäusevangeliums," *BZ* 4 (1960): 19–38.

49. Josef Kürzinger, "Die Aussage des Papias von Hierapolis zur literarischen Form des Markusevangeliums," *BZ* 21 (1977): 245–64. Cf. T. Y. Mullins, "Papias on Mark's Gospel," *VC* 14 (1960): 216–24, which proposes a more speculative theory, involving Mark's translation of Peter's written testimony.

50. *Contra* Arthur Wright, "*Taxei* in Papias," *JTS* 14 (1913): 298–300; and,

more recently, Rupert Annand, "Papias and the Four Gospels," *SJT* 9 (1956): 55; and Körtner, *Papias von Hierapolis,* 212.

51. Kürzinger, "Die Aussage des Papias," 256–58. An overview of the *chreiai* is provided by Vernon K. Robbins, in Aune, *Greco-Roman Literature and the New Testament,* 1–23. Burton L. Mack and Vernon K. Robbins, *Patterns of Persuasion in the Gospels,* FFLF (Sonoma, Calif.: Polebridge, 1989), is a thorough exploration of the Synoptics' use of this literary form. Generations of North American schoolchildren have been taught the virtue of honesty through a *chreia* popularized by Parson Weems: George Washington's youthful confession of chopping down a cherry tree.

52. Kürzinger, "Das Papiaszeugnis," 30–36; "Die Aussage des Papias," 260–64.

53. For a different assessment, which places a higher premium on distinguishing the Elder's testimony from its interpretation by Papias, see Benjamin Wisner Bacon, *The Gospel of Mark: Its Composition and Date* (New Haven: Yale University Press, 1925), 22–34.

54. Representative of this common assumption is Helmut Koester's comment, in reference to *H.E.* 3.39.15: "Thus *Mark's Gospel* was known by the name of its author no later than the middle of the 2d century" (*Ancient Christian Gospels: Their History and Development* [Philadelphia and London: Trinity Press International / SCM, 1990], 274 [emphasis added]).

55. Eusebius may have made such a connection (see *H.E.* 2.15.1, a passage that will be taken up in chap. 5). To be sure, widely discrepant scholarly reconstructions have been grounded in this assumption: among others, H. E. W. Turner, "Modern Issues in Biblical Studies: The Tradition of Mark's Dependence on Peter," *ExpTim* 71 (1960): 260–63; Kurt Niederwimmer, "Johannes Markus und die Frage nach dem Verfasser des zweiten Evangeliums," *ZNW* 58 (1967): 172–88. Well-founded uncertainty about Papias's knowledge of Synoptic traditions in their literary form is expressed by Richard Heard, "Papias' Quotations from the New Testament," *NTS* 1 (1954–55): 130–34.

56. On the basis of passages like Quintilian's *Education of the Orator* 7.Pr.3, Schoedel has suggested that the muted critique of Mark's order amounts to a complaint about its incompleteness (*Apostolic Fathers,* 106). A related problem is implied by Papias's seeming assertion that Matthew composed "a Hebrew Gospel": Greek is the language of the Christian canon's First Gospel—if that is the document Papias had in mind.

57. Thus, see Tolbert, *Sowing the Gospel* (N.B. 311–15). On this score, however, Tolbert evinces some ambivalence: elsewhere she suggests that Mark's Gospel is a "simple, fairly crude, synthetic narrative" (78), far below the standard of subtlety and sensitivity set by comparable works in antiquity (59).

58. C. D. F. Moule and A. M. G. Stephenson, "R. G. Heard on Q and Mark," *NTS* 2 (1955): 114–18. Moule and Stephenson are not in every respect convinced by Heard's findings, which they published after his death.

59. Mullins, "Papias on Mark's Gospel," 216–24; David G. Deeks, "Papias Revisited," *ExpTim* 88 (1977): 296–301, 324–39.

60. George A. Kennedy, "Classical and Christian Source Criticism," in *The Relationships among the Gospels: An Interdisciplinary Dialogue,* ed. William O. Walker, Jr. (San Antonio: Trinity University Press, 1978), 125–56. Adumbrated by Robert M. Grant, *The Earliest Lives of Jesus* (New York: Harper & Brothers, 1961), 14–18, Kennedy's thesis has been given a cautiously favorable reception: see the reviews by Wayne A. Meeks, *"Hypomnēmata* from an Untamed Skeptic: A Response to George Kennedy," in Walker, *Relationships,* 157–72; and Reginald H. Fuller, "Classics and the Gospels: The Seminar," in Walker, *Relationships,* 173–92.

61. For example, Taylor, *Gospel according to St. Mark,* 2–3; Cranfield, *Gospel according to Saint Mark,* 3–4.

62. As he acknowledged, Kürzinger's suggestions were not without precedent: cf. F. H. Colson, *"Taxei* in Papias (The Gospels and the Rhetorical Schools)," *JTS* 14 (1912): 62–69; and Taylor, *Groundwork of the Gospels,* 29–30, 75–90 (on the *chreiai*). Yet it is Kürzinger's elaboration of this rhetorical perspective which has exerted the greatest influence on recent scholarship.

63. George Kennedy, *The Art of Rhetoric in the Roman World, 300 B.C.–A.D. 300* (Princeton: Princeton Univesity Press, 1972); Kennedy, *Greek Rhetoric under Christian Emperors* (Princeton: Princeton University Press, 1983).

64. Cf. the corroborative conclusions of Johannes Behm, *"hermēneuō, k.t.l.,"* *TDNT* 2 (1964): 661–66, esp. 663; Gerhard Kittel et al., *"legō, k.t.l.,"* *TDNT* 4 (1967): 69–192 (s.v. *logion* [137–41]); Roger Gryson, "A propos du témoignage de Papias sur Matthieu: Le sens du mot *LOGION* chez les Pères du second siècle," *ETL* 41 (1965): 530–47. Schoedel, however, argues that *hermēneutēs* should be rendered "translator" in *H.E.* 3.39.15 (*Apostolic Fathers,* 106–8).

65. Among others, W. D. Davies and Dale C. Allison, Jr., are unsure that this aspect of Kürzinger's translation can bear the weight placed upon it (*A Critical and Exegetical Commentary on the Gospel according to Saint Matthew,* ICC [Edinburgh: T & T Clark, 1988], 1:16). Although Kürzinger has argued that Irenaeus (*Adv. Haer.* 3.1.1) supports such a translation ("Irenaeus und sein Zeugnis zur Sprache des Matthäusevangeliums," *NTS* 10 [1963]: 108–15), Matthew Black finds it uncorroborated in all subsequent patristic traditions, even those traceable to Papias ("The Use of Rhetorical Terminology in Papias on Mark and Matthew," *JSNT* 37 [1989]: 31–41, esp. 33–34).

66. One of the most difficult phrases to translate in *H.E.* 3.39.14–17 is *pros tas chreias*: Did Peter adapt (his) teachings "to the *chreiai* [i.e., in anecdotal form]" or "toward the needs [of his audience]"? In context either would make sense, though the alternatives suggest very different meanings. Favoring the latter possibility are: (1) the usual sense of the preposition *pros*; and (2) the modern, form-critical presumption that Christian traditions were indeed accommodated to the liturgical and catechetical requirements of primitive churches. Favoring the former alternative are: (1) the likely rhetorical context

of Papias's observations (note the immediate contrast with *syntaxis*, "a systematic arrangement"); and (2) the remarkably precise correspondence in the wording of Papias's defense (*H.E.* 3.39.15) with two of Theon's criteria in the *Progymnasmata* (ca. first century A.D.) for proper *chreiai*: truth and relative completeness (as perceptively argued by Grant, *Earliest Lives of Jesus,* 18, citing *Rhetores Graeci,* ed. Leonard Spengel [Leipzig: Teubneri, 1853], 2:104.15–18). This is a very close call indeed. Being guardedly inclined toward Kürzinger's general approach, I might give a slight edge to the "rhetorical" reading; as with most questions concerning Papias, however, it is impossible to be certain.

67. *Pace* Sanders and Davies (*Studying the Synoptic Gospels,* 10–11), who suggest that Papias's primary purpose was to establish the authorship of the Second Gospel. It is also hard for me to concur with W. C. van Unnik that the substance of Mark's interpretive effort, not the manner of its performance, is what Papias considers important ("Zur Papias-Notiz über Markus (Eusebius H.E. III 39,15)," *ZNW* 54 [1963]: 276–77). As far as I can see, the questions stimulated by the form and content of Mark's literary product are, for Papias, inseparable.

68. Among those who argue that Luke's Gospel is the standard against which Mark has been measured are Robert M. Grant, "Papias and the Gospels," *ATR* 25 (1943): 218–22; and Ralph P. Martin, *Mark: Evangelist and Theologian* (Grand Rapids, Mich.: Zondervan, 1972), 80–83. For the case that Papias defends Mark against the Fourth Gospel, see (among others) Wright, "*Taxei* in Papias," 298–300; James Moffatt, *An Introduction to the Literature of the New Testament,* ITL (Edinburgh and New York: T & T Clark / Charles Scribner's Sons, 1918), 185–91; and the fairly elaborate theory of Alfred Loisy, *The Origins of the New Testament* (London: George Allen & Unwin, 1950), 63–70. A renewed defense of Papias's knowledge and use of John's Gospel has recently been offered by Folker Siegert, "Unbeachtete Papiaszitate bei armenischen Schriftstellern," *NTS* 27 (1981): 605–14; however, the primary evidence on which Siegert bases his argument is very late (early seventh century).

69. Cf. Deeks, "Papias Revisited," 299–300. Scholars have also debated the degree to which Papias's comments connote a polemical purpose (against protognostics or even against various canonical writers): thus, see Charles M. Nielsen, "Papias: Polemicist against Whom?" *TS* 35 (1974): 529–35; "Polycarp and Marcion: A Note," *TS* 47 (1986): 297–99. For a judicious assessment of the possibilities and attendant problems, consult Körtner, *Papias von Hierapolis,* 167–72.

70. The earlier that Papias is dated, the less certainly we can presume his and other Christians' widespread knowledge of documents like Matthew, Luke, or John, which themselves were written probably not earlier than 80–100.

71. Though not original (cf. Kenneth L. Carroll, "The Creation of the Fourfold Gospel," *BJRL* 37 [1954–55]: 68–77, esp. 70), such a suggestion has perhaps been too often neglected in recent scholarship. Bacon (*Gospel of*

Mark) suggests that the Elder John also was biased toward the living voice of tradition: "To learn the real meaning of the sacred tradition, one should apply at [Petrine] headquarters" (31).

72. If *dialektos* suggests not only "language" but "discourse"—a nuance of the word that dates back to Plato (*Symposium* 203a; *Theaetetus* 146b [cf. *dialexis*, Eusebius, *H.E.* 5.26.1])—is it possible that Papias could have been making an analogous assertion about Matthew (*H.E.* 3.39.16)?

73. Davies and Allison, *Gospel according to Saint Matthew*, 1:16.

74. See Heard, "Papias' Quotations from the New Testament," 133–34, who suggests that Papias's remarks signify an important transition from apostolic persons to apostolic documents (cf. Körtner, *Papias von Hierapolis*, 226–31). In the light of form criticism we may wonder if Papias has telescoped historical reality by speaking of Mark's allegiance to Peter rather than to Petrine tradition (even as late first-century Paulinists probably penned communications like Ephesians and 1 Timothy in their mentor's name). At any rate Papias's statement does not necessarily imply a history of transmission so oversimplified as some have suggested (see Werner H. Kelber, *The Oral and the Written Gospel: The Hermeneutics of Speaking and Writing in the Synoptic Tradition, Mark, Paul, and Q* [Philadelphia: Fortress, 1983], 212–14).

75. Eric Francis Osborn, *Justin Martyr*, BHT 47 (Tübingen: Mohr [Siebeck], 1973), provides a comprehensive overview.

76. A thorough canvassing of relevant primary materials, plus a careful overview of research, is offered by Niels Hyldahl, "Hegesipps Hypomnemata," *ST* 14 (1960): 70–113.

77. For a different view, which sees little relationship between the Gospels and what Justin says about them, consult Kee, *Jesus in History*, 137–38.

78. See Luise Abramowski, "The 'Memoirs of the Apostles' in Justin," in *The Gospel and the Gospels*, ed. Peter Stuhlmacher (Grand Rapids, Mich.: Eerdmans, 1991), 323–35, esp. 332–34.

79. For Justin's comments about "inspiration," or "divine empowerment," see *Apol.* 1.33.5 (with reference to the Old Testament prophets); 1.39.3 (in regard to the Twelve and their proclamation of the [oral] gospel). As Gamble notes (*New Testament Canon*, 29 n. 18, citing Eusebius, *H.E.* 4.23.11), the use of a document in early Christian worship did not necessarily signify its scriptural status.

80. On two other occasions in Justin's writings (*Dial.* 10.2, 100.1) the term *Gospel* refers to writings that can be read. For discussion of these passages, plus the possibility that *Apol.* 1.66.3 is a later gloss, consult Abramowski, " 'Memoirs of the Apostles' in Justin," 323–35.

81. Osborn, *Justin Martyr*, 87.

82. Abramowski, " 'Memoirs of the Apostles,' in Justin," 327–29.

83. Schoedel, *Apostolic Fathers*, 108. Cf. Richard Heard, "APOMNĒMO-NEUMATA in Papias, Justin, and Irenaeus," *NTS* 1 (1954): 122–29, who argues that, for this understanding, Justin was directly dependent on Papias. Interestingly, in a recent study of the Second Gospel, Vernon K. Robbins has pointed

up formal and material similarities between Mark's presentation of Jesus and the Socratic memoirs collected by Xenophon (*Jesus the Teacher: A Socio-Rhetorical Interpretation of Mark* [Philadelphia: Fortress, 1984], 60–67).

84. The standard monograph on this difficult subject is Arthur J. Bellinzoni, *The Sayings of Jesus in the Writings of Justin Martyr*, NovTSup 17 (Leiden: E. J. Brill, 1967). Cf. also Gamble, *New Testament Canon*, 29.

85. C. E. B. Cranfield, "Mark, Gospel of," *IDB* 3 (1962): 267–68. Although Cranfield does not argue for Justin's dependence on Papias, that possibility is recognized by Sanders and Davies, *Studying the Synoptic Gospels*, 11–12.

86. Grant, *Earliest Lives of Jesus*, 119.

87. Thorough discussions of the versions of the *Diatessaron* and the problems surrounding their interpretation are provided by Bruce M. Metzger, *The Early Versions of the New Testament: Their Origin, Transmission, and Limitations* (Oxford: Clarendon, 1977), 10–36; and William L. Petersen, "Tatian's *Diatessaron*," in Koester, *Ancient Christian Gospels*, 403–30.

88. On the possibility that Tatian may also have used apocryphal Gospels, see Gamble, *New Testament Canon*, 30–31, and the secondary literature cited there.

89. William L. Petersen, "Textual Evidence of Tatian's Dependence upon Justin's ΑΡΟΜΝΕΜΟΝΕΥΜΑΤΑ," *NTS* 36 (1990): 512–34.

90. The importance of Mark, relative to the other Gospels, may be suggested by the pattern of their appropriation by Tatian: the *Diatessaron*'s basic structure appears to have been adopted from Matthew and John then filled in with details drawn from Luke and, to a lesser degree, from Mark (see, e.g., Dura-Europos fragment reproduced in Metzger, *Early Versions*, 11). Already in the mid-second century Mark was being ranged with, yet practically subordinated to, the other three Gospels that ultimately were canonized.

91. Adopting and elaborating an earlier suggestion by Albert C. Sundberg, Jr. ("Canon Muratori: A Fourth-Century List," *HTR* 66 [1973]: 1–41), Geoffrey Mark Hahneman has recently mounted a painstaking challenge against the consensus dating and provenance of the Muratorian fragment. See Hahneman's monograph, *The Muratorian Fragment and the Development of the Canon* (Oxford: Clarendon, 1992), which argues that the fragment is a fourth-century Eastern list.

92. The translation is that of Gamble, who reproduces the entire text of the Muratorian catalog (*New Testament Canon*, 93–95).

93. This, in my judgment, is a problematic aspect of Arnold Ehrhardt's indispensable discussion of "The Gospels in the Muratorian Fragment," in *The Framework of the New Testament Stories* (Cambridge, Mass.: Harvard University Press, 1964), 11–36. It may be reasonably conjectured that the linkage here between Mark and Peter has not been wrought as a deduction from 1 Peter 5:13, since the Muratorian Canon does not recognize that document.

94. For example, the claim that "everything is declared in all [four Gospels]" is a considerable overstatement, since neither Mark nor John preserves a narrative "concerning [Jesus'] birth."

95. As Gamble (*New Testament Canon*, 33) perceptively notes.

96. A judicious examination of Irenaeus's writings and theology may be found in Johannes Quasten, *Patrology*, vol. 1: *The Beginnings of Patristic Literature* (Utrecht-Antwerp and Westminster, Md.: Spectrum/Newman, n.d.), 287–313.

97. For more detailed consideration of this topic, see Denis Farkasfalvy, "Theology of Scripture in St. Irenaeus," *RBén* 78 (1968): 328–30. I am indebted to William S. Babcock for alerting me to this article and its relevance to the present discussion.

98. Thus, see Heard, "APOMNĒMONEUMATA in Papias, Justin, and Irenaeus," 127; *contra* Perumalil ("Are Not Papias and Irenaeus Competent to Report on the Gospels?" 332–37), who argues that Irenaeus received traditions about the Gospels from Polycarp, independently of Papias.

99. Cf. also Irenaeus's comments about Matthew, which portrays the First Gospel's composition as coincidental with the preaching of Peter and Paul in Rome.

100. I understand neither the reason for Reicke's suggestion (*Roots of the Synoptic Gospels*, 154) that "[Irenaeus] connected [the four Gospels] with Syria, Asia, Greece, and Italy to get an even distribution on four Christian countries," nor the textual basis for his comment (*Adv. Haer.* 2.1.1: a misprint, perhaps?). As far as I can tell, in this passage at least, Irenaeus clearly associates only one Evangelist (John) with a particular locale (Ephesus, Asia; *Adv. Haer.* 3.1.1).

101. The translation, to which I have made minor modifications, is by Edward Rochie Hardy in *Early Christian Fathers*, ed. Cyril C. Richardson et al., LCC 1 (Philadelphia: Westminster, 1953), 382–83.

102. For the formulation of this paragraph I am especially indebted to the discussions in Gamble, *New Testament Canon*, 31–32; and Hans von Campenhausen, *The Formation of the Christian Bible* (Philadelphia: Fortress, 1972), 181–209.

Chapter Four

Sketches of an Apostolic Evangelist (I)

The Figure of Mark in Western Christianity
of the Third and Fourth Centuries

When the second century had melted into the third, the lines of a sketch of the Evangelist Mark had been roughed in within two narrow but significant bands of primitive Christianity: Asia Minor and Europe, particularly in Rome. With Papias in Hierapolis (Asia Minor) we can chart the beginnings of a putative literary association of Mark with the apostle Peter: the former regarded as faithful interpreter of remembered oral traditions, ascribed to the latter. Cognate with, if not directly dependent on, the tradition presented by Papias is the more general portrayal of the Gospel writers as memoirists of Jesus and the Twelve, suggested by Justin, who had taught for a time in Ephesus, Asia Minor, before opening a school in Rome. One of Justin's pupils in that city, Tatian, ended up in Syria; there his *Diatessaron* offered little if any embellishment to the figure of Mark but did confer a measure of credibility to the Gospel associated with Mark, by consolidating its presentation of Jesus with those of several other Gospels.

Whereas Tatian's "Gospel harmony" remained popular in the Syrian church until the fifth century (when its author's ascetic sectarianism became insuperably suspect), the Muratorian fragment reflects another theological strategy, probably employed in the Western church: the movement toward a normative canon—including four different Gospels, each with a particular apostolic pedigree. Because of its lamentably mutilated state, we cannot know as precisely as we would like the claims made by the Muratorian Canon of Mark's Gospel. For that we must turn to Irenaeus, a child of Eastern Christianity (Smyrna, Asia Minor) and later a bishop in the West (Gaul, a Roman province that included modern-day France). Claiming acquaintance with Papias's work, Irenaeus refines some of the features of what by now was a discernible cameo: Mark, portrayed as the disciple of Peter, late of Rome, who literarily transmitted Petrine preaching in the Second of four indispensable and mutually self-correcting Gospels.

114

In this chapter and the next we shall trace the figure of Mark as it continued to evolve in Christian reflection and imagination during the two centuries that followed. Unlike the previous chapter, which permitted us to travel within a more or less restricted geographical ambit, along a roughly continuous chronology, we shall now take multiple soundings, repeatedly across the third and fourth centuries, in five major centers of early Christianity. Partly for reasons of continuity with some paths already traversed, we shall begin with early third-century traditions about the Second Evangelist which may be associated particularly with Rome, or (where such precision is denied us) European Christianity in general, then pick up two more representatives of Western (or Latin) Christianity in North Africa. In chapter 5 we shall move eastwardly, gathering some traditions in Egypt and Syria, before coming to rest in the first cradle of Christianity, Palestine. In globe-trotting the ancient Mediterranean basin, we shall look, wherever appropriate, for possible links among the portraits of Mark which arise from these various centers. Where that project seems futile or ill advised we shall be content to observe and to enjoy the kaleidoscopic figures of Mark which emanate, then retract, from the traditions and legends of patristic Christianity.

STUMPY-FINGERED BUT APOSTOLIC: MARK IN ROME AND WESTERN EUROPE

Befitting its early eminence and strategic position in the imperial capital (cf. Rom 1:8–15), Roman Christianity was either the stage or the backdrop for the work of most of the church fathers whom we have considered thus far. The last years of Justin's life as schoolmaster and apologist were played out in Rome. There Irenaeus visited, and Tatian was educated. Most scholars agree that, if it was not assembled in Rome, the Muratorian Canon likely bespeaks a Roman or at least Latin Christian evaluation of some literature that was esteemed among second-century Christians. On the other hand, during our period, "the Eternal City" was not an overly productive center of Christian scholarship; as a result, we have rather less material from this region to sift. Among that material, however, the figure of Mark bobs to the surface in some intriguing and unexpected ways.

Hippolytus of Rome

For the next brush stroke in the patristic portrait of Mark we turn to Hippolytus (ca. 170–236), third-century Rome's most prolific and perhaps most significant Christian author. In the midst of a remarkably checkered career that included election as the first anti-pope, imperial exile to Sardinia, and posthumous beatification, Hippolytus produced a ten-book treatise entitled *Kata Pasōn Haireseōn Elenchos (Refutation of All Heresies), otherwise known as the Philosophoumena, or Exposition of Philosophical Tenets.*[1] Owing something in spirit and substance to "the blessed presbyter Irenaeus" (*Refut.* 6.42.1, 55.2),[2] Hippolytus's object in this work was to discredit all heretics as unchristian by demonstrating that their tenets "[take] nothing from the holy scriptures—nor is it from preserving the succession of any saint that they have rushed headlong into these opinions—but their doctrines originate from the wisdom of the Greeks, from the deductions of those who have created philosophical systems, and from would-be mysteries and astrologers' vagaries" (*Refut.* 1. Pref. 8).

Hippolytus's basic strategy, as well as his contribution to the present study, can be witnessed in a comment about one of the earliest and most noteworthy of Christian Gnostics, Marcion of Pontus (d. ca. 160):

> Whenever Marcion or any of those dogs would howl about the demiurge, fobbing off contrasting statements of good and evil, one must say of them that neither Paul the apostle nor Mark the stumpy-fingered [*Markos ho kolobodaktylos*] corroborated such things—for nothing of this is written in the Markan Gospel—but rather Empedocles of Acragas [in Sicily], whose appropriation has until now gone unnoticed. [Marcion] seized upon the arrangement of every one of his heresies, transferring these sayings from Sicily over to the evangelical words. (*Refut.* 7.30.1)

This, the only reference to Mark the Evangelist in Hippolytus's *Refutation,* is odd. For the first time since the composition of the Lukan Acts and the Pauline corpus, we observe here an association of Mark with Paul, not Peter. Completely without precedent is the association of Paul with the author of Mark's Gospel. Less subtle but no less mysterious is the characterization of "Mark the stumpy-fingered."

On its own terms, apart from our particular concerns, at least one other aspect of this refutation of Marcion seems puzzling: whereas Hippolytus suggests that Marcion coated Paul's letters and Mark's Gospel with a thick veneer of plagiarized Greek philosophy, both Irenaeus (*Adv. Haer.* 1.27.2) and Tertullian (*Adv. Marc.* 4.2.4; cf. 4.3.1–2) are clear that Marcion bowdlerized those Epistles and Luke's Gospel and cut out everything else—including, presumably, Mark. Assuming (as do most scholars) that Irenaeus and Tertullian were right about this, has Hippolytus confused Mark with Luke, or is this evidence of his cavalierness with the facts about those whom he excoriates?[3] As posed, such questions are impossible to answer: nothing has survived from among Marcion's own writings against which we might measure the accuracy of his opponent's castigations. And Hippolytus himself does not elaborate his meaning, beyond the useful clarification that the "Mark" he (like Irenaeus) has in mind is the alleged author of the Second Gospel.

Regardless of how fairly Marcion's perspective is represented in the *Refutation,* the affiliation of Mark with Paul is intriguing. Of course, by this association nothing more consequential may be intended than Hippolytus's attempt to preserve the integrity of two orthodox figures, thought to have been commandeered and besmirched by a known heretic. If so, this in itself markedly corroborates a tendency that we have already witnessed in (at least) Irenaeus and the Muratorian fragment: in the West, by the turn of the third century, the figure of Mark had become securely connected with a written Gospel that was considered to be as ecclesiastically normative as the letters of Paul. Indeed, despite its curt ellipticalness, the statement about Mark in the *Refutation* may suggest a notable turning point for our investigation: whereas Hippolytus, like Irenaeus, accords to Mark's Gospel an orthodox stature and disciplinary authority, comparable to that of the Epistles, Hippolytus expresses greater interest than Irenaeus and most of his patrisitc predecessors in the *figure* of Mark, the putative author behind the Gospel. Strictly speaking, with Hippolytus the persona of Mark *the Evangelist,* though far from fully developed, begins to come into its own.

And how intriguing is that persona! For the first time in our study the author of the Second Gospel is not clearly joined with Peter (though an assumed linkage is conceivable, if not verifiable). Neither, in fact, is Mark joined with Paul, in the sense that the former acquires his "identity" through association with the latter: unlike the Pauline epistolary corpus or the Lukan Acts, Hippolytus's *Refutation* does not identify Mark as Paul's associate or onetime traveling companion. Rather, Paul and Mark now stand together, though from all appearances independently of each other, as recognizable figures within Christian tradition. Indeed, Hippolytus seems to assume of his readers an acquaintance with the figure of Mark no less ready or sharply etched than their knowledge of Paul: support for Marcion's heresy is provided by neither "Paul the apostle nor Mark the stumpy-fingered." From the casual manner in which Hippolytus states this, one would think that *kolobodaktylos,* "the stumpy-fingered," had become as much a "title" for Mark as *apostolos*, "the apostle," had become for Paul!

Other words compounded with *kolobo-* ("curtailed," "truncated") appear in Greek literature; only here, however, does *kolobodaktylos* occur. Its meaning is clear enough—but what is its intended significance? Later we shall consider some of the suggestions that were proposed in the ensuing decades of Latin Christianity. As early as the fifth century, and in the modern period as well, the term has been interpreted as a metaphorical allusion to Mark's Gospel, whose beginning is abrupt and whose ending is bobtailed. The palm for the most ingenious solution probably should go to J. L. North,[4] who has proposed that *kolobodaktylos* is a carryover into Greek of the Latin term *murcus*: a sardonic sobriquet given by Gallic soldiers to those among their Italian comrades who disqualified themselves from hazardous military service by cutting off their thumbs. Attachment of this piece of army slang to Mark, either by Hippolytus or in a tradition he inherited, could be explained (North theorizes) on the basis of Acts 13:13 and 15:36–39: remembered as a craven deserter, Mark was given a nickname to match that characterization, which coincidentally, if insolently, created a pun on his name—*Markos/Marcus*, the *murcus*.

Less important than adjudicating among these interpretations of *kolobodaktylos*, all of which are unavoidably speculative, is observing that which they hold in common: the nuance of diminished integrity, whether in regard to physical or moral capacities.[5] A term like *kolobodaktylos*, with its connotations of deformity or cowardice, probably would have registered among listeners or readers in Mediterranean antiquity as a slur or (at best) as a lament, not as a compliment. Just at this point, perhaps, the cameo of Mark in the *Refutation* curiously coincides with the traditions from which it otherwise diverges: Mark's apostolicity (though not his apostleship) is granted, guardedly, by Hippolytus. Behind a Gospel now recognized as a touchstone of orthodoxy stands, for Hippolytus and the tradition that he assumes, an apostolic "personality" who, as it were, may be praised with faint damnation.

The "Anti-Marcionite" Gospel Prologue

Even as the editors of some modern translations of the Bible offer their readers brief introductions to its various books, providing some historical context for their composition and correcting anticipated misinterpretations, such prologues also were attached to the canonical Gospels in a number of Old Latin manuscripts. In the early decades of this century many scholars believed that the best known among the old

Gospel prologues were originally and collectively composed in Greek, probably at Rome, around 160–80, in direct opposition to a set of unorthodox prologues created by Marcion.[6] Since about 1930 confidence in this scholarly consensus has gradually eroded. In 1969 the *coup de grâce* was administered by a German scholar, Jürgen Regul, who persuasively argued that the so-called anti-Marcionite prologues probably originated with different authors and were neither Roman, second-century, nor even anti-Marcionite in character.[7] A prologue to Matthew is missing. The Markan prologue is the shortest of the survivors, in a state so fragmentary that neither Regul nor any scholar since has been able to date and to ascertain its origin with confidence.[8] Its comments about Mark the Evangelist, however, seem to evince some affinities with Western Christianity:

> . . . Mark related, who was called "stumpy-fingered" [*colobodactylus*], because for the size of the rest of his body he had fingers that were too short. He was Peter's interpreter [*interpres*]. After the departure [or "death," *post excessionem*] of Peter himself, the same man wrote this Gospel in the regions of Italy.[9]

This sketch of the Second Evangelist offers at least six specific details, four of which we have previously encountered: that Mark's nickname was "Stumpfinger" (see Hippolytus), that he was Peter's interpreter (see Papias and Irenaeus),[10] that he penned a Gospel (thus, implicitly, Irenaeus) after Peter's "departure" or "death" (thus, see Irenaeus). Given the length of the fragment, its wording is so remarkably close to the statement of Irenaeus, and at one point exactly identical with that of Hippolytus (with the non-Latin loanword *colobodactylus* left untranslated in Greek), that we may assume either that these two Western fathers are the prologue's primary sources (the simpler explanation), or (should we wish to hedge our bets) that the prologue is closely entwined with Western traditions at virtually the same stage of growth.[11]

Two things in this statement are new, though both may be explained as inferences from the old. One is the locale of Mark's compositional activity: "in the regions of Italy." Vague, perhaps—yet it is the most precise indication we have been given for the supposed provenance of Mark's Gospel. If the author of the prologue knew and used Irenaeus (*Adv. Haer.* 3.1.1), this *could* be a deduction from the latter's comment that Mark wrote down Petrine preaching after Peter and Paul departed from Rome. But, if that were the case, then why did not the prologue simply tie the knot and locate Mark's Gospel in the capital city ("support" for which could have been drawn from 1 Peter's reference to "Babylon" [5:13])? Naturally, a confident answer cannot be given. It may be that here we are observing the tradition at a barely perceptible, transitional phase: groping for an otherwise uncertain location for Mark's work, the author of the prologue traveled with Irenaeus as far as *Against Heresies* would carry him, then left the matter vaguely intelligible but purposely unresolved. To the degree that this accurately portrays its ground and strategy, the prologue would emerge as a rather circumspect statement, not recklessly legend mongering.

The other tidbit that we garner from this prologue is an explanation for *colobodaktylus*, which Hippolytus never volunteered: Mark's nickname derived from a natural defect, "his fingers [being] too short for the rest of his body." Of all possible reasons this is probably the most neutral that could have been offered for an Evangelist's deformity; whether it was intended to absolve the Evangelist from suspicions of mutilation or desertion, it surely has that effect.[12] Yet, however respectful this explanation may be toward an author now regarded as the creator of a canonical product, to have ignored an awkward matter altogether would have been even more so. As with the proposed locale of the Gospel, again we may see the tradition at this point evolving, clearly yet with restraint, from its antecedents:[13] "with just cause" (a congenital defect and a mentor's death) Mark the Evangelist was both physically deformed and separated from Peter.

Though incomplete and rather simple, the "anti-Marcionite" prologue sums up much of what we have witnessed in the evolution of the figure of Mark in the West. Some inherited details are dutifully reported: Mark as the author of a literary work, by now clearly regarded as a Gospel, which interpreted Peter at some remove from the apostle. New tendrils of tradition slowly uncurl: a bland explanation for a nickname, a vague provenance for the Gospel. Finally, a concern for the personality of the Evangelist, marginally latent in the second-century fathers and cursorily patent in Hippolytus, is evident here: Mark the stumpy-fingered apostolic interpreter and author. In the latter regard the anti-Marcionite prologue may mark yet another turning point in the tradition: a heightening of interest in the Evangelist in his own right. In fact, it is rather striking that, in the extant fragment of this Gospel prologue, so little is said about the Second Gospel, so much about the Second Evangelist.

The Monarchian Gospel Prologue

Lest the reader conclude that tentative circumspection was the hallmark of all early Christian interpretation, we complete our review of

patristic European traditions about Mark with another statement that
prefaces a number of Latin manuscripts of the Second Gospel (positioned, interestingly, as *last* among the four). The origins of the
Monarchian prologues are almost as obscure as those of the anti-
Marcionite prologues; as we shall see, the former may even have been
dependent to some degree on the latter. Many historians' best guess is
that the Monarchian arguments (as they are sometimes called) contain
traditions that may be related to a form of late fourth-century Spanish
Gnosticism.[14] The customary rubric applied to these prologues (for all
four Gospels) refers to a theological movement, "Monarchianism,"
which so emphasized the monotheistic unity (or "monarchy") of the
Godhead that it came to be regarded with suspicion by proponents of
an emergent, Trinitarian orthodoxy.

The Monarchian prologue to Mark's Gospel certainly is not lacking
a point of view, with respect either to Christology or to the figure of
the Second Evangelist. That perspective is, however, singularly bi-
zarre. In the judgment of Dom John Chapman (to whom I am indebted
for the translation that follows) the Monarchian prologue to Mark "is
the most curious of all [these prologues], for its heresy is the most
patent, its obscurity is the blackest, and the thumb of Mark suggests
an apparently insoluble problem:"[15]

> Mark, the evangelist of God, and the son by baptism of
> Peter and his disciple in the divine word, exercising the
> priesthood in Israel, being a Levite after the flesh, after he
> had been converted to the faith of Christ, wrote his Gospel
> in Italy, showing in it what he owed to his birth and what to
> Christ. For he commenced the beginning of his introduction
> with the voice of the prophet's cry, thus showing the order
> of his Levitical election, so that, by pronouncing the predes-
> tined John, son of Zacharias, to have been sent out as the
> voice of an angel, he showed as the beginning of the Gospel
> preaching not simply the Word made flesh, but also the
> Body of the Lord having the Word of the Divine Voice for
> all the functions of a soul; so that any who reads this might
> know how to recognize to whom he owed the beginning of
> flesh in the Lord, and the Tabernacle of God coming among
> men, being himself flesh, and might find in himself through
> the Word of the Voice what he had lost in the consonants.
> Thereafter, entering upon the work of the perfect Gospel,
> and beginning to preach God from the Baptism of the Lord,
> he did not labour to mention the birth of the flesh which he

had already conquered in what preceded, but with his whole strength [*totus*] he produced the expulsion into the desert, the fast for a mystic number of days, the temptation by the devil, the fellowship with the wild beasts, and the ministry of the angels, that, by teaching us to understand, and describing each point briefly, he might at once establish the truth of the facts, and affirm the fullness of the work that was to be perfected. Further, he is said to have cut off his thumb after he had received the faith, in order that he might be accounted unfit for the priesthood. But the predestined election which corresponded to his faith so prevailed, that even by this he did not lose in the work of the Word what he had formerly received by his birth; for he was bishop of Alexandria, whose [i.e., a bishop's] work it is to know in detail and dispose the sayings of the Gospel in his heart, and recognize the discipline of the law in himself, and understand the Divine Nature of the Lord in the flesh; which things we ourselves also desire to be searched for, and after having searched for to be recognized, having as a reward of this exhortation, that "he that planteth and he that watereth are one, but it is God that giveth the increase." [cf. 1 Cor 3:6–8]

It is easy to be struck by the novelty, both in detail and in general conception, of a statement so fantastic as this. That Mark was baptized by Peter; that he had at once time exercised the Levitical priesthood, from which he later disqualified himself by self-mutilation; that he came to be a bishop in Alexandria—all of this is "news" to the unsuspecting reader. Moreover, had not the author of this prologue told us, we might never have "recognized" how Monarchian was Mark's theology: "In the Incarnation God assumed a human body, of which the Divine Nature was the soul—the vowel, to which the body supplied as it were the consonants, thus making the 'Word.' "[16]

However improbably fabricated all this may appear to us, I would suggest that, on closer examination, it is not entirely without precedent. In fact, once we allow for its distinctive theological perspective the Monarchian prologue remains intriguingly connected to bits of tradition, either already witnessed or yet to be encountered. Moreover, and equally notable, the *manner* in which those traditions are developed here is analogous (though not identical) to what we have already seen, however different the *substance* of those elaborations may be.

First, Mark's relation to Peter, as disciple to mentor, remains intact.

The datum that sonship was conferred on Mark through his baptism by Peter might be a remote inference from 1 Peter 5:13. More immediately, it could be a deduction from Jerome's (roughly contemporaneous?) comment that Mark was Peter's "son, not by the flesh, but by the Spirit" (*Homily* [75] *on Mark*: 1.1–12, to be examined in chap. 5). However the detail is to be explained, it is worth noting that this writer has some investment in apostolic (and specifically Petrine) continuity, comparable to that of an orthodox church that would brand this prologue as heretical.

While completely unexpected, the identification of Mark as an erstwhile Levitical priest may reflect a harmonizing of the Pauline and Lukan traditions of the New Testament. To end up, as has the Monarchian prologue, with Mark as priest and Levite, a complex chain of deductions and connections may have been wrought: if Mark was Barnabas's cousin (see Col 4:10), and if Barnabas was a Levite (Acts 4:36), then Mark, too, was a Levite; and, if Levitical descent was tantamount to priestly responsibility (a fallacious but understandable assumption), then Mark, *ex hypothesi*, "exercis[ed] the priesthood in Israel." From our point of view the reasoning may be specious and the outcome farfetched, but the process is quite intelligible: no more here than elsewhere, elements of Markan "portraiture" appear not to have been cut from whole cloth but were creatively spun out of traditional (and, in this case, ultimately biblical) antecedents. If the progression I have suggested accurately charts the traditional undercurrents of "Mark the Levitical priest," then the really surprising thing is that the Monarchian argument at no point overtly maintains Mark's apostolicity through his association with *Paul*. Evidently, by the late fourth century the presumed alliance in the European church of Mark with Peter (and of Luke with Paul)[17] was too firm to be shaken, in spite of the murmurings of traditional alternatives.

Second, Italy (though not Rome in particular) is listed as the provenance for Mark's Gospel. This vague location comports with the Latin tradition that we have witnessed in Irenaeus and the anti-Marcionite prologue. In one respect the Monarchian argument is even less forthcoming than its predecessors: here no mention is made of the Gospel's being written after Peter's departure or death.

Third, the Monarchian prologue records two other items that show up elsewhere in previous traditions. Like Hippolytus and the anti-Marcionite fragment, the Monarchian argument preserves the tradition of "stump-fingered Mark" (though apparently scrambling for its explanation, even more so than the earlier prologue). The identification of Mark as Alexandria's bishop is new to us, at this stage in our investigation; however, as we shall witness shortly, this too is already present in Jerome (in the preface to his *Commentary on Matthew*).

In themselves these details are probably not as important as what they may signify: namely, that in European Christianity at the end of the fourth century the rudiments of a roughly defined personality of Mark were in place and were not easily obliterated, even among Western Christians who stood boldly outside the orthodox mainstream. Concomitant with this "sketch" of the Evangelist, indeed its apparent *raison d'être,* was a growing interest in, first (with Irenaeus), the distinctiveness of the Markan Gospel and, later (with Hippolytus and the anti-Marcionite prologue), the personality of the one who was believed to have written it.

Indeed, with the Monarchian argument we observe the next stage in that evolution: an elaborated and coherent "biography" of Mark the Evangelist. To a degree heretofore unprecedented in the tradition of Latin Christianity, Mark in this prologue is regarded as *an authorial personality,* whose own life and experience has shaped the manner in which his Gospel has been composed, "showing in it what he owed to his birth and what to Christ." When did Mark write his Gospel? According to this prologue, "after he had been converted to the faith of Christ." Why does this Gospel begin with John the baptizer? For two entwined reasons: christologically, to symbolize "the voice" (cf. Mark 1:2–3), the divine nature of Christ; autobiographically, to represent through Zechariah's son (cf. Luke 1:5–80) Mark's own predestined origins, "the beginning of flesh in the Lord," in the Levitical priesthood. Why does not Mark narrate Jesus' birth or elaborate the story of the temptation, as do Matthew and Luke? Because Mark himself "had already conquered the flesh" and needed only "[to describe] each point briefly" in order "to affirm the fullness of the work that was to be perfected." For what reason was Mark called "Stumpfinger"? It was a function of his conversion and his predestined election: "he is said to have cut off his thumb after he had received the faith, in order that he might be accounted unfit for the [Jewish] priesthood," to the ultimate end that "the work of the Word" might be consummated in his Alexandrian (Christian) episcopacy.

Let us make no mistake: by critical standards in the twentieth century (and even in the fourth) the exegesis and theology here are problematic to the point of despair. That, however, should not blind us to the *process* whose outcome is stunningly represented by this prologue. After centuries of concern, first over a written Gospel, later over its apostolic pedigree, the Monarchian argument tacitly considers those matters closed. Its spotlight now is thrown on the figure that has been darting backstage: Mark the Evangelist, with a definable (albeit unorthodox) ecclesiastical, literary, and theological profile.[18] Modern expositors of the Gospels may find something vaguely familiar in the general approach, though not the exact reconstruction, of this author: viewed from one angle the Monarchian prologue is a fascinating specimen of ancient Markan redaction criticism.

DEFENDER OF THE FAITH
OR OBEDIENT EPITOMIZER?
MARK IN NORTH AFRICA

During the period under investigation Carthage was second only to Rome in metropolitan stature, and surely the African church exceeded that of the imperial capital in its contribution to early Christian literature and theology. "During the course of her history," as Hans Lietzmann has commented, "from Tertullian to Cyprian and then to Augustine, [the church in North Africa] was the teacher of the entire Christian Church in the west."[19] Of the three church fathers mentioned by Lietzmann the first and third applied their brushes to the patristic canvas of Mark. From the former the Markan Gospel received praise. If the latter did not bury it, his comments may have contributed to such an effect.

Tertullian

Except for Augustine, whom we shall meet momentarily, Tertullian (ca. 160–225) was probably the most original thinker and influential author in Latin Christianity. Revealing his superb education in philosophy, literature, rhetoric, and law, Tertullian's literary output was largely polemical, defending the church's faith while savaging its heretics.[20] By far the longest of his works was a five-volume treatise *Against Marcion* (*Adversus Marcionem*, published ca. 212), in which we learn much about the Marcionite movement and a smidgen of how the Evangelist Mark was regarded within African Christianity of the early third century:

> Every sentence, indeed the whole structure, arising from Marcion's impiety and profanity, I now challenge in terms of that gospel [Luke] which he has by manipulation made his own. . . . I lay it down to begin with that the documents of the gospel have the apostles for their authors, and that this task of promulgating the gospel was imposed upon them by our Lord himself. If they also have for their authors apostolic men [*si et apostolicos*], yet these stand not alone,

but as companions of apostles or followers of apostles [*cum apostolis et post apostolos*]. . . . In short, from among the apostles the faith is introduced to us by John and by Matthew, while from among the apostolic men Luke and Mark give it renewal, [all of them] beginning with the same rules [of belief]. . . . It matters not that the arrangement of their narratives varies, so long as there is agreement on the essentials of the faith—and on these they show no agreement with Marcion. . . . If Marcion's complaint is that the apostles are held suspect of dissimulation or pretense, even to the debasing of the gospel, he is now accusing Christ, by thus accusing those whom Christ has chosen. . . .

That same authority of the apostolic churches will stand as witness also for the other gospels, which no less [than Luke's] we possess by their agency and according to their text—I mean John's and Matthew's, though that which Mark produced is stated to be Peter's, whose interpreter Mark was [*cuius interpres Marcus*]. Luke's narrative also they usually attribute to Paul. It is permissible for the works which disciples published to be regarded as belonging to their masters. And so concerning these also Marcion must be called to account, how it is that he has passed them over, and preferred to take his stand upon Luke's, as though these too, no less than Luke's, have not been in the churches since the beginning. . . . (*Adv. Marc.* 4.1.1, 2.1–2, 3.4, 5.3–4)[21]

It is important to bear in mind the antagonistic context of these comments. Here and elsewhere Tertullian's presiding aim is less to construct a systematic theology of scripture, still less to persuade an interlocutor, but to smite an enemy through theological counterargument.[22] His opponent, Marcion, has had the gall to shrink the Gospel canon to a bowdlerized Luke. Hence Tertullian's reprisal: exclusive seizure of Luke is utterly indefensible, since, as "apostolic men," Luke and Mark renewed the faith that had been introduced by the apostles John and Matthew. How dare Marcion abridge or impugn any of the Gospels? They concur with one another in faith's essentials; all of them flout Marcion's bastard confession; all were promulgated at the Lord's behest and carry the inviolable warrant of Christ and the apostolic churches.

The tenor of this argument may help in explaining what is here retained and enhanced in the patristic picture of Mark and, even more obviously, why Tertullian adds so little. *Preserved* in Tertullian's depiction is Mark the interpreter of Peter. *Deepened* in that portrayal is the apostolicity [*apostolicos*] of Mark, through his association with an actual apostle, Peter. *Effaced* from the portrait, ironically, is the individuality of the Evangelist. Within Tertullian's overall conception of scripture Mark is all but transparent to the figure of Peter which underwrites his work. Ultimately, Mark's Gospel is really Peter's, just as Luke's Gospel is really Paul's, because "the works which disciples published [may be credibly ascribed] to their masters." The principle is the same as that of Irenaeus, though perhaps here more explicitly articulated. Ultimately, for both Tertullian and Irenaeus the gospel and its documentations belong to Christ and to the delegated agency of the apostolic churches, from whom and from which Marcion has severed himself.[23] The existence of a fourfold Gospel canon seems, for Tertullian, less a phenomenon to be explained (thus Irenaeus), more an unexceptionable resource in the defense of catholic faith.

Tacitly, Tertullian's remarks crack open a mare's nest of theological issues, including the character of scripture and the inspiration of its witness, from which the modern church has yet to extricate itself.[24] Of course, such matters cannot be tackled here; indeed, one wonders how Tertullian himself might have refined and dovetailed the implications of his comments. Suffice it to say that from this author we receive the scantest of sketches of the Evangelist Mark, familiar and without particularization.[25] To have accented the differences of Mark and the Markan Gospel from the other Evangelists and their works, without the sort of countervailing coordination of their emphases which Irenaeus provides, could have undermined the case for a unified rule of faith. And to have done that would have amounted to playing into his adversary's hands—the last thing that a canny theologian like Tertullian would ever have done.

Augustine

Elsewhere in North Africa, at the very end of the fourth century (ca. 400), Bishop Augustine of Hippo Regius (354–430) added to his prodigious body of theological writings *The Harmony of the Evangelists* (*De consensu evangelistarum*), a defense of the historical veracity of the canonical Gospels against "calumnious charges by certain persons [of] impious vanity or . . . ignorant temerity" (*De con. evang.* 1.7.10; see also 2.1.1). Since most of these allegations apparently had revolved around the differences among the Gospels, Augustine's aim was to demonstrate that, in matters touching the integrity of Christian faith, the Evangelists were in essential agreement. In a word Augustine assumed the validity of the kind of project executed by Tatian and gave it a reasoned justification, which (so far as we know) the *Diatessaron* lacked.

The result is a meticulous literary analysis that compares, contrasts, and invariably reconciles the narratives of the four Gospels. Among Augustine's prefatory remarks are some comments on the character and purposes of their authors:

> Now these four Evangelists . . . are believed to have written in the order which follows [*hoc ordine scripsisse perhiben-tur*]: first Matthew, then Mark, thirdly Luke, lastly John. . . . As far, indeed, as concerns the acquisition of their own knowledge and the charge of preaching, those unquestionably came first in order who were actually followers of the Lord when he was present in the flesh, and who heard him speak and saw him act. . . . For the first place in order was held by Matthew, and the last by John. And thus the remaining two [Mark and Luke], who did not belong to the number referred to, but who at the same time had become followers of the Christ who spoke in these others, were supported on either side by the same, like sons who were to be embraced, and who in this way were set in the midst between these twain. . . . For Matthew is understood to have taken it in hand to construct the record of the incarnation of the Lord according to the royal lineage [of David]. . . . Mark follows him closely, and looks like his attendant and epitomizer [*Marcus eum subsectus, tanqum pedisse-quus et breviator ejus videtur*]. For in his narrative he gives nothing in concert with John apart from the others: by himself separately, he has little to record; in conjunction with Luke, as distinguished from the rest, he has still less; but in concord with Matthew, he has a very large number of passages. . . . Luke, on the other hand, had no one connected with him to act as his summarist in the way that Mark was attached to Matthew. . . . For it is the right of kings not to miss the obedient following of attendants; and hence the Evangelist, [i.e., Matthew,] who had taken it in hand to give an account of the kingly character of Christ, had a person attached to him as his associate who was in some fashion to follow in his steps [*habuit sibi tanquam comitem adjunctum qui sua vestigia quodammodo sequer-etur*]. (*De con. evang.* 1.2.3–4; 3.6)[26]

Augustine's portrayal of Mark and the other Evangelists is probably more complex than even this lengthy excerpt might suggest. For example, it is far from clear that he thought of Mark as simply drafting the Second Gospel with a copy of Matthew before him, boiling down the latter as he went. Elsewhere in the same treatise (2.42.90) Augustine claims that the Evangelists "preferred to keep by the [historical] order in which these events were recalled to their own memory." Moreover, differences of style among those authors can account for divergences in their wording: "whichever of the Evangelists may have preserved for us the words as they were literally uttered by the heavenly voice [at Jesus' baptism], the others have varied the terms only with the object of setting forth the same sense more familiarly" (*De con. evang.* 2.14.31). However differently Mark and the others narrated what they recalled, their empowerment by the Holy Spirit has secured their presentation "with respect to the facts and the sentiments themselves" (*De con. evang.* 2.12.28). Toward the end of the *Harmony* Augustine seems even to have reconsidered his position on the Synoptics' literary interrelationship:

> And in this way, Mark . . . either appears to be preferentially the companion of Matthew, . . . as I have stated in the first book, . . . or else, in accordance with the more probable account of the matter [*vel quod probabilius intelligitur*], he holds a course in conjunction with both [the other Synoptists]. For although he is at one with Matthew in the larger number of passages, he is nevertheless at one rather with Luke in some others. (*De con. evang.* 4.10.11)

In short, the last word on Augustine's comprehensive view of the Evangelists and their Gospels' interrelationships has not been written,[27] and the following observations should be received with tentativeness equal in measure to that with which they are offered.

To begin with, several of Augustine's general comments may remind us of paths already traveled. The assumption that Mark's Gospel was written after Matthew's finds precedent in Irenaeus (*Adv. Haer.* 3.1.1).[28] Tertullian's shadow seems to loom large in some broader conceptions: the support of Mark and Luke, apostolic followers, by canonical Gospels believed to have been penned by apostles (Matthew and John); the Holy Spirit's power to maintain the fidelity of Mark's memory and the consequent veracity of his report (and those of the other Evangelists). Independent of the wildly unorthodox Monarchian prologues, yet reminiscent of their tenor, is Augustine's appeal to differences in authorial personality to explain divergences among the

Gospels: "For it is evident that the Evangelists have set forth these matters just in accordance with the recollection each retained of them, and just according as their several predilections prompted them to employ greater brevity or richer detail on certain points, while giving, nevertheless, the same account of the subjects themselves" (*De con. evang.* 2.12.27).

Yet I think it fair to say that Augustine's comments about Mark are most striking for their divergence from what we have seen. Whereas not a word of the Second Gospel's place or time of composition is mentioned in Tertullian, but only the Evangelist's linkage with Peter, even that lonely datum is now missing from Augustine's discussion.[29] In its place stands the heretofore unprecedented identification of Mark as the obedient follower, epitomizer, companion and "court-attendant" of *Matthew* (and, in *De con. evang.* 4.10.11, the fellow traveler with both Matthew and Luke).

How are we to account for what seems so jarring a turn in this presentation of Mark the Evangelist? Evidently, for Augustine, the terms of the discussion have changed and the portrayal of Mark has been shifted accordingly. For such early fathers as Papias, Irenaeus, and Tertullian the critical questions in this conversation appear to have been the tradition and theological grounds by which Mark and his writings could be validated as trustworthy and (later) normative. The chief points at issue have been, in other words, the canonicity of the four Gospels and the definition of the apostolic tradition. The association of Mark with Peter has been pressed to address these concerns, which, for Augustine, are now essentially resolved: "The whole canon of the Scriptures on which we say that this consideration of the step of knowledge should depend is contained in the following books: [those of the Old Testament, plus] the New Testament [, which] contains the four evangelical books, according to Matthew, Mark, Luke, and John" (*De doctrina Christiana* 2.8.13).[30]

The rather different question with which Augustine is grappling in *The Harmony of the Evangelists,* signaling the rather significant turn that medieval commentary will henceforth take, involves *literary relationships among the Gospels*: here, in particular, the Markan Gospel's literary character with respect to the other three Gospels and the theological problems attending the similarities and differences among these four canonical narratives. Accordingly, Augustine ignores the putative association of Mark and Peter (as well as the putative association of Luke and Paul) and takes up, instead, the question of the Evangelists' relationships to one another. This issue he tackles by exploring the literary relationships that apparently obtain among the

Gospels attributed to them.[31] And, because he had apparently inherited a tradition that accepted the canonical order of the Gospels as describing the chronology in which they were composed, Augustine deduced that Mark was Matthew's summarizer.

In the late fifth century an Antiochene presbyter named Victor bemoaned the complete lack of a commentary on Mark. The situation was no better by the middle of the sixth century, when Cassiodorus Senator cataloged three separate commentaries on Matthew (by Jerome, Hilary, and Victorinus), one commentary each for Luke (by Ambrose) and John (by Augustine), but *none* for Mark.[32] The suggestion is sometimes made that the cause of Mark's neglect within the medieval commentary tradition was Augustine's depiction of Mark, Evangelist and Gospel.[33] After all, who needs a derivative epitome (Mark) if one has access to an original, unabridged version (Matthew)?[34] If responsibility for the Second Gospel's desuetude is laid at Augustine's doorstep, it is by no means clear that such was his intention: as we have witnessed, his understanding of both the process and outcome of the Evangelists' work was a good deal more complicated than that assumption would suggest. Throughout patristic Christianity, and into the medieval era in the West, it nonetheless remains the case that appeals to the Second Gospel were strikingly less frequent, even among Mark's defenders, when compared with citations drawn from Matthew, Luke, and John. Early on, in both common worship and constructive theology, Mark's Gospel became something of the stepchild among the canonical four. By focusing on Mark's diminished status among the Evangelists, Augustine thus may have indirectly rationalized and to that degree unintentionally ratified what had been, and would long continue to be, a practical reality.

NOTES

1. A long scholarly debate over the authorship of this work seems generally, if not universally, to have been resolved in favor of Hippolytus. See the comments of Miroslav Marcovich in the introduction to his critical text of *Hippolytus: Refutatio Omnium Haeresium*, Patristische Texte und Studien 25 (Berlin and New York: Walter de Gruyter, 1986), 7–18. For a concise discussion of Hippolytus's life, works and theology, consult Johannes Quasten, *Patrology*, vol. 2: *The Ante-Nicene Literature after Irenaeus* (Utrecht-Antwerp and Westminster, Md.: Spectrum/Newman, 1953), 163–207.

2. In his comparative study of early Christian heresiologists, Gérard Valée has argued that Hippolytus did not achieve Irenaeus's sophistication (*A Study in Anti-Gnostic Polemics: Irenaeus, Hippolytus, and Epiphanius,* Studies in Christianity and Judaism 1 [Waterloo, Ont.: Canadian Corporation for Studies in Religion / Wilfrid Laurier, 1981], 41–62).

3. Cf. Henry Barclay Swete, *The Gospel according to St. Mark: The Greek Text with Introduction, Notes, and Indices*, 3d. ed. (London: Macmillan, 1927), with Vallée, *Study in Anti-Gnostic Polemics*, esp. 48–56. Vallée doubts that the Gnostics in general, and Marcion in particular, would have recognized themselves in Hippolytus's defamatory presentation.

4. J. L. North, "MARKOS HO KOLOBODAKTYLOS: Hippolytus, *Elenchus*, VII.30," *JTS* 28 (1977): 498–507, a learned and fascinating study to which I am indebted for much of the contextual information presented in this paragraph.

5. On the other hand, North ("MARKOS HO KOLOBODAKTYLOS," 504) notes a few scraps of evidence, mostly from rabbinic sources, that within clearly defined (usually extenuating) contexts associate self-mutilation with valor.

6. The key scholar here is Donatien de Bruyne, "Les plus anciens prologues Latines des Evangiles," *RBén* 40 (1928): 193–214. Cf. Dom Gregory Dix, *Jew and Greek: A Study in the Primitive Church* (Westminster: Dacre, 1953), 73; Quasten, *Patrology*, 2:210–11.

7. Jürgen Regul, *Die antimarcionitischen Evangelienprologe*, Vetus Latina 6 (Freiburg: Herder, 1969), esp. 266–67; cf. Benjamin Wisner Bacon, "The Anti-Marcionite Prologue to John," *JBL* 49 (1930): 43–54; Wilbert Francis Howard, "The Anti-Marcionite Prologues to the Gospels," *ExpTim* 47 (1935–36): 534–38; Robert M. Grant, "The Oldest Gospel Prologues," *ATR* 23 (1941): 231–45; Richard G. Heard, "The Old Gospel Prologues," *JTS* 6 (1955): 1–16.

8. Regul, *Die antimarcionitischen Evangelienprologe*, 97–99. The earliest firm date for a manuscript of the prologues seems to be ca. 521–32 (see North, "MARKOS HO KOLOBODAKTYLOS," 505–6), though they were probably written earlier than that (see n. 13). The language in which they were originally composed remains uncertain; in favor of Greek is the appearance of *colobodactylus* in the Markan prologue and a complete Greek version of the Lukan prologue.

9. Translated here is the version of the "anti-Marcionite" prologue that is usually regarded as earliest. An eighth-century Spanish manuscript adds considerably more material, apparently drawn from other patristic sources. On the textual traditions of the prologues, see Regul, *Die antimarcionitischen Evangelienprologe*, 15–74.

10. In the prologue one might note that Mark is described as the interpreter of Peter, not of "the things preached by Peter"; in this respect the wording is somewhat closer to Papias than to Irenaeus. Notice also that Paul has again dropped out of the picture and compare with this our earlier suggestion that Hippolytus's mention of Paul and Mark serves strictly to score a point against Marcion, not to identify Mark the Evangelist.

11. In this connection recall that the prologue says nothing of Paul's death (as does Irenaeus). Furthermore, since we cannot be utterly sure of our chronology, arguments for literary dependence can be made in either direction: if the prologue is earlier than the third century, Hippolytus could have borrowed from it the *colobodactylus* reference (rather than the other way around).

12. On this point, especially within conservative scholarship, more than one modern interpreter has effectively followed the lead of the "anti-Marcionite" prologue. Thus, Swete (*Gospel according to St. Mark,* xxvi–xxvii), who regards *kolobodaktylos* as a "personal reminiscence of St. Mark," speculates: "Such a defect, to whatever cause it was due, may have helped to mould the course of John Mark's [*sic*] life; by closing against him a more ambitious career, it may have turned his thoughts to those secondary ministries by which he has rendered enduring service to the Church." See also Vincent Taylor, *The Gospel according to St. Mark,* 2d. ed., Thornapple Commentaries (1946; reprint, Grand Rapids, Mich.: Baker Book House, 1981), 3–4; Joseph F. Kelly, "The Patristic Biography of Mark," *Bible Today* 21 (1983): 42.

13. Possibly this might favor a date for this prologue in the third century rather than the fourth (when, as we shall observe, the traditions tend to encompass greater detail). At any rate, questions of dating need not be labored here.

14. John Chapman, *Notes on the Early History of the Vulgate Gospels* (Oxford: Clarendon, 1908), 238–53; Quasten, *Patrology,* 2:211–12; Regul, *Die antimarcionitischen Evangelienprologe,* 197–265.

15. Chapman, *Notes,* 233 (quotation), 235–36 (translation). Note also Chapman's valiant attempt at commentary on the prologue, 233–35.

16. Chapman, *Notes,* 236.

17. Thus, see the Monarchian prologue to the Third Gospel: "Luke, a Syrian of Antioch by nation, by profession a physician, a disciple of the apostles, later followed Paul until his confession, serving God without blame" (in Chapman, *Notes,* 231).

18. Within Christian legend even the death of Mark takes on a curious life of its own: beyond Jerome's testimony to his interment at Alexandria (*De vir.* 8, to be discussed in chap. 5), later traditions portray the transfer of Mark's body to Venice. To this day Venice regards Mark as its patron saint, honored especially at the famous San Marco Church, on San Marco Square. For an overview of medieval legends surrounding Mark, especially in Coptic and Latin Christianity, see the brief but lavishly illustrated work by Jürgen Schultze and Leonhard Küppers, *Mark* (Recklinghausen: Aurel Bongers, 1966).

19. Hans Lietzmann, *The Founding of the Church Universal: A History of the Early Church* (New York: Charles Scribner's Sons, 1950), 2:276.

20. Later (ca. 207), after he had embraced a form of ascetic apocalypticism known as Montanism, Tertullian redirected some of that vilification against the church's hierarchy (*De pudicitia* 22; *De ieiunio adversus psychicos* 12; see Quasten, *Patrology,* 2:290–317). For a general consideration of Tertullian's life and thought, consult Timothy David Barnes, *Tertullian: A Historical and Literary Study* (Oxford: Clarendon, 1971).

21. Translated by Ernest Evans in *Tertullian: Adversus Marcionem, Books 4 and 5* (Oxford: Clarendon, 1972), 256–73.

22. For further discussion of Tertullian's tactics, see Lietzmann, *Founding*

of the Church Universal, 218–25; Quasten, *Patrology,* 2:246–48, 255–90. On the degree to which classical rhetoric molded Tertullian's formulation of arguments and disposition of debates, see Robert Dick Sider, *Ancient Rhetoric and the Art of Tertullian* (Oxford: Oxford University Press, 1971).

23. Tertullian's argument here is reminiscent of the preemptive strike in his renowned treatise, *De praescriptione haereticorum (The Prescription of Heretics* [ca. 200]): all appeal to scripture by heretics is precluded, simply because the Bible does not belong to them.

24. For considerations of some of these broader issues, see Hans von Campenhausen, *The Formation of the Christian Bible* (Philadelphia: Fortress, 1972), 274–91 (on Tertullian); and Paul J. Achtemeier, *The Inspiration of Scripture: Problems and Proposals* (Philadelphia: Westminster, 1980).

25. One might compare Tertullian's more extensive representation of Paul, deftly traced by Robert Dick Sider, "Literary Artifice and the Figure of Paul in the Writings of Tertullian," in *Paul and the Legacies of Paul,* ed. William S. Babcock (Dallas: Southern Methodist University Press, 1990), 99–120.

26. The translation of *De consensu evangelistarum,* excerpted here and elsewhere (with minor stylistic adjustments), is that of S. D. F. Salmond in *Saint Augustin: Sermon on the Mount, Harmony of the Gospels, Homilies on the Gospels,* ed. M. B. Riddle (*NPNF* 6, 1st ser. [reprint 1980]: 77–236).

27. A helpful introduction to some of these problems is David Peabody, "Augustine and the Augustinian Hypothesis: A Reexamination of Augustine's Thought in *De Consensu Evangelistarum,*" in *New Synoptic Studies: The Cambridge Gospel Conference and Beyond,* ed. William R. Farmer (Macon, Ga.: Mercer University Press, 1982), 37–64. For examples of Augustine's treatment of additions and omissions with respect to Matthew and Luke, see *De con. evang.* 2.5.14, 16; 19.44.

28. Augustine's discussion (*De con. evang.* 1.2.3) of the appropriateness of four Gospels on the basis of four terrestrial divisions suggests that he probably knew the similar defense of Irenaeus (*Adv. Haer.* 3.11.8).

29. This detail is also lacking from Hippolytus's *Refutation* (7.30), in which the omission is far less glaring than in the context of Augustine's argument.

30. Translated by David W. Robertson, Jr., *On Christian Doctrine: Saint Augustine,* Library of Liberal Arts (Indianapolis: Bobbs-Merrill, 1958), 41–42.

31. For this insight I am indebted to Peabody, "Augustine and the Augustinian Hypothesis," 41–42.

32. Cassiodorus Senator, *An Introduction to Divine and Human Readings,* ed. and trans. Leslie Webber Jones (1946; reprint, New York: W. W. Norton, 1969), 89. I owe this datum and its attestation to William Babcock.

33. For example, see Robert Henry Lightfoot, *The Gospel Message of St. Mark* (Oxford: Clarendon, 1950), 1–14.

34. This, in essence, is the view of Euthymius Zigabenus, a twelfth-century monk in Constantinople (*PG* 129 [1864]: 765–852). Though they require leaps across the centuries for their recovery, medieval commentators on Mark can be numbered on the fingers of a hand: Paterius and Alulfus, who compiled the

detached comments on Mark of their teacher, Gregory the Great (ca. 540–604 [*PL* 79 (1903): 1051–58, 1137–40, 1177–1200]); England's Venerable Bede (ca. 673–735 [*PL* 92 (1862): 131–302]); the eleventh-century Byzantine exegete Theophylact (*PG* 123 [1864]: 487–682); and Euthymius Zigabenus. For selected examples of their Markan interpretation, consult Seán P. Kealy, *Mark's Gospel: A History of Its Interpretation from the Beginning until 1979* (New York and Ramsey, N.J.: Paulist, 1982), 28–30.

Chapter Five

Sketches of an Apostolic Evangelist (II)

The Figure of Mark in Eastern Christianity
of the Third and Fourth Centuries

By the end of the fourth century, among churches in the West, an impressionistic portrait of Mark has taken shape. Its primary features are entwined, consistent, and recurrent though subjected and adjusted to the tendencies, subtle or outrageous, of various patristic media.

First, Mark is regarded as a literary figure, usually as the author of the Second Gospel (thus Irenaeus, the Muratorian Canon, Hippolytus, the anti-Marcionite and Monarchian prologues, Augustine).

Second, Mark is presented as a figure of reliable, albeit derived and sometimes mitigated, apostolicity. Usually, Mark is depicted as Peter's protégé or interpreter (Irenaeus, Tertullian, the prologues). In Augustine Mark is aligned with another apostolic figure, Matthew; in Hippolytus he stands alongside, yet evidently independent of, Paul. Often some attenuation of Mark's apostolic pedigree seems evident: thus, Mark wrote after Peter's leave-taking (Irenaeus, the anti-Marcionite prologue); alternatively, Mark, like Luke, basks in the reflected apostolic glory of Matthew and John (Tertullian, Augustine).

Third, other touches of the Second Evangelist's personality have been applied to the portrait. Perhaps following a lead implied by Irenaeus, the prologues have located Mark's literary transcription of Peter's preaching in "[the regions of] Italy." For different reasons, or no suggested reason whatever, Mark has emerged from certain traditions with an unsavory nickname, Stumpy-fingered (Hippolytus, the Gospel prologues). Notably, with the North African theologians these more definite (and probably legendary) features of Mark's persona seem to have waned as a more overarching concern for the inspiration of Mark's Gospel has waxed (Tertullian, Augustine).

Whither the figure of Mark in the contemporaneous Christianity of Egypt, Syria, and Palestine?

136

ATTENDANT TO THE APOSTLES:
THE ALEXANDRIAN TRADITIONS

Among the Mediterranean cities of antiquity Alexandria was second only to Rome in size, economy, and cultural importance. In such respects, by the end of the fourth century, Alexandria was probably second to none. That early Christian missionaries could have bypassed Egypt's one major metropolitan crossroads is virtually inconceivable, and some indirect testimony justifies that skepticism.[1] Nevertheless, for reasons as obscure as they are debatable,[2] no direct evidence has survived of the origins of Egyptian Christianity in the first century and a half of its existence. Later in this chapter we shall observe how some of the church fathers postulated an answer to this historical enigma and how the figure of Mark was implicated in that postulate. Our present task is to note the references to Mark by three notable personages, whose writings document our earliest, firm knowledge of Alexandrian Christianity.[3]

Clement

An early leader of ancient Christianity's renowned school in Alexandria,[4] Titus Flavius Clemens, bridges the second and third centuries (ca. 150–215). Whereas his older, European contemporary, Irenaeus, hewed closely to ecclesiastical tradition and regarded deviations from that norm with suspicion, Clement positioned himself on the cutting edge of scholarship, attempting to defend and to deepen Christian faith through philosophy. For our purposes, Clement throws considerable light on the appropriation of Mark, both that figure and its associated Gospel, by seekers like himself of a perfect, "catholic Gnosis," as well as by those who overstepped the bounds of even Clement's more expansive understanding of orthodoxy.

Clement offers three, and possibly four, comments on Mark. Two of these, included in Clement's lost work, *Hypotypōseis (Outlines,* or *Sketches)*, have survived in Eusebius's *Church History.* Apparently, Clement's aim in the *Outlines* was to provide selected, allegorical expositions of "all the canonical scriptures" (*pasēs tēs endiathēkou graphēs* [see also Eusebius, *H.E.* 6.14.1]), among which Clement numbered "the four Gospels that have been handed down to us" (*Strom.* 3.93.1).[5] The following excerpt suggests that Clement also demonstrated some interest in traditions concerning the Gospels' authorship and provenance:

> Now again in the same books [that is, *Hypotypōseis*] Clement has put down a tradition of the elders of old concerning

the order of the Gospels, which goes like this: "The earlier among the Gospels to have been written," he said, "were those that contained the genealogies, but the one according to Mark was administered in this way. When Peter had preached [*kēryxantos*] the word publicly at Rome, and by the Spirit had proclaimed the Gospel, those present, who were many, implored [*parakalesai*] Mark (as one who had followed [*akolouthēsanta*] him for a long time and remembered what had been spoken) to record what was said; and he did, and shared the Gospel among his petitioners; and when the matter came to Peter's knowledge, he neither actively prevented nor promoted it. But last of all John, taking a general view that the bodily facts had been disclosed in the Gospels, was urged on by his acquaintances and, divinely inspired, composed a spiritual Gospel [*pneumatikon euangelion*]." So says Clement. (*H.E.* 6.14.5–7)

Here, obviously, Mark's Gospel is being compared and contrasted with the other three canonical Gospels. Earlier in the *Church History*, following a statement about Peter's preaching in Rome, Eusebius also attributes to Clement's *Outlines* the following, more specific anecdote about the Second Evangelist:

So brilliant was the light of piety that shone on the minds of Peter's hearers that they were not satisfied with only a single hearing or with the unwritten teaching of the divine proclamation [*kērygmatos*]; but with all sorts of appeals [*paraklēsesin*] [they] earnestly entreated Mark, whose Gospel is extant, who was Peter's follower [*akolouthon onta Petrou*], to leave them in writing a memorandum [*hypomnēma*] of the teaching relayed to them by word; nor did they let up until they had prevailed upon the man, and thus they became the occasion of the scripture called the Gospel according to Mark. And they say that the apostle, who knew through spiritual revelation to him what had been done, was delighted with the men's zeal, and authorized the scripture for concourse in the churches. Clement cites the story in the sixth book of the *Hypotypōseis*. . . . (*H.E.* 2.15.1–2)

Both of the preceding excerpts may be compared with Clement's expository comments (*Adumbrationes*) on 1 Peter 5:13, known to us only through a sixty-century Latin translation by Cassiodorus, the founder of a monastery at Vivarium, in Italy:

> Mark, Peter's follower [*sectator*], while Peter was preaching [*praedicante*] publicly the Gospel at Rome in the presence of certain of Caesar's equestrians [*equitubus*, i.e., members of the equestrian order] and was putting forward many testimonies concerning Christ, being requested [*petitus*] by them that they might be able to commit to memory the things that were being spoken, wrote from the things that were spoken by Peter the Gospel that is called, "According to Mark."[6]

To these fragments may be added a fourth, doubtless the most provocative of all. In 1958, while examining ancient manuscripts at the monastery library of Mar Saba (near Jerusalem), the late Morton Smith of Columbia University discovered a copy of an incomplete and theretofore unknown Epistle of Clement, addressed to an otherwise unidentified Theodore.[7] The authenticity of this document remains in dispute; however, many patristic scholars tend to concur with Smith that the letter was, indeed, written by Clement.[8] For our purposes only a portion of it need be reproduced here:

> As for Mark, then, during Peter's stay in Rome he wrote an account of the Lord's doings, not, however, declaring all of them, nor yet hinting at the secret ones [*tas mystikas*], but selecting what he thought most useful for increasing the faith of those who were being instructed. But when Peter died a martyr, Mark came over to Alexandria, bringing both his own notes [*hypomnēmata*] and those of Peter, from which he transferred to his former book the things suitable to whatever makes for progress toward knowledge [*peri tēn gnōsin*]. Thus he composed a more spiritual Gospel [*synetaxe pneumatikōteron euangelion*] for the use of those who were being perfected. Nevertheless, he yet did not divulge the things not to be uttered, nor did he write down the hierophantic teaching of the Lord, but to the stories already written he added yet others and, moreover, brought in certain sayings of which he knew the interpretation would, as a mystagogue, lead the hearers into the innermost sanctuary of that truth hidden by seven veils. Thus, in sum, he prepared matters, neither grudgingly nor incautiously, in my opinion, and, dying, he left his composition to the

church in Alexandria, where it even yet is most carefully
guarded, being read only to those who are being initiated
into the great mysteries. (*To Theodore* 1[recto].15–
1[verso].2)[9]

What was in this "more spiritual Gospel"? Judging from Clement's
comments, it included, after Mark 10:32–34, a story about Jesus'
raising from the dead a rich young man of Bethany, who subsequently
came to Jesus by night, "wearing a linen cloth over his naked body,"
and was taught by Jesus "the mystery of the kingdom of God."[10]
Overall, the purpose of this *Letter To Theodore* appears to have been
the acknowledgment, defense, and orthodox interpretation of Mark's
Secret Gospel, into which had been interpolated "the unspeakable
teachings" and "utterly shameless lies" of the Carpocratians, a group
of second-century libertine Gnostics (cf. Irenaeus, *Adv. Haer.* 1.25;
Clement, *Strom.* 3.2–6; Hippolytus, *Refut.* 7.32).

So intriguing is this discovery, so tantalizing are its details, and so
controversial was Smith's own interpretation of them[11] that it would be
easy for us to become sidetracked from our present investigation.
Beyond the debate over its authenticity the Mar Saba letter triggers a
spate of questions, involving such things as the reliability of its quotations from Mark's *Secret Gospel*, the textual relationship of that
document to the canonical Second and Fourth Gospels (cf. John 11:1–
44), and the clandestine character of some expressions of early Christianity. Though indubitably fascinating, such questions need not concern us here: not only have they been explored elsewhere (and often
found to be critically resistant, if not practically insoluble),[12] they are
not germane to our purpose: to ascertain Clement's depiction of the
figure of Mark. To this end the *Letter to Theodore* enriches, but
ultimately should not be positioned apart from, Clement's other,
better-known statements.

Some scholars have leaped so quickly to the question of how well
(or how poorly) Clement's comments harmonize with other patristic
traditions about Mark[13] that they have neglected the question of internal consistency: Can these several Clementine statements be synchro-
nized with one another? All four possess some similarities; none is
simply identical or interchangeable with the others, however, and one
(in the *Letter to Theodore*) is very different indeed. In this connection
we would do well to bear in mind that none of Clement's comments
about Mark has survived in a state that is not fragmentary. Two (from
the *Outlines*) are rough extracts, embedded secondhand into another
author's historical commentary; a third stands within an apparently

incomplete commentary, translated into Latin some centuries later; the fourth, while more abundant than the rest, also derives from an incomplete letter (whose authenticity remains contested by some experts). However copious the Clementine testimonies to Mark collectively may seem when compared with the patristic snippets that we have previously examined, in fact we possess precious little *context* from Clement in which to coordinate and to interpret them. By this our analysis need not be paralyzed, but it ought to be chastened.

Four specific details recur in all four of Clement's extant remarks about the putative author of a Markan Gospel: (1) Mark, (2) in association with Peter (3) at Rome, (4) prepared a written transcript (of something). This appears to be the basic tradition preserved by Clement, from which variations or amplifications evolved. Alternatively, if one wishes to consider the traditional development from the other end, it is to this common denominator that different, more complex traditional fields attested by Clement may be reduced.

Among the three traditions witnessed in the *Outlines* and comments on 1 Peter, an additional four details are shared (expressed in closely cognate terminology): (1) As a follower [*akolouthēsanta; akolouthon; sectator*] of Peter, Mark wrote down (2) at the request [*parakalesai; paraklēsesin; petitus*] of Peter's auditors (3) the apostle's public preaching [*kēryxantos; kērygmatos; praedicante*], (4) which eventually was distributed as a written Gospel. While none of these details is explicit in the *Letter to Theodore,* nothing in that document contradicts them; conceivably, all or most of these elements could have been implied in that rather different statement. In any case, it should be noted that Clement's *Comments on 1 Peter,* which contains what is probably the clearest, synthetic epitome of these four details, appears to be the earliest patristic record of an *explicit* linkage of 1 Peter 5:13 with a tradition about the authorship of the Second Gospel.[14]

Beyond this point each of Clement's four statements becomes more elaborate, either subtly or extravagantly, and accordingly drifts away from the others. The divergences can be grouped into three categories.

First, when the accounts are viewed synoptically, *precisely what Mark wrote* becomes somewhat fuzzy. The most straightforward statement among the four appears to be that in the comments on 1 Peter: "Mark . . . wrote from the things spoken by Peter the Gospel that is called, 'According to Mark.' " This seems to be echoed in the excerpt reported by Eusebius in *Church History* 6.14.6 ("[Mark] shared the Gospel among his petitioners"). The latter report, however, lacks the explicit identifier, "According to Mark"; moreover, it is impossible to assert, with confidence, that Clement is speaking specifically of *a book* ("the Gospel"), not of evangelical proclamation in general ("the [message of the] gospel").[15] Eusebius's other extract from the *Outlines* is even more intriguing: Mark is requested to render "a note," or "memorandum" (*hypomnēma*), which request "became the occcasion of the Scripture called the Gospel according to Mark" (2.15.1). In this statement the memorandum and the Gospel need not be equated; the former could be a preliminary draft or outline of the latter. Nor is this fanciful speculation, since just such a process seems to be suggested, in a different context, in the *Letter to Theodore*. There Mark is portrayed as having compiled his own notes (*hypomnēmata*), which in Rome were fashioned into a book; later, in Alexandria, that book was revised (*synetaxe*, "composed"), with material from both his notes and those of Peter, into "a more spiritual Gospel." The kind of procedure suggested by Clement is actually prescribed by his older contemporary, Lucian of Samosata (ca. 120–80), in a work entitled *How to Write History*:

> By all means [the historian] should be an eyewitness; but, if this is impossible, he should listen to those who relate the more impartial account. . . . When he has gathered all or most [of the facts], first let him weave them together into some notes [*hypomnēma ti*] and fashion a body [of material] still charmless and disjointed. Then, having laid order [*taxin*] upon it, let him bring in beauty and ornament it with style and figuration and rhythm. (47–48)[16]

If, in the excerpt from *H.E.* 2.15.1 and in *To Theodore*, Clement imagined Mark's composition of a work in multiple stages, then it is *possible* to read his other comments (in *H.E.* 6.14.6 and *Adumbr. ad 1 Pet* 5:13) as telescoped assessments that assume the more complicated process intimated elsewhere. To understand the kind of literary judgments that Clement made is not, of course, the same thing as concurring with them in all respects. Most modern critics would disagree with Clement's attribution of the *Secret Gospel* to the author of the Second Gospel of the canon, even as they would part with his belief in the authenticity of the apocryphal *Preaching of Peter* (*Kerygma Petrou*, an early second-century document, perhaps of Egyptian origin [see *Strom.* 2.15.68, 6.5.39]) or in the Pauline authorship of the canonical Epistle to the Hebrews (*H.E.* 6.14.1–4). More important for our purposes is recognizing a pattern of description: for Clement, no less than for his patristic predecessors and contemporaries, the figure of Mark is involved in a broader interpretation of the shift, whether simple or complex, from oral tradition to written Gospel.

A second area of divergence among the four Clementine reports concerns *the circumstances attending Mark's literary project*. Here the statements ramify in ways great and small which are impossible to explain confidently, with the fragmentary evidence at our disposal. Who requested Mark's written transcript of Peter's preaching in Rome: many who were present (*H.E.* 6.14.6),[17] Caesar's equestrians (*Adumbr. ad 1 Pet* 5:13), or no one in particular (*To Theodore*)? Who was tacitly resistant to the enterprise: Mark, who had to be nagged into it by Peter's hearers (*H.E.* 2.15.1), or Peter, who, on learning of Mark's activity, "neither actively prevented nor promoted it" (*H.E.* 6.14.7)? Was Peter's reception so guarded, or "was [he] delighted with [his listeners'] zeal and authorized the scripture for concourse in the churches" (*H.E.* 2.15.2), or is nothing more to be said of Peter (*Adumbr. ad 1 Pet* 5:13) beyond the fact that afterward he was martyred (*To Theodore*)? It is barely possible that the report of Peter's delight and endorsement is actually Eusebius's, who may have broken into Clement's account with a "footnote" to other traditions ("And they say . . .": *H.E.* 2.15.2);[18] if so, then Clement's clearest statement of Peter's response to Mark would be that of indifference (*H.E.* 6.14.7). Again, however, our evidence is so fragmentary and lacking in context that it is exceedingly difficult to establish how Clement harmonized— if indeed he did—what may appear to us as divergent traditional testimonies.

We can, however, discern at least two "circumstantial" items about Mark in the Clementine traditions which are heretofore unprecedented: (1) that his (initial) transcription of Peter's preaching was *coincidental* with the apostle's Roman mission (contradicting Irenaeus and the anti-Marcionite prologue); (2) that this literary enterprise encountered either subsequent apostolic detachment or preliminary resistance by the Evangelist himself. The first element has been explained by some scholars as the result of an ancient tradition that increasingly tended to position the figure of Mark more closely to an apostolic patron;[19] the second, as mirroring the admittedly lukewarm reception given to Mark's Gospel in Egyptian churches.[20] Both suggestions have merit. What has been neglected, I think, is the possible *relationship* between these two developments in the tradition. It is as though the more closely some traditions, to which Clement testifies, correlate the personalities of Mark and Peter, the more powerfully a counteracting force is exerted to distance them, without dissociating them outright. This is but the latest variation on a theme that has pervaded the patristic testimony: the curious tension created by an *attenuated linkage* of Peter and Mark.

Last, and most obviously, Clement's account in the *Letter to Theodore* differs from the other three excerpts in describing *the aftermath of Mark's literary work in Rome*. Here we find the remarkable and heretofore unparalleled story of Mark's activity in Alexandria, expanding his earlier book for Roman catechumens into "a more spiritual Gospel for the use of those who were being perfected." Perhaps at this point it should be recalled that Clement considered himself among those advanced Christians of Alexandria who were "progress[ing] toward knowledge" (*peri tēn gnōsin*), according respect if not reverence to Mark's *Secret Gospel*.[21] Unlike his patristic contemporaries within nascent catholic orthodoxy, Clement overtly aligned himself with a kind of Gnosis—knowledge founded upon faith, perfected in love and moral conduct—while attacking other Gnostic systems that he deemed heretical (thus, the burden of his major work, *Stromata* [N.B. 2.2–4, 19–20]). Likewise, as the *Letter to Theodore* makes clear, Clement's censure was heaped not upon Mark's *Secret Gospel* (whose leadership of enlightened readers into the holiest of holy truth was worthy of most careful protection and discrete use) but, rather, upon blasphemous Carpocratians who had corrupted it.

One of the more interesting features of *Theodore* which seems to have escaped sustained attention is an issue raised by our present study: Clement's labored defense of an "authorial personality" underlying both canonical Mark and the *Secret Gospel*. However divinely inspired is this literature (a point forthrightly granted by Clement),[22] neither that assumption nor the sheer content of the works is sufficient to authorize their proper use and interpretation. The latter depends, at least in part for Clement, on recollection of the circumstances by which these Gospels came to be created: namely, the Evangelist Mark, drawing upon apostolic tradition, carefully ("neither grudgingly nor incautiously") tailored evangelical literature to the different needs of audiences at different stages of faith. Elsewhere in *Theodore* Clement is noticeably concerned to preserve the integrity not only of the *Secret Gospel* but also of its author: when the Carpocratians present their "Gospel of Mark," not the corrupted document but, rather, its authorship *by Mark* should be disavowed, even on oath.[23] It could be that the Carpocratians invested some importance in the "traditional pedigree" of their version of Mark's Gospel, even as another of Clement's Gnostic opponents, Basilides, professed to have been instructed by a certain Glaucias, who, like Mark, was styled as an interpreter of Peter (*Strom.* 7.17). In any case, both Clement and his antogonists appear not to have regarded prized Christian documents as utterly self-warranting but, rather, to have validated them on the basis of their demonstrable apostolicity, the tradition regarding their authoritative derivation (which was typically, and tautologously, believed to be confirmed by the documents' content). And when additions to Mark's Gospel were made, by Alexandrian Gnostics, either Clementine or Carprocratian, the tradition about Mark, the late Peter's secretary, was fleshed out accordingly.[24]

Origen

Origen (ca. 185–254), Clement's successor as head of Alexandria's Catechetical School, was early Christianity's most prolific, and arguably most technically proficient, biblical interpreter. To the patristic portrait of Mark, Origen adds only the faintest of brush strokes; even this, unfortunately, is known to us only secondhand through an excerpt by Eusebius:[25]

> Now in the first of his [commentaries] on [the Gospel] according to Matthew, defending the ecclesiastical canon, [Origen] testifies to knowing only four Gospels, writing somewhat as follows: ". . . having learned by tradition about the four Gospels, which alone are undeniable in the church of God under heaven, that written first was that [Gospel] according to Matthew, who was at one time a tax-collector but afterwards an apostle of Jesus Christ. For those who from Judaism came to believe, [Matthew] published it, composed in the Hebrew language. And second, the one according to Mark, as Peter guided [hyphēgēsato] him. In the Catholic Epistle he [Peter] also acknowledged him as a son through this assertion: 'She who is in Babylon, chosen together with you, sends you greetings; and so does my son Mark.' And third, the one according to Luke, the Gospel commended by Paul for those who, from the Gentiles, [came to believe]. After them all, the one according to John." (H.E. 6.25.3–6)

Origen's comments carry the ring of familiarity. In general presentation and even specific wording they bear an especially marked resemblance to Irenaeus's statement in *Adversus Haereses* 3.1.1 (cf. Eusebius, *H.E.* 5.8.2–3; see chap. 3). This may not be complete happenstance: a papyrus fragment of *Against Heresies* appears to have reached the community of Oxyrhynchus, southeast of Alexandria, within only twenty to fifty years of that work's composition.[26] Very likely, then, the tradition about Mark to which Origen acknowledges indebtedness is essentially that of Irenaeus and the West. Origen's testimony is not, however, "just the same old thing." On closer inspection it introduces a couple of delicate and interesting modifications.

First, Origen's statement assumes that which, some eighty years earlier, Irenaeus thought needful to prove: the "undeniable" existence of a catholic canon of four (and only four) Gospels, among which Mark's is now securely nestled. Whatever particulars about its origin are recounted, Mark's Gospel as an individual statement and, concomitantly, the Evangelist Mark as an individualized author seem less absorbing to Origen than Mark's location within an inviolable, evangelical quadrumvirate. In this respect, and for basically the same reasons, Origen is rather like his older contemporary in North Africa, Tertullian: both held an elevated doctrine of scriptural inspiration, against which the literary and religious endeavors of the several Evangelists tend to pale in importance. As elsewhere Origen pointedly puts it: "For Matthew and Mark and John and Luke did not 'make an attempt' [literally, "take in hand"] to write; on the contrary, filled with the Holy Spirit they wrote Gospels" (Homily on Luke 1; cf. Luke 1:1).[27] Mirroring this assumption is a leveled uniformity in the parallel style of Origen's description of Mark and the other Synoptists: first, Matthew, an apostle of Jesus Christ, who composed for those who came to Christianity by way of Judaism; second, Mark, guided by Peter; third, Luke, commended by Paul, for the Gentiles who came to Christian faith.

Among Origen's observations about Mark, second, is a novel item that seems to bob among the traditions we have heretofore witnessed yet ultimately floats away from them: the assertion that Mark wrote as Peter guided him. Doubtless behind this comment is the belief, as old as Papias and John the Elder, that Mark was Peter's interpreter (and thus enjoyed derivative apostolicity). Unlike them, however, as well as unlike Irenaeus and the anti-Marcionite prologue, is Origen's suggestion that Mark wrote while Peter was active (not after his death). Such a coincidence of Mark's and Peter's activities was first encountered, we may recall, in Clement of Alexandria. Given the fact that Origen immediately cites 1 Peter 5:13 in support of his statement, it is reasonable to suppose that he is in touch with Clement's Comments on 1 Peter (or a tradition within Alexandrian Christianity which would have inclined both Clement and Origen to interpret that verse as a reference to the Second Gospel's authorship). On the other hand, Origen also veers away from another Clementine testimony: Peter's reserve toward Mark's composition (H.E. 6.14.7). Even in Clement's more positive presentation of the reception accorded Mark's Gospel by Peter, there is no suggestion that the Evangelist acted under the apostle's leadership or instruction; the existence of the Gospel is, rather, made known to Peter "through spiritual revelation," only after which the apostolic commendation is forthcoming (*H.E.* 2.14.2).

Because Origen's statement is, like so much of our patristic evidence, incomplete and secondhand, we should beware of claiming more than can be known with confidence. Still, as far as I can tell, Origen's distinctive contribution to our patristic panorama appears to be *the unreserved association of Mark with the apostolic witness represented by Peter*, unmitigated and unimpaired by either death, diffidence, or disfigurement.

Dionysius

Last among the Alexandrian fathers in our survey is Dionysius (d. ca. 265), whose contribution to our study is largely negative but critically constructive. Origen's most able student, and his successor as head of Alexandria's Catechetical School, Dionysius was later appointed bishop (or patriarch) of the church in that city. For most of what has survived of his writings we have again to thank Eusebius, who devoted the bulk of book 7 of his *Church History* to Dionysius. The following excerpt from Dionysius' work, *Peri Epangeliōn* (*On Promises*), occurs in the context of a sophisticated rhetorical argument against the authorship of the Johannine Apocalypse by the writer of the Fourth Gospel or of 1 John:

> I consider there to have been many [persons] of the same name as John the apostle, who, out of love and admiration and esteem for him, as well as the desire to be loved, like him, by the Lord, welcomed the same given-name—just as many a child among believers is named "Paul" or even "Peter," for that matter. So then, there is also another John in the Acts of the Apostles, who was surnamed "Mark," whom Barnabas and Paul took with themselves, concerning whom it also says, moreover, "And they also had John as an attendant." But whether it was he who wrote [Revelation], I should think not. For it is written that he did not arrive with them in Asia; rather, "Having set sail," it says, "from Paphos, Paul and his companions came to Perga in Pamphylia. But John left them and returned to Jerusalem." Now I think that there was some other [John] among those in Asia, since it is said both that there were two tombs in

Ephesus, and that each of the two is said to be John's. (*H.E.* 7.25.14–16)

Obviously, Dionysius' citation of Acts 13:5, 13, adds little to the patristic depiction of Mark, nor are his comments so intended: he is trying to make a point about the authorship of Revelation, not about the Second Gospel or the figure of Mark as such. Indirectly, however, Dionysius' comments inform our investigation in at least two ways. First, he testifies to the fact that, in Christian antiquity, it was easy for different personages who shared the same name to be confused or conflated into one figure: thus, John of Patmos, who wrote Revelation (1:4, 9), came to be identified without textual warrant as the otherwise anonymous author of the Fourth Gospel (which early Christian tradition had further ascribed to the son of Zebedee). Similarly, in the late fourth-century Monarchian prologue we have witnessed a similar chain of improbable but explicable identifications wrought for Mark: the various "Marks" we have encountered in the New Testament could be, and sometimes were, blended into one legendary figure.

Second, and equally important, Dionysius' critical judgments testify to the ability of at least some patristic writers *to distinguish* traditions and legendary figures that were easily mixed up. Not only does Dionysius dispute the identification of John Mark with John, the apostle and Evangelist;[28] interestingly, he also prescinds (at least in this extant excerpt) from identifying John Mark of Acts either with "Peter's son in Babylon" (1 Pet 5:13) or with the Second Evangelist, as denominated in Christian tradition. So too, for that matter, has the majority of patristic interpreters whose comments we have examined. Could an identification of the figure in Acts 12 and 13 as "John," not "Mark," have been more customary within patristic traditions, thus retarding an association of John Mark with the author of the Second Gospel?[29]

Barring the recovery of additional texts from his pen, Dionysius' reserve in characterizing Mark, like all forms of silence, is patient of various, equally unverifiable explanations. Yet, for our purposes, his statement is important nonetheless. It warns the more sanguine among us that ancient Christian traditions were subject to careless consolidations; at the same time it reminds the more skeptical that ancient Christian traditionists were capable of careful distinctions, to the contrary notwithstanding.

Summary

On balance, to the degree that the fragmentary evidence has been fairly interpreted, the Alexandrian testimonies reflect both the constancy and mutability of early Christian traditions about Mark. Maintained are some familiar features: Mark again surfaces as the faithful communicator of Petrine tradition in Rome, creatively yet appropriately tailoring a written Gospel to the needs of an authorial audience. Added are new details, either soft or stark, intelligible if at times unpredictable: the Gospel's composition as concurrent with Peter's career (Clement), indeed under the apostle's direct supervision (Origen); Mark's subsequent creation, in Alexandria, of a secret, more spiritual Gospel (Clement). Through Dionysius we are privy to one scholar's concern for critical discrimination among the traditions flowering about figures like Mark. Beyond the fourth century the figure of Mark held an ongoing position of prominence in Alexandrian Christian liturgy and legend;[30] even before that century's close Mark's supposed association with Alexandria was cultivated further, as we shall presently see.

THE RETURN OF THE PAULINE COLLABORATOR: THE SYRIAN TRADITIONS

According to Josephus, the first-century Jewish historian, Syrian Antioch was the third greatest city of the Roman Empire, after Rome and Alexandria (*J.W.* 3.2.4). Christianity spread to Antioch quite early (Gal. 2:11–14; Acts 11:19–30) and, somewhat later, to the eastern city of Edessa. During the first four centuries A.D. the religion appears to have proliferated, in forms both orthodox and heretical, among a considerable portion of the region's inhabitants.[31] What, if anything, did a vibrant Syrian Christianity contribute to the emerging picture of Mark in Christian antiquity?

"Adamantius"

For the answer to that question we must wait until the early fourth century and the composition of *De recta in Deum fide* (*The Dialogue on the Orthodox Faith*). The origins of this five-volume work are cloaked in an obscurity almost as thick as that enshrouding the Gospel of Mark. Most scholars, however, regard its place of composition as either Asia Minor or Syria and usually refer to its writer as "Adamantius," the leading interlocutor in "the dialogue."

The Dialogue on the Orthodox Faith dramatizes a disputation between Adamantius, the "diamond-hard" defender of orthodoxy,[32] and several heretics, among whom is a disciple of Marcion, Megethius (the "Great," or "Loud," One). Adjudicating the debate is Eutropius ("Well-Balanced"), a pagan whom both Adamantius and Megethius attempt to persuade:

MEGETHIUS: . . . So tell me first the names of those who wrote the Gospels.

ADAMANTIUS: The disciples of Christ have written them: John and Matthew, Mark and Luke.

MEGETHIUS: Christ had no disciples, "Mark and Luke," so you are convicted of fraud. For why didn't the disciples whose names are written in the Gospel write them, rather than those who were not disciples? Who, then, is Luke or Mark? By this you are convicted of bringing forward names that haven't been written in Scripture.

EUTROPIUS: Since he had disciples, was not Christ more likely to entrust [the writing of the Gospel] to them than to those who were not disciples? This does not appear to me to get it right, for the disciples themselves ought to have been trusted more.

ADAMANTIUS: These are also disciples of Christ.

MEGETHIUS: Have the Gospel read, and you will find that these names aren't written in it.

EUTROPIUS: Let it be read.

ADAMANTIUS: The names of the twelve apostles have been read, but not of the seventy-two [cf. Luke 10:1].

EUTROPIUS: How many apostles did Christ have?

ADAMANTIUS: First he sent out twelve and, after that, seventy-two to preach the gospel. Therefore, Mark and Luke, who are among the seventy-two, preached the gospel together with Paul the apostle.

MEGETHIUS: It is impossible that these [two] ever saw Paul.

ADAMANTIUS: I can show the apostle himself testifying to Mark and Luke.

MEGETHIUS: I don't trust your forged apostolicon [a group of Pauline letters, accepted into a scriptural canon].

ADAMANTIUS: Bring forward *your* apostolicon, even though it is exceedingly mutilated, and I can prove that Mark and Luke worked together with Paul.

MEGETHIUS: Prove it.

ADAMANTIUS: I am reading the closing comments of Paul's letter to the Colossians [Col 4:10–11, 14 is quoted]: I have produced the proofs of the Epistle. You see: the apostle himself testifies to them.

EUTROPIUS: The proof in their case is clear.[33]

This is a fabulous addition to the lore about Mark. Like many of our witnesses thus far, Adamantius is concerned to justify the apostolic character of Mark's Gospel. Unlike the majority, however, he appeals not to its Petrine background but, instead, to the Pauline corpus: the strand of tradition, examined in chapter 2, which has been by far the least exploited. Indeed, so "adamant" is "Adamantius" about the Second Gospel's apostolicity that, for the first time in our study, all distance between the Second Evangelist and his apostolic patron has been obliterated. Here Mark is promoted to the rank of apostle—which, in this discourse, is regarded as tantamount to having been "a disciple of Jesus."

How do we account for a presentation so unprecedented? The clues, I think, are woven into the fabric of "the dialogue" itself. Although Adamantius and Megethius differ on the authority of Mark and Mark's Gospel (as well as that of Luke), we might begin by observing how radically they *agree* on the argument's fundamental assumptions. Neither Adamantius nor Eutropius challenges the premises of Megethius's case: (1) the Gospels should have been written by "apostles" or "disciples of Christ"; (2) some record of that authorship, in particular the authors' names, should have been left in the Gospels, or elsewhere in scripture. In accordance with these mutually accepted axioms, Adamantius asserts (1) that Mark and Luke, no less than Matthew and John, are disciples of Christ, and (2) that the evidence for this claim resides in their inclusion among the seventy-two other missionaries whom Jesus reportedly dispatched *en route* to Jerusalem. Since Luke 10:1[34] explicitly identifies none of these other apostles, Adamantius is proposing an invalid "argument from silence." However fallacious the logic, apparently the parties in the debate find the evidence of Luke 10:1 more relevant than an appeal to the Second Gospel's traditional attribution, "According to Mark." Indeed, that title or superscript is neglected altogether: as Megethius asserts (and Adamantius concedes), "Have the Gospel read and you'll find that these names"—Mark and Luke—"are not written in it."[35]

But why the appeal to a proof text so filigreed as Luke 10:1? Evidently, Admantius is a tactician who believes that "the best defense is a good offense": the most powerful rebuttal is that which not only answers Megethius but also undermines the latter's own Marcionite warrants, which employed expurgated versions of Paul's letters and Luke's Gospel.[36] Though allowance must be made for the apologists' own tendentiousness, Adamantius tacitly concurs with Irenaeus's complaint: "[Marcion] persuaded his disciples that he himself was more worthy of credit than are those apostles who have handed down the Gospel to us" (*Adv. Haer.* 1.27.2).[37] In this context the issue of *authority* has become bound up with particular claims of *authorship*, much as we witnessed in Clement's wrangling with the Carpocratians. Accordingly, Adamantius moves not just to any Gospel but to *Luke's*—

and to a passage (10:1) whose wording is uniquely Lukan—to "find," from among that larger company of apostles, the two unnamed Evangelists. These two, Adamantius argues, in tandem receive their corroborative identification not merely from any scripture but *from Paul himself* (thus, the appeal to Col 4:10, 14). Most likely it is for this reason, then, that *The Dialogue on the Orthodox Faith* breaks with most patristic traditions elsewhere by summoning, as Mark's referee, Paul and not Peter: although Petrine traditions were conspicuously strong in Syria,[38] the Pauline tradition about Mark was more directly serviceable for the defense against Marcionism that Adamantius was burdened to build.

In this matter, as at the end of the debate, Eutropius ruled in Adamantius's favor. Had one of Marcion's sympathizers constructed this dialogue, very likely a different verdict would have been rendered! Frustrated by the fragile assumptions and wobbly arguments that unfold here, many modern readers may be tempted to call down a plague on both houses. In our haste to disparage Megethius's and Adamantius's illogical sleights of hand, perhaps we should not overlook their minutely reasoned appeals to biblical evidence, including (for Adamantius) the figure of Mark, in the defense of orthodoxy. While Adamantius's construction of Mark is in some respects decidedly different from others that we have seen, ultimately his objectives and craftsmanship are similar: here, as elsewhere in early Christian testimony, the apostolicity and personality of Mark have been carefully tailored to clothe a particular body of religious and theological commitments—and, as sometimes happens, to strip another naked.

The *Apostolic Constitutions*

Probably from Syria, during the latter half of the fourth century, comes Christian antiquity's largest compilation of church law and liturgical practice, apocryphally addressed from "the apostles and elders to all who from among the Gentiles have believed in the Lord Jesus Christ" (1.1.Pref.).[39] In the midst of detailed prescriptions for the proper conduct of Christian worship, "the apostles" authorize readings from the Old Testament (characterized as the books of Moses and Joshua; Judges, Kings, and Chronicles; the postexilic books; Job, Solomon, and the prophets), then Acts, then the Pauline Epistles; "and afterwards let a deacon or a presbyter read the Gospels, both those which I, Matthew, and John have delivered to you, and those which the fellow-workers of Paul received and left to you, Luke and Mark" (*Const. Ap.* 2.7.57).

When compared with their expanded portrayal in *The Dialogue on the Orthodox Faith,* here Mark and Luke have returned to their traditional status as apostolic associates, not apostles themselves. Like Adamantius, however, the *Apostolic Constitutions* recall Mark's affiliation with Paul, not Peter. Specifically, the document's reference to Mark as Paul's coworker suggests an interaction with the Pauline tradition (Philem 24; Col 4:10–11), rather than with the Lukan alternative in Acts 12–15.[40] Since it is not developed within the *Constitutions*, the reason for this cannot be certainly known. One possibility is that the text is dependent here on an earlier tradition that espoused Mark's association with Paul, whether that of Adamantius (the evidence for which is meager) or of Hippolytus (which is only slightly more plausible).[41] Another possibility, which the context and wording of this passage may suggest as more likely, is that the *Apostolic Constitutions* have been colored by an interpretation of that canonical ordering of the Gospels with which its author was familiar: Matthew, John, Luke, and Mark is the order preserved in old Western codices and canonical catalogs (including Tertullian), on the principle that Gospels attributed to apostles were ranked ahead of those ascribed to apostolic followers.[42] Although the *Apostolic Constitutions* do not appeal, in support of this principle, to either Colossians 4:10, 14; 2 Timothy 4:11; or Philemon 24, it is not hard to imagine that such texts would have been presupposed.

Before leaving the *Constitutions,* we should note its discrimination of four Gospels and differentiation of four Evangelists. Such a conclusion was by no means foregone in fourth-century Syria: the *Diastessaron* was still regarded highly by orthodox Syrian scholars such as Ephraem of Nisibis (ca. 306–73), who prepared an extensive commentary on Tatian's masterwork.[43] By contrast, the *Apostolic Constitutions* were intended to cultivate within Syrian Christianity the canon and practice of the church catholic, "the plantation of God and His beloved vineyard" (*Const. Ap.* 1.1.Pref.). Thus, the sheer identification of Mark the Evangelist, coworker with Paul, may have contributed in a minor way to a major ecclesiastical endeavor.[44]

John Chrysostom

The last of our representatives of Syrian Christianity may be that region's most famous "doctor of the church." During his tenure as parish priest (386–98), John of Antioch (ca. 347–407) delivered a series of sermons, at once technically expository and morally edifying, which earned for him the nickname by which he is best known: Chrysostom, or the "Golden-Mouthed." Among his homilies was a lengthy series on Matthew, the first of which introduces that Gospel by comparing it with another:

> Of Matthew again it is said that when those who from amongst the Jews had believed came to him, and besought him to leave to them in writing those same things, which he had spoken to them by word, he also composed his Gospel in the language of the Hebrews. And Mark too, in Egypt, is said to have done this self-same thing at the entreaty of the disciples. (*Homily* [1:7] *on Matthew*)[45]

In his fourth homily on Matthew (1:17) Chrysostom compares the genealogy of Jesus in that Gospel with both its Lukan counterpart and Mark's account, which contains no genealogy:

> "Why, then," one may say, "does not Mark do this, nor trace Christ's genealogy, but utter everything briefly?" It seems to me that Matthew was before the rest in entering on the subject (wherefore he both sets down the genealogy with exactness, and stops at those things which require it): but that Mark came after him, which is why he took a short course, as putting his hand to what had already been spoken and made manifest. How is it then that Luke not only traces the genealogy, but does it through a greater number? As was natural, Matthew having led the way, he seeks to teach us somewhat in addition to former statements. And each too in like manner imitated his master; the one Paul, who flows fuller than any river; the other Peter, who studies brevity. (*Homily* [4:1] *on Matthew* 1:17)

Chrysostom's comments on Mark may sound familiar, and for good reason: they closely resemble Clement's account in the *Hypotypōseis*, as mediated to us by Eusebius (*H.E.* 6.14.5–6). Common to both are the claims that Mark's project was undertaken (1) after the composition of Matthew and Luke, the Gospels recounting genealogies of Jesus, and (2) by popular demand. Other details seem analogous to, though not identical with, Egyptian traditions: the location of the Evangelist in Alexandria (see Clement's *Letter to Theodore*) and the close alignment of his literary product with the character of Peter (see Clement's *Comments on 1 Pet* 5:13; Eusebius's quotation of Origen in *H.E.* 6.25.5).

Some small differences are detectable as well. First, in comparison with Eusebius's account of Clement (*H.E.* 2.14.1–2, 6.14.5–6), Chrysostom is much clearer that the *vox populi* gave rise to Mark's *Gospel*, not to *hypomnēmata*. Second, according to Chrysostom, those to whom Mark acceded were "the disciples," a reference that, while vague, is more specific than the Clementine traditions. Third, and most startling, the identification of Rome as the place of Mark's composition has dropped out; in its place an *Alexandrian* provenance has been entered. It is difficult to know just what lies behind this change: whether the usual story has been somewhat garbled by Chrysostom (or his traditional sources) or whether the account that we know from Clement's *Letter to Theodore* has been radically compressed and thus fundamentally altered.

A final point of comparison is a bit more subtle. Chrysostom is perhaps less like Clement, and more like his slightly younger contemporary in the West, Augustine (cf. *De con. evang.* 2.12.27), in projecting a cameo of the Evangelist's personality from the overall literary character of the Gospel ascribed to that figure. On the assumption that Matthew was written first, to what do we attribute Mark's conspicuous brevity? This, by the way, remains a very good question: twentieth-century scholars who assume that Mark was written after Matthew continue to grapple with it.[46] While his underlying assumptions would be troublesome for most modern critics, Chrysostom's twofold answer has the merit of proposing a literary solution to a literary problem. First, assuming that Mark's audience would have known Matthew's Gospel, the Second Gospel is shorter because a reproduction of the bulk of Matthew would have been redundant. Second, just as the novice imitates the master, so too does Mark's Gospel reproduce the brevity of Peter's composition (and, similarly, the longer Lukan Gospel mirrors Paul's loquaciousness).[47] With this second, admittedly undeveloped, point Chrysostom creatively brings the assumption of Mark's Petrine authorization (and Luke's Pauline warrant) directly to bear on the question that vexed Augustine: the literary relationships among the Gospels.[48]

With some adjustments and little embellishment, then, Chrysostom relays several of the traditions we have already analyzed. To the extent that these prolegomena fairly represent his overall approach, Chrysostom seems less interested in the supposed Evangelists and more engaged with the Gospels themselves. Confirmations for this judgment recur in Chrysostom's extant homilies on Acts (13:13), Colossians (4:10), and 2 Timothy (4:11): precisely at those points at which a character named Mark appears, and could easily have been embroidered in accordance with the patterns of tradition involving Mark the Evangelist, Chrysostom never rises to the bait.[49]

Summary

In some respects Chrysostom may be representative of some general tendencies in the Syrian traditions regarding Mark: an evidently marginal interest in an apostolically accredited Evangelist, whose personality was sometimes pressed in the attempted illumination of the Markan Gospel and its apologetic, liturgical, or homiletic applications. Though broadly replicative of traditions surveyed elsewhere in the West and East, the Syrian witnesses attest to some variations on those traditions: the attribution of apostleship to Mark (Adamantius); the location of his Gospel's composition in Alexandria (Chrysostom); the recrudescence of the New Testament's Pauline tradition about Mark (Adamantius, the *Apostolic Constitutions*; though cf. Chrysostom). Another century or two would pass before such elements were recombined and adorned in the apocryphal *Acts of Barnabas,* which may be of Cypriot origin.[50] In this legendary elaboration of Acts 13–15 John Mark purportedly narrates his own visionary vocation to preach the gospel, Barnabas's marvelous adventures and eventual martyrdom in Cyprus, and Mark's subsequent evangelization of Alexandria. But all of this comes later. In the third and fourth centuries, by comparison, the Syrian traditions about Mark are considerably more pallid.[51]

AN IMPERFECT MARRIAGE: THE PALESTINIAN TRADITIONS

If any region could lay stronger claim than Syria to being "the cradle of Christianity," it would be Palestine, from which "the Jesus movement" sprang and primitive Christianity subsequently evolved.[52] Palestine was also the home of the last three patristic writers whose work we shall consider. Again, our informants stand among the church's elite: two were bishops; the third, Christian antiquity's most accomplished biblical scholar.

Eusebius

Caesarea's patriarch, Eusebius (ca. 260–340), is no stranger to this study. His *Church History*, discussed in some detail in chapter 3, has been for us an invaluable source for the views of others: Papias (*H.E.* 3.39.1–7, 14–17), Irenaeus (5.8.1–5), Clement (2.15.1–2, 6.14.5–7), Origen (6.25.3–6), and Dionysius of Alexandria (7.25.1–27).

In addition to summaries of others' opinions, Eusebius contributes at least two other pieces of tradition regarding Mark. After rehearsing one of the Clementine testimonies (2.15.1–2) and before his presentation of Papias (3.39.1–7, 14–17), Eusebius compares John's Gospel with that of the canon's other three:

Not without experience of the same things were the rest of those who resorted to our Savior: twelve apostles and seventy disciples and myriad others on top of them. All the same, from among those who encountered and remained with the Lord, only Matthew and John have left behind for us notes [*hypomnēmata*], which of necessity they put into writing (according to the prevalent report [*katechei logos*]). Now Matthew had preached first to Hebrews . . . ; Mark and Luke already had published the Gospels according to them; but John, they say, used all the time an unwritten proclamation. . . . [T]he cause for [the Gospel] according to Mark has been set forth in the preceding. (*H.E.* 3.24.5–6, 7, 14)

Most likely, the earlier explanation to which Eusebius refers, at the end of this excerpt, is the story of Peter's delight in learning of his auditors' zealous request for a memorandum (*hypomnēma*) of his teaching (*H.E.* 2.15.1–2).[53] "In the sixth book of the *Hypotypōseis*" Eusebius states, "Clement cites [this] story,"

and the bishop of Hierapolis, named Papias, corroborates his witness, which calls to mind Peter's reference to Mark in the first Epistle [*tou de Markou mnēmoneuein ton Petron en tō protera epistolē*] This also, they say, was composed in Rome itself, as signified by his own figurative reference to the city as Babylon in this way: "The co-elect in Babylon sends you greetings, as does my son Mark."

This Mark, who was the first, they say, to be dispatched [*steilamenon*] to Egypt to preach the gospel which he also composed, was in addition the first to establish churches in Alexandria itself. So great was the multitude of both men and women there who came to believe at the first attempt, and so philosophical and inordinate their asceticism, that Philo thought fit to write of their pastimes and assemblies and symposia, and all the rest of their way of life. . . . In the eighth year of the reign of Nero, Annianus was the first of the successors of Mark the Evangelist to the parish [*paroikias*] ministry in Alexandria. (*H.E.* 2.15.2–16.1–2; 2.24.1)

Repeatedly in this study we have observed how a given presentation of Mark bespeaks something of the presenter's own interests and inclinations. In at least three significant ways the same can be said of the author of these extracts.

First, for Eusebius *the figure of Mark is of only minor concern, secondary to other historical preoccupations.* Although the *Church History* has proved to be a mine of traditions about Mark and other personalities of the apostolic age, nowhere in that work does Eusebius devote a section to Mark as a leading character in his own right. In some measure this may be owing to Eusebius's awareness, derived from his oral and written sources,[54] that Mark simply was not "a leading character" in ancient Christianity: thus, in the first passage quoted above, Eusebius differentiates Mark from recognized apostles Matthew and John. Although he recalls the Lukan tradition (10:1) of "the seventy" missionaries of Jesus, to say nothing of "myriad others on top of them," Eusebius does not pursue Adamantius's strategem in numbering Mark (or Luke) among this larger coterie beyond the Twelve. Rather, "from among those who encountered and remained with the Lord, only Matthew and John have left behind for us notes" (*H.E.* 3.24.5). In Eusebius the figure of Mark retains a derivative status.

Beyond what his sources suggested, Eusebius's minimal interest in Mark is more obviously indicated by the specific contexts in which his references to that figure occur. In every section of the *Church History* in which Mark is mentioned, Eusebius concentrates not on Mark himself but, instead, on some other person or place whose significance, in Eusebius's judgment, may be better understood through recalling a pertinent Markan tradition. Accordingly, in *Church History* 3.24.7 Mark (and Luke) are mentioned in passing within a much longer narrative about the apostle John (3.23.1–24.18). Similarly, the focus of *Church History* 2.14.1–18.9 is on early developments in the churches of Rome and Alexandria; because of his traditional associations (at least as far back as Clement of Alexandria) with both of those cities, Mark serves Eusebius's purposes as a transitional figure that advances the chronicle from one stage to another (*H.E.* 2.15.1–16.1). This squares with what we already have observed of Eusebius's procedure: his scant references to Mark in *Church History* 3.39.14–17, 5.8.1–3, 6.14.5–7, 6.25.3–6, and 7.25.14–16 serve primarily to illuminate not the Second Evangelist and Petrine or Pauline associate but, rather, the perspectives, respectively, of Papias, Irenaeus, Clement, Origen, and Dionysius.[55]

Second, *regarded cumulatively, many of the traditional pieces about Mark, reported by Eusebius, do not interlock into a coherent picture,*

notwithstanding Eusebius's occasional comments to the contrary.
Several examples may clarify some dimensions of the problem:

1. At different points in his narrative (*H.E.* 3.24.7, 6.25.4–5)
Eusebius records two seemingly incompatible assessments of the
order in which the Gospels of Matthew, Mark, and Luke were
written. The first suggests that the composition of Mark and Luke
preceded that of Matthew; the second reproduces, without rectification, Origen's judgment that the Gospels were produced in the order
in which they have been canonically preserved.

2. The timing of the composition of Mark's Gospel, viewed apart
from the others, is hard to pin down from Eusebius's synthesis of
traditions. Bracketing his first reference to the writing of Mark (*H.E.*
2.15.1–2) is a narrative hodgepodge of Peter's missionary endeavors
in Rome, including his response to Mark's Gospel, during the reign
of Claudius (41–54; see *H.E.* 2.14.6, 17.1). Elsewhere, however,
Eusebius simply reproduces Irenaeus's statement that Mark's Gospel was written in Rome during Nero's reign (54–68), following the
deaths of Peter and Paul (*H.E.* 5.8.1–3; see also 2.25.5, 3.1.2–3).

3. Even among the traditions (ascribed by Eusebius to Clement's
Outlines) which fix Mark's composition during Peter's lifetime, two
anecdotes remain difficult to coordinate, if not mutually exclusive:
on the one hand, Peter's ratification of the Markan Gospel (*H.E.*
2.15.2); on the other, his queer neutrality toward it (*H.E.* 6.14.7).

4. After recounting the story of Peter's more gracious reception
and acclamation of Mark's work, Eusebius claims that Papias confirms Clement's witness (2.15.2); however, at least that part of
Papias's testimony quoted by Eusebius (3.39.1–7, 14–17) really does
nothing of the sort.[56] Common to both passages is the portrayal of
Mark as Peter's follower and interpreter (2.15.1, 3.39.15); beyond
that lonely datum the testimonies attributed to Papias and Clement
are different and noncorroborative.[57]

5. Similarly, when one tries to reconcile a number of Eusebius's
historical judgments, related to Mark, with other evidence within or
beyond the Bible, the results are at best equivocal, outrageous at
worst. Take, for example, Eusebius's statement that Mark was the
first to establish churches in Alexandria. This not only recalls
Clement's comment to Theodore about the esteem in which Mark's
activity, following Peter's martyrdom, was held in that city; it also
ratchets up the association between Mark and Alexandria, which
later figures significantly in Christian traditions both Eastern and
Western. On the other hand, that datum sits rather uneasily beside

Luke's suggestion of a much earlier Christian evangelization of Egypt (Acts 2:10).[58] More famous, not to say infamous, is Eusebius's astounding statement (in *H.E.* 2.16.2–18.8) that Philo's treatise *On the Contemplative Life* (*De vita contemplativa*), which portrays a group of monastic Jews in Egypt called the "Therapeutae," is in fact a description of Mark's Alexandrian converts.[59]

In his handling of Markan traditions, therefore, we witness another facet of Eusebius's "very desultory treatment" of Christian history.[60] That is to say, the structure of the *Church History* is loosely anthological, not systematically historical, and Eusebius's detached comments on Mark should be interpreted in that vein.[61]

Third, *the traditions about Mark, preserved in this history, appear to serve Eusebius's larger theological commitment to the principle of an apostolic succession.* Except for a quotation from Dionysius in which John Mark just happens to crop up (*H.E.* 7.25.15), the only "Mark" in whom Eusebius seems the least bit interested is Mark the Evangelist and associate of Peter, sometimes regarded (after Clement) as the founder and first patriarch of Alexandrian Christianity.[62] Surely, this is no coincidence. The object of Eusebius's history was to preserve "the successions from the Savior's apostles, . . . at least the most renowned among them, throughout those churches whose significance is still remembered" (*H.E.* 1.1.4)—namely, the Christian congregations at Alexandria, Jerusalem, Antioch, and Rome (see *H.E.* 2.16.1, 17.23; 3.23.2, 6; 5.6.1). Nor was Eusebius's interest in preserving this material dispassionately archival or antiquarian. It flowed, rather, from his apologetic aim to demonstrate God's gracious foundation and guidance of the church, up to its ultimate triumph over the pagan state through the conversion of Constantine, the first Christian emperor (see *H.E.* 1.1.1–8, 9.8.15–9.11).

Accordingly, so minor a figure as the Second Evangelist is shown to have been caught up in the larger, rushing tide of providence. Mark is depicted as having been "dispatched" to Egypt,[63] to inaugurate what would become a renowned church (*H.E.* 2.16.1–2) with its own succession of distinguished leaders, such as Annianus (*H.E.* 2.24).[64] Implied in this concern for communities with an apostolic lineage is, moreover, an apostolic canon: those writings, attested by "the most ancient ecclesiastical elders and authors," which bound together particular urban expressions of the church catholic (*H.E.* 3.3.3., 5.8.1). Notably, therefore, Eusebius highlights those patristic traditions that portray Mark and the other Evangelists as authors of scriptural Gospels (e.g., *H.E.* 2.15.1–2, 3.24.1–18, 3.39.14–16, 5.8.1–4, 6.25.3–6). On balance, from among the traditions on Mark at his disposal, Eusebius appears to have selected and stressed precisely those that supported his hypothesis of an apostolic succession,[65] as manifested in Christianity's leading sees (such as Alexandria) and canonical scriptures (such as the Second Gospel).

Epiphanius

The venerable tradition of Christian heresiology—the description and refutation of religious views regarded as dangerous by an author who considers himself orthodox—flourished in the encyclopedic, aspersive work of Epiphanius (ca. 315–403), a native Palestinian, who for thirty-six years served as bishop of Salamis, on the island of Cyprus. Epiphanius's most significant literary effort was the *Panarion*: literally, "the medicine chest of antidotes" against the viperous doctrines of some eighty heretical groups.[66] Like Irenaeus, Tertullian, and Hippolytus, Epiphanius demonstrates some uses for which even a minor figure like Mark could be enlisted in the reinforcement of sound doctrine.

Mark as Evangelist enjoys at least two curtain calls in the *Panarion*. The first appearance, in no more than a "cameo role," supports Epiphanius's attack on the Nazoraeans (also styled by him as "the Jessaeans"), Christian groups of Syriac Jewish origin which continued to adhere to the Jewish law (*Pan.* 29.1.1–9.5):[67]

> If you enjoy study and have read about them in Philo's historical writings, in his book entitled "Jessaeans," you may discover that, in his account of their way of life and hymns, and his description of their monasteries in the vicinity of the Marean marsh, Philo described none other than Christians. . . . So in that brief period when they were called Jessaeans—after the Savior's ascension, and after Mark preached in Egypt—certain other persons seceded, though they were followers of the apostles if you please. I mean the Nazoraeans, whom I am presenting here. (*Pan.* 29.5.1, 4)[68]

Little comment is required here. Epiphanius knows, and here relays, the tradition (traceable at least as far back as Clement) which relates Mark with Alexandrian Christianity.[69] The collocation of Mark's preaching in Egypt with Philo's report of a group of Jewish monastics who were taken actually to have been Christian is too precise, and too precisely incorrect (at least with respect to Philo), to be reckoned as sheer coincidence: for this portrayal Epiphanius is almost certainly indebted to Eusebius (*H.E.* 2.16.1–17), whom he explicitly cites elsewhere in the *Panarion* (29.4.3; 66.21.3; 68.8.2–5; 69.4.3, 6.4).

Rather more novel is the discussion of Mark and the other Evangelists in Epiphanius's diagnosis and treatment of a sect of Asian Christians who, because of their spurning of John's Gospel and Apocalypse, were branded by their opponents as "the Alogoi": "the unreasonable ones" who repudiated the characteristically Johannine belief in Christ as the incarnate *logos* (*Pan.* 51.1–34). According to Epiphanius, one bone of contention for the Alogoi was the striking difference between the Fourth Gospel and the others: "For they say . . . that [John's] books do not accord with the rest of the apostles" (*Pan.* 51.4.5: cf. 51.4.6–9, citing John 1:1, 14, 17, 29, 38, 43; 2:1–2). To this charge—which of course is accurate, to a considerable extent—Epiphanius offers an interesting rejoinder: he minimizes the divergence of John from the Synoptics by magnifying the abundantly productive differences among *all* of the Gospels. "Has not God apportioned [the task] to each [of them]," he asks rhetorically, "in order that the four Evangelists, who were obligated to preach, might every one carry out what they discovered and might proclaim those things harmoniously and equally?" (*Pan.* 51.6.2).[70] From that standpoint the openings of the Gospels of Matthew, Mark, and John are admittedly different, mutually supportive, and problematic only for heretics, whose cockeyed assumptions are bound to lead to error (*Pan.* 51.6.3–9). As a refutation, more than a few questions are begged in this argument; it is, nevertheless, not merely an exposé of irregular doctrine but a reasoned response to it.[71]

On the subject of the Second Evangelist, Epiphanius continues:

> And following immediately after Matthew, Mark was entrusted by the holy Peter in Rome to set out the gospel; and when he had written it, he was sent by the holy Peter to the region of Egypt. Now he happened to be one of the seventy-two who were scattered abroad on account of what the Lord said: "Unless you eat my flesh and drink my blood, you are not worthy of me" [cf. John 6:53], as the banishment [should be] clear to readers of the Gospels. Nevertheless, through Peter he was brought back and considered worthy [*kataxioutai*] to write a Gospel, after being filled with the Holy Spirit. He begins his proclamation at the point from which the Spirit exhorted: from the fifteenth year of Tiberius Caesar, thirty years after Matthew's treatment. But since he was the second evangelist to write and did not

distinctly signify the descent from above of God the Word—
but [did so] plainly in all sorts of ways, though without such
verbal precision—he became for the aforementioned be-
guiled a second "mind-clouder" [*eis deuteron skotosis ton
dianoēmaton*], so that they would not be deemed worthy
[*kataxiōthēnai*] of the gospel's illumination. (*Pan.* 51.6.10–
13)

On a first reading these comments may seem unprecedentedly
strange. On closer inspection Epiphanius's rendering of Mark offers
yet another specimen of discernible fidelity to traditions that by now
have come to cling to that figure as well as their adaptation and
development for particular religious and theological purposes.

Perhaps most familiar in this statement is its association of Mark
with Peter and Rome, then Alexandria: these elements have been in
place at least as early as the second century. The creative difference
in Epiphanius's portrayal lies in *the explicit apostolic authorization of
Mark the Evangelist,* who was both *entrusted* with the writing of a
Gospel and *delegated* to Alexandria by "the holy Peter." This ampli-
fies, by at least one degree, the testimonies of both Origen (who
assumes Peter's guidance of Mark's Gospel) and Eusebius (who suggests a rather formal dispatch of Mark to Egypt, without naming the
authority behind it). The effect of these elaborations is to position
Mark more closely within an "apostolic succession," without claiming
apostleship as such for the Evangelist. More likely than not, Epiphanius intended such an effect, even as he deliberately portrayed heresy
as an aggregative process, a worldwide genealogy of poisonous lies: to
detoxify a *successio haeraticorum,* only a *successio apostolorum*
would do.[72]

More than once in this study we have witnessed a peculiar tension
in patristic literature which distances Mark from Peter while at the
same time affiliating them. Epiphanius executes a different variation
on that familiar theme by casting *Peter as instrumental in Mark's
redemption, after the latter's temporary fall from grace.* Though it
does not qualify him for the title of "apostle," as in Adamantius's
Dialogue, Mark is again ranged among the seventy-two whom Jesus
appointed and sent out (cf. Luke 10:1). Unlike the Third Evangelist,
who depicts that band as returning with joy from a successful mission
(10:17), Epiphanius identifies this larger group, including Mark, with
the "many disciples" who turned back and abandoned Jesus, upon
hearing his discourse on the necessity of (eucharistically)[73] partaking
of the Son of Man for eternal life (John 6:52–71).

A modern interpreter may be forgiven for wondering just how all of this "[should be] clear to readers of the Gospels." An appeal to Johannine theology to explain, and indeed to revamp, a Lukan anecdote (which is presumed, moreover, to imply the Evangelist Mark) is, by modern scholary standards, woefully illegitimate. Even by the norms of fourth-century exegesis Epiphanius's comment on the clarity of Mark's banishment in John 6 would have been debatable, and perhaps more intelligible as a rhetorical flourish. Whatever its problems, this exposition does achieve several objectives that are important to Epiphanius's argument. Most obviously, it positions Mark among Jesus' more attenuated followers, while preserving the traditional authorization of Mark's subsequent Gospel by Peter, spokesman for the Twelve, who (at that point in the Johannine narrative) "[did] not also wish to go back home" (John 6:66–69).[74] More subtly, but maybe no less significantly, Mark is thus cast by Epiphanius as one who was reclaimed for the catholic faith after having rejected a difficult, and uniquely Johannine, teaching that many of Jesus' disciples could not take. This characterization, of course, typifies the overall recalcitrance of the Alogoi toward the Fourth Gospel, according to Epiphanius. An implicit parallel, drawn between the once lapsed Mark and still stubbornly unorthodox Alogoi, may also be suggested by a delicate verbal correspondence in the passage quoted above: through Peter's ministrations ultimately Mark was brought back to the fold and considered worthy (*kataxioutai*) to write a work that would fog the minds of errorists deemed unworthy (*mē kataxiōthēnai*) of the gospel's piercing radiance.

Finally, to judge from this excerpt the *Panarion*'s presentation of Mark appears not to be driven by purposes that are predominantly hagiographical. Like other patristic treatments that we have observed, the figure of Mark affords Epiphanius a convenient way of construing, even legitimating, the distinctiveness of a normative religious document in comparison with another three. For Epiphanius that which binds together and finally validates four different Gospels is their common sanction and direction by the Holy Spirit. But the same Spirit compelled different Evangelists to discharge their assignments variously: hence, four presentations that are dissimilar, more (in the case of John) or less (among the Synoptics). Although such a position does not originate with Epiphanius, he does give it an imaginative wrinkle: *Rather than something to be defended (thus Irenaeus) or assumed (so Origen), here a four-Gospel canon—interpreted as the inspired production of Mark and the other Evangelists—becomes a paradoxically constructive occasion for the consternation of heretics.* While this might be applauded for its cleverness, there is a hermeneutical hook here: because the Gospels, like the rest of the Bible, tend to be regarded by Epiphanius as oracles of truth, the burdens of interpretation are shifted almost entirely away from the transmitting witnesses in scripture onto its receivers, whether orthodox or heretic.[75]

Even more so than that of Tertullian, Epiphanius's deeply felt and deliberately unyielding position exacts a high cost intellectually, no less for moderns than for those ancients who might scarcely have recognized themselves from his sometimes invidious characterizations.[76] That is grist for another book's mill. For us this conclusion must suffice: once again the figure of Mark has retained familiar features, while nonetheless assuming the particular shape of particular concerns, held by the commentator responsible for its figuration.

Jerome

We complete our survey of patristic portrayals of Mark with the comments of Eusebius Hieronymus (ca. 342–420), who, next to Origen, was early Christianity's most sophisticated biblical scholar.[77] Jerome, as he is better known, was a bridge between Eastern and Western Christianity: he received his secondary education in Rome, though his later and most productive years were spent in a monastery that he founded in Bethlehem. Although best known for a Latin translation of the Bible which weathered initial controversy to become the "Vulgate" (or "common [edition]") within Roman Catholicism, Jerome also produced a voluminous body of commentaries, homilies, treatises, and correspondence.

The most noteworthy of Jerome's references to the figure of Mark appear in various writings that may be dated within the last two decades of the fourth century. The earliest among these works is probably the *Commentary on Philemon* (ca. 387).[78] Interpreting verse 24 of that letter, Jerome identifies Paul's partner, "Mark," with the one "who is, I reckon [*puto*], the founder [or "author," *conditorem*] of the Gospel." Since elsewhere (as we shall see) Jerome follows the prevailing precedent of associating Mark with Peter, not with Paul, this reference is as anomalous as it is scant. Unfortunately, we cannot correlate this passing comment with Jerome's treatment of, say, Colossians 4:10 or 2 Timothy 4:11: after having completed commentaries on Philemon, Galatians, Ephesians, and Titus, Jerome abandoned whatever plans he may have had for commentaries on all of the letters attributed to Paul (cf. *Comm. on Philemon* 1).

Around the year 393 Jerome published a catalog of early Christianity's *Famous Lives* (*De viris illustribus*), an attempt to persuade the

church's cultured critics of its bountiful literary heritage.[79] Its review
of Christian authors and writings, including the Evangelists (see *De
vir.* 3, 7, 9), contains this entry concerning Mark:

> Mark, Peter's disciple and interpreter, wrote a brief Gospel
> in accordance with what he had heard Peter relating, on the
> request of his comrades in Rome. When Peter heard of this,
> he approved it and authorized its reading in the churches,
> as Clement writes (in the sixth book of the *Hypotypōseis*),
> as well as Papias, the Hieropolitan bishop. Peter mentions
> this Mark in his first Epistle, where he figuratively signifies
> Rome under the name of "Babylon": "The co-elect in
> Babylon sends you greetings, as does my son Mark" [5:13].
> With the Gospel that he had himself composed, he went to
> Egypt and, [being] the first to proclaim Christ in Alexandria,
> he founded a church with such teaching and such conti-
> nence of life that he brought all the followers of Christ to
> [adhere to] his own example. Finally Philo, the most elo-
> quent of the Jews, seeing that the first church in Alexandria
> was still judaizing as if in praise of his own people, wrote a
> book on their way of life; and as Luke tells that, in Jerusa-
> lem, the faithful held all things in common [Acts 2:43–47,
> 4:32–37], so [Philo] recorded for Alexandrian posterity what
> he saw taking place under Mark as teacher [*doctore*]. But
> he died in Nero's eighth year and was buried at Alexandria,
> Annianus succeeding him. (*De. vir.* 8)[80]

A more compressed statement about Mark, presented as the second
among four Evangelists, appears in the preface of Jerome's *Commentary on Matthew*, which was published toward the end of the fourth
century:[81]

> Second, [there is] Mark, interpreter of the apostle Peter and
> first bishop of the church of Alexandria, who himself did
> not see the Lord, the very Savior, but narrated those things
> which he had heard his master preaching, with greater
> fidelity to the deeds performed than to [their] order. (*Comm.
> on Matt.* Pref.)

To this "thumbnail sketch" Jerome adds slight shadings within some
of his shorter works. First, in a letter addressed to two noble Roman
friends, Pammachius and Marcella (ca. 402), Jerome encloses an episcopal letter by Theophilus of Alexandria, expressing the hope that,
"by its preaching, may the chair of the apostle Peter [i.e., the Roman

pontiff] confirm the chair of the Evangelist Mark" (*Ep.* 97.4).[82] Second, in correspondence with a learned Frenchwoman named Hedibia (ca. 407) about the meaning of 2 Corinthians 2:16, Jerome draws a comparison between Paul, who had Titus as his interpreter, with "the blessed Peter [who] had Mark, whose Gospel was composed by Peter's dictation and [Mark's] transcription" (*cuius evangelium Petro narrante et illo scribente compositum est*). The point of this analogy, which Jerome bolsters with appeal to 1 and 2 Peter, is to demonstrate how different interpreters necessarily lend variations in literary style and character to works attributed to one and the same author (*Ep.* 120.11).[83] Interestingly, in a homily (75) on Mark 1:1–12 Jerome expatiates on the differences, even mistakes, which can be introduced into the process of such presumed transcription:

> Now, as far as I can recall by going back in my mind and sifting carefully the work of the seventy translators [i.e., the Septuagint] as well as the Hebrew scrolls, I have never been able to locate in Isaiah the prophet the words: "Behold I send my messenger before thee," but I do find them written near the close of the prophecy of Malachi [3:1]. If, therefore, this statement is written at the end of Malachi's prophecy, on what grounds does Mark the Evangelist take for granted here: "As it is written in Isaiah the prophet" [Mark 1:2]? The utterances of the Evangelists are the work of the Holy Spirit. This Mark who writes is not to be esteemed lightly; in fact, Peter the apostle says in his letter: "The Church chosen together with you greets you; and so does my son Mark" [1 Pet 5:13]. O Apostle Peter, Mark, your son—son, not by the flesh, but by the Spirit—informed as he is in spiritual matters, is uninformed here, and credits to one prophet of Holy Writ what is written by another." (*Hom.* 75)[84]

Many of the preceding comments have a familiar ring, and for good reason: whereas Jerome acknowledges indebtedness to Clement and Papias, his dependence on Eusebius is virtually verbatim, following the latter's presentation of details in identical order:

Famous Lives 8	**Church History 2.15–17, 24**
Mark, Peter's disciple and interpreter,	Mark, Peter's follower,
Wrote a Gospel in accordance with Peter's account, at the request of Roman comrades.	At the request of Peter's Roman auditors, wrote his Gospel from the apostle's preaching.

On hearing of it, Peter approved and authorized its reading in the churches,

On learning of it, Peter was pleased and authorized its study in the churches,

As written by Clement (*Hypotypō-seis*, bk. 6), and confirmed by Papias of Hierapolis.

As quoted by Clement (*Hypotypō-seis*, bk. 6), and confirmed by Papias of Hierapolis.

Mark is mentioned in 1 Peter 5:13 (quoted), which figuratively signifies Rome as "Babylon."

Mark is mentioned in 1 Peter 5:13 (quoted), which metaphorically refers to Rome as "Babylon."

With his completed Gospel, Mark went to Egypt, the first to preach Christ in Alexandria and to found its church,

With his written Gospel, Mark was the first sent to Egypt to preach and the first to found Alexandrian churches,

Whose judaizing and continence of life Philo described.

Whose asceticism was described as that of the Therapeutae, in Philo's treatise.

In Nero's eighth year, Mark was succeeded by Annianus at Alexandria.

In Nero's eighth year, Mark was succeeded by Annianus in the Alexandrian diocese.

Likewise, the depiction of Mark in Jerome's *Commentary on Matthew* essentially reproduces Eusebius's quotation of Papias:

Commentary on Matthew (Preface)

Church History 3.39.15

Mark, interpreter of the apostle Peter,

Mark became Peter's interpreter.

Did not himself see the Lord

He had not heard the Lord, nor had he followed him,

But narrated those things that he heard the master preach,

[But wrote] down single points as he remembered them [from Peter's teaching],

With greater fidelity to deeds performed [by Jesus] than to their order.

Not, indeed, in order, of the things said or done by the Lord.

While numbering the *Church History* among his sources in the preface to *Famous Lives*, nowhere in his comments on Mark does

Jerome suggest that he was so heavily dependent on Eusebius. In a way this incidentally may be typical of Jerome's efforts at historical bibliography and biblical commentary: while he was among the most erudite of scholars in the fourth century, he was hardly Augustine's equal in venturesome originality.[85] In that light it may not be fortuitous that Jerome's unsurpassed *métier* was in translating the words of others.

On the other hand, Jerome does more than parrot the opinions of his predecessors: from some testimonies he tries to draw inferences about Mark, which carry stronger or weaker conviction. For instance, on the basis of Philemon 24, he opines that this Mark, Paul's associate, may have been Mark the Evangelist—while quickly conceding that such a connection is speculative (*Comm. in Philem* 24). From Eusebius's statement, otherwise uncorroborated, that in 61–62 Annianus immediately succeeded Mark the Evangelist in supervising the Alexandrian diocese (*H.E.* 2.24), Jerome evidently deduces, equally without corroboration, (1) that Mark was the Alexandrian church's first bishop (*Comm. in Matt.* Pref.), and (2) that Mark, therefore, died "in the eighth year of Nero's reign" and was buried in Alexandria.[86] These new data are somewhat equivocal. On the one hand, they arguably culminate the developing tradition of Mark's intimate association with Alexandrian Christianity. On the other hand, this very tradition is difficult to meld with earlier testimonies that (1) Mark was a minor, not to say dubious, figure in ancient Christianity (which does not sit comfortably beside his elevation to the episcopacy),[87] and (2) Mark outlived Peter (cf. Irenaeus, *Adv. Haer.* 3.1.1; Clement, *To Theodore*), whose death by martyrdom during the Neronian persecution of Roman Christians (in the year 64) is usually assumed among patristic witnesses after the late second century.[88] Likewise, Jerome's opinion that Mark took down his Gospel from Peter's direct dictation (*Ep.* 120.11)[89] recalls, while significantly embellishing, the assumption of Petrine oversight of the Second Gospel, found in Origen (Eusebius, *H.E.* 6.25.5) and Epiphanius (*Pan.* 51.6.10). Once again the Petrine apostolicity of Mark's Gospel is being firmly underscored. Yet this particular way of linking Evangelist with apostle cannot be easily squared with a claim for the Second Gospel's creation after the departure of Peter and Paul (Irenaeus, *Adv. Haer.* 3.1.1; Eusebius, *H.E.* 5.8.3). In these respects Jerome emerges as an interesting example of how one learned author, on the threshold of the early Christian Middle Ages, attempts to consolidate some divergent traditions about Mark, which have evolved to some degree separately and by this time simply refuse to gel.

For all of that, Jerome's portrayal of Mark rings yet another change, or series of changes, in the patristic tendency to recast the Evangelist's figure in his interpreters' mold. Thus, it is no surprise that Jerome, a one-time monastic in the desert of northern Syria (ca. 375–77) and a lifelong "champion of chastity,"[90] would focus on an exemplary ascet-icism that Mark supposedly promulgated among Egyptian Christians (*De vir.* 8). If the reputations of non-Christians such as Philo (*De vir.* 11), Seneca (12), Josephus (13), as well as arch-heretics like Eunomius (120), could be drafted in Jerome's defense of an elevated Christian culture, then the promotion of a traditionally minor figure like Mark to the ranks of "Illustrious Gentlemen" would have been easy to justify. Similarly, to strengthen an alliance between the fifth-century sees of Alexandria and Rome, the figures of "Bishop Mark" and his father in the faith, "Bishop Peter," could be deftly capitalized by Jerome (*Ep.* 97.4), who knew firsthand something of ecclesiastical politics by virtue of his tenure as secretary to Pope Damasus (ca. 382–85). And when Mark's abilities as an Old Testament exegete were suspect (see Mark 1:2) no one could call an inspired Evangelist on the carpet with greater independence of judgment or more disarming arrogance than Jerome (*Hom.* 75), who centuries later would be styled within Catholicism as *doctor maximus in sacris scripturis explanandis* ("supreme doctor in the interpretation of sacred scripture").[91] Like others among his patris-tic forebears, from Jerome we learn something of the Mark of Christian tradition,[92] and not a little about the patristic interpreter in question.

Summary

Third- and fourth-century Palestinian traditions about Mark exhibit a pattern with a quartet of regular features. First, Mark remains a minor figure, in which Eusebius and Epiphanius demonstrate little interest beyond its usefulness in their larger ecclesiastical or theological projects. Similarly, an "illustrious life" is ascribed to Mark by Jerome, but only because that is dictated by the propagandistic slant of *Famous Lives*. Second, tiny adornments are added incrementally by these authors to the standing traditional presentations. Thus, Mark's associ-ation with Peter (repeatedly recalled by Eusebius) is amplified by claims that the apostle, after rescuing Mark from apostasy, authorized him to write a Gospel and to missionize Alexandria (Epiphanius), or that with occasional errors Mark recorded his Gospel through apostolic dictation (Jerome). Likewise, the Egyptian traditions of the Evange-list's connection with Alexandria are extended: Mark was dispatched to that city to establish its churches (Eusebius), by Peter's authoriza-tion (Epiphanius), and ultimately became the first patriarch of Alexandria, where he died and was buried (Jerome). Third, as such details are fused with existing traditions, the result is a discernible degree of incoherence in the overall picture of Mark (especially in Eusebius and Jerome; less pronounced in Epiphanius's more modest portrayal). Fourth, and by now not surprising, the depiction of Mark by Eusebius, Epiphanius, and Jerome tends to echo, either softly or forcefully, each author's particular perspectives, interests, and concerns.

NOTES

1. One might instance Acts 18:24, in which Apollos is described as an Alexandrian Jewish convert to Christianity.

2. Earlier in the twentieth century Walter Bauer proposed that the roots of Egyptian (or Coptic) Christianity were thoroughly heretical, an embarrassment that was effectively suppressed when nascent Catholicism finally took hold in the second century (*Orthodoxy and Heresy in Earliest Christianity*, ed. by Robert A. Kraft and Gerhard Krodel, 2d. German ed. [Philadelphia: Fortress, 1971], 44–60). Although the adequacy of this theory has been challenged on several fronts, scholarship since Bauer has confirmed the hybrid character of orthodoxy and heresy, and its mutual fructification, in ancient Egyptian Christianity. For discussion, see Colin H. Roberts, *Manuscript, Society and Belief in Early Christian Egypt* (London: British Academy / Oxford University Press, 1979), 49–73; Helmut Koester, *Introduction to the New Testament,* vol. 2: *History and Literature of Early Christianity* (Philadelphia, Berlin, and New York: Fortress / Walter de Gruyter, 1982), 219–39. Coptic Christianity's origins in Jewish Christianity are investigated in several essays from among the important collection, *The Roots of Egyptian Christianity,* ed. Birger A. Pearson and James F. Goehring, SAC (Philadelphia: Fortress, 1986). See, in particular, Henry A. Green, "The Socio-Economic Background of Christianity in Egypt" (100–113); Birger A. Pearson, "Earliest Christianity in Egypt: Some Observations" (132–59); and A. F. J. Klijn, "Jewish Christianity in Egypt" (161–75). Two different reconstructions of early Egyptian Christianity's rootage in distinctively Palestinian Judaism are proposed by L. W. Barnard, "Saint Stephen and Early Alexandrian Christianity," *NTS* 7 (1960): 31–45; and Roberts, *Manuscript, Society and Belief,* 71–72. Aziz S. Atiya (*History of Eastern Christianity* [Notre Dame, Ind.: University of Notre Dame Press, 1967], 13–166), offers a thorough, somewhat more traditional, overview of Coptic Christianity from its origins up to the modern era.

3. The literature from the Christian monastery at Nag Hammadi (southeast of Alexandria, in the Nile Valley) dates to about the middle of the fourth century; however, the oral and literary traditions underlying those texts are in many cases considerably earlier, some perhaps contemporaneous with the writings of the New Testament.

4. The precise character of the school of Alexandria is a matter of some debate. For a treatment of the problem and a proposal for its resolution, see Robert L. Wilken, "Alexandria: A School for Training in Virtue," in *Schools*

of Thought in the Christian Tradition, ed. Patrick Henry (Philadelphia: Fortress, 1984), 15–30.

5. Clement knew of other written Gospels, such as the *Gospel of the Egyptians* (for the fragments of which see *The Other Gospels: Non-Canonical Gospel Texts*, ed. Ron Cameron [Philadelphia: Westminster, 1982], 49–52), but accorded precedence to the canonical four.

6. Fragments of Clement's comments on selected biblical books are translated by William Wilson in *ANF* 2 (1913): 571–87. At several points I have modified Wilson's translation of *Adumbr. ad 1 Pet* 5:13.

7. Fifteen years after the manuscript discovery Smith's findings were doubly published: a technical volume, *Clement of Alexandria and a Secret Gospel of Mark* (Cambridge, Mass.: Harvard University Press, 1973); a popularization, *The Secret Gospel: The Discovery and Interpretation of the Secret Gospel according to Mark* (New York: Harper & Row, 1973).

8. Saul Levin, "The Early History of Christianity, in Light of the 'Secret Gospel' of Mark," *ANRW* 2.25.6 (1988): 4272–75.

9. The translation is Smith's (*Clement of Alexandria*, 446–47). A transcription of the Greek text, plus reproductions of the ancient documentary finds, are available in the same volume (448–53).

10. The young man in the linen cloth, in the *Secret Gospel*, may refer to a nameless character similarly (and uniquely) described in Mark's Gospel (14:51–52; cf. 16:5). One proposal for the relationship between *Secret Mark* and canonical Mark, centered on this character, has recently been suggested by Marvin W. Meyer, "The Youth in the *Secret Gospel of Mark*," *Sem* 49 (1990): 129–53. According to Clement, after the statement of Jesus' entry to Jericho in Mark 10:46, the *Secret Gospel* included, moreover, the following insertion: "And there were the sister of the youth that Jesus loved, and his mother and Salome, and Jesus did not receive them" (*Letter to Theodore* 2 [recto]. 15–18).

11. Smith's thesis, presented in *Secret Gospel* and developed in *Jesus the Magician* (San Francisco: Harper & Row, 1978), is that the Jesus of history founded an esoteric mystery cult, characterized by nocturnal baptism in the nude (perhaps accompanied by sexual contact) and libertine behavior. While granting that Smith has helpfully reopened the subject of magic in the Greco-Roman world, few scholars have been persuaded by his reconstruction of Jesus' career. Representative of most critics' response are the reviews of Smith's 1973 volumes by Robert M. Grant ("Morton Smith's Two Books," *ATR* 56 [1974]: 58–65) and R. P. C. Hanson (*JTS* 25 [1974]: 513–21).

12. Levin, "Early History of Christianity," 4270–92, offers a helpful review of pertinent scholarship and a judicious assessment of the various questions raised by Smith's discovery. Six years earlier Smith's own reassessment and rebuttal to his critics was published as "Clement of Alexandria and Secret Mark: The Score at the End of the First Decade," *HTR* 75 (1982): 449–61. Both articles provide thorough bibliographies of secondary research.

13. As one might expect, the answers vary: from those who try to smooth

over the discrepancies between Irenaeus and Clement (Donald Guthrie, *New Testament Introduction* [Downers Grove, Ill.: Inter-Varsity, 1970], 73) to those who favor the historical likelihood of one patristic tradition over the other (Vincent Taylor, *The Gospel according to St. Mark*, 2d. ed., Thornapple Commentaries [1946; reprint, Grand Rapids, Mich.: Baker Book House, 1981], 6). Ultimately, such questions may be less fruitful, or patient of resolution, than asking how and why the traditions in question may have evolved in the ways that they did.

14. Eusebius (*H.E.* 2.15.2) regards this connection, established by Clement, as worthy of special notice: "[Clement's story about Peter and Mark] calls to mind Peter's reference to Mark in the first Epistle; this also, they say, was composed in Rome itself, as signified by his own figurative reference to the city as Babylon in this way: 'The co-elect in Babylon sends you greetings, as does my son Mark.' " It is possible, of course, that the specter of 1 Peter 5:13 may have been hovering about the testimonies of Papias and Irenaeus concerning the authorship of Mark's Gospel. To the best of my knowledge, however, it is with Clement's comments on the verse itself that for the first time we can actually document the influence of 1 Peter 5:13.

15. Evidently, Eusebius (*H.E.* 6.14.4–5) seems to think that Clement was speaking of the written Gospel of Mark, relative to the others in the canon. Still, there is no way to ascertain from the Greek text (*euangelion*, uncapitalized) whether an oral or a literary product is intended by Clement himself.

16. For this reference to Lucian I am indebted to Wayne A. Meeks, "*Hypomnēmata* from an Untamed Skeptic," in *The Relationships among the Gospels: An Interdisciplinary Dialogue*, ed. William O. Walker (San Antonio, Tex.: Trinity University Press, 1978), 168. For a comparison of the Papias and Clementine traditions, centered on the subject of *hypomnēmata*, see T. Y. Mullins, "Papias and Clement and Mark's Two Gospels," *VC* 30 (1976): 189–92.

17. Cf. the slightly different statement in *H.E.* 2.15.1, which emphasizes the height of the appeal, not the number of solicitors.

18. In support of this possibility is the seemingly discrepant description, in *H.E.* 2.15.2, of Mark's literary work: as "scripture authorized for concourse in the churches," not as a *hypomnēma* (*H.E.* 2.15.1). For Clement the latter may have been the occasion for what ultimately came to be "the Gospel according to Mark"; if so, then Clement's point was misunderstood by Eusebius, who simply equated *aides-mémoire* with a more polished product. Since, however, we are entirely dependent on Eusebius for Clement's point of view in this matter, such a reconstruction is inescapably tenuous.

19. The understandable, though apocryphal, culmination of this tendency occurred in the Middle Ages, when 1 Peter 5:13 was interpreted as meaning that Mark was Peter's son *by blood*, the brother of the apostle's (equally apocryphal) daughter "Petronilla" (Joseph F. Kelly, "The Patristic Biography of Mark," *Bible Today* 21 [1983]: 43).

20. Thus, John A. T. Robinson, *Redating the New Testament* (Philadelphia:

Westminster, 1976), 108. To judge from the manuscript evidence, the Gospels of John and Matthew, as well as the Gnostically oriented apocryphal Gospel of Thomas, appear to have been especially popular in Alexandrian Christianity of that period. By contrast, the only surviving Egyptian manuscript of Mark, prior to Constantine, is the early third-century Chester Beatty codex of the Gospels and Acts. According to scholarly tabulations, fourth-century Coptic manuscripts exhibit sixty quotations from Matthew, fifteen from Luke, fifteen from John, and none from Mark (Roberts, *Manuscript, Society and Belief*, 61, following T. Lefort). Extant from among Clement's own writings is a homily on Mark 10:17–31 (*Who Is the Rich Man That Is Saved?*); nevertheless, in Clement's *Stromata* quotations from Mark (about 29) are less frequent by far than his citations from Matthew (approx. 281), Luke (127), and John (111).

21. With his characterization of the Alexandrian recension of Mark as "a more spiritual Gospel" (*pneumatikōteron euangelion*) one might compare Clement's similar evaluation of John as a *pneumatikon euangelion* (*H.E.* 6.14.7).

22. *Letter to Theodore* 1 [recto]. 11–12.

23. *Letter to Theodore* 1 [verso]. 11–12.

24. This assessment would hold, I think, even if the majority of scholars ultimately judged the *Letter to Theodore* as inauthentically Clementine.

25. Since its publication after the year 244 only eight of the twenty-five books in Origen's *Commentary on St. Matthew* appear to have survived (bks. 10–17 on Matt 13:36–22:33).

26. Roberts, *Manuscript, Society and Belief*, 23, 53. Roberts also adduces evidence that suggests early contact between the Roman and Alexandrian churches (59).

27. On Origen's doctrine of inspiration, consult R. P. C. Hanson, *Allegory and Event: A Study of the Sources and Significance of Origen's Interpretation of Scripture* (London and Richmond, Va.: SCM / John Knox, 1959), 187–209.

28. Oddly enough, just the opposite of Dionysius' judgment—that John Mark was the author of the Fourth Gospel—has been proposed by a modern interpreter (see Pierson Parker, "John and John Mark" *JBL* 79 [1960]: 97–110, N.B. 108).

29. G. M. Lee ("Eusebius on St. Mark and the Beginnings of Christianity in Egypt," *Studia Patristica* 12, TU 115 [Berlin: Akademie, 1975], 422–31, esp. 424–25) cites evidence suggesting that churches in Egypt and Syria tended to differentiate between John Mark and Mark the Evangelist. Apparently, however, some writers of Christian antiquity were inclined to identify John Mark with the apostle John, the son of Zebedee (which figure was ultimately equated with the Fourth Evangelist): thus, J. Edgar Bruns, "John Mark: A Riddle within the Johannine Enigma," *Scripture* 15 (1963): 88–92; "The Confusion between John and John Mark in Antiquity," *Scripture* 17 (1965): 23–26. See also the volume in the present series by R. Alan Culpepper, *John, the Son of Zebedee: The Life of a Legend* (Columbia: University of South Carolina Press, 1994).

30. A liturgy of the Alexandrian church, of old but indeterminate age, honors "our holy father Mark, the apostle [*sic*] and evangelist, who has shown us the way of salvation"; in like manner it is styled as "The Divine Liturgy of the Holy Apostle and Evangelist Mark, the Disciple of the Holy Peter" (translated in *ANF* 7 [1899]: 551–60). As early as the seventh century (with the *Chronicon Paschale*), Mark was regarded in the Byzantine church as a martyr. This tradition appears to stem from a colorful fifth-century Alexandrian apocryphon, the *Acts of Mark,* which recounts an early mission to Alexandria by Mark, his performance of miracles and his appointment of ecclesiastical leaders, and his noble death by the hand of a pagan mob (*Die apokryphen Apostelgeschichte und Apostellegenden* ed. Richard Adelbert Lipsius [1887; reprint, Amsterdam: APA—Philo, 1976], vol. 2, pt. 2, 321–53, esp. 332–36). Although its historicity is problematic (see the balanced discussion by Pearson, "Earliest Christianity in Egypt: Some Observations," 137–45), this legend has exerted a significant influence on Coptic Christian tradition: see Atiya, *History of Eastern Christianity,* 25–28; and the more popular treatment, *St. Mark and the Coptic Church* (Cairo: Coptic Orthodox Patriarchate, 1968). Why Mark and not Apollos (Acts 18:24; see n. 1) became fixed within the apostolic aspirations of Alexandrian Christian folklore remains an unsolved mystery (thus, also F. F. Bruce, *Stephen, James, and John: Studies in Early Non-Pauline Christianity* [Grand Rapids, Mich.: Eerdmans, 1979], 84).

31. In two of his Antiochene sermons, delivered during the years 386–98, John Chrysostom placed the membership of the city's principal church at over 100,000, about one-half of Antioch's total population except for children and slaves (*Hom. in Ignat.* 4.85). On the motley character of Syrian Christianity during this period, see Bauer, *Orthodoxy and Heresy in Early Christianity,* 1–43; Hans Lietzmann, *The Founding of the Church Universal: A History of the Early Church* (New York: Charles Scribner's Sons, 1950), 2:258–74; Helmut Koester, "*Gnomai Diaphoroi*: The Origin and Nature of Diversification in the History of Early Christianity," in *Trajectories through Early Christianity,* James M. Robinson and Helmut Koester (Philadelphia: Fortress, 1971), 114–57, esp. 119–43; Wayne A. Meeks and Robert L. Wilken, *Jews and Christians in Antioch in the First Four Centuries of the Common Era,* SBLSBS 13 (Missoula, Mont.: Scholars Press, 1978).

32. The name is symbolic and obviously cognate to the English word *adamant,* which has a double etymology. Its Latin root refers to that which is "hard as a diamond"; its Greek equivalent suggests "[something] unvanquished."

33. The Greek text of this portion of *De recta in Deum fide,* plus a slightly archaizing translation, are provided by Henry Joel Cadbury in *The Beginnings of Christianity,* pt. 1: *The Acts of the Apostles,* ed. F. J. Foakes Jackson and Kirsopp Lake (London: Macmillan, 1922), 2:240–43.

34. The ancient testimonies to Luke 10:1 split rather evenly on the number appointed and sent out by Jesus: like Adamantius, the primary manuscripts from Alexandria and the West support the numeral "seventy-two," while other

Alexandrian and Caesarean evidence give the number as "seventy." The latter reading may have been slightly favored in the majority of patristic references (including Irenaeus [Latin recension], Tertullian, Clement of Alexandria, Origen, Eusebius).

35. This rather curious fact does not necessarily flout Hengel's argument for an early attachment of superscriptions to the Gospels, but it does cast a shadow of doubt on the probative weight accorded to such titles, at least by some Christians during the patristic era. See Hengel, "The Titles of the Gospels and the Gospel of Mark," in *Studies in the Gospel of Mark*, 64–84.

36. Irenaeus, *Adv. Haer.* 1.27.2; Tertullian, *Adv. Marc.* 4.2–3.

37. Megethius's accusation of the forged authorship of the Second and Third Gospels (*De recta in Deum fide*) is also reminiscent of "Marcion's complaint . . . that the apostles are held suspect of dissumulation or pretense, even to the debasing of the gospel" (Tertullian, *Adv. Marc.* 4.3.4).

38. Syria appears to have been the home of such apocryphal works as the *Kerygmata [Proclamations] of Peter* and the *Gospel of Peter* (see Eusebius, *H.E.* 6.12.2–6), as well as Matthew's Gospel, which emphasizes the role of Peter among the Twelve (see Matt 16:13–19). On the other hand, as early as 100, Pauline Christianity played an important role in Antioch; see Rudolf Bultmann, "Ignatius and Paul," in *Existence and Faith: Shorter Writings of Rudolf Bultmann*, ed. Schubert M. Ogden (Cleveland and New York: Meridian/World, 1960), 267–77. Interestingly, in Galatians 2:11 Paul himself bears witness to Peter's (Cephas's) presence in Antioch.

39. Here and elsewhere the translation is that of James Donaldson in *ANF* 7 (1899): 387–508. For thorough investigation of the critical problems associated with this text, see the classic study by Franz Xaver Funk, *Die Apostolischen Konstitutionen: Eine Litterar-Historische Untersuchung* (1891; reprint, Frankfurt am Main: Minerva, 1970).

40. For a summary of suggested differences between these traditions on the figure of Mark, see the conclusions drawn at the end of chapter 2.

41. Hippolytus's important presentation of primitive church orders, *The Apostolic Tradition*, is generally regarded as a source for the *Apostolic Constitutions* (N. B. bk. 8). I know of no evidence, however, that supports the latter document's dependence on Hippolytus's *Refutation of All Heresies* (7:30).

42. Henry Barclay Swete, *The Gospel according to St. Mark: The Greek Text with Introduction, Notes, and Indices*, 3d. ed. (London: Macmillan, 1927), xxxv–xxxvi.

43. Appendices to different versions of Ephraem's commentary on the *Diatessaron* offer thumbnail sketches of the Evangelists. Of Mark it is said, in the Latin version, that "[he] followed Simon Peter. He went to Rome, and the believers [there] persuaded him to write, so that the tradition would be remembered and not fall into oblivion over the passage of time. Thus he wrote what he retained." In later, Armenian translations of the commentary, this testimony, already a blend of Western and Eastern elements, is extended and

sounds even more Clementine: Mark composed his Roman Gospel in Latin [*sic*] and preached the gospel in Egypt. Some experts doubt that Ephraem wrote these appendices; if inauthentic, they are probably later than the fourth century. For further discussion, see *Éphrem de Nisibe: Commentaire de l'Évangile concordant ou Diatessaron,* ed. and trans. Louis Leloir, SC 121 (Paris: Cerf, 1966), 25–32, 409. Other pseudo-Ephraemic testimonies are reproduced in *Synopsis Quattuor Evangeliorum,* ed. K. Aland, 10th rev. ed. (Stuttgart: Deutsche Bibelstiftung, 1976), 544.

44. The struggle to supplant the *Diatessaron* with a four-Gospel canon is manifest in the comments of the fifth-century Syrian bishop, Theodoret of Cyrus (ca. 393–466): "Not only Tatian's group have used [the *Diatessaron*], but the adherents of the apostolic teaching also have innocently employed the book as a convenient compendium, since they did not recognize the deception of the compilation. I myself found more than two hundred such books which were being held in honor in the congregations of our region; I collected and destroyed them and in their place introduced the Gospels of the four Evangelists" (*Haer. fab.* [*Haereticarum fabularum compendium (Compendium of Heretical Fables)*] 1:20; quoted by Bauer, *Orthodoxy and Heresy in Earliest Christianity,* 32).

45. Translation by George Prevost in *NPNF,* 1st ser., 10 (1986 [rpt.]): 3–4. The translation, below, of Chrysostom's *Homily* [4:1] *on Matthew* 1:17 is also that of Prevost (20), with slight modifications.

46. For instance, see C. S. Mann, *Mark: A New Translation with Introduction and Commentary,* AB 27 (Garden City, N.Y.: Doubleday, 1986), 80–81, who accepts as historically probable far more of the traditions about the Second Gospel's Petrine and Roman origins than would many modern investigators. Lest unintended confusion creep in here, it should be noted that Chrysostom is not proposing, before Johann Jakob Griesbach (1745–1812), the theory that Mark's Gospel was derived from Matthew's: according to Chrysostom, Mark was ultimately dependent on *Peter's* preaching, not the First Evangelist's. Chrysostom recognizes a literary problem attending the Matthean and Markan Gospels (the former's length, the latter's brevity); his response to that problem does not necessarily presuppose those documents' literary interrelationship. One might observe a similar distinction, recently limned with respect to another patristic citation, by Denis Farkasfalvy, "The Presbyters' Witness on the Order of the Gospels as Reported by Clement of Alexandria," *CBQ* 54 (1992): 260–70.

47. I take Chrysostom's statement in *Homily* [4.1] *on Matthew* 1:17 to refer to the Petrine and Pauline corpora, which by now were firmly ensconced among most canonical listings in the East: thus, for example, its secure position within the "festal canon" promulgated in 367 by Alexandria's bishop, Athanasius (reprinted in *New Testament Apocrypha,* vol. 1: *Gospels and Related Writings,* ed. by W. Schneemelcher, rev. ed. (Cambridge and Louisville, Ky.: James Clarke / Westminster / John Knox, 1991], 49–50).

48. For this observation I am indebted to William Babcock.

49. At relevant points in his exposition (*Homilies on Acts* [13:4, 5] 28; *On Colossians* [4:5, 6] 11; *On 2 Timothy* [4:9–13] 10) Chrysostom essentially restates the biblical texts with colorless comment. Portraits of Paul and Barnabas, though not of John Mark, are developed by Chrysostom from Acts 15:37–38, in order to score moral points: Paul's anger was justified by the need to teach Mark an important lesson; "[Paul and Barnabas took] themselves so as to instruct and make perfect, by their separation, them that need the teaching which was to come from them" (*Homily on Acts* [15:36–41] 34). On the other hand, Chrysostom appears to have identified John Mark with John the apostle, "that John who was always with [the other apostles]" (*Homily on Acts* [12:12]).

50. An English translation of this curious text of uncertain origin is provided by Alexander Walker in *ANF* 8 (1899): 493–96. I am indebted to R. Alan Culpepper for first alerting me to the relevance of this apocryphal work for the present study.

51. The association of Mark with Paul is also recalled, though not elaborated, in the apocryphal *Apocalypse of Paul* (late fourth or early fifth century; provenance unknown). Based on other Christian apocalyptic traditions, this text purports to be a narration, transcribed by Mark and Timothy, of Paul's vision in the third heaven (2 Cor 12:1–10). For the text and its discussion, see *New Testament Apocrypha*, vol. 2: *Writings Relating to the Apostles, Apocalypses, and Related Subjects*, ed. Wilhelm Schneemelcher (Philadelphia: Westminster, 1965), 755–98.

52. Gerd Theissen, *Sociology of Early Palestinian Christianity* (Philadelphia: Fortress, 1978), is a trailblazing sociological analysis of the movement founded by Jesus. Though inevitably dated, Adolf von Harnack's overview of Palestinian Christianity until 325 remains a useful synthesis and interpretation of many primary sources (*The Expansion of Christianity in the First Three Centuries* [New York and London: G. P. Putnam's Sons / Williams and Norgate, 1905], 2:247–71).

53. Compared with *H.E.* 2.15.1 and Lucian's norms of ancient historiography (discussed earlier in this chapter), note in *H.E.* 3.24.5 the recurrence of the term *hypomnēmata* and the intimation of more than one stage in the composition of the Gospels of Matthew and John.

54. Robert M. Grant (*Eusebius as Church Historian* [Oxford: Clarendon, 1980], 3–9, 61–72) provides an overview of Eusebius's sources, oral and written. For an argument that the idiom "they say" (*phasi*) refers to more than merely hearsay evidence, see Lee, "Eusebius on St. Mark," 425–27.

55. Like Augustine and Chrysostom, Eusebius evinced interest in the literary relationships among the canonical Gospels: thus, his compilation of *The Evangelical Canons* (*PG* 22 [1857]: 1275–92), an early synopsis of the four Gospels. However, neither in these ten Eusebian canons nor in his letter to Carpianus (1275–78), which serves as a kind of introduction to these canons, does Eusebius correlate his literary findings with the assumption of the Second Gospel's Petrine derivation (as does Chrysostom).

56. For another example of a Eusebian "nonconfirmatory confirmation," see Grant, *Eusebius as Church Historian,* 73 (on *H.E.* 2.17.1). For an attempt to reconcile the comments about Papias in *H.E.* 2.15.2 and 3.39.14–15, see A. Delclaux, "Deux Témoignages de Papias sur la Composition de Marc?" *NTS* 27 (1981): 401–11.

57. In *H.E.* 2.15.2 Eusebius does indicate his reason for concluding otherwise: namely, an interpretation of the Papias-notice (in 3.39.15) by way of 1 Peter 5:13 (following Origen [cf. 6.25.5] and, perhaps, Clement).

58. Thus, Lee, "Eusebius on St. Mark," 430–32. Eusebius openly acknowledges his dependence on the Lukan Acts as well as on Josephus's historical books (*H.E.* 1.5.3–6.11). Had he remembered Egyptians as being among the witnesses to the miracle at Pentecost in Acts 2:9–11, surely he would have regarded their presence as historical, notwithstanding doubts cast by modern redaction critics (e.g., Ernst Haenchen, *The Acts of the Apostles: A Commentary,* trans. Bernard Noble et al [Philadelphia: Westminster, 1971], 166–75).

59. For consideration of Eusebius's remarkable treatment of Philo, see the comments of F. H. Colson in *Philo,* vol. 9: *Every Good Man Is Free; On the Contemplative Life; On the Eternity of the World; Against Flaccus; Apology for the Jews; On Providence,* LCL (Cambridge, Mass., and London: Harvard University Press / William Heinemann, 1960), 104–11 (cf. 105–69). See also Grant, *Eusebius as Church Historian,* 72–76.

60. Cf. Grant, *Eusebius as Church Historian,* 1–2, 127. Grant offers additional examples of Eusebius's discrepant explanations of events and phenomena (97–113, 126–41): reasons for the fall of Jerusalem (cf. *H.E.* 2.5.6–10, 10.1; 3.5.2–8, 11) and circumstances attending the composition of various New Testament books (cf. *H.E.* 3.18–31).

61. This is not to suggest that Eusebius's history is to be dismissed as completely idiosyncratic and utterly unreliable. To take but one example to the contrary: his report of a traditional association of Mark the Evangelist with Alexandria, without extant precedent until 1958, appears now to have been anticipated in Clement's *Letter to Theodore.* (Of course, Clement corroborates only the tradition that Eusebius appears to have known; the historical circumstances underlying either attestation are practically impossible to verify.) For a positive estimate of Eusebius as historian, see Lee, "Eusebius on St. Mark," 422–31; for a more reserved assessment, cf. Grant, *Eusebius as Church Historian,* 164–69.

62. Some aspects of this major tradition are recalled in n. 30.

63. The elevated tenor of Mark's commission to Alexandria may be hinted by Eusebius's use of *steilamenon* ("having been sent" or "dispatched"), a form of the verb *stellō* which appears in Greek epic (e.g., *Iliad* 1.433; *Odyssey* 14.248; see LSJ 2.1637b).

64. Nero's "eighth year," to which *H.E.* 2.24 refers, was from 62 to 63. For information on episcopal and imperial successions Eusebius was probably dependent on sources such as the *Chronographies* of Julius Africanus (ca. 160–240), which appear to have been constructed somewhat artificially and, to

that degree, unreliably (Grant, *Eusebius as Church Historian,* 51–53). With the patriarch Demetrius (d. ca. 231–32) our historical footing in Alexandrian Christianity becomes a good deal surer.

65. For a useful discussion of this important theme in Eusebius's work, see Grant, *Eusebius as Church Historian,* 45–49, 84–96, which also considers Eusebius's other principles of historical composition (22–32).

66. A concise overview of the *Panarion*'s structure and intent is provided by Gérard Vallée, *A Study in Anti-Gnostic Polemics: Irenaeus, Hippolytus, and Epiphanius* (Waterloo, Ont.: Canadian Corporation for Studies in Religion / Wilfrid Laurier, 1981), 63–91.

67. Though Epiphanius does not do so, Origen, Eusebius, and Jerome quote from a *Gospel of the Nazoraeans,* which appears to have been an annotated expansion of Matthew's Gospel (cf. *Pan.* 29.9.4). For a standard reconstruction of its fragments, see Cameron, *Other Gospels,* 99–102.

68. *The Panarion of Epiphanius of Salamis: Book I (Sects 1–46),* trans. Frank Williams, Nag Hammadi Studies 35 (Leiden, New York, København, Köln: E. J. Brill, 1987), 115–16.

69. Although Epiphanius does not explicitly credit his precursors with this portrayal of Mark, elsewhere in the *Panarion* (29.4.3, 31.33.3) he acknowledges familiarity with the works of Irenaeus, Clement, Hippolytus, and Eusebius.

70. One might recall the similar point, emphasized by Irenaeus in *Adversus Haereses* (3.11.8): each of the four Evangelists communicates distinctive, yet mutually complementary, dimensions of Christ's comprehensive activity.

71. Epiphanius tends to insist that heresy is self-refuting (*Pan.* 21.6.1, 25.5.4, 26.3.2, 31.34.1, 44.1.3) or self-evidently contradicted by scriptural truth (21.5.1; 24.8.8, 9.1; 56.2.11, 12; see Vallée, *Study in Anti-Gnostic Polemics,* 83–87). Nevertheless, his argumentative use of acknowledged differences among the Gospels suggests that Epiphanius's polemic was not entirely bereft of creativity.

72. For an illuminating discussion of this component of Epiphanius's method, consult Vallée, *Study in Anti-Gnostic Polemics,* 69–74.

73. On the eucharistic overtones of John 6:35–59 consult the discussion in Raymond E. Brown, *The Gospel according to John (i–xii),* AB 29 (Garden City, N.Y.: Doubleday, 1966), 268–94.

74. Interestingly, a similar scenario is rehearsed later by Epiphanius with reference to the Third Evangelist: also among the seventy-two who were scattered abroad by what the Savior had said was Luke, who was returned to the Lord by Paul and bidden to write a Gospel (*Pan.* 51.11.6).

75. For further reflection on this problem, see Vallée, *Study in Anti-Gnostic Polemics,* 84–87.

76. Epiphanius's predilection for the scurrilous is admitted even by some of his sympathetic interpreters: thus, Williams, *Panarion of Epiphanius of Salamis,* xxv–xxvi.

77. For an insightful analysis of "Jerome as Biblical Scholar," see H.F.D. Sparks's contribution to *The Cambridge History of the Bible,* vol. 1: *From the*

Beginnings to Jerome (Cambridge: Cambridge University Press, 1970), 510–41. The place of biblical interpretation within Jerome's life and career is assessed by John Norman Davidson Kelly, *Jerome: His Life, Writings, and Controversies* (London: Duckworth, 1975).

78. For this reference, as well as that to Jerome's *Homily* (75) on Mark 1:1–12, I am indebted to Séan P. Kealy, *Mark's Gospel: A History of Its Interpretation from the Beginning until 1979* (New York and Ramsey, N.J.: Paulist, 1982), 24–25.

79. The standard critical edition of this major work is that of E. C. Richardson in TU 14 (1896). It has been translated into German and Italian, although I do not know of an English version of this work.

80. I am grateful to William S. Babcock for his help in preparing this translation.

81. The Latin text, accompanied by Émile Bonnard's introduction, notes, and translation (in French), is available in SC 242 (*Saint Jérôme: Commentaire sur S. Matthieu,* bk. 1 (Paris: Cerf, 1977).

82. Trans. W. H. Fremantle in *NPNF*, 2d. ser., 6 (1989 [reprint]): 188.

83. For the Latin text (with a French translation), see *Saint Jérôme: Lettres,* ed. Jérôme Labourt, Collections des Universités de France (Paris: Société d'Edition / "Les Belles Lettres," 1958), 6:156.

84. *The Homilies of Saint Jerome,* trans. Marie Ligouri Ewald, vol. 2 (Homilies 60–96), (The Fathers of the Church; Washington, D.C.: Catholic University of America Press, 1966), 121–22. I have made minor, stylistic adjustments to the translation.

85. See the discussion in Kelly, *Jerome,* 144–78, 222–25.

86. The suggestion that Jerome may have made "an unsound inference from the Eusebian date for the succession of Annianus" was made at least as early as Swete (*Gospel according to St. Mark,* xxvii).

87. For this statement the closest parallel, which is scarcely exact, may be Clement's remark *To Theodore* that the *Secret Gospel of Mark* was bestowed both reverance and careful protection by Alexandrian Christians.

88. The tradition of Peter's martyrdom in Rome antedates its specific placement during the Neronian persecution (see Eusebius, *H.E.* 3.1.2–3; and, perhaps indirectly, *1 Clem.* 5 and Ignatius, *Rom.* 4.3). For a critical assessment of the relevant traditions, see Oscar Cullmann, *Peter: Disciple-Apostle-Martyr: A Historical and Theological Study* (Philadelphia: Westminster, 1953), 70–152.

89. As Babcock has suggested to me, the allusion to Mark's secretarian transcription may reflect Jerome's own practice of dictating to scribes.

90. The epithet is Kelly's (*Jerome,* 179–94; see also 46–56).

91. The sobriquet was given to Jerome at the Council of Trent (1545–63). As Kelly notes (*Jerome,* 334 n. 8), papal encyclicals have consistently presented Jerome as the model Roman Catholic exegete.

92. As was noted in chapter 3, Irenaeus, not Jerome, appears to have initiated the conventional characterization of the Evangelists as the four visionary creatures (man, lion, ox, eagle) described in Ezekiel 1:4–14 and

Revelation 4:6b–8 (*Adv. Haer.* 3.11.8). Nor was Jerome the first to liken Mark with the lion: that identification is made in a third-century commentary on Revelation by Victorinus of Pettau (*Scholia in Apocalypsin Beati Joannis* in Migne, *PL* 5 [1984]: 324–25). However, the more consistent association of Mark with the lion—reflected in Christian art of the medieval, Renaissance, and modern periods—may owe largely, if at times indirectly, to Jerome's influence: "Mark uttered the voice of the lion, roaring in the wilderness: 'Prepare the way of the Lord; make straight his paths'" (*Comm. in Matt.* Pref. [citing Mark 1:3]; see Schultze and Küppers, *Mark*). As Swete has demonstrated (*Gospel according to St. Mark*, xxxvi–xxxviii), until Jerome popularized this particular symbolism Mark's Gospel was variously likened by the church fathers to all four biblical creatures (cf., among others, Irenaeus, *Adv. Haer.* 3.11.8 [Mark as the eagle]; Augustine, *De con. evang.* 1.6 [Mark as the man]). On the other hand, Matthew, Luke, and John rather quickly and consistently were typified (respectively) as the man, the ox, and the eagle. From this Swete concludes, rightly I think, that the church of the first four centuries experienced difficulty "in forming a definite judgment as to the place and office of [Mark's] Gospel" (xxxviii).

Chapter Six

Gathering the Threads
A Patristic Conspectus

In the three chapters preceding, we have canvassed some of the portrayals of Mark among Christian interpreters of the second, third, and fourth centuries. I should emphasize that our survey has been selective, not complete. Given the vastness of patristic literature, we have aspired to consider not every testimony to Mark but only the best known among those witnesses. Nor have we considered whatever folk traditions about Mark and the other Evangelists may have been propagated among early Christianity's rank and file: whatever was not written, and even much that was, is lost to the ages. My aim in this chapter is not to rehash previous summaries but, instead, to offer some general observations on the more salient features and broader trends suggested by this slender segment of the history of biblical interpretation.

First, *only partial "pictures" of Mark, assembled mostly from fragmentary texts, have survived from the patristic era.* In general, we have been compelled to work with dribs and drabs of evidence (like that of Justin Martyr, Tertullian, and Origen), often in scrappy condition (recall Papias, the Muratorian Canon, Clement of Alexandria). Even when we have enjoyed relatively more abundant traditions about Mark—as in the case of authors such as Eusebius and Jerome—we have noticed some basic tensions among particular features within their presentations. Moreover, among those church fathers whose writings have survived in bulk (including Irenaeus, Chrysostom, and Augustine), the figure of Mark occupies a minor, if not trivial, position, when viewed in the context of those authors' overarching purposes or most pressing concerns. For them Mark was scarcely a leading figure or major personality. Consequently, little hagiographical and practically no antiquarian interest is demonstrated in Mark, even among those church fathers (such as Eusebius) who made it their business to collect and to transmit such things.[1] Whatever significance was accorded by these patristic interpreters to the figure of Mark served religious or theological concerns that transcended sheer interest in that figure in its own right.

Second, *the extracanonical presentations of Mark demonstrate tendencies toward both the conservation of, and discriminations among, other patristic traditions.* In some cases, for particular aspects of their portrayal of Mark, we may reasonably infer some patristic interpreters' reliance on their predecessors or contemporaries, or at least on the traditions that they represent (e.g., a dependence of the anti-Marcionite prologue and Origen on Irenaeus; of Chrysostom on Clement; of Epiphanius and Jerome on Eusebius). In other cases lines of derivation are more nebulous, and we can safely speak only of "family resemblances" among parallel traditions (cf. Papias and Justin). Either way, the portrayal of Mark among Christian authors of the second, third, and fourth centuries tends to assume a familiar shape, whose outline we shall momentarily trace. To that sketch are made adjustments small and great; typically, however, these alterations tend to be not brand-new creations but, rather, elaborations of elements previously introduced. For instance, one might recall the evolution of Mark's association with Alexandria: the tradition seems to have blossomed from a germinal assertion of the Evangelist's relocation and honored career there (Clement) to his having been dispatched there by Peter (Epiphanius) to establish churches (Eusebius), over which he exercised episcopal authority (Jerome, the Monarchian prologue).

On the other hand, patristic portrayals of Mark do not appear to be indiscriminately aggregative, as though all later writers simply harmonized, with supplements, all features of their precursors' portrayals. In this case, as perhaps in others within Christian history and tradition, what is "later" is not necessarily tantamount to what is "more developed": Chrysostom (ca. 386–98), for example, offers a much sketchier depiction of the Second Evangelist when compared with that of Clement, formulated some two centuries previously. With no little sophistication Dionysius of Alexandria attempts to sort out the different personalities named "John" within Christian tradition (including "John Mark"), without lumping them all together. In different ways Eusebius and Jerome exhibit both a greater inclination than some to amalgamate divergent traditions about Mark as well as the increasing impracticality of such an endeavor in the fourth century. The exception to the general rule here is the Monarchian prologue, which more than any other patristic witness attempts to consolidate almost everything that, by the end of the fourth century, had ever been said about any Christian figure named Mark. Yet even the Monarchian argument, which creaks under its own weight, offers nothing so agglomerative as the familiar maximal reconstruction with which we inaugurated this study. In retrospect such elaborations as that are a product of modernity, not of the patristic period. In early Christianity traditions about Mark appear to be, within limits, more fluid and less predictably unilinear.

Third, as suggested earlier, *the portrayal of Mark in patristic Christianity tends to assume a basic shape*. Allowing for the variety just mentioned, we may note five features that recur in most of the traditions surveyed:

1. *Typically, Mark is portrayed as a "literary figure" or evangelical author,* the conveyor of oral proclamation, possibly in the form of preliminary memoranda (see Papias, perhaps, and Clement), ultimately in the form of the Second Gospel of the Christian canon (e.g., Adamantius and Jerome). While a simple progression from apostolic preaching to written Gospel is suggested by many patristic testimonies (thus, Irenaeus; the Gospel prologues; Hippolytus), a more complex movement—from oral traditions through written notes to eventual refinement into "The Gospel according to Mark"—may be intimated elsewhere (Clement, *To Theodore*; perhaps Augustine). Still other traditions are tantalizingly vague on the subject of what Mark supposedly wrote (Papias; other comments of Clement). Nor, we might recall, does the New Testament provide any help in assessing this datum: however commonplace it might seem to us, the ascription of literary activity to "Mark" is attested neither in Acts nor in the canonical letters, much less in the Second Gospel.

2. *Normally, Mark is associated with the apostle Peter, often as the latter's adherent, interpreter, or transcriber.* Along with the aforementioned portrayal of Mark as a literary Evangelist, this feature, introduced very early (with Papias, who refers it to John the Presbyter), is probably the most consistent within patristic traditions (thus, see Irenaeus, the Gospel prologues, Tertullian, Clement, Origen, Eusebius, Epiphanius, Chrysostom, Jerome).

Both to scholars and to laity, this aspect of the tradition is so well known that its *oddity* probably no longer surprises. The most highly elaborated of New Testament traditions about someone named Mark, the Lukan portrayal of John Mark in Acts, is *least* exploited in patristic ruminations on the Second Evangelist; it is altogether ignored in Dionysius's mention of John Mark and implicit only in the late Monarchian prologue.[2] The close association of a Mark with the apostle Paul, known to us through the Pauline epistolary traditions, is alluded to by Adamantius, the *Apostolic Constitutions,* and Jerome (who, in commenting on Philemon 24, expresses uncertainty that its Mark authored the Markan Gospel). The least developed of New Testament traditions about Mark, which couples him with Peter (only at 1 Peter 5:13), is, ironically, *the most persistent and developed* among the fathers of the early church. Nor is that development usually accomplished through a blending of the several New Testament traditions: except for the Monarchian prologue, the patristic sources that we have studied tend to elaborate only a Petrine tradition about Mark the Evangelist, disregarding the Lukan and Pauline alternatives.

To my mind a satisfying explanation for the origin of this tradition that associates Mark with Peter is still forthcoming. Biblical scholars usually have regarded its earliest patristic expression (in Papias) as a deduction from 1 Peter 5:13.[3] As we have seen, it is not at all clear that Papias made such an inference on that basis (even if *H.E.* 3.39.17 implies that Eusebius thought so). With Clement and Origen we can document an unwarranted deduction from 1 Peter of the Markan Gospel's authorship. Yet a linking of the Second Evangelist with Peter—usually not with the Paul of Acts or of the Pauline Epistles— appears to have firmly settled into the tradition long before any "biblical proof" was proffered in the late second or early third century. In other words, the interpretation of 1 Peter 5:13 as a reference to the Second Evangelist may not have triggered patristic reflection on Mark; that exegesis may have become customary and intelligible only after the association of the Markan Gospel with Peter had *already* been popularized within Asian and European Christianity. Indeed, though impossible to prove, the alignment of Mark with Peter in 1 Peter 5:13 conceivably could have been yet another precipitate, not the catalyst, of the same popular tradition. At the end of the day we may never be able to identify the origin of the portrayal of Mark as Peter's interpreter, so popular in patristic Christianity.

3. *Usually, the linkage of Mark with an apostle reflects widespread patristic concerns about the fidelity of the Markan tradition to the church's proclamation of Jesus.* Because it is so persistent among the fathers, and effectively incorporates other aspects that we have encountered, this feature is of unusual importance. From the earliest testimonies onward patristic portrayals of Mark were not crafted for their own sake. In every case they appear to have served the church's quest for *memory* of particular traditions about Jesus and *warrant* for their propagation, orally or literarily. This holds no less for patristic mavericks (like the author of the Monarchian prologue) than for the proponents of formative catholicism (such as Papias, Justin, Irenaeus, Clement, Origen,[4] Tertullian, the anti-Marcionite prologue, the *Apos-*

tolic Constitutions, Epiphanius, Jerome). In patristic Christianity these issues of recollection and authorization are frequently resolved into the concept of apostolicity. Accordingly, the Evangelist Mark is considered the satellite of an apostle (usually Peter); ranged alongside an apostolic figure (Paul, for Hippolytus and the *Apostolic Constitutions*; Matthew and John, for Tertullian and Augustine); interpreted within theological frameworks of apostolic succession (Irenaeus and Eusebius); or, in its most exaggerated expression, identified *as* an apostle (Adamantius).[5]

At this point, however, there is an interesting catch in most of the fathers' interpretations of Mark. Frequently, indeed too often to seem merely accidental, Mark's apostolicity is somehow chastened even as it is avowed. This takes many different forms: from Papias's early, defensive comments about Markan style to Augustine's later portrait of Mark as Matthew's epitomizer. In between we find all manner of supposed deviations of Mark from an unblemished apostolic norm: Peter's distance or death (Irenaeus, the anti-Marcionite prologue), the apostle's diffidence (Clement), the Evangelist's disfigurement (Hippolytus, the Gospel prologues), even Mark's onetime apostasy (Epiphanius) or exegetical inaccuracy (Jerome). Though not universal (see Tertullian and Origen), this enigmatic tendency is captured in the most ragged of our fragments, from the Muratorian Canon: here, as elsewhere, with Mark it is "yes, but"—even when the substance of the reservation is unclear or disputed.

4. *Commonly, Rome (in particular), Italy (more generally), is identified as a locale either for Mark's literary activity or for his association with Peter.* With 1 Peter, the conjunction of Mark-Peter-Rome can be documented at least as early as perhaps the last decade of the first century. It is recalled by Irenaeus a century later. The location of Mark's Gospel in Europe, after Peter's death or departure, may have been postulated in stages of increasing precision: the anti-Marcionite and Monarchian prologues' obscure and undatable suggestion of provenance ("in [the regions of] Italy") may have arisen as a cautious inference from 1 Peter and Irenaeus, which, in Eastern Christianity by the third century, was further reworked into the assertion that Mark's Gospel was composed in the city of Rome, contemporaneous with Peter's ministry (Clement, Origen, Eusebius, Epiphanius, Jerome).[6] Interestingly, Western traditions that more vaguely locate Mark's Gospel also tend to fix its composition after Peter's death; Eastern traditions that more precisely place the Gospel in Rome also tend to synchronize its composition with the career of that see's legendary patriarch.

5. Once introduced into its traditions (at least as early as the late second century), *an association of Mark, though usually not Mark's Gospel, with Alexandria is typically maintained in Eastern Christianity* (thus, Clement, Eusebius, Epiphanius, Jerome; though cf. Origen). As demonstrated by the Monarchian prologue (here and elsewhere, probably through Jerome's influence), this aspect of the tradition is not unknown in Western Christianity; neither, however, does it seem widespread in the West (cf. Hippolytus, the anti-Marcionite prologue, Tertullian, Augustine). Alexandria also tends to drop out of the Markan picture among the few Eastern witnesses that coordinate the Evangelist with Paul, not with Peter (Adamantius, the *Apostolic Constitutions*). Whereas Mark's relationship with Rome appears generally among traditions in both the West and the East, his connection with Alexandria tends to be emphasized in the East. Clement reports that Mark wrote a second, more spiritual Gospel in Alexandria; that city is assumed to be the provenance of the canonical Markan Gospel only by Chrysostom, probably through his misunderstanding of either Clement or Eusebius.

Whereas Mark's Roman association may well have been an extrapolation from the tradition concerning Peter's later career,[7] it is hard to say why a putative relationship between Mark and Alexandria would ever have been forged to start with. A venerated "Secret Gospel," thought to be a recension of the Second Gospel by the Second Evangelist, might suffice to explain Clement's view of Mark's prominence in Alexandria. This explanation, however, is not corroborated by Clement's successors, many of whom remembered Mark's tie with Egyptian Christianity but reported nothing of his "more spiritual Gospel" (owing, perhaps, to its Gnostic affinities). Once Mark's derivative apostolicity becomes established in the tradition the connection between Mark and Alexandria can be generally, and I think accurately, understood as a way of providing an apostolic foundation for a major church. Nevertheless, the precise reasons for *Mark's* linkage with Alexandria remain, in my judgment, opaque. The reasons for this affiliation, like the Evangelist's supposed relationship with Peter, may be forever lost to us.[8]

Fourth and finally, *the portraits of Mark in patristic Christianity often appear to have been accommodated to the specific leanings of the various portraitists*. At a superficial level the figure of Mark sometimes attracts, and effectively sanctions, the perspectives of those who assume responsibility for that Evangelist's figuration. Thus, Mark can be portrayed alternately as an illustrious ecclesiarch (Jerome) or Peter's shadow (Tertullian), as an advocate of either catholic orthodoxy

(Hippolytus, Adamantius, Epiphanius), catholic Gnosticism (Clement), or dynamic Monarchianism (the Monarchian prologue).

More generally, and perhaps more profoundly, patristic interest in Mark as an "authorial personality" tends to be secondary to, and commensurate with, a primary interest in the distinctive literary or religious characteristics of a written Gospel attributed to him. We observe this as early as Papias, who defends the disorganization of Markan composition on the basis of its correspondence with equally disarrayed teachings of Peter, whose interpreter Mark was presumed to be. Though much later and materially uncommon, the Monarchian prologue exhibits the same tendency by essaying an interpretation of the Second Gospel which purportedly accords with a "biographical profile" of its "priestly Evangelist." Likewise, a sketch of Mark proves serviceable for Clement's explanation of the *Secret Gospel*'s divergence from its canonical precursor. Analogously, Mark's relationship with an apostolic forebear, whether Peter (Chrysostom) or Matthew (Augustine), is summoned to account for his Gospel's brevity, or for its status within a fourfold Gospel canon (the Muratorian fragment, Irenaeus, Eusebius). Perhaps in a few cases (Hippolytus, the anti-Marcionite prologue) we can detect traces of fledgling curiosity in Mark's persona, as it was being crafted by patristic commentators; by and large, however, "the personality of Mark" is invoked, interpreted, and refashioned to make sense of some literature that was religiously important to early Christians. When the fathers' concerns shift to matters, like scriptural inspiration or the unity of Christian witness, which tend to downplay the individuality of apostolic writings, the figure of Mark correlatively recedes (thus, see Justin, Tatian, Tertullian, Origen, Augustine).

Here, strictly speaking, our investigation of the figure, or figures, of Mark in Christianity of the first four centuries draws to a close. Nowhere is that personality planted, much less cultivated, in the Second Gospel that was canonized as scripture by and for the Christian church. Nor is the attachment of this persona with that Gospel expressed or necessarily assumed by any of the New Testament authors.

Yet, early on and pervasively, a relationship between an anonymous Evangelist, denominated as Mark, and a particular Gospel, written in the first century, was presupposed and pondered by Christian interpreters. This we have witnessed in the preceding three chapters. Moreover, it is self-evident from the very title that was given by the church to that book: "The Gospel according to Mark." Had not a connection between this authorial figure and that literary work been remembered or imagined, even to the present day, it is improbable that so negligible a character as Mark would ever be ranged among those "personalities of the New Testament" thought worthy of study in the late twentieth century. Indeed, save for that association, surely Mark would have been buried among those "trivial personalities decomposing in the eternity of print," whose sight so nauseated Virginia Woolf.[9]

Accordingly, in the next two chapters we turn to the Gospel attributed to Mark, inquiring about the *consonance* of its own concerns with patristic presentations of Mark the Evangelist. Differently phrased, we shall raise a difficult question, or cluster of related questions, in which the Markan Gospel does not, indeed could not, express any interest whatever: Was the patristic ascription of this Gospel to Mark meaningful or significant in any historical, social, religious, or theological sense?

NOTES

1. The exception here may be Jerome (*De vir.* 8). On the other hand, as I have already suggested, in *De viris illustribus* Jerome was inclined, for apologetic reasons, to err on the side of comprehensiveness in recounting Christianity's "famous men" (numbering among them even non-Christians such as Josephus and Philo). Also, at this point in Christian history, the New Testament Evangelists could hardly be ignored in a work that attempted to persuade pagans of the riches of Christian literature.

2. As discussed in chapter 4, the remembrance of John Mark's defection in Acts may underlie the later characterization of the Second Evangelist's "stump-finger(s)."

3. Representative in this respect is Rudolf Pesch, "Die Zuschreibung der Evangelien an apostolische Verfasser," *ZTK* 97 (1975): 56–71; Pesch, *Das Markusevangelium*, HTKNT (Freiburg: Herder, 1976), 1:3–11.

4. Though Origen's orthodoxy was challenged even during his own lifetime (as evidenced by his excommunication from the Alexandrian church in 231), we need not debate that question here. As Quasten notes (*Patrology*, vol. 2: *The Ante-Nicene Literature after Irenaeus* (Utrecht-Antwerp and Westminster, Md.: Spectrum/Newman, 1953), 39–40, citing *De princ.* Pref.2), Origen endeavored to be orthodox; for our purposes that suffices to warrant his inclusion among these representatives of formative Catholicism.

5. In the conclusion we shall ponder, at somewhat greater length, the intersection of apostolicity and portrayals of the Evangelist.

6. The fact that the more general reference to "Italy" even enters the tradition at all, after "Rome" had long been considered the place of association of Mark with Peter, may indirectly support an earlier suggestion: 1 Peter 5:13 was not the fount from which gushed all patristic speculation about the composition of the Gospel of Mark.

7. See chapter 8.

8. Secondary studies treating this question are quite sparse. Myrtle Strode-Jackson offers a lively and entertaining, but generally uncritical, chapter on "Mark the Evangelist and the Church in Egypt" in her *Lives and Legends of Apostles and Evangelists* (London: Religious Tract Society, 1928), 99–116. A disciplined review of the relevant primary sources in the patristic period and beyond is presented by John J. Gunther, "The Association of Mark and Barnabas with Egyptian Christianity (Parts I and II)," *EvQ* 54 (1982): 219–33; 55 (1983): 21–29.

9. Virginia Woolf, *The Common Reader* (New York: Harcourt, Brace and Company, 1925), 301. In its proper context Woolf's barb is aimed not at biblical authors but, instead, at incompetent essayists.

The Second Gospel and
Its Evangelist

Chapter Seven

The Second Gospel
and the Traditions about Mark (I)
Evangelical Author and Petrine Authority

Why was the New Testament's Second Gospel, an anonymous document, attributed by patristic Christianity to Mark? In what sense, if any, was this ascription meaningful?

These are the questions of modern critical readers. As such, they are not framed in patristic literature; naturally, Mark's Gospel does not pose them at all. Such queries as we address to ancient texts are neither illegitimate in principle nor superior to those of their own authors. They are simply different, and that difference should be recognized and respected. So, if we compare the Second Gospel with what some early Christians said about Mark the Evangelist, and contemplate the significance of that association, at the outset we should bear in mind that this is *our* question, not that of the texts that constitute the basis of our inquiry.

Clarity is necessary on another matter. Over the decades in which Mark's Gospel has been compared with later statements about its authorship, the question of historicity has tended to engross scholarly attention. In general, critics have usually settled into one of two camps. More conservative researchers have perceived some correspondence between patristic claims about Mark the Evangelist and the Gospel according to Mark, sometimes interpreting such coherence as historical authentication of that Gospel's portrayal of Jesus. More liberal investigators have often discerned little or no such coherence and, not infrequently, have regarded patristic comments about Mark and the Second Gospel as historically worthless figments of early Christians' pious imaginations. Some caricature may lurk in this characterization, but I think not much.

In comparing ancient religious literature with religious traditions about its production, historical questions are valid and signficant. Indeed, they are inevitable, insofar as the traditions in question fasten one's mind upon a document's origins within a religion's past. These, however, are not the only questions worth raising, much less the questions of supreme importance. When reading testimonies to the circumstances attending the creation of Mark's Gospel, we should keep in mind that patristic concerns are preeminently *religious* in nature. In a word, the fathers were engaged in the enterprise of making sense, religiously, of a document that for them had come to execise considerable influence on their understanding of Christian faith.[1] Their location of the Second Gospel within Christianity's formative history is, in itself, an important index of that religious endeavor; accordingly, it merits our attention. On the other hand, comparison of different religious phenomena, such as religious texts and the traditions about their origins, need not have as their sole or even primary goal the confirmation (or disproof) of their "genealogical" relationship. On this point Jonathan Z. Smith offers us some conceptual clarity:

> This is to say, comparison does not necessarily tell us how things "are" (the far from latent presupposition that lies behind the notion of the "genealogical" with its quest for "real" historical connections); like models and metaphors, comparison tells us how things might be conceived, how they might be "redescribed," in Max Black's useful term. A comparison is a disciplined exaggeration in the service of knowledge. It lifts out and strongly marks certain features within difference as being of possible intellectual significance, expressed in the rhetoric of their being "like" in some stipulated fashion. Comparison provides the means by which we "re-vision" phenomena as our data in order to solve our theoretical problems.[2]

In this chapter and the next we shall compare, from different angles of vision, two sets of religious phenomena: (1) the Gospel according to Mark and (2) the cluster of traditions associated by the early fathers with Mark the Evangelist. As suggested in the synopsis in chapter 6, the salient features in the patristic portrayal of Mark are five:

1. Mark is a literary figure, or evangelical author,
2. whose relationship to the apostle Peter
3. accredits, to a chastened degree, his Gospel's presentation of Jesus.
4. Mark's association with Peter, or his literary activity, is typically localized in Rome,

5. though Mark, if not the Second Gospel, is sometimes associated with Alexandria.

In "re-visioning," or "redescribing," the literary phenomena of the Second Gospel in the light of these patristic traditions, we need to stipulate some general ways in which their likeness or difference may be explored. Here, I propose, are four potentially fruitful, and appreciably overlapping, areas of questioning:

1. Historical: To what degree, if any, can the early fathers' statements about the Markan Gospel and Evangelist be confirmed?
2. Sociological: To what degree, if any, do patristic traditions about the provenance of that Evangelist or Gospel cohere with the evidence suggested by the Gospel itself?
3. Theological: To what degree, if any, are these traditions about Mark consistent with the theology of the Second Gospel?
4. Religious: How do patristic references to the figure of Mark or to the Gospel of Mark function within the larger framework of early Christian belief and practice?

What follows, therefore, is a comparison of the Second Gospel with what some early Christians believed to be true of its author. Let us make no mistake: we are trafficking in the realm of "disciplined exaggeration," not merely because that is Smith's overall assessment of comparison in the study of religion but, more fundamentally, because such distortion is endemic to our task. After all, a profile of the Evangelist no more arises from the exegesis of Mark's Gospel than such exegesis ostensibly guided the fathers to their conclusions about the legendary figure behind the Second Gospel. Whether the ensuing exercise yields knowledge of interest or intellectual significance, we shall see.

THE EVANGELIST MARK AS AUTHOR

While patristic sources vary in the degree to which they comment on Mark's personality, the description of Mark as a literary figure is probably the most prevalent, and often dominant, aspect of their presentations. In Christian traditions of the second, third, and fourth centuries Mark is usually considered to be an author of Christian literature about Jesus. Those traditions tend not to focus on the portrayals of Mark in Acts, Philemon, Colossians, 2 Timothy, or 1 Peter; instead, the characterization of Mark as a writer, which is mentioned nowhere in the New Testament, is precisely the feature on which most of the fathers concentrate.

The Historical Conundrum

Historically, little may be said with confidence on this subject. That a document like Mark's Gospel[3] was composed with care, perhaps even sophistication, is widely accepted within the scholarly guild, simply because that judgment can be confirmed on the face of the text itself. Appreciation is commonplace among Markan commentators for the various techniques that have been used in adapting the Gospel's likely traditions: arrangements of similar stories that build to a climax (e.g., 2:1–3:6, 11:27–12:37), creative juxtapositions of disparate materials (e.g., 3:1–6, 19–35; 5:21–43; 11:12–25), and repetitive cycles of confessional and didactic discourse (8:31–9:1, 9:30–37, 10:32–45).[4] Although no consensus exists on the narrative's precise structure, its central portion (8:22–10:52) is generally regarded as pivotal for interpretation.[5] The Second Gospel even seems to demonstrate some awareness and deployment of classical rhetoric.[6] Such literary results do not happen randomly: responsibility for them surely fell to some person or persons, significant among whom could have been someone named Mark. This mundane possibility is conceded even by commentators who dispute the reliability of much patristic tradition about the Second Gospel.[7]

For at least two reasons, however, establishing the historicity of this ascription is, in my judgment, practically impossible. First, the church fathers themselves offer no support for this identification (other than their own traditional antecedents, which could be as easily grounded in legend as in fact). Second, and most problematically, the Gospel itself never reveals the identity of its author. Because of its presumption of a "criterion of dissimilarity,"[8] the strongest argument in favor of the Second Gospel's having been written by someone named Mark may still be that of Burnett Hillman Streeter: precisely because the primitive church tended to regard significant writings as the work of apostles, "the burden of proof is on those who would assert the traditional authorship of Matthew and John and on those who would deny it in the case of Mark and Luke."[9] On the other hand, so leery of patristic biases have many scholars become that the burden of proof tends to be shifted onto those who would give any credence whatever to the fathers' comments on the Gospel's authorship.[10] On balance, to the historicity of assigning the Markan Gospel to Mark—whoever that may have been or may have been imagined to be—we must render a verdict of *non olet sed non liquet*: it may not smell fishy, but it can't be proven.

Some Social and Preliterary Considerations

All is not bleak, however: with regard to the social and literary environment that conditioned the Second Gospel, some critics, patristic and modern, point in some common directions. Without pretending to summarize the intricacy of Markan tradition criticism,[11] we can simply point out that Mark's Gospel appears not to have sprung, pristine and without precedent, from the inventive genius of a creative composer. Although Mark's sources are indeterminate and the subject of considerable debate, probably underlying the Gospel are primitive traditions about Jesus, permeated with overt or covert interpretations of the Old Testament (e.g., 1:2–3, 11; 15:24, 29, 34), which could have circulated orally or in writing among early Christians and which may have been known to Mark's audience in either piecemeal form or smaller collections.[12] When subjected to careful scrutiny the narrative of the Second Gospel appears to contain materials of different literary genres: sayings (e.g., 9:42–50) and parables (4:3–32, 12:1–12) attributed to Jesus, miracle stories (4:35–5:43), stylized controversies between Jesus and his adversaries (3:22–30, 12:13–27), an apocalyptic farewell discourse of Jesus to his disciples (13:1–37), and accounts of Jesus' last days in Jerusalem (14:1–15:39).

Naturally, these categories are modern inventions that were neither conceived nor employed by patristic interpreters. On the other hand, we have seen that Papias's remarks, for example, can be interpreted as indirectly corroborating the tendency of these modern scholarly appraisals of the Second Gospel—if Papias was defending a Markan literary enterprise that (1) is not necessarily to be equated with the Second Gospel that we know and (2) bespeaks, in any case, a circuitous yet significant transition from oral to written transmission of traditions about Jesus.[13] Of course, even if we decide that Papias subscribed to a rather more complex theory of the Markan Gospel's origins, a simpler if not simplistic formulation seems to be presumed by some other church fathers (Irenaeus, the Gospel prologues, Hippolytus), if not by all (Clement, Augustine). On a related matter there is greater concord: most of the patristic testimonies regard Mark's Gospel as a product, as it were, "of the church, by the church, and for the church." With some demurrals,[14] that judgment is probably shared by the majority of modern critics as well.

Some Literary and Religious Implications

Although often overlooked amid controversy over the fathers' historical veracity, some other implications of their interest in Mark as an evangelical author seem to me complex and worth pondering. For

example, patristic concentration on the authorship of the Second
Gospel (or, possibly, its literary predecessors), often to the neglect of
its actual contents, signals a departure from the book's own probable
intentions. Mark's Gospel says nothing of its own authorship yet much
about the significance of Jesus.[15] To the degree that many of the earliest
commentators become less engaged with Mark's content, and more
absorbed with its apostolic authorization, a measure of incoherence
may have crept between the Second Gospel and patristic reflections on
it.

Yet the matter is not so simple. On the one hand, the fathers'
concern for apostolicity appears not to have been for its own sake but,
rather, in the interest of securing the authority of Mark's content, that
Gospel's presentation of Jesus.[16] On the other hand, by executing
another kind of shift—away from an oral to a written narrative—the
author of Mark's Gospel effectively invited, even if he did not promote,
that reflection on authorship with which patristic interpreters were
engaged. The writer of the Second Gospel creates less explicit distance
between himself and the story that he recounts than, say, the Fourth
Evangelist, who intermittently suspends his narrative for commentary
aimed at his audience (see John 1:1–18; 2:11, 21–22; 4:54; 5:18; 11:13;
12:16). Moreover, the writers of the Third and Fourth Gospels also
reveal more overtly their literary intentions, in address directed to
their readers (Luke 1:1–4; John 20:30–31), than does the author of
Mark. Still, when Jesus' Olivet address to the disciples is interrupted
with the urgent counsel "Let the reader understand" (13:14, to take
one of the most obvious instances),[17] an author has deliberately distanced himself from sheer narration and has flung down a challenge to
his book's readers, whose own existence is simultaneously acknowledged.[18] Thus, if the content of the Second Gospel does not encourage,
much less guide, later patristic speculation on its authorship, its very
acknowledgment of *having* an author arguably opens the door to those
ruminations.

Embedded in this literary decision are theological consequences.
The moment that a religious document like Mark acknowledges, however elliptically, that behind it stands an author, its temporality is
implicitly conceded and something of its transcendent quality is diminished. Although the reader of Mark is maneuvered into accepting its
author's point of view as faithful to God's own (see Mark 1:1, 11; 8:31;
9:7), the perspective remains nonetheless that of a particular author
who narrates the story of Jesus, not from some timeless Olympian
vantage point but, rather, within the context of human circumstances.[19]

> We read the story of Jesus Christ in a different way from
> the mighty acts of Yahweh [in the Old Testament] precisely
> because it reads like the experiences authenticated by the
> very persons who underwent them, or at least by persons in
> direct contact with the original witnesses. . . . Such a person
> [as Mark] may, in fact, have had little or nothing to do with
> the text as we now have it. Nevertheless, the point remains,
> and we cannot and should not escape it, that the gospels are
> presented to us as the works of particular "authors" and
> this is a significant, inescapable fact about the kind of books
> the Gospels are, however complex the process by which
> they came to be formed.[20]

If Brian Wicker's appraisal is sound, then the church fathers' tendency to read the Second Gospel as the work of an author was by no means naive or inappropriate, however historically problematic some of their judgments about that author may have been. In fact, by focusing on the religious considerations of Mark's author—fidelity in transmitting apostolic beliefs about Jesus the Christ—patristic observers may have been rather more perceptive than those modern interpreters who have tried to discern the author's concerns from this Gospel's "exceptional vividness" and "unmistakable aroma of [historical] truth."[21] To the contrary, as Benjamin Wisner Bacon observed almost seventy years ago, "Only those whose exposition of [Mark] proceeds on the principle that its anecdotes are arranged primarily in the interest of religious edification (including apologetic), and only secondarily in the interest of biography or history, will do real justice to the facts. On this point [John] the Elder's criticism is more penetrating than most of that put forward today."[22]

MARK AND PETER

Some Attempts at Historical Reconstruction

Second only to his being identified as an author of evangelical proclamation, Mark's association with Peter is an unusually persistent feature in patristic traditions Eastern (Papias, Clement, Origen, Eusebius, Epiphanius, Chrysostom, Jerome) and Western (Irenaeus, the Gospel prologues, Tertullian). Historically, are there warrants for the linkage of Peter with the Second Evangelist?

1. Some scholars think so.[23] For example, Ralph P. Martin has argued that from the references to Mark in the New Testament there arises a consistent picture, which goes unchallenged during the patristic age: "John, whose other name was Mark" (Acts 12:25) not only

traveled with Paul and Barnabas but also was in Rome with Peter (as suggested by 1 Peter 5:13). To refute Marcion's Gnostic appropriation of Luke's Gospel, Papias stressed Mark's Petrine association, thus obscuring Mark's closer ties with Paul; still, "The testimonium of Papias (recorded in Eusebius HE xxxix) that situates Mark at Rome with Peter . . . thus confirms the authenticity of Mark's authorship of his Gospel, since authenticity depends on his intimate association with Peter, whose teaching he purportedly related."[24]

This is a coherent reconstruction, granting certain premises. Yet the thrust of our examination thus far has cast doubt upon many of those assumptions. First, certainly within the New Testament and largely within patristic tradition of the first four centuries, the coherence perceived by Martin among the Lukan, Pauline, and Petrine depictions of Mark cannot be clearly demonstrated. To be sure, a historian can synthesize those traditions and can formulate, as Martin has done, a reasonable harmony among the portrayals of Mark in Acts and the New Testament letters. However, such a cross-canonical harmony is neither attempted nor even suggested within either Acts, the Pauline corpus, or 1 Peter,[25] nor do most of the early fathers blend these apparently separate traditions about Mark.[26] Strictly speaking, "the consistent picture" of Mark to which Martin refers is found nowhere in the New Testament; that consistency is a product of a particular historian's interpretation of the evidence.

Second, even if Martin's minority judgment regarding the authorship of 1 Peter were sustained (namely, that the letter was indeed written by that apostle), this in itself would not demonstrably bear on the alleged association of Peter with the author of Mark's Gospel. (1) On the one hand, nowhere in the Second Gospel is the claim for such a relationship ever made or even hinted. (2) Nowhere in 1 Peter, on the other hand, is Mark ever associated with the Second Gospel or any other literature. (3) Nor is it clear that Papias—a source for some later patristic assessments of the Gospels[27] and the linchpin of Martin's own thesis—has in mind Mark's Gospel or has drawn any conclusions on the subject of Mark's literary activity from 1 Peter or is preoccupied by the question of the Second Gospel's authenticity as such.[28] More-over, contrary to Martin's proposal, the Papias-fragment says nothing about Rome (the "Babylon" of 1 Peter 5:13). In any case, Papias attributes his information about Mark and Peter to the Elder John, not to 1 Peter. Strictly speaking, therefore, neither Papias nor 1 Peter authenticates the authorship of Mark's Gospel by an associate of Peter; on that specific topic neither witness corroborates the testimony of the other.

Third, it seems to me that the question of historicity is not so much resolved as begged by Martin's conclusion: "The testimonium of Papias . . . confirms the authenticity of Mark's authorship of his Gospel, since authenticity depends upon his intimate association with Peter."[29] Even if Papias had been primarily concerned with the Markan/Petrine authenticity of the Second Gospel, as Martin believes,[30] such authenticity would not be substantiated by the belief that Mark and Peter were closely related: those two convictions may have mirrored each other while proving nothing. That is to say, the conclusion that Mark's Gospel enjoys a kind of "authenticity" could easily and understandably have been fathered by the prior—but perhaps historically unwarranted—belief that Peter and Mark were indeed so closely related. In that way some patristic Christians, if not Papias, might have "noodled through" the matter; if so, however, this would teach us something about circular reasoning among early Christians, little or nothing about the historicity of the supposed Markan-Petrine axis of the Second Gospel.

2. Martin's hypothesis well exemplifies a case for the historicity of the Second Gospel's Petrine derivation that tries to bring patristic traditions into direct alignment with the New Testament evidence. Another kind of historical argument attempts to discern a Petrine "homiletical" template underlying the structure of the Second Gospel. Thus, William Lane has proposed that the basic outline of Mark is encapsulated by Peter's sermon in Acts 10:36–41: an introduction to the message of Jesus Christ (Mark 1:1/Acts 10:36); the original spread of that message from Galilee (Mark 1:14/Acts 10:37); the anointing of Jesus with the Holy Spirit (Mark 1:10/Acts 10:38); Jesus' divinely directed ministry of healing, attending the rout of demonic forces (Mark 1:16–10:52/Acts 10:38); Jesus' ministry in Jerusalem (Mark 11–14/Acts 10:39a), culminating in his crucifixion (Mark 15:1–39/Acts 10:39b) and resurrection (Mark 16:1–8/Acts 10:40). For Lane the implication of these parallels is that the content of Mark derives from the preaching of Peter, much as the church fathers asserted.[31]

Like others who have undertaken such analyses,[32] Lane points up some interesting parallels. In pondering them and their putative historical importance, at least two questions should be raised.[33] First, are the parallels between Acts 10:36–41 and the Gospel of Mark sufficiently extensive to be significant? For instance, does the general statement in Acts 10:38 (that Jesus "went about doing good and healing all who were oppressed by the devil, for God was with him") precisely correspond with the diverse stories and sayings contained in Mark 1:16–10:52? What do we make of those features in the Second Gospel which do not correspond with the substance of the sermon in Acts 10 (such as Jesus' repeated controversies with the religious establishment [Mark 2:1–3:6, 7:1–22, 8:11–13]), or those aspects of Peter's preaching in Acts 10 without parallel in Mark (like the appearances and missionary commission of the risen Jesus [Acts 10:40b–42])?[34] Second, and more burdensome for the question of historicity, is the fact that in its present form in Acts 10:34–43 we have not Peter's preaching as such but, rather, *Luke's portrayal* of Peter's preaching. Indeed, all of the speeches and sermons in Acts have been filtered through the mind of another and recast in a form appropriate to the story of the church as that later author wished to tell it.[35] Would we really expect Luke, in Acts, to attribute to the apostles a presentation of Jesus' ministry which was inconsistent with that presented by Luke himself in the Third Gospel—a narrative, moreover, whose basic structure was very likely appropriated from Mark?[36]

3. A similar though more indirect tack has been taken by other interpreters: the tendency to see Peter's own hand upon the Second Gospel's portrait of that disciple, "warts and all." Along with his brother Andrew, Peter is the first of the disciples to be called in Mark (1:16–18); he stands at the head of the list of the Twelve (3:16–19a) and is always the first to be mentioned among an inner group of disciples (1:29, 5:37, 9:2, 13:3, 14:33). Typically, he serves as spokesman for the Twelve (1:36, 8:29, 9:5–6, 10:28, 11:21, 14:29–31). Though his desertion is predicted and reported at length (14:30, 66–72), Peter, from among all of the Twelve, follows Jesus longest (14:54), openly repents of his apostasy (14:72), and is singled out as an intended recipient of the news of Jesus' resurrection (16:7). Nevertheless, in Mark's Gospel Peter is a blemished figure, who responds vapidly or contrarily to Jesus (8:32, 9:5–6, 14:29–31). His opposition to Jesus is characterized as satanic (8:33), his inconstancy at Gethsemane is pointedly chastised (14:37), and his defection from Jesus is recounted in unflattering detail (14:66–72). Although much of this mottled characterization of Peter is found also in Matthew and Luke, those later Gospels tend to delete or tone down these harsher features as well as to supplement Mark's presentation with more complimentary touches (e.g., Matt 16:16b–19, 17:24–27; Luke 5:1–11; 22:31, 45; 24:34).[37]

Most readers of Mark will concede that its presentation of Peter is somewhat scrambled; where they diverge is in their explanations for this ambivalence. Some, like Béda Rigaux, have ventured a historical solution to this literary phenomenon: if Peter is prominent, for good or ill, in the Second Gospel, and if one assumes that Mark was not out to denigrate the apostle, then Mark's source for these Petrine passages must have been Peter himself (a conclusion that accords with patristic testimonies).[38] The capstone of this argument, for others than Rigaux, lies in the vivid, terse style of the Second Gospel, "the presence [within it] of those descriptive touches which reproduce for us not only the event, but the scene and the surroundings as well."[39] According to J. B. Phillips, "[w]e cannot help feeling the presence of Peter, the man who was there at the time."[40]

Beyond the subjectivism implied in the preceding quotations, the principal difficulty with this kind of analysis is, once again, the practical impossibility of its verification. Quite possibly, a degree of historical reminiscence does lie behind the variegated picture of the apostle in Mark: after all, the inconstancy of Simon Peter in the Second Gospel seems not all that far removed from the waffling of which Cephas is accused by Paul in Galatians (2:1–14, although Paul's judgment of character at Antioch was hardly dispassionate).[41] On the other hand, we must reckon with other factors. Between the Peter of history and the Gospel of Mark intervened thirty to forty years of Christian tradition, some of which probably layered legendary or tendentious accretions onto the image of Peter. Could the discrepancies in Mark's depiction of the apostle be partially attributed to tensions between an anti-Peter strain in some of those traditions and the Evangelist's own, more favorable, perspective on Peter?[42] Perhaps so, even though this reconstruction is as practically unverifiable as the other explanations we have just reviewed.[43] Easier to substantiate is a strictly literary datum: in Mark's Gospel Peter's blend of attributes, favorable and unfavorable, is not unique to him but, instead, embodies the general virtues and failings of the Twelve (see, e.g., 1:16–20; 3:13–19a; 4:35–41; 6:6b–13, 30; 8:14–21; 9:33–41; 10:35–45). Exactly how one should assess the significance of this characterization for Markan theology has been among scholars a subject of heated debate.[44] For our purposes we need note only that the presentation of Peter in the Second Gospel can be attributed to the Evangelist's (or his sources') theological interests, beyond, if not apart from, whatever historical reality may underlie that presentation.

To me it seems, on balance, that we lack enough hard, pertinent evidence to confirm the historicity of the connection between the apostle Peter and the Second Evangelist or his Gospel. That association is neither inconceivable nor implausible; neither, however, do we possess the resources by which it might be historically verified. Some scholars have wondered how a Gospel, given such short shrift by the fathers as was Mark's, could ever have survived had it not been based on Peter's reminiscences.[45] As historical explanation, a rhetorical question of this kind will not ultimately satisfy—though it may point us in the direction of a more fruitful line of inquiry.

Some Religious and Theological Dimensions

Whatever its historical basis, there can be no doubt that the fathers of the church tended to relate the figure of Mark with a tradition closely associated with the apostle Peter. Indeed, as we have witnessed,[46] some of the earliest patristic testimony to Mark the Evangelist appears far less concerned with his personality or biography, as such, and far more interested in his Petrine apostolicity: that is to say, the location of that figure within a circle of early Christianity considered to be Petrine in some theological or more generally religious sense.

Some recent trends in scholarship suggest that the situation of the Markan Gospel within a broader stream of early Petrine Christianity is intelligible and hardly farfetched. John H. Elliott has called attention to an impressive range of affinities between 1 Peter and the Gospel of Mark, which suggest their participation in a common tradition.[47]

1. With respect to social conditions both 1 Peter and the Second Gospel appear to have emerged from marginal, perhaps even sectarian, communities that were attempting to stake out their identities over against both Jewish and Greco-Roman society (1 Pet 2:7–8, 4:3–6; Mark 4:11–12, 7:1–30, 10:42), while at the same time motivated by a more ecumenical, missionary impulse (1 Pet 2:12, 3:1; Mark 11:17; 13:10, 27; 14:9).[48] "Both [documents] distinguish those who heed the call of Jesus in faith and follow him from those who reject him, the righteous elect from the unrighteous sinners, those who live by the will of God from those who follow human ordinances and conventions, insiders from outsiders."[49] On the one hand, both 1 Peter and Mark betoken a conservative Christian response to the Roman government (1 Pet 2:13–14, 3:14b–16; Mark 12:13–17, 15:39); on the other hand, both documents reflect the perspective that tension exists between nonbelieving outsiders and Christian believers, resulting in the latter's innocent suffering (1 Pet 3:8–4:2; Mark 4:13–20, 10:29–30, 13:9–13).

2. Also revealed in these writings is at tacit dependence on particular religious resources, whose appropriation contributed to the catalysis of their social stance. The communities implied by both 1 Peter and Mark's Gospel appear to draw from some common Palestinian and Diaspora Christian traditions (1 Pet 2:25, 3:22, 5:4; Mark 12:36; 14:27, 62), which come specifically into focus on the proclamation of Jesus' suffering, death, and resurrection (1 Pet 2:21–25; Mark 8:31, 9:31, 10:33–34), and the interpretation of Jesus' passion as a ransom or redemption for sin (Mark 10:45; 1 Pet 1:18–19, 2:24). This *kerygma*, in

turn, becomes crucial among believers for interpreting their own suffering (1 Pet 2:4–10, 4:13–14; Mark 8:34–37, 12:1–12).

3. Kindred theologies in Mark and 1 Peter arise from this nexus of tradition and social setting. For example, both documents betray commitments to the community's upbuilding and universal mission, undertaken on the eve of Jesus' imminent, revelatory return (Mark 13:10, 24–27; 1 Pet 1:6–7, 4:7–12).[50] Both writings portray faithful religious adherence as the obedience of God's "elect" to the doing of God's will (Mark 3:35, 12:28–34, 13:22; 1 Pet 1:2, 14–16, 22; 2:9–10). Typically, such obedience is characterized as an affirmative response to the call to follow Jesus, focused on the acceptance of innocent suffering and ultimate vindication by God, much as Jesus experienced (Mark 8:34–9:1; 1 Pet 2:21). Both documents refer to Christians' sustenance by the Holy Spirit in times of persecution (1 Pet 4:14; Mark 13:11). In addition, both 1 Peter and Mark adopt two social metaphors as illustrative of an appropriate Christian stance: the status and conduct of the servant (1 Pet 2:22–25;[51] Mark 9:35, 10:43) and life within the household or family of God (1 Pet 2:5, 4:17; Mark 3:33–34, 10:29–30).

As Ernest Best has demonstrated,[52] the similarities between 1 Peter and the Second Gospel are not adequately explained by the proposal that one document is literarily dependent on the other. While there are a number of allusive "echoes" of Mark's Gospel in 1 Peter (e.g., 1 Pet 4:14/Mark 13:11; 1 Pet 5:8/Mark 13:37), the wording in question is similar but not identical. In fact, the closest parallels between the Epistle and any of the Gospels are those between portions of 1 Peter and the Sermon on the Mount (in Matthew) or the Sermon on the Plain (in Luke); even there, however, it is difficult to trace a direct literary dependence (e.g., Matt 5:10; Luke 6:22/1 Pet 3:14; Matt 5:11/1 Pet 4:14a; Luke 6:28/1 Pet 3:9, 16). Likewise, 1 Peter and Mark appear not so much to have directly borrowed from each other as to share discernible affinities in their social and religious outlook, their traditional resources, and their theological articulation. Whatever may have been the relationship between these documents and the Peter of history, to whose own theology we no longer have direct access,[53] both Mark's Gospel and 1 Peter seem to define points along a late first-century Christian trajectory that was styled by its adherents or observers as Petrine.[54] Therefore, in effect and perhaps by accident, some evidence from the New Testament seems to cohere with patristic assessments of the Second Gospel's Petrine lineage—this despite the fact that the fathers seem roundly uninterested in Mark's "Petrinism" as such (that is, the use of the Gospel in reconstructing Peter's preaching, theology, or "school").

At least indirectly, this judgment may throw less heat and more light on a critical debate that has sporadically flared over the alleged "Paulinism" of the Second Gospel. On occasion throughout the history of New Testament interpretation the suggestion has been ardently defended that Mark's Gospel is steeped in Pauline theology, particularly with respect to such concepts as fulfillment, concealment and revelation, faith and discipleship, and Jesus' defeat and victory as concentrated on the cross.[55] Other scholars, probably in the majority, have found the terminological coincidences between Mark and Paul too imprecise, and the absence in Mark of many characteristically Pauline concepts too gaping, to support any dependence of the Evangelist on the apostle beyond their common indebtedness to some Christian traditions.[56] In a way an analogous puzzlement has bedeviled the interpretation of 1 Peter, which also contains many Pauline themes (such as the notion of believers' existence "in Christ" [1 Pet 3:16; 5:10, 14; cf., e.g., Rom. 3:24; 1 Cor 1:2; 2 Cor 5:17, 19; Gal 2:17] or Christ's atoning death [1 Pet 1:18–19, 2:24; cf. Rom 3:25; 1 Cor 15:3]) as well as a socially conservative attitude toward the Roman state (1 Pet 2:13–17; cf. Rom 13:1–7). As with Mark and Paul, so also here: it is hard to deny that some kind of relationship exists between 1 Peter and Pauline theology, yet the case for a direct dependence of 1 Peter on any of Paul's letters is even harder to make.[57] Perhaps the best explanation is that first-century Pauline and Petrine Christianities intertwined, religiously and theologically, and traces of this hybridization can be detected in documents within a Petrine circle, like Mark's Gospel and 1 Peter. Such a reckoning would jibe with the assessment of those scholars who suspect Petrine Christianity to have been highly synthetic of other primitive forms of the religion.[58] Corroborating this possibility is a snatch of oblique and quite minor evidence, previously discussed in chapter 2 of our study: the cameo of Mark, Peter's "son," appears to have been appropriated from the Pauline tradition and adapted for the edification of 1 Peter's recipients in Asia Minor.

So agglomerative was Petrine Christianity that the stamp of the apostle Peter was claimed by the literature of many Christians during the patristic period, some of whom were later judged heretical. With some difficulty, and after much time,[59] the Epistle known as 2 Peter was accepted by the early catholic church as orthodox, even canonical.[60] A different fate befell other works within the ideologically amorphous Petrine circle, such as the *Preaching of Peter* (ca. 100–50), the *Apocalypse of Peter* (ca. 135), the *Gospel of Peter* (ca. 150), and the

Acts of Peter (ca. 180–90).[61] So wide ranging is the theological perspective of these works that generalizations about their contents or religious outlook are hazardous. This much may be said: the figure of Peter appears to have occupied the center of considerable controversy during the first two centuries of the church. Only later was Peter construed as an epitome of orthodox Christianity.[62]

The implications of this fact for our study of the image of Mark are difficult to pin down. Conventionally, scholars have tended to suppose that an association with Peter probably rescued the Second Gospel from that oblivion suffered by other early Christian writings of dubious authorship.[63] Up to a point this explanation satisfies and is probably correct. It does not explain, however, why the sheer ascription of Petrine authority to other documents, like the apocryphal works just mentioned, was not sufficient to accredit them throughout the church. In the case of the *Gospel of Peter*, we know the answer to that question: notwithstanding its apostolic ascription, the book's irregular teachings (*heterodoxous didaskalias*) rendered it objectionable.[64] Apostolic figures were esteemed by both the orthodox and the heterodox; when tarred by a heretical brush even the figure of Peter could be rendered suspect.

By inverting the conventional wisdom, a less frequently asked question could be framed: Is it possible that Peter's apostolic reputation in the first and second centuries might have enjoyed a measure of reciprocal confirmation by virtue of its association with a Gospel, attributed to Mark, whose content was more consistent with emerging Christian orthodoxy? The investigation of that question in its own right would require yet another book. Here I would simply suggest that one index of Mark's value in consolidating an orthodox image of Peter may well have been that Gospel's use by the authors of the First and Third Gospels. Adopting the Markan narrative (and its depiction of Peter) as their baseline, Matthew and Luke embellish Mark's portrait not only of Jesus but also of Peter (see Matt 16:16b–19, Acts 1–12) and give to that apostle's image a sheen that would acquire additional luster in the orthodox tradition of post-Nicene Christianity.[65] In any event, and for reasons more overtly religious than demonstrably historical, the figures of Peter and Mark appear to have been correlatively supportive, and perhaps mutually interpretive, in emerging Catholic Christianity: within the canon materially similar writings were attributed to them (1 Peter and the Second Gospel); beyond the canon the figure of Mark was persistently, though not universally, associated with Peter, rather than with Paul or any other apostolic personality.

A LIMITED WARRANTY

As we have observed throughout this study, the personality of Mark in patristic tradition was not crafted and propagated for the sake of hagiography, the collection of legends about a saint. To the contrary, Mark appears to have been regarded as a figure too minor to merit such attention in his own right. Rather, the connection between the Evangelist and an apostle—usually Peter, sometimes Paul—reflected the early fathers' interest in the Second Gospel's apostolicity: its presentation of Jesus in a manner considered by them as conformable with, and corroborative of, particular (sometimes varying) interpretations of the claims of Christian faith. Implicit in patristic musings about Mark's relationship with the apostle Peter, therefore, was a kind of historical interest that was motivated primarily by religious, not strictly biographical, concerns. For them remembrance of Christian history was not an end in itself but, rather, a means to ends that were basically religious.

A Kind of Authorization

The significance of this motivation appears not to have been fully appreciated, even by some of the New Testament's more perceptive critics. We may take one example as representative. In his standard introduction to the field Werner Georg Kümmel comments that "Papias' representation of the reproduction of the preaching of Peter by Mk [sic] is false, because the material in Mk 'is the product of a complicated, in part contradictory tradition history.' "[66] In chapter 3 I have suggested that Papias's remarks may acknowledge greater sensitivity to the complexity of Gospel traditions than criticisms such as Kümmel's may assume, but here we may let that issue pass. Of equal concern is (or should be) the almost reflexive scholarly tendency simply to dismiss Papias's representation as historically false without inquiring into the *religious function* of such assessments by Papias and other patristic commentators.

In a recent work throwing light on pagan criticism of Christianity from the early second to the late fourth centuries,[67] Robert L. Wilken has noted that the Romans' religious tendencies were strongly conservative and distrustful of novelty. For a world in which religious observance was regarded as vital in sustaining the social commonweal, "the primary test of truth in religious matters was custom and tradition, the practices of the ancients."[68] Just here, in the minds of their despisers, cultured and otherwise, Christians fell short on several counts. Not only did their religion appear to have severed itself from its Jewish parentage; the link with their founder, Jesus, was compromised by unreliable Gospels, based on hearsay and unsubstantiated evidence.[69] Moreover, to its critics—many of whom were exceptionally religious—Christians also seemed fanatically, even self-righteously, convinced that their beliefs were innovative and uniquely true. No wonder that pagan observers such as Pliny (*Epistle* 10.96) and Tacitus (*Annals* 13.32) branded Christianity as impious superstition: such a term aptly characterized a religion whose claims affronted the empire's social and religious sensibilities, its "civil religion."[70]

We need not, indeed should not, force patristic comments on Peter, Mark, and the Gospel of Mark squarely at the center of some single, imagined debate between pagans and Christians over the validity of Christianity. For our topic the general relevance of this religious and social context should be clear enough, especially given the manifest apologetic endeavors of most of the patristic authors whose works we have reviewed (Papias, Justin, Irenaeus, Hippolytus, Tertullian, Augustine, Clement, Origen, Eusebius, Epiphanius, Jerome). The propagation of comments on the Evangelist Mark was one small expression of a larger process by which patristic Christians interpreted, for themselves and for others, the claims and warrants of Christianity. And, while the Second Gospel is not substantively preoccupied with the fathers' interest in its origins, in a way it formally anticipates their concerns and strategies: both the Gospel (about Jesus) and patristic reports (about Mark) frame traditional anecdotes about a notable figure, situated in secular and religious history, in order to convey particular interpretations of the Christian faith and to defend certain claims made of those interpretations. This is not to suggest that patristic authors elevated the figure of Mark (or any of the Evangelists) to the same level of significance as Jesus. It is to suggest, rather, that some of the same social, religious, and theological pressures that prompted Christians to remember and craft stories about Jesus also prompted them to remember and craft stories about those to whom Gospels were later attributed. This, in my opinion, is a crucial factor, to which we shall return in this volume's conclusion.

From their inception patristic traditions about Mark's Gospel tended to associate its composition not with an apostle but, rather, with an apostolic surrogate.[71] It is often conjectured, or assumed, that Mark's Gospel was so named as a way of distinguishing it from, or even legitimating it alongside, other Gospels. But why *this* manner of identification and accreditation? Other roads could have been taken. The Second Gospel could have been attributed directly to Simon Peter: a far more parsimonious solution, since most of the fathers accepted his authority, not Mark's, as underwriting the book. Streeter's suggestion is, after all, not without merit: the early church may have inherited a Gospel already bearing attribution to Mark, which motivated the fathers to account for the apostolicity of that figure.

Whatever may have been the historical circumstances conditioning the early fathers' more circuitous identification of the Second Gospel's authorship, perhaps something may be said about its religious consequence. Contemporaneous, and at least to some degree parallel, with early Christian ascriptions of their writings to apostolic authors (or apostolic associates) is the tendency in rabbinic Judaism to attribute Mishnaic traditions to individual rabbinic masters.[72] As William Scott Green has shown, [73] conventional and intellectual biographies of early rabbinic figures—that is, descriptions of their life and thought—are impossible to produce, because our available sources are too fragmentary, scattered, and stylized to support such a task. Yet it is not the lives of people, even the lives of notable masters, so much as the preservation of their names which is religiously significant in rabbinic Judaism:

> It is the preservation of the names of individual masters that gives rabbinic Judaism its diachronie, its "pastness," its traditionality. It is primarily because of the names that rabbinic Judaism appears to unfold and we are able to chart change and movement in it through time. . . . The presence of the names of rabbinic masters, then, provides a tangible connective between the present and the past, and the demarcation of the past in terms of generations not only avoids one sort of temporal vertigo, it also palpably establishes the inter–generational chain of communication fundamental to a traditional culture. These are not inconsequential functions.[74]

Although the Mishnah and *Tosefta* are very different, both generically and materially, from the sources with which we have been working, there may be an intriguing point of intersection in their preservation of the names of figures—some prominent, others obscure—to whom were ascribed memorable articulations of the theology or practice of rabbinic Judaism and patristic Christianity. As with the rabbis, so also with Mark: their biographies cannot be produced, primarily because our sources do not permit such. As with the rabbis, so also with the church fathers: patristic literature tells us less of who Mark was and more of how Mark functioned—namely, as a second-generational link in the chain of religious memory and communication, extending backward through Peter to Jesus and forward through the

Elder John to Papias and his successors. As Green says of the names of rabbinic masters, so also may we say the name of Mark: these are not inconsequential functions. Indeed, such functions would have been especially vital for Christianity: in comparison with a religion of antiquity like Judaism, it had been "born yesterday" and was in the process of constructing its own transgenerational tradition from Judaism to Jesus, from Jesus to the Twelve, from the Twelve to the apostles and to the Evangelists, such as Mark.[75] Interestingly, a trace of this concern is expressed in the introduction to Luke, another Gospel of which immediate apostolic authority was never claimed: in describing his sources, the Third Evangelist appeals to the credibility of "eyewitnesses and servants of the word" (Luke 1:2).

A Perceptible Hesitation

Within such a framework the attempts by Tertullian and others to draw Mark more closely to his apostolic patron are easily understandable. What is hard to fathom is why the figure of Mark, in whom such authority is vested, is treated throughout patristic tradition with conspicuous reserve: as writing after Peter's death (the anti-Marcionite prologue) or with the apostle's indifference (Clement), as disfigured (Hippolytus) or apostate (Epiphanius). The details vary widely, almost at random, but an ill-defined pattern of dubious features persists.[76] Here one might wish that Jonathan Smith's caveat might be overriden, that we could trace a clear genealogy of this aspect back to its origin. Given the nature of our sources, however, I do not see how that can be done.

Yet we might close this chapter with an unanswerable question: Is there a coherence between the diffidence with which the fathers regarded Mark the Evangelist and their own rather chilly reception of the Gospel of Mark? It is not until the late fifth century, with Victor of Antioch, that a commentary on the Second Gospel can be documented. Until then, and even afterward, Mark's Gospel was overshadowed by the others, for reasons not clearly expressed but probably not difficult to infer. After all, when compared with Matthew and Luke, Mark contains little of the teaching associated with Jesus (cf. Matt 5:3–7:21; Luke 13:22–18:14) and none of the stories, so prominent in the church's liturgical year, of his birth and resurrection appearances (cf. Matt 1:18–2:23, 28:16–20; Luke 1:5–2:52, 24:13–53). For the inculcation and nurturance of Christian piety Mark offers less obvious help than either Matthew or Luke, both of which portray Jesus' disciples more favorably and seem more sanguine about their foibles (e.g., Matt 13:51–52, 14:22–33; Luke 5:1–11, 22:31–32). Unlike the Fourth Gospel, whose Jesus unveils and proclaims himself at length (e.g., John 6:35–51, 10:1–18, 15:1–7), the Markan Jesus is a remarkably cryptic figure, who conceals as much as he reveals (e.g., Mark 3:11–12, 4:10–12, 9:2–9). It would outrun the evidence to suggest that the church fathers deliberately or even consciously queered their developing portrayal of the Second Evangelist in accordance with their reading of the mysterious Second Gospel (especially since they tended to ignore Acts and its immediately accessible presentation of the recalcitrant John Mark). Still, the early church's acceptance and disregard of the Gospel of Mark can no more be denied than its attraction to and distance from the figure of Mark the Evangelist. Whether these expressions of ambivalence may be justifiably correlated, or are purely coincidental, is and must remain an open question.

NOTES

1. Germane to this point is Jacob Neusner's observation: "Even though, through philology, we understand every word of a text, and, through history, we know just what happened in the event or time to which the text testifies, we still do not understand that text. A religious text serves not merely the purposes of philology or history. It demands its proper place as a statement of religion. Read as anything but a statement of religion, it is misunderstood" ("Judaism within the Disciplines of Religious Studies: Perspectives on Graduate Education," *CSRBul* 14 [1983]: 143).

2. Jonathan Z. Smith, *Drudgery Divine: On the Comparison of Early Christianities and the Religions of Late Antiquity* (Chicago: University of Chicago Press, 1990), 52. The context of these remarks is the enterprise of comparing different religions; however, Smith's judgment holds, I think, for comparisons of different phenomena within a given religion, like primitive Christianity.

3. As noted by critics both ancient (Clement, *To Theodore*) and modern (Helmut Koester, *Ancient Christian Gospels: Their History and Development* [Philadelphia and London: Trinity Press International / SCM, 1990], 295–303), the Second Gospel of the Christian canon was not the only edition of Mark and, therefore, not necessarily the Markan Gospel presupposed by all patristic authorities. Nevertheless, I shall assume a basic consonance between the Markan literature, considered by the early fathers, and the Markan Gospel that was canonized, unless there are demonstrable grounds for judging otherwise (such as Clement's comments on the *Secret Gospel of Mark*).

4. Like the descendants of Abram, literary analyses of Mark and the other Gospels have become as numerous as the stars in heaven. Among such studies of the Second Gospel, Mary Ann Tolbert's *Sowing the Gospel: Mark's World in Literary-Historical Perspective* (Minneapolis: Fortress, 1989), is the most recent and comprehensive, thoroughly interactive with the literature of both secular literary and biblical scholarship. Still very useful as a summary of

Mark's style and structure is Howard Clark Kee's discussion in *Community of the New Age: Studies in Mark's Gospel* (Philadelphia: Westminster, 1977), 50–76.

5. An influential treatment of this important section is Norman Perrin's "Towards an Interpretation of the Gospel of Mark," in *Christology and a Modern Pilgrimage: A Discussion with Norman Perrin*, ed. Hans Dieter Betz (Claremont, Calif.: New Testament Colloquium, 1971), 1–78.

6. I have argued for this position in "An Oration at Olivet: Some Rhetorical Dimensions of Mark 13," in *Persuasive Artistry: Studies in New Testament Rhetoric in Honor of George A. Kennedy*, ed. Duane F. Watson, JSNTSup 50 (Sheffield: Sheffield Academic Press, 1991), 66–92.

7. Among others, Harold A. Guy, *The Origin of the Gospel of Mark* (London: Hodder & Stoughton, 1954), 142; Dennis Eric Nineham, *The Gospel of St. Mark*, PGC (Baltimore: Penguin, 1963), 39; Reginald H. Fuller, *A Critical Introduction to the New Testament* (London: Duckworth, 1971), 105; Dieter Lührmann, *Das Markusevangelium*, HNT 3 (Tübingen: Mohr [Siebeck], 1987), 5.

8. Predicated on the tendency of early Christians to mold their presentations of Jesus in their own image, the principle of dissimilarity has proved to be especially important for assessing the historical authenticity of traditions attributed to Jesus in the Gospels. As the axiom has been enunciated by one of its most rigorous practitioners, "the earliest form of a saying we can reach may be regarded as authentic if it can be shown to be dissimilar to characteristic emphases both of ancient Judaism and of the early Church" (Norman Perrin, *Rediscovering the Teaching of Jesus* [New York: Harper & Row, 1976], 39).

9. Burnett Hillman Streeter, *The Four Gospels: A Study of Origins* (New York: Macmillan, 1925), 562.

10. See, for example, Hans Conzelmann, *History of Primitive Christianity*, trans. John E. Steely (Nashville: Abingdon, 1973), 148–62.

11. The classic works in this area include Martin Dibelius, *From Tradition to Gospel* (New York: Charles Scribner's Sons, n.d. [German original, 1919]); and Rudolf Bultmann, *The History of the Synoptic Tradition* (New York: Harper & Row, 1963 [German original, 1921]). A major, recent contribution to this subdiscipline is Gerd Theissen, *The Gospels in Context: Social and Political History in the Synoptic Tradition*, trans. Linda M. Maloney (Minneapolis: Fortress, 1991). For a brief description of form and redaction criticism of the Gospels, see the introduction to the present study and the other secondary treatments cited there.

12. For representative attempts to discern pre-Markan collections of various traditions about Jesus, see Heinz-Wolfgang Kuhn, *Ältere Sammlungen im Markusevangelium*, SUNT 8 (Göttingen: Vandenhoeck & Ruprecht, 1971); and Egon Brandenburger, *Markus 13 und die Apokalyptik*, FRLANT 134 (Göttingen: Vandenhoeck & Ruprecht, 1984). Brandenburger (among others) posits a pre-Markan form of Jesus' apocalyptic discourse in Mark 13; Kuhn,

the existence of preliterary chains of controversy stories (see Mark 2:1–12, 15–28), miracle tales (Mark 4:35–6:52), parables (Mark 4:1–32), and didactic anecdotes (10:13–31). Werner Kelber, Anitra Kolenkow, and Robin Scroggs, "Reflections on the Question: Was There a Pre-Markan Passion Narrative?" SBLSP 2 (1971): 503–85, provides a careful, critically equivocal assessment of the question raised by that essay's title.

13. See chapter 3; also Harold A. Guy, *The Origin of the Gospel of Mark*, 15–35. Often this possibility has been overlooked, or at least underestimated, by scholars preoccupied by Papias's linkage of Peter with Mark the Evangelist (thus, e.g., Dennis Eric Nineham, "Eyewitness Testimony and the Gospel Tradition. I, II, III," *JTS* n.s. 9 [1958]).

14. Cf. Tolbert, *Sowing the Gospel*, 303–6, which argues that Mark was written not for a local community but, rather, for the entertainment, encouragement, and proselytization of individuals.

15. In this connection one is reminded of the poet's self-surrender to that "consciousness of the past," which, as described by T. S. Eliot, "is more valuable. The progress of an artist is a continual self-sacrifice, a continual extinction of personality" (*The Sacred Wood: Essays on Poetry and Criticism*, The Fountain Library [London: Methuen, 1920], 52–53).

16. I am grateful to William Babcock for helping me to see this rationale more clearly.

17. Just what the reader of Mark 13:14 should understand remains a riddle. Elsewhere (Black, "An Oration at Olivet," 89–90) I have suggested that this statement intends to be provocatively obscure; for other interpretive possibilities, consult Morna D. Hooker, *A Commentary on the Gospel according to St. Mark*, BNTC (London: A & C Black, 1991), 314–15.

18. This, I think, would hold even if Mark 13:14 originally stemmed from a source used by the Evangelist (thus, Brandenburger, *Markus 13 und die Apokalyptik*, 43–73): in that case a later editor has let the direct address stand in application to a subsequent audience. Nor, in this connection, need we become unduly troubled to distinguish between "real" (flesh-and-blood) authors and readers and those authors and readers normatively "implied" by their narrative (Seymour Chatman, *Story and Discourse: Narrative Structure in Fiction and Film* [Ithaca and London: Cornell University Press, 1978], 147–58; also see, in the present study, chap. 1 n. 10). Modern literary critics of the Bible may decide that, in fabricating real authors out of the Gospel narratives' implied authors, the church fathers were naive. Perhaps they were, and for reasons appropriate to the intellectual conventions of their day. Still, readers of late antiquity perused the Gospels with sufficient discernment to recognize the "authorial voices" implicit in those narratives.

19. Many scholars suspect that veiled references to the evangelist's contemporary situation may be detectable in Mark 13 (N.B. vv. 5–6, 9–13); see, for instance, Theissen, *The Gospels in Context*, 125–65. We shall pursue this line a bit further in chapter 8.

20. Brian Wicker, *The Story-Shaped World. Fiction and Metaphysics: Some Variations on a Theme* (London: Athlone, 1975), 102–3 (emphasis added).

21. Wolfgang Schadewaldt, "The Reliability of the Synoptic Tradition," in Hengel, *Studies in the Gospel of Mark,* 89–113 (quotations on 102, 105).

22. Benjamin Wisner Bacon, *The Gospel of Mark: Its Composition and Date* (New Haven: Yale University Press, 1925), 46–47. The Elder's criticism, to which Bacon alludes, is that Mark, following Peter, "used to offer the teaching in anecdotal form but not making, as it were, a systematic arrangement of the Lord's oracles" (Eusebius, *H.E.* 3.39.15).

23. In addition to Martin (see n. 24 and the discussion that follows), consult, for example, Birger Gerhardsson, *The Gospel Tradition* (Lund: Gleerup, 1986); and Augustine Stock, *The Method and Message of Mark* (Wilmington, Del.: Michael Glazier, 1989).

24. Martin, "Mark, John," *ISBE* 3 (1986): 259–60 (quotation on 260), which draws on his discussion in *Mark: Evangelist and Theologian,* 80–83. Martin acknowledges two contrary arguments: one against 1 Peter's apostolic authorship, the other against a secure identification of Mark in 1 Peter 5:13 (owing to the innumerable "Marks" in Roman antiquity). Both challenges are dismissed by Martin as inconclusive: the first because the postapostolic origin of 1 Peter remains unproved; the second because of the "consistent picture" of John Mark which emerges (in Martin's view) from the New Testament ("Mark, John," 260).

25. See the conclusions drawn in chapter 2.

26. See the conclusions drawn in chapter 6.

27. Precisely because some second-century testimonies (like those of Papias and Irenaeus) became the basis for other traditions throughout Mediterranean Christianity (see chap. 6) the multiplication of witnesses to the Second Gospel's Petrine derivation is historically inconclusive (*contra* A. Robert and A. Feuillet, *Introduction to the New Testament* [New York: Desclée, 1965], 216).

28. See chapter 3.

29. Martin, "John Mark," 260 (emphasis added).

30. Alongside others Martin suggests that Papias's comments on Mark were intended to challenge the credibility of Marcionism (which appealed to Pauline authority). Though that may have been the case, such an estimate invites an open question: Why would Papias not have bolstered his rebuttal by appealing to at least some of those New Testament traditions in which Mark is aligned with Paul (Acts 12:25, 13:5; Col 4:10; 2 Tim 4:11; Philem 24)? Were such appeals made in those portions of Papias's *Expositions* which did not survive?

31. William L. Lane, *The Gospel according to Mark,* NICNT (Grand Rapids, Mich.: Eerdmans, 1971), 10–11.

32. A classic essay in this vein is Charles Harold Dodd's "The Framework of the Gospel Narratives," *ExpTim* 43 (1932): 396–400. See also Martin Hengel, *Acts and the History of Earliest Christianity,* trans. John Bowden (Philadelphia: Fortress, 1980), 24.

33. A detailed critique of Dodd's proposal highlights these and other considerations, which are equally relevant to Lane's argument: Dennis E. Nineham, "The Order of Events in St. Mark's Gospel—An Examination of Dr. Dodd's

Hypothesis," in *Studies in the Gospels: Essays in Memory of R. H. Lightfoot,* ed. D. E. Nineham (Oxford: Basil Blackwell, 1957), 223–39. Note also the perceptive comments of David E. Aune, *The New Testament in Its Literary Environment,* LEC (Philadelphia: Westminster, 1987), 24–25.

34. Again, the oldest and best manuscripts of Mark's Gospel end at 16:8. See the introduction to the present study, n. 13.

35. The parallels between (on the one hand) the presentations of Peter and Paul within Acts and between (on the other hand) Jesus and the apostles in Luke and Acts are carefully analyzed in Charles H. Talbert, *Literary Patterns, Theological Themes, and the Genre of Luke-Acts,* SBLMS 20 (Chico, Calif.: SBL / Scholars Press, 1974). See also my remarks, in part 1, on the critical disposition of Luke's point of view throughout Acts.

36. For this reason Robert Guelich attempts a meticulous though inevitably speculative reconstruction of the history of pre-Lukan tradition underlying Acts 10:34–43, a passage that (in his judgment) constitutes a significant formal and material precedent for the Gospel of Mark ("The Gospel Genre," in *The Gospel and the Gospels,* ed. Peter Stuhlmacher (Grand Rapids, Mich.: Eerdmans, 1991), 173–208, 198–202). *Pace* Lührmann (*Das Markusevangelium,* 5), Guelich does not employ such an analysis to advance a hypothesis for Mark's derivation from Petrine preaching, a proposition that Guelich explicitly disavows elsewhere (*Mark 1–8:26,* WBC 34A [Dallas: Waco, 1989], xxxiv).

With Lane's proposal one might compare a recent suggestion by A. Lancellotti ("La casa di Pietro a Cafarnao nei Vangeli sinottici: redazione e tradizione," *Antonianum* 58 [1983]: 48–69, for knowledge of which I am indebted to *NTA* 28 [1984]: 245). Lancellotti suggests that the tradition of a house in Capernaum (Mark 1:29–34; 2:12; 3:20–21, 31–35; 4:10–11; 9:33) is pre-Markan and actually goes back to Peter (whose house, allegedly, has been recovered by archaeologists in northeastern Israel). While not outrageous, this suggestion stimulates a host of difficult questions. For example, how do we know that "the house" theme in Mark flowed from tradition and not from Mark's own pen? Even if traditional, how do we know that Peter was its source? Even if Petrine, is that tradition necessarily related to an ancient abode in Capernaum (which may or may not have been the historical Peter's house)? Alternatively, could the significance of "the house" in Mark's Gospel be theological, rather than historical (see, e.g., Christopher Burdon, *Stumbling on God: Faith and Vision in Mark's Gospel* [Grand Rapids, Mich.: Eerdmans, 1990], 53–55)?

37. Reinhard Feinmeier, "The Portrayal of Peter in the Synoptic Gospels," in Hengel, *Studies in the Gospel of Mark,* 59–63, 161–62.

38. Béda Rigaux, *The Testimony of St. Mark* (Chicago: Franciscan Herald, 1966), 49. On the other hand, Rigaux recognized some qualifications to this conclusion, necessitated by form criticism: because other sources can be discerned within Mark, that Gospel can no longer be regarded as the uninterrupted literary transcription of eyewitness testimony. Petrine associations within Mark cannot be simply assumed throughout; the probabilities in each suspected case must be carefully weighed (49–50).

39. E. P. Gould, *A Critical and Exegetical Commentary on the Gospel according to Mark*, ICC (New York: Charles Scribner's Sons, 1896), xii; see also H. E. W. Turner, "Modern Issues in Biblical Studies: The Tradition of Mark's Dependence upon Peter," *ExpTim* 71 (1960): 260–63.

40. J. B. Phillips, *Peter's Portrait of Jesus: A Commentary on the Gospel of Mark and the Letters of Peter* (London: Collins & World, 1976), 10. This way of reading the Gospel (if not its roots in Peter) may find its consummation in an essay by Edmund D. Jones, "Was Mark the Gardener of Gethsemane?" *ExpTim* 31 (1921–22): 403–4: "[The Second Gospel] employs words and expressions that reveal an intimate knowledge of plant life and garden operations"(!)

41. Similarly, C. K. Barrett posits of Peter's position, at Antioch, a well-intentioned but impulsive instability (*Freedom and Obligation: A Study of the Epistle to the Galatians* [Philadelphia: Westminster, 1985], 99–100).

42. A possibility proposed by Rudolf Bultmann, "Die Frage nach dem messianischen Bewusstein und das Petrusbekenntnis," *ZNW* 19 (1919–20): 165–74, which is carefully, albeit cursorily, assessed by Ernest Best, "Peter in the Gospel according to Mark," *CBQ* 40 (1978): 547–58.

43. Similar doubts becloud Étienne Trocmé's suggestion that Acts's John Mark was the later redactor of an already heavily edited Second Gospel: "the ideal person to translate and edit for Greek-speaking Christians the Jerusalem Passion story of which Peter was, if not its author, at least its principal guarantor" (*The Formation of the Gospel according to Mark* [Philadelphia: Westminster, 1975], 247–48 [quotation on 247 n. 2]). A perceptive appraisal of this and other aspects of Trocmé's proposal is offered by T. Alec Burkill, "The Formation of St. Mark's Gospel," in his *New Light on the Earliest Gospel: Seven Markan Studies* (Ithaca and London: Cornell University Press, 1972), 180–264.

44. As I have attempted to chronicle and assess in *The Disciples according to Mark: Markan Redaction in Current Debate*, JSNTSup 27 (Sheffield: Sheffield Academic Press, 1989).

45. For instance, Alfred Loisy, *L'Évangile selon Marc* (Paris: Émile Nourry, 1912), 44–53; C. S. Mann, *Mark: A New Translation with Introduction and Commentary*, AB 27 (Garden City, N.Y.: Doubleday, 1986), 80–91. A more guarded assessment, with which many New Testament historians might sympathize, would posit the Second Gospel's survival on the strength of sheer belief that it contained Petrine reminiscence. While certainly intelligible, such a position seems to me less an explanation, more a restatement, of the problem: Was that patristic belief utterly arbitrary, founded in nothing other than religious frivolousness?

46. See, for instance, my remarks in chapter 3 on Papias and Irenaeus.

47. John H. Elliott, "The Roman Provenance of 1 Peter and the Gospel of Mark: A Response to David Dungan", in *Colloquy on New Testament Studies: A Time for Reappraisal and Fresh Approaches*, ed. Bruce C. Corley (Macon, Ga.: Mercer University Press, 1983), 181–94; Elliott, "Backward and Forward

'In His Steps': Following Jesus from Rome to Raymond and Beyond. The Tradition, Redaction, and Reception of 1 Peter 2:18–25," in *Discipleship in the New Testament*, ed. Fernando F. Segovia (Philadelphia: Fortress, 1985), 184–209. In the summary that follows I have made some additions to the parallels drawn by Elliott as well as supplemented his documentation from Mark and 1 Peter.

48. On this point Elliott's lead may be followed for the moment, notwithstanding some critical questions (to be raised in chap. 8) concerning the inference of such precise sociological data from a religious text like Mark's Gospel.

49. Elliott, "Backward and Forward," 196.

50. *Pace* J. S. Setzer, "A Fresh Look at Jesus' Eschatology and Christology in Mark's Petrine Stratum," *LQ* 24 (1972): 240–53, apocalyptic eschatology seems to characterize at least some sections of Mark in which Peter plays a role (Mark 9:2–13, 13:3–37, 14:22–31).

51. Although 1 Peter does not use the term *diakonos* ("servant") and Mark's Gospel does not explicitly refer to Isaiah 53, both documents may be indebted to the motif, in Deutero-Isaiah, of the innocent righteous one (or community) who suffers for the nation. See Elliott's discussion ("Backward and Forward," 191–93).

52. Ernest Best, "I Peter and the Gospel Tradition," *NTS* 16 (1970): 95–113.

53. That the Gospel of Mark is the most valuable source for Peter's theology is, accordingly, a considerable overstatement (P. Wernle, *Die Synoptische Frage* [Freiburg: Mohr, 1899], 200).

54. Thus, among others, Elliott, "Peter, Silvanus and Mark in 1 Peter and Acts: Sociological-Exegetical Perspectives on a Petrine Group in Rome," in *Wort in der Zeit. Neutestamentliche Studien: Festgabe für Karl Heinrich Rengstorf zum 75*, ed. W. Haubeck and M. Bachmann (Leiden: E. J. Brill, 1980), 250–67; Rudolf Pesch, *Das Markusevangelium*, HTKNT (Freiburg: Herder, 1976), 1:9; E. Earle Ellis, "Gospels Criticism: A Perspective on the State of the Art," in *The Gospel and the Gospels*, ed. Peter Stuhlmacher (Grand Rapids, Mich.: Eerdmans, 1991), 26–52. The existence of a Petrine circle, in which the figure of Mark and Gospel of Mark were implicated, seems to me better supported by the wide-ranging social, traditional, and theological consonance between 1 Peter and the Second Gospel than by the recurring character of Peter in portions of Mark's narrative (cf. Schweizer, *Good News according to Mark*, 25; Koester, *Introduction to the New Testament,* 2: 167).

55. I know of no more thorough attempt in English to demonstrate the consanguinity of Pauline and Markan theologies than John C. Fenton, "Paul and Mark," in Nineham, *Studies in the Gospels*, 89–112. Of course, the resemblances have been noticed and judged significant by an earlier generation of scholarship. The most extreme assertion of this position may have been that of Gustav Volkmar (in *Die Religion Jesu* [Leipzig: Brockhaus, 1857]), who considered Mark "far from being a life of Jesus [to be] actually a life of Paul."

More moderate assessments of Pauline influence on the Second Gospel are found in Alfred Loisy, *Les Évangiles Synoptiques* (Haute-Marne: Ceffonds, 1907), 112–19; Benajmin Wisner Bacon, *The Beginnings of the Gospel Story* (New Haven: Yale University Press, 1909), xxvii–xxviii; Bacon, *Gospel of Mark*, 228–74; Willi Marxsen, *Mark the Evangelist: Studies on the Redaction-History of the Gospel*, trans. James Boyce et al (New York and Nashville: Abingdon, 1968), 126–38; and Albert C. Outler, "The Gospel according to St. Mark," *PSTJ* 33 (1980): 3–90.

56. The most forceful denial of Pauline influence on Mark may be found in Martin Werner, *Der Einfluss paulinischer Theologie im Markusevangelium: Eine Studie zur neutestamentlichen Theologie*, BZNW 1 (Giessen: Töpelmann, 1923). More recent assessments, returning a similarly negative verdict, are K. Romaniuk, "Le Problème des Paulinismes dans l'Évangile de Marc," *NTS* 23 (1977): 266–74; and Andreas Lindemann, *Paulus im ältesten Christentum: Das Bild des Apostels und die Rezeption der paulinischen Theologie in der frühchristlichen Literatur bis Marcion*, BHT 58 (Tübingen: Mohr [Siebeck], 1979), 151–54. In English, see the useful presentations by F. C. Grant, *The Earliest Gospel: Studies of the Evangelic Tradition at Its Point of Crystallization in Writing* (New York: Abingdon, 1943), 188–206; and Howard Clark Kee, *Jesus in History: An Approach to the Study of the Gospels*, 2d. ed. (New York: Harcourt Brace Jovanovich, 1977), 122–32.

57. Consult the treatments of the subject in Ernest Best, *1 Peter*, NCB (Grand Rapids, Mich., and London: Eerdmans / Marshall, Morgan & Scott, 1971), 32–36; and J. Ramsey Michaels, *1 Peter*, WBC 49 (Waco, Tex.: Word Books, 1988), xliii–xlv.

58. Thus, Dunn: "Similarly [as with Matthew and Hebrews], Mark and Paul seem to be fulfilling a similar function, holding together Gentile Christianity and diaspora Jewish Christianity. . . . [Yet] it was Peter who became the focal point of unity in the great Church, since *Peter was probably in fact and in effect the bridge-man who did more than any other to hold together the diversity of first-century Christianity*" (*Unity and Diversity in the New Testament*, 384–85). See also my remarks in chapter 2.

59. For more extensive treatment of the letter's attestation in patristic Christianity, consult Richard J. Bauckham, *Jude, 2 Peter*, WBC 50 (Waco, Tex.: Word Books, 1983), 162–63.

60. Compared with Mark's Gospel, 2 Peter evinces far less similarity, either traditional or literary, than does 1 Peter (which in turn serves as a useful reminder that the Second Gospel was not so closely affiliated with *all* expressions of Petrine Christianity). Indeed, the stylistic and terminological dissimilarities between 1 and 2 Peter are striking and have long been recognized (see, e.g., Jerome, *De vir.* 1; *Ep.* 120.11). For a thorough discussion, see Bauckham, *Jude, 2 Peter*, 138–51.

61. These ancient texts are handily collected, with commentary, in *New Testament Apocrypha*, ed. Hennecke and Schneemelcher, 1:216–27; 2:88–102, 259–322, 663–83. Some of these Petrine pseudepigrapha, and others with

Gnostic colorings, are helpfully analyzed in Pheme Perkins, *The Gnostic Dialogue: The Early Church and the Crisis of Gnosticism* (New York and Ramsey, N.J.: Paulist, 1980), 113–30.

62. This is the conclusion drawn, and carefully substantiated, by Terence V. Smith, *Petrine Controversies in Early Christianity: Attitudes towards Peter in Christian Writings of the First Two Centuries*, WUNT 15 (Tübingen: Mohr [Siebeck], 1985).

63. See, for instance, Hengel, *Acts and the History of Earliest Christianity*, 9; Hooker, *St. Mark*, 7.

64. Serapion, Bishop of Antioch (ca. 200), sanctioned the reading of the *Gospel of Peter* in the church at Rhossus—until he read it. Afterward he collected and attempted to refute its Gnostic statements (Eusebius, *H.E.* 6.12.1–6).

65. See Raymond E. Brown, Karl P. Donfried, and John Reumann, *Peter in the New Testament* (Minneapolis and New York: Augsburg/Paulist, 1973), 39–56, 75–107, 157–68. Another (and to my mind less persuasive) interpretation of the significance of the Petrine tradition for the question of Synoptic Gospel interrelationships has been proposed by those scholars who regard Mark's Gospel as a condensation of Matthew and Luke: William R. Farmer, "Modern Developments of Griesbach's Hypothesis," *NTS* 23 (1976–77): 275–95; David L. Dungan, "The Purpose and Provenance of the Gospel of Mark according to the 'Two-Gospel' (Griesbach) Hypothesis," in *Colloquy on New Testament Studies*, ed. Bruce C. Corley, 133–56; Mann, *Mark*, esp. 60–81. Strictly speaking, however, an argument for the intersection of Mark's Gospel with Petrine Christianity is far too oblique, and probably too conjectural, to be used as *proof* either that Matthew and Luke employed Mark as a source or that Mark used them.

66. Werner Georg Kümmel, *Introduction to the New Testament*, trans. Howard Clark Kee, 17th rev. ed. (Nashville: Abingdon, 1973), 95–96, quoting Kurt Niederwimmer, "Johannes Markus und die Frage nach dem Verfasser des zweiten Evangeliums," *ZNW* 58 (1967): 185.

67. Robert L. Wilken, *The Christians as the Romans Saw Them* (New Haven and London: Yale University Press, 1984).

68. Wilken, *Christians*, 62.

69. Both charges were leveled by the Platonist philosopher Celsus, whose critique of Christianity, *True Doctrine* (ca. 170), was the object of extensive rebuttal by Origen of Alexandria (*Against Celsus*, ca. 247). For discussion, see Wilken, *Christians*, 94–125.

70. Wilken, *Christians*, 48–67.

71. Thus, Willi Marxsen: "It appears that even before the time of Papias Mark was considered to be the author [of the Second Gospel] (otherwise Papias would presumably have suggested Peter himself as the author)" (*Introduction to the New Testament*, trans. G. Buswell [Philadelphia: Fortress, 1968], 143).

72. The Mishnah, a collection of authoritative Jewish legal traditions, was

developed in Pharisaic and rabbinic Judaism and codified in the early third century A.D. Along with the *Tosefta*, a corpus of supplementary traditions, the Mishnah was the basis of two Talmuds, which began to be produced somewhat later by Babylonian and Palestinian rabbis.

73. William Scott Green, "What's in a Name?—The Problematic of Rabbinic 'Biography,' " in *Approaches to Judaism: Theory and Practice*, ed. W. S. Green, BUJS 1 (Missoula, Mont.: Scholars Press, 1978), 77–96.

74. Green, "What's in a Name?" 88–89.

75. Could it have been due to this tendency to locate Mark the Evangelist in a "third generation" of Christianity which led the early fathers away from attributing the Second Gospel to another Petrine associate—Andrew, Simon's brother (Mark 1:16–18, 3:18)?

76. Everett R. Kalin's essay, "Early Traditions about Mark's Gospel: Canonical Status Emerges, the Story Grows" (*CurTM* 2 [1975]: 332–41) helpfully summarizes these shifts in the patristic portrayal of Mark.

Chapter Eight

The Second Gospel
and the Traditions about Mark (II)

Ubi et Unde?

We continue our "re-visioning" of the Second Gospel, in the light of
traditional portrayals of the Second Evangelist. As in the preceding
chapter, we are comparing the biblical and patristic phenomena with
attention to their possible coherence in four interpenetrating areas: the
historical, the sociological, the religious, and the theological. Again it
should be stressed that in only one of these domains, that of historical
inquiry, shall we be exercised by the question of a genealogical
development from, or lacuna between, Mark's Gospel and the traditions about its author. Otherwise, our inquiry will be directed toward
the meaning or significance—the social, theological, or religious "fit-
tingness"—of the fathers' attribution of this Gospel to Mark.

ALL ROADS LEAD TO ROME?

As we have seen, the conjunction of the Second Evangelist with
Christianity in Rome is persistent in patristic anecdotes about Mark's
Gospel. As it happens, of all things attributed by the early fathers to
that document its origination in Rome may be the datum accorded
greatest plausibility at the bar of critical scholarship.[1] To the minds of
modern critics, however, the most persuasive reasons for associating
that Gospel with Rome are not those suggested by patristic sources,
which tend, for their part, toward another possibility that is roundly
rejected by most moderns.

Perplexities for the Historian

To come straight to the point: the connection of Mark, both Evangelist
and Gospel, with Rome appears to have been sustained in Christian
tradition by means of Mark's prior association with Peter. In their
comments on Mark the majority of the fathers yoke Peter and Rome
(Irenaeus, Clement,[2] Origen, Eusebius, Epiphanius, and Jerome) or

Peter and Italy (the anti-Marcionite and Monarchian Gospel prologues). For these details, naturally, several testimonies appear to be
dependent on each other (Origen and the anti-Marcionite prologue, on
Irenaeus; Eusebius, on Irenaeus, Clement, and Origen; Epiphanius,
on Clement; Jerome, on Eusebius; the Monarchian prologue, on Jerome[?]). Moreover, all of these witnesses have access to 1 Peter's
concatenation of Peter, Mark, and Rome (= Babylon [5:13]).[3] Some
patristic authors link Mark with Peter, but not with Rome (Papias,
Tertullian, John Chrysostom); others associate Mark with neither Peter
nor Rome (Hippolytus [of Rome!], Adamantius, the *Apostolic Constitutions,* Augustine). *However, in none of the patristic materials that
we have examined is a link between Mark and Rome ever wrought in
the absence of a coinciding connection of Mark with Peter.* Among the
fathers of the first four centuries Rome seems never to have been the
point of entry for Mark's association with Peter. Just the reverse:
Rome appears to have entered the traditions about Mark only by way
of Peter's association with that city.[4] In other words, in patristic
reflection the Second Gospel's Roman origin appears to have been a
function of the tradition of Mark's Petrine authority.[5] And there's the
rub: as we have seen in chapter 7, the Gospel's affinity with a Petrine
circle or tradition is the most that can be securely claimed; its actual
derivation from the apostle Peter is seriously contested within critical
scholarship. Consequently, more recent appraisals of a Roman provenance for Mark's Gospel tend to be made not on the face but, rather,
in the teeth of the early fathers' similar conclusions.

From these comments it should be evident that the historicity of
patristic presentations of Mark and Rome is exceedingly difficult,
perhaps impossible, to verify. Partly this stems from the derivative
quality of our source material, as we have just observed: the assertion
of the Gospel's composition in Rome appears to have been an offshoot
of those traditions that envisioned its creation under Petrine patronage.
That a critical eye is appropriate in the weighing of such traditions for
historical reconstruction is further suggested by the rather divergent
character of those traditions: as we have witnessed in previous chapters, patristic sources do not present an entirely consistent picture of
the circumstances attending the Gospel's composition. This, in itself,
suggests that the historian should allow for a considerable, if not
precisely determinate, degree of folklore and legend in the patristic
coupling of Mark with Rome.

The Shape of Early Roman Christianity

Nevertheless, the matter should not be prematurely dropped. Let us
consider whether the fathers' association of Mark's Gospel with Rome

makes sense in the light of what we know about (1) the social and religious setting of first-century Roman Christianity and (2) the content of the Second Gospel. Is the situation of Mark's Gospel in Rome a claim that is, if not historically *demonstrable,* at least *coherent* with what can be reasonably inferred about the social, religious, and political circumstances of the first Christians in that area?[6]

In pondering this question, we are the beneficiaries of several recent studies that throw considerable light on the character of primitive Roman Christianity.[7] With allowance for expected differences in critical assessment of finer details a fairly sharp and rather textured reconstruction of first-century Christianity in the imperial capital seems now to be emerging.

1. *Ethnicity and social background.* From the second century B.C. onward a substantial portion of Rome's population consisted of non-Romans who, as enslaved war captives, had been imported from their homelands in the Hellenized East (Greece, Asia Minor, Syria, Judea, Egypt, as well as Africa, Spain, and elsewhere). One of the largest segments of that foreign population consisted of Jews, who by the first century A.D. numbered around forty to fifty thousand.[8] Paul's Epistle to the Romans, written in the late fifties of the first century, presumes a similar ethnic mix among Christians in the capital: accordingly, at different points in that letter, Paul directs his comments to Jews (2:1–3:20) or Gentiles (11:13).[9] Moreover, the names mentioned in Paul's concluding salutations[10] reflect a significant, if arguably minority, portion of Jews (Prisca and Aquila, Rom 16:3 [cf. Acts 18.2]; Andronicus, Junia, and Herodion, Paul's "relatives," Rom 16:7, 11),[11] as well as a heavy concentration of Christians in Rome whom Paul had met during his missionary travels (Prisca [or "Priscilla," as she is called in Acts 18] and Aquila [Rom 16:3]; Epaenetus, "the first convert in Asia for Christ" [Rom 16:5]; Andronicus, Junia, Urbanus, Rufus[12] and his mother [Rom 16:7, 9, 13]). Eleven of the twenty-six persons in Romans 16 bear names that are held by slaves in literary references or inscriptions associated with Rome (Mary, Junia, Ampliatus, Tryphaena, Tryphosa, Asyncritus, Phlegon, Hermes, Philologus, Julia, Nereus [Rom 16:6, 7, 8, 12, 14, 15]).[13]

2. *Economic and social standing.* In an exhaustive analysis of the available archaeological, epigraphical, and literary evidence, Peter Lampe has made a convincing case for the relatively low economic status of the first Christians in Rome. Roman Christianity appears to have been centered in two swampy, urban districts: the harbor of Trastevere (west of the Tiber River), one of the city's most densely populated, heavily Jewish, and rundown areas; and beyond the Porta

Capena around the heavily traveled Appian Way (to the southeast). Collectively, the population in these areas consisted of laborers, artisans, traders, transport workers, and, in general, some of the poorest from among Rome's citizenry. On the other hand, traces of a Christian presence also linger from the city's more affluent Aventine district, which was located in a southwestern sector between Trastevere and Porta Capena. Christians there may have enjoyed better prospect for upward mobility, whether as freedmen or as the slaves of Roman aristocrats.[14] Although the evidence is ambiguous, Christians of senatorial rank, including women, can perhaps be documented at least as early as the first century's last decade.[15] James S. Jeffers has suggested that these different social levels among Roman Christians tacitly inform two documents, issuing from Rome in the late first and early second centuries: *1 Clement* (ca. 93–97), which to a considerable degree assumes the values of an educated elite (*1 Clem* 37.4, 62.3), and the *Shepherd of Hermas* (ca. 135), which may exhibit a more pervasive advocacy for destitute Christians (*Herm Mand* 2.4; 8.3, 4, 10; *Herm Sim* 5.3.7, 9.27.2; *Herm Vis* 3.9.5,6).[16]

Even earlier than those writings Paul's letter to the Roman church suggests a compatible picture. Numbered among those greeted in chapter 16 are several persons who were able either to own or to rent houses in which Christians might gather for worship: Prisca and Aquila (v. 5); Asyncritus and Phlegon, among others, "and the brothers and sisters who are with them" (v. 14); and Philologus and Julia, among others, "and all the saints who are with them" (v. 15). Women are conspicuously present among the persons addressed by Paul in Romans 16: Phoebe, who was coming to Rome from Cenchreae in Corinth (vv. 1–2); Prisca (v. 3); Mary (v. 6); Junia (v. 7); Tryphaena and Tryphosa (v. 12); Persis (v. 12); the mother of Rufus (v. 13); Julia (v. 15); and the sister of Nereus (v. 15). In addition, Paul's reference to the property of Prisca and Aquila as "their house" (Rom 16:5; see also 1 Cor 16:19) implies that Prisca's social standing was at least the equal of Aquila's. Indeed, the fact that her name is usually listed before his throughout the New Testament (Acts 18:18, 26; Rom 16:3; 2 Tim 4:19; cf. Acts 18:2; 1 Cor 16:19) could suggest that her status was remembered as having been higher than that of her husband.[17]

3. *Religious organization.* Although our sources yield scant information on the subject, worship among early Christians in Rome appears to have been heterogeneous, even fragmented. In this respect Christianity mirrored its parent Judaism in that city, which was divided into about a dozen synagogues, each of which was supervised by a local council of elders but none of which was directly connected with

the others through centralized governance.[18] From the range of available evidence Lampe deduces that Roman Christians congregated in a half-dozen Christian circles, located in houses and somewhat separated from one another geographically, socially, and intellectually.[19] Glimmers of this situation may be perceptible in Romans 16, in which Paul explicitly identifies three (different) house congregations, one of which is led by a Jewish couple (Prisca and Aquila [vv. 3–5]), the others organized around persons with Greek or Latin names (Asyncritus and company [v. 14]; Philologus and Julia, among others [v. 15]).[20] Paul encourages Christian solidarity among these various groups (Rom 16:16), an ideal that, by the second century, had begun to run aground on the shoals of ethnic and ideological diversity.[21] By that time a countervailing pull was being exerted toward a more centralized, even hierarchical, administration among Roman congregations: thus, *1 Clement* (written between A.D. 80 and 140) presumes as its provenance "*the* church of God that sojourns in Rome" (Pref.) and emphasizes an apostolic succession of authority (42.4, 44.1–2). Ultimately, a single-bishop pattern of leadership prevailed in Rome, though probably not before the mid-second century.[22]

4. *Political turbulence.* Long before that time conflicts for Roman Christians were aborning, and the earliest to be documented are traceable to the religion's rootage in Judaism. Relations between the empire and Roman Jews, in their own right, had tended at best toward uneasiness: though the Jews had been conceded various religious privileges (such as exemption from military service and freedom to collect taxes in support of the Jerusalem temple [Josephus, *Ant.* 14.10.1–8]), their religious insularity made them objects of suspicion and ridicule (Cicero, *For Flaccus* 28,69; Juvenal, *Satires* 3.14, 6.542–548, 14.105–106). By around the year 49 there was enough tension in Rome to provoke the Emperor Claudius (41–54) to expel from the capital a large number of Jews (Suetonius, *Claudius* 25.4;[23] cf. Acts 18:2), who were not allowed to return until five years later. The effect of this imperial ban for the future of Roman Christianity was profound: it pushed to the outer edges its indigenous Jewish quality, which had already been marginalized by the preponderance of foreign Gentiles among Christian converts in Rome.

By the mid-sixties a distinction between Christians and Jews in the imperial capital was recognizable even to such pagan historians as Tacitus, who chronicled the next major chapter in Roman Christianity's stormy political history (*Annals* 15.44):[24]

> But neither all human endeavor, nor all imperial largess,
> nor all the modes of placating the gods, could stifle scandal

or banish the belief that the [great Roman] fire had taken place by order. Therefore, to scotch the rumor, Nero substituted as culprits, and punished with the utmost exquisite cruelty, a class loathed for their abominations, whom the crowd styled Christians. Christus, from whom the name is derived, had undergone the death penalty in the reign of Tiberius, by sentence of the procurator Pontius Pilate. Checked for the moment, this pernicious superstition again broke out, not only in Judea, the home of the disease, but in the capital itself [Rome]—that receptacle for everything hideous and degraded from every quarter of the globe, which there finds a vogue. Accordingly, arrest was first made of those who confessed [to being Christians]; next, on their disclosures, vast numbers were convicted, not so much on the charge of arson as for hatred of the human race. Every sort of derision was added to their deaths: they were wrapped in the skins of wild beasts and dismembered by dogs; others were nailed to crosses; others, when daylight failed, were set afire to serve as lamps by night. Nero had offered his gardens for the spectacle and gave an exhibition in the circus, mingling with the people in the costume of a charioteer or mounted on a car. Hence even for criminals who merited extreme and exemplary punishment, there arose a feeling of pity, due to the impression that they were being destroyed, not for the public good, but to gratify the cruelty of a single man.

Tacitus's report harmonizes with several things we have already noted. Here, as we have observed elsewhere, many pagans were inclined to regard Christian beliefs and practices as eccentric, even pernicious.[25] Interestingly, Trastevere, the harbor in which many poor Christians were concentrated, suffered no damage from the great fire, which may partially account for how Nero was able to make his scapegoating stick.[26] Moreover, the grotesque punishments suffered by Roman Christians at the hand of Claudius's successor, Nero (54–68), tallies with our earlier inferences of their social standing: Roman law forbade such means of execution for citizens of the state.[27] For its part Christian tradition located the martyrdom of the apostles Peter and Paul within this persecution of Christians in Rome (ca. 64–67; *1 Clem* 5.4–7; 6.1; Ignatius, *Rom* 4.2–3; Irenaeus, *Adv. Haer.* 3.3.2; Eusebius, *H.E.* 2.25.7). Though mantled from the third century onward in ever more elaborate legend, this basic tradition is credible and generally accepted by many scholars.[28]

If Christians in Rome were not the target of imperial animosity by the end of the sixties, they were surely caught up in the general social and political upheavals that roiled the empire.[29] Following military and senatorial revolt against him, Nero killed himself in 68; within the following year four emperors were installed in rapid succession, only to die by murder or suicide. By the time a degree of stability was restored under Vespasian (69–79) the state's economy and spirit had been depleted by civil war. Part of the internal hemorrhaging was a disastrous Jewish insurrection against Rome, triggered in 66 by the avarice and short temper of a Roman procurator in Judea. Although fighting dragged on until 74, with the suicide of the Jewish garrison at Masada, the climax of this war came in 70, when Jerusalem was first starved, then slaughtered, and its temple burned by order of Vespasian's son, Titus. No less for the empire than for Jews, these events were of more than regional significance: Titus's quelling of the Judean uprising was commemorated both in late first-century Roman coinage and in the Arch of Titus, which still may be seen in the ancient Roman Forum.

For reasons disputed among historians evidence for contemporaneous Jewish or Gentile Christian reactions to its ambient turmoil is hard to come by.[30] Contrary to the once popular notion that Christianity was the seedbed for a social unrest that ultimately toppled the empire, Christians of this and subsequent periods adopted a rather low political profile.[31] For instance, Jewish Christians in Jerusalem did not participate in the revolt against Rome but fled to Gentile territory (Eusebius, *H.E.* 3.5.2–3). This, in a sense, was symptomatic of Christianity's destiny: years before 70, as suggested by Paul's letters and corroborated by the Book of Acts, the fledgling religion had already flown beyond Israel, both deliberately and in popular perception, and was nesting in numerous Gentile regions throughout the Mediterranean basin. Between Paul's letter to Roman Christians during the fifties and the Roman Clement's letter to Corinthian Christians in the nineties, there emerges an impression of Christians attempting to sculpt a new religious identity from the materials of their religious heritage. To that end, though in very different ways, both Paul and Clement explore some common themes: the question of Christianity's relationship with Judaism (Rom 9:1–11:36; *1 Clem* 40.1–5, 41.2), the distinctive structure of Christian belief (Rom. 3:21–31, 5:1–8:39) and practice (*1 Clem* 42.4, 44.1–4), and a stance of reflective compliance with the Roman government (Rom 13:1–7; *1 Clem* 60.4–61.2).[32]

5. *Summary*. Though lacking much of the clarity that we would like, a snapshot of some of the conditions under which first-century Chris-

tians lived in Rome can probably be developed. It seems reasonable to imagine a religiously kindred circle of separate communities, varying in social and educational levels, whose worship was convened in houses and governed by leadership that was local (with apparent tendencies toward centralization). Ethnically and culturally, the roots of Christianity in Rome (as elsewhere) were Jewish; already in the first century, however, the movement was becoming preponderantly Gentile and increasingly remote from its Jewish origins. Our available evidence further suggests that Roman Christianity was predominantly a lower-class phenomenon, in which slaves and menial laborers were included, yet some members may have enjoyed the potential to improve their economic lot. Both women and men seem to have played a noteworthy role in sustaining the movement, which was subject to different degrees of various pressures: the empire's political instability during the decade of the sixties; distrust among pagans; tensions with erstwhile Jewish coreligionists; and apparently some internal discord among Christians during their targeted harassment by Nero. In a word, Roman Christianity in the first century appears to have been a rather conflicted movement, both within and without—ethnically, socially, religiously, and politically.

The Shape of Christianity in the Second Gospel

Do the message of Mark's Gospel and its manner of presentation comport with first-century Roman Christianity, thus reconstructed? I think that an affirmative verdict may be rendered.

1. With regard to its *ethnic and religious assumptions*, the Second Gospel presents Christian traditions that originated in Palestinian Judaism, interpreted for an audience that would no longer find some of its Jewish references intelligible or sufficient.[33] Jesus in Mark's Gospel travels the countryside and urban areas of Israel, interacting with basic Jewish institutions like synagogue and temple, in a narrative laced with biblical quotations (thus 1:2-3, 7:6-7, 12:10-11, 12:36) and riddled with biblical imagery (see, e.g., 1:6 [2 Kings 1:8; Zech 13:4], 12-13 [Exod 19-24, 34:28]; 6:30-44; 8:1-10 [Exod 16:13-35; Num 27:15-17]; 9:2-8, 9-13 [Mal 3:1-2, 4:5-6]).[34] The resemblance between Judaism and Markan Christianity is not superficial: although proximity to God's kingdom is authoritatively judged by Jesus, he and a sincere scribe concur on the first principles of a life lived in accordance with God's will (Mark 12:28-34, working out of Lev 19:18; Deut 4:35, 6:4-5; 1 Sam 15:22; Isa 45:5).

On the other hand, the Second Gospel bears the vestiges of a community distanced from Judaism, both ethnically and religiously.

Thus, the author considers it needful to translate Semitic expressions (5:41; 7:11, 34; 11:9–10; 14:36; 15:22, 34, 42) and to explain Jewish customs (7:3–4, 11, 19b).[35] Indeed, so opaque are several of the Gospel's explanations that one may question the depth of its author's own knowledge about matters Jewish: the suggested translation of *Boanerges* as "sons of thunder" (3:17) is as obscure as many of the Gospel's renderings of Palestinian geography are incomprehensible, as a glance at any map of biblical Palestine will confirm (5:1, 6:53, 7:31, 10:1). In addition, the author's grasp of Jewish scripture (1:2 [cf. Exod 23:20; Mal 3:1];[36] 2:25–26 [cf. 1 Sam 21:1–6]) and religious practice (7:3 [cf. Lev 22:1–16]) sometimes seems unsure.[37]

Even as new wine inevitably bursts from old wineskins (Mark 2:22), the movement inaugurated by Jesus in Mark's Gospel has spilled out of Judaism into the Gentile world, whose communities figure conspicuously in the narrative (3:8; 5:1, 20; 7:31; 8:27). As a result of altered social conditions and religious assumptions, inherited traditional directives appear to have been reconsidered and modified. Thus, while divorce is rigorously forbidden by Jesus (Mark 10:2–9; cf. Deut 24:1–4), even the possibility of its initiation by a wife (Mark 10:12) apparently presumes the stipulations of Roman law, not of its Palestinian Jewish counterpart.[38] Of more fundamental religious significance is Jesus' dismissal of Levitical discriminations between what is clean and unclean (7:14–23; cf. Lev 11:1–47), which signals for Mark both a clear break from Pharisaic tradition (Mark 7:1–9)[39] and an effective justification for "the proclamation of the gospel to all nations" (13:10, 14:9). Ironically, that mandate is explicitly executed by a Gentile: the only human being in Mark's Gospel to acclaim Jesus as "truly God's son" is the centurion, upon seeing how Jesus had died (Mark 15:39).[40] Nevertheless, the shift in Mark from a Jewish past to a Gentile future is navigated with considerable resistance, both among Jews (2:1–3:6, 12:1–9) and toward Gentiles (7:24–30).[41] The same transition, as we have seen, was no smoother for first-century Christians in Rome.

2. Positive interactions with Jesus are typically displayed in the Second Gospel by characters whose *social identity or standing* is roughly analogous to that which appears to have been characteristic among Christians in Rome. While largely rural in orientation, in Mark Jesus' mission is extended to towns (1:38) and attracts adherents from a mixture of urban and rural settings (1:45; 6:32–33, 56). The condition for entrance into God's kingdom is described by Jesus as being childlike in receptivity (10:15; cf. 9:36–37), which may refer (albeit ambiguously) to the powerlessness, or lack of status, attributed to children in antiquity.[42] Clearly, however, sparks of discipleship in the

Second Gospel are struck by a band of nameless minor characters: "little people"[43] living on society's margins (1:40–45, 2:1–12, 8:22–26, 10:46–52), many of whom are women (5:25–34, 7:24–30, 12:41–44, 14:3–9, 15:40–41, 16:1).[44] The social stability created by possessions is actually or potentially manifest among some of Jesus' disciples and would-be followers (1:16–20,[45] 10:17–22), yet "the lure of wealth and the desire for other things" stymies discipleship and must be extirpated (4:18–19, 10:23–31). Jesus' models of discipleship consistently subvert conventional assumptions about social power: many who are first will be last, and the last—those who are others' servants and slaves—will be first (9:35; 10:31, 43–44).

3. *Religious organization.* Another cluster of images in Mark surely would not have gone unnoticed by Christians, at Rome and elsewhere, who gathered for worship in houses as real and surrogate families. Repeatedly, Jesus is portrayed as interacting with his followers in "a house" (1:29, 32–33; 2:1, 15; 3:19b; 7:24b); pointedly, Jesus satisfies a hungry horde that is away from home (8:1–10, N.B. v. 3). This motif meshes with another that suffuses the Second Gospel, namely the constitution of Jesus' disciples into a new family: "houses, brothers and sisters, mothers and children" who do God's will in this age (3:33–35, 10:29–30).[46] The absence in Mark 10:29 of the *paterfamilias,* the customary patriarch of the clan, is conspicuous yet arguably coherent with this Gospel's egalitarian tendencies (which, as we have just noted, elevates slaves, embraces children, and recognizes women). Accordingly, disciples who bicker among themselves over greatness, or clamber over one another for exalted positions, are immediately reproved by Jesus (9:33–37, 10:35–45). Although consideration for one's natural parents fulfills the commandment of God and is thus no negligible matter (7:9–13), divisions among families over the pursuit of Jesus' way are painfully real, even predictable (3:21, 31–32; 6:1–6a; 10:28–30). Indeed, Mark also is aware of divisions that can occur among those surrogate families who follow Jesus: thus, as readers we encounter houses that may refuse hospitality to his disciples (6:7–13), an exorcist who invokes Jesus' name without belonging to a particular group of adherents (9:38–41), and those among Jesus' auditors who could trip up the "little ones who believe in [him]" (9:42–48). Rectified communion among Christians entails judgment, repentance, and prayerful forgiveness (6:11–12, 11:25): "Have salt in yourselves, and be at peace with one another" (9:50b).

4. Probably no feature in the Gospel has garnered a greater degree of interpretive consensus than Mark's acknowledgment of the *turmoil,* even *persecution,* to which Jesus' followers are inevitably subject.

From the early arrest and subsequent execution of John the baptizer (1:14, 6:14–29) to the plot hatched early against Jesus (3:6, 19a; 11:18; 12:12; 14:1; see also 1:37, 2:20, 3:9); from repeated promise of his disciples' torment (4:16–17; 8:34–9:1; 10:30, 38–39; 13:9–13) to the anguished abandonment and death ultimately endured by Jesus (8:31–33; 9:30–32; 10:32–34; 12:1–8; 14:27, 32–52; 15:21–37)—no Gospel probes more relentlessly than Mark the implications of "proclaim[ing] Christ crucified" (1 Cor 1:23).

Hostility to Jesus and his followers assumes manifold social shapes in Mark, all of which appear to have had counterparts among Roman Christians in the first century. First, Jesus and the Twelve are perpetually at loggerheads with their fellow Jews. Most obviously, this is dramatized through Jesus' repeated conflicts with Jewish leaders (2:6–10; 3:6, 22–30; 7:1–13; 8:11–13, 31; 9:14; 10:2–9, 33; 11:27–12:27, 38–40; 14:1–2, 43, 53–65; 15:31–32). However, the contretemps may also be conveyed through other media: the sometimes conflicted response of Israel to the gospel's incursion (4:13–20, 5:14–20, 7:36); the presence of demonism in the synagogue (1:23–24) and the absence of "fruit" in the temple (11:15–19; cf. 11:12–14, 20–21; see also 13:1–2, 15:38); John's inaugural call to the country of Judea to repent of its sins (1:4–5).

Second, in Mark, Jesus and his followers are at odds with the forces of the Roman state. Though favorably disposed toward Gentiles, Mark harbors no illusions about "those whom they recognize as their rulers": they are "tyrants" who "lord it over them" (10:42). Jesus predicts his deliverance into the hands not only of Jewish authorities but of Gentiles as well (10:33–34; cf. 15:16–28), and the same is forecast of the disciples (13:9). Precisely because their message constituted an implied challenge to the religious and political claims of the imperial cult, those who proclaimed "the gospel of God's Son and God's kingdom" (cf. 1:1, 11, 15; 4:26–32; 9:1, 7, 47; 11:9–10; 15:39)[47] would inevitably fall afoul of the Roman authorities.

Whereas one Rubicon—the separation of Christians and Jews—has begun to be crossed, the Second Gospel draws on traditions that effectively attempt repair of Christians' relationship with the empire: thus, the delicacy of Jesus' response to the question of paying imperial taxes (12:13–17) and the presentation of Caesar's procurator, Pilate, as sympathetically feckless but not malicious (15:1–15). And, though its theological reasons are many, complex, and irreducible to purely political motivations, surely the mystery in which the Second Gospel enshrouds Jesus' identity as Christ and Son of God (1:34, 3:11–12, 8:27–30) has the practical effect of defusing, among Mark's contemporaries, any charge that Jesus and his successors were outrightly seditious. That is to say, one implication, among others, of the so-called messianic secret in Mark[48] is probably made explicit in the characteristic blatancy of the Johannine Jesus: "My kingdom is not from this world. If my kingdom were from this world, my servants would be fighting to keep me from being handed over to the Jews. But as it is, my kingdom is not from here" (John 18:36). The "low profile" adopted by Jesus in Mark's Gospel is congruent with the sectarian tendencies that have been attributed by some scholars to Markan Christianity:[49] a group that evidently regarded itself, under threat, as "elect insiders" in apocalyptic tension with the general public (cf. Mark 4:10–12, 21–25, 33–34). While not necessarily localized in first-century Rome, the adoption of such a perspective by Christians in that time and place is neither implausible nor hard to imagine.[50]

Some of the threats to Mark's readers are poignant but ill defined,[51] much as the experience of first-century Roman Christians appears to have been. To be sure, Jesus' warnings to his followers on Olivet are clothed in the stock motifs of prophecy and apocalypticism (2 Chron 15:6; Isa 13:13, 14:30, 19:2; Jer 22:23; Rev 6:8, 11:13, 16:18). On the other hand, some of these cautions may not be merely imaginative: according to both Jewish and Roman historians, "nation [did] rise against nation" during the sixties (cf. Mark 13:8), and the Gospel's readers may well have been shaken by political turmoil and in need of settling down (thus see 13:6–7, 14–23).[52] To "be hated by all because of [Jesus'] name" (13:13) need not be taken as either a rhetorical flourish or an expression of religious paranoia: Pliny and Tacitus remind us of the indiscriminate contempt heaped upon Christians by many pagans.[53] Although fraternal betrayal doubtless occurred in various historical contexts, Tacitus's record of the persecution of Roman Christians could be interpreted as confirmation of the fact that "brother [did] betray brother to death" (Mark 13:12). If its substance is more than biblically allusive (cf. Mic 7:6; 2 Esd 6:24), such a comment could help to explain why Jesus' disciples in Mark are characterized as such craven, faithless incompetents (4:35–41; 6:45–52; 8:14–21; 9:18; 10:35–41; 14:10–11, 17–21, 26–31, 66–72): it was indeed the experience of some early Christians, in Rome and elsewhere,[54] that, "when trouble or persecution [arose] on account of the word, immediately they [fell] away" (4:17).[55]

5. *Summary.* If the emphases of the Second Gospel permit such deductions about its original readership, then we may infer that Mark was apparently written for early Christians of low to middling social status, who may have gathered for worship in independent house

churches. By the time of the Gospel, Markan Christianity evidently had begun to break away, ethnically and religiously, from its roots in Palestinian Judaism. The tension presumably experienced between Markan Christians and their erstwhile Jewish coreligionists was but one element in a larger panorama of turmoil and persecution, in which the Roman state and even other Christians were also implicated. In short, between the social, political, and religious conditions suggested by Mark's Gospel and what we may infer about first-century Roman Christianity, there are some interesting if not striking parallels. If Mark may be justifiably located within a Petrine circle of tradition (as was suggested in chap. 7), and if at least one stream of Petrine Christianity can be located in Rome (as John Elliott has argued),[56] then a tie between the Second Gospel and Roman Christianity would seem even more plausibly cinched.[57]

Lingering Caveats

One might ask: If the parallels are so suggestive, why not cut the Gordian knot, vindicate the majority patristic opinion, and flatly assert that Mark's Gospel was written in Rome? At least three factors, in my judgment, prevent us from drawing a conclusion with such strong claims for historicity.

First, for the location of Mark in Rome we cannot summon the kind of firm, corroborative evidence that is the historian's bread and butter. If other Christian documents, issuing from Rome during the late first or early second century, registered demonstrable use of the Second Gospel, then that would be a significant point in support of its Roman provenance. Such documents we have (1 Peter; *1 Clement*; the *Shepherd of Hermas*); indisputable references to Mark within them we lack.

Second, the social, religious, and political factors that we have inferred from Mark are subject to plausible, alternative interpretations, which do not necessitate the Gospel's having originated in Rome. For example, while many interpreters believe that Mark would have been read most meaningfully in a situation of actual persecution, there is nothing in the Gospel that demands such a reading. Conceivably, the book could have been written for a community for which the threat of persecution loomed on the horizon, or in any place that pondered the meaning of suffering within the Christian confession.[58] Precisely because Mark does not necessarily point to any particular provenance (as Paul, e.g., identifies Ephesus as the origin of 1 Cor [16:8]), modern scholars, appraising the evidence differently, have proposed other homes for the Gospel. Forceful arguments have been articulated for its origin somewhere in Syria,[59] while a Galilean provenance has received minority support.[60] Many commentators consider the Gospel's evidence so ambiguous and our knowledge of the diverse circumstances of first-century Christians so incomplete that any certainty of Mark's origins is precluded.[61]

Third, more fundamental questions can, and perhaps should, be raised about the overall method by which *any* assessment of Mark's provenance is made. On the one hand, social-scientific analysis of ancient documents, of which this chapter has offered an elementary example, is anything but an exact science.[62] On the other hand, as Dan Via has cautioned, the manifest content of Mark's Gospel is far less *descriptive* of where its community actually was, historically and sociologically (to say nothing of geographically), and far more *prescriptive* of what that community might and should be, religiously and theologically.[63] Insufficient appreciation of these factors can lead readers of the Gospels to tumble into what has been called "the referential fallacy": the assumption that there is a one-for-one correlation between a Gospel's story line and the actual world, in time and space, from which that story issued.[64] As we are reminded by the Spanish philosopher, José Ortega y Gasset, "The person portrayed and the portrait are two entirely different things"[65]—and the same truth holds for artistic representation of historical and social circumstances.

On balance I think that our relevant evidence is strong enough to lend support to a location of Mark's Gospel in Rome; at the same time it remains too equivocal to nail that theory down. Given our present state of knowledge, we can nevertheless speak of *an appreciable social, religious, and theological congruity* between the Second Gospel and first-century Christianity in that region. "Whence" (*unde*) the Gospel's association with Rome is intelligible, even if the actual "where" (*ubi*) of its origin be ultimately unverifiable. If they were indeed as much in the dark about the book's historical origins as we, then the church fathers could have reasoned their way to an intelligible conclusion (the consonance of Mark's Gospel with Roman Christianity) on the strength of a fallacious premise (a legendary connection between the apostle Peter and the Second Evangelist). On the other hand, it is worth remembering that the sheer connection of Mark with that apostle need not have necessitated a secondary derivation of Mark *from Rome*. After all, the figure of Peter was exceedingly significant in Syrian Christianity, but none of the early fathers, even those from Syria themselves, located the composition of the Second Gospel there.[66] What suggested, or at least bolstered, the triangulation of Peter-Mark-Rome appears to have been the strong testimony not to Peter's mere presence in Rome (much less the later tradition of his

Roman pontificate) but, rather, to his Roman *martyrdom*.[67] In other words, the fathers seem to have been impressed not only with the Second Gospel's Petrine derivation but also with its strong overtones of suffering and death for the Christian cause, an impression shared by a host of modern scholars. In any case, the association between Mark's Gospel and Rome, drawn by most patristic interpreters and perpetuated by some of their modern counterparts, is, if not proven, then at least not improbable.

MARK AND ALEXANDRIA

With one exception in third- and fourth-century Eastern traditions, the association of Alexandria with Mark pivots on stories of the Second *Evangelist* and not, strictly speaking, on considerations of the Second *Gospel*. For this reason there is little call for inquiry into the consonance of Mark's Gospel with patristic traditions about the Evangelist and Alexandria. The exception, of course, is occasioned by John Chrysostom's remark that "Mark too, in Egypt, is said to have [composed his Gospel] at the entreaty of the disciples" (*Homily* [1:7] *on Matthew*). As we have seen, there is nothing in this passing comment to suggest that Chrysostom was referring to anything other than the Markan Gospel of the Christian canon.[68] Unfortunately, a responsible inquiry into the Second Gospel's alleged Alexandrian affinities is impossible to undertake, since practically nothing about Christianity in this significant region can be documented much earlier than A.D. 200, a date far too late for the canonical Gospel of Mark.

If the document implied by Chrysostom's comment is actually the *Secret Gospel of Mark,* known to us through the Alexandrian Clement's *Letter to Theodore,* then some connections might be drawn, religiously if not historically, between *that* ancient text and its patristic commentary: as Helmut Koester has noted, Mark's *Secret Gospel* suggests an esoteric rite of initiation into a form of Christianity compatible with the theology and practice of Egyptian Gnostic sects.[69] Intriguing though it be, that possibility poses a topic for an essay other than this.[70]

SOME CONCLUSIONS:
THE NEW TESTAMENT'S GOSPEL
AND THE FATHERS' EVANGELIST

Part 3 of this study was introduced with a query: Is there meaningful consonance between patristic portrayals of Mark the Evangelist and the concerns of the Gospel according to Mark? This, I have suggested, is a complex question that requires division and consideration at different levels.

1. *Historically,* the results of our investigation have been equivocal and somewhat negative. (a) The Second Gospel bespeaks the handiwork of a creative traditionist, arguably a stylist and religious thinker of merit, who may have been named Mark. Nevertheless, the author's identity is irrecoverable, and the historicity of that ascription cannot be verified. Even though reference to a singular author has become a popular and scholarly convention, we cannot know for sure whether Mark's Gospel is the product of one writer or several. (b) Although not inconceivable, a direct historical connection between the apostle Peter and either the Second Evangelist or the Second Gospel cannot be established. (c) While by no means improbable, the location of that book's composition in Rome is, likewise, practically impossible to confirm.

With each of these issues we have run headlong against recurring problems: our sources are too spotty, too sparsely corroborated, too heavily coated with religious or theological preoccupations to be successfully penetrated and appraised for their historicity. Relatively speaking, Mark's putative association with Roman Christianity probably enjoys the highest degree of the historian's confidence. Yet even for that datum our evidence is tangential and ambiguous, our methods of analysis relatively crude. The origin of Mark's Gospel remains a small piece in the larger puzzle of primitive Christian origins; it profits us nothing to pretend to knowledge in matters in which even reasonable certainty is, at least for now, unattainable.

2. If we shift gears and inquire into the broader *social* significance of patristic ascription of the Second Gospel to Mark, as that figure is couched by most of the fathers, the results are more promising. Whatever historical circumstances may have conditioned its creation, Mark's Gospel presumes a discernible pattern of social identities and relationships which is compatible with what may be inferred of Christianity in the region with which its alleged author is most closely associated. (a) "Following Jesus," in the Second Gospel, is the challenge issued to both men and women, to persons of varying ethnic origins, social standings, and economic levels. So it was in Rome, and elsewhere in the empire. (b) The interaction of Roman Christians with other social groups in the first century appears to have been dissonant: engaged with a culture in which they felt marginalized; nurtured in, but increasingly divorced from, Judaism; striving to achieve critical stability within an empire with which they were in confrontation; struggling toward Christian solidarity among themselves. A similar

profile of Jesus' adherents emerges from the Gospel of Mark. (c) Beyond that document itself the patristic depiction of Mark the Evangelist as responsible trustee of apostolic traditions about Jesus probably served, in part, an ancient social function: as a warrant, among both pagans and Christians, for the claims of the religious perspective espoused by the Second Gospel.

3. Pondering such factors as these directs us toward some specifically *religious* functions of the fathers' alignment of the Second Gospel with an authorial figure. (a) For one thing, the attribution of this Gospel to a particular Evangelist, Mark, afforded a means by which patristic Christians could construe that document's distinctive harvest of traditions about Jesus. (b) Imputing the Second Gospel to Peter's surrogate also added a "link" in a chain of apostolic witness to Jesus, thereby enhancing the perceived depth and credibility of emergent Christian tradition. (c) Moreover, the ascription of that Gospel to Mark oriented its readers toward the appropriation of the book's content from within a definable circle, or heritage, of Christian antiquity. Much as North Americans may tag a political legacy as that of Roosevelt or of Reagan (even when speaking of matters in which those presidents may not have been personally involved), many patristic Christians formulated their understanding of the Second Gospel's significance with reference to the apostle Peter. We have entertained the further possibility that the figures of Mark and of Peter may have been reciprocally interpretive of that particular expression of Christianity with which both were associated.

4. Characteristic of that tradition were some *theological* tendencies, whose manifestation in the Second Gospel may have bolstered the intelligibility of that book's attribution to a Petrine protégé. (a) Like the theology of 1 Peter, which was probably authored not by the apostle but, rather, by a later individual or group in Rome, Markan theology appears to have been richly amalgamative, grounded in Palestinian Judaism yet receptive to a range of Hellenistic Christian ideas and practices. (b) Both Mark's Gospel and 1 Peter attempt to equilibrate some common theological tensions: the edification of Christian communities with parochial tendencies, coupled with a more expansive mission for "the elect"; faithful adherence to God's will in an age thought to be passing away; a belief in Christians' vindication by means of, not apart from, torments social and political. (c) First Peter and the Second Gospel commonly speak of Jesus' death in a way that integrates what modern thinkers might call "theology and praxis": the Christ's suffering service both interprets and normatively models the Christian's own conduct in a world regarded as potentially or actually

hostile. Interestingly enough, it is precisely at this point—the perceived importance of faithful martyrdom—that the theologies of 1 Peter and Mark most profoundly intersect not only with each other but also with the thrust of our earliest traditions about Peter in Rome.

Forty years ago the British scholar Austin Farrer concluded his assessment of patristic testimony about Mark with some observations that would doubtless ring true for many New Testament critics: "The outlook is discouraging. For we have seen that the whole substance of what [Papias] gives us is neither more nor less than an ingenious but false historical hypothesis. . . . The hypothesis was an invention, but it was invented to account for something."[71] By attributing to Papias a false historical hypothesis, Farrer may have been correct. Not infrequently, as we have observed, historical probabilities weigh against the comments of Papias and others on Mark. In any case, such historical considerations are certainly complex, possibly to a considerable extent unresolvable.

On the other hand, in reckoning this patristic opinion as *neither more nor less* than historically false, Farrer himself may have strayed into overstatement. Patristic reflections on the authorship of Mark's Gospel suggest a good deal more than historical dubiety: they convey an intricate pattern of resonance with at least some of the social, religious, and theological dimensions of that document. Whatever may have been the proportions of remembrance and invention, of fact and fancy, in patristic conjectures about the Second Evangelist and his Gospel, those hypotheses did account, or at least tried to account, for some things of consequence. Our own outlook need not be quite so dispirited, notwithstanding Farrer's estimate to the contrary.

NOTES

1. Rome prevails as the likely, though not indisputable, origin of the Second Gospel in scholarship old and recent. Among standard introductions to the field, see W. D. Davies, *Invitation to the New Testament: A Guide to Its Main Witnesses*, Anchor Books (Garden City, N.Y.: Doubleday, 1969), 198; James L. Price, *The New Testament: Its History and Theology* (New York and London: Macmillan/Collier, 1987), 124; Robert A. Spivey and D. Moody Smith, *Anatomy of the New Testament: A Guide to Its Structure and Meaning*, 4th ed. (New York: Macmillan, 1989), 63–64. Among commentaries, see Henry Barclay Swete, *The Gospel according to St Mark: The Greek Text with Introduction, Notes, and Indices*, 3d. ed (London: Macmillan, 1927), xxxix–xliii; A. E. J. Rawlinson, *St. Mark, with Introduction, Commentary, and Additional Notes*, WC (London: Methuen & Co., 1925), xxvi; B. Harvie Branscomb, *The Gospel of Mark*, MNTC (London: Hodder & Stoughton,

1937), xv–xviii; Vincent Taylor, *The Gospel according to St. Mark*, 2d. ed., Thornapple Commentaries (1946; reprint, Grand Rapids, Mich.: Baker Book House, 1981), 32; C. E. B. Cranfield, *The Gospel according to Saint Mark*, CGTC (Cambridge: Cambridge University Press, 1959), 8–9; Dennis Eric Nineham, *The Gospel of St. Mark*, PGC (Baltimore: Penguin, 1963), 42; Rudolph Pesch, *Das Markusevangelium*, HTKNT (Freiberg: Herder, 1976), 1: 3–11; Joachim Gnilka, *Das Evangelium nach Markus*, EKKNT 2 (Zurich and Neukirchener Vluyn: Benzinger/Neukirchener, 1978), 1: 34. Studies of Mark that favor a Roman provenance include Benjamin Wisner Bacon, *Is Mark a Roman Gospel?*, HTS 7 (Cambridge, Mass.: Harvard University Press, 1919); Curtis Beach, *The Gospel of Mark: Its Making and Meaning* (New York: Harper & Brothers, 1959), 54–63; Ralph P. Martin, *Mark: Evangelist and Theologian* (Grand Rapids., Mich.: Zondervan, 1972), 61–69; Raymond E. Brown and John P. Meier, *Antioch and Rome: New Testament Cradles of Catholic Christianity* (New York and Ramsey, N.J.: Paulist, 1983), 191–201; Ernest Best, *Mark: The Gospel as Story* (Edinburgh: T & T Clark, 1983), 21–36. Martin Hengel, *Studies in the Gospel of Mark*, trans. John Bowden (Philadelphia: Fortress, 1980), 1–30, 117–38, offers the most extensive defense, known to me, of the historicity of Mark's Roman origin.

2. It might be recalled that Mark's linkage with Rome (and Peter) are among the few details that remain constant within the disparate Clementine witnesses. See chapter 5.

3. The use of *Babylon* as a code name for Rome (see also Rev 14:8; 16:19; 17:5; 18:2, 10, 21; *2 Apoc. Bar.* 11.1; 67.7; *Sib. Or.* 5.143, 159) apparently arose from those empires' conquests of Jerusalem and destruction of the Jewish temple in, respectively, 587 B.C. and A.D. 70. A convincing argument for this suggestion is provided by Claus-Hunno Hunzinger, "Babylon als Deckname für Röm und die Datierung des 1. Petrusbriefs," in *Gottes Wort und Gottes Land*, ed. Henning Graf Reventlow (Göttingen: Vandenhoeck & Ruprecht, 1965), 67–77.

4. In this regard a pair of conclusions in chapter 6 might be recalled, but inverted: in those (primarily Eastern) traditions in which Peter's career and Mark's composition are more closely coordinated, the location of the Gospel is more precisely identified as Rome. Correlatively, in those (Western) traditions in which the activities of Mark and Peter overlap less, the Gospel's provenance becomes vaguer ("in the regions of Italy").

5. Thus, see, among others, Gnilka, *Das Evangelium nach Markus*, 1:33; Dieter Lührmann, *Das Markusevangelium*, HNT 3 (Tübingen: Mohr [Siebeck], 1987), 5.

6. To frame the question in this way differentiates the following discussion from such learned but inevitably dated surveys as George Edmundson's Bampton Lectures, given earlier in this century at Oxford, *The Church in Rome in the First Century: An Examination of Various Controverted Questions relating to Its History, Chronology, Literature and Traditions* (London: Longmans, Green, 1913). Taking the New Testament and patristic traditions largely

at face value, Edmundson's remarks on John Mark's influence upon Roman Christianity now seem naive, even antique, in their critical premises. More discerning is Walter Bauer's classic volume, *Orthodoxy and Heresy in Earliest Christianity*, ed. Robert A. Kraft and Gerhard Krodel, 2d. ed. (Philadelphia: Fortress, 1971; on Roman Christianity, see esp. 95–129), which, though still instructive, labors under the weight of its comprehensive hypothesis that Christian orthodoxy was the development of older positions that later were branded as heretical.

7. The standard work in this area is Peter Lampe, *Die stadtrömischen Christen in den ersten beiden Jahrhunderten: Untersuchungen zur Sozialgeschichte*, WUNT 18 (Tübingen: Mohr [Siebeck], 1987), to which my treatment is prinicipally indebted. Less ambitious but informative for the discussion are James S. Jeffers, *Conflict at Rome: Social Order and Hierarchy in Early Christianity* (Minneapolis: Fortress, 1991); Jeffers, "Pluralism in Early Roman Christianity," *Fides et Historia* 22 (1990): 5–17 (which condenses the thesis of Jeffers's monograph); and Raymond Brown's analysis of Roman Christianity's theological traditions in Brown and Meier, *Antioch and Rome*, 87–210. The volumes by Lampe and Jeffers contain copious bibliographies of other relevant research.

8. George La Piana, "Foreign Groups in Rome during the First Centuries of the Empire," *HTR* 20 (1927): 183–403; La Piana, "The Roman Church at the End of the Second Century," *HTR* 18 (1925): 201–77.

9. Even more explicitly and extensively, Romans 9–11 is devoted to the relationship between Christian Jews and Gentiles in God's impartial plan for human salvation.

10. Exactly where Romans ends and whether chapter 16 was originally part of that letter are points long debated in the history of New Testament scholarship. Naturally, if one judges the end of the letter to have been at Romans 15:33, the pertinence of Romans 16 for discerning anything about the church at Rome is moot. The most extensive study of the textual problem, which favors the inclusion of Romans 16:1–23 as part of the original letter, is Harry Y. Gamble, Jr., *The Textual History of the Letter to the Romans*, SD 42 (Grand Rapids, Mich.: Eerdmans, 1977).

11. Corroboration for the Jewish tenor of Roman Christianity is provided by Ambrosiaster, the name given to a fourth-century Latin commentator: "it is generally admitted that in the time of the apostles there were Jews . . . living in Rome; those among them who had become believers delivered to the Romans the tradition that while professing Christ they should keep the law. . . . [T]hey accepted faith in Christ, though according to a Jewish rite" (cited in F. W. Beare, "Rome (Church)," *IDB* 4 [1962]: 123).

12. Commentators on Romans are divided on whether "Rufus," greeted by Paul (in Rom 16:13), refers to the son of Cyrenian Simon, Alexander's brother (in Mark 15:21). Beyond the fact that the name was quite common, doubts surround the original readership of *both* Mark's Gospel and Romans 16 (see n. 10); thus, it is probably well that we note the coincidence without building anything upon it.

13. Consult Lampe, *Die stadtrömischen Christen*, 135–53, for a thoroughly documented treatment of the names in Romans 16 within their Greco-Roman social context.

14. Lampe, *Die stadtrömischen Christen*, 36–52. A similar, more general assessment of early Christians' mixed socioeconomic status enjoys consensus among many social scientific critics of the New Testament. See Robin Scroggs, "The Sociological Interpretation of the New Testament: The Present State of Research," *NTS* 26 (1980): 164–79, esp. 169–71.

15. This conclusion follows if, as Christian tradition holds, two Roman aristocrats executed by the emperor Domitian (81–96), Titus Flavius Clemens and his wife Flavia Domitilla, were Christians (see the ill-defined reports of Suetonius, *Domitian* 15; Dio Cassius, *Roman History* 67.14). See Lampe, *Die stadtrömischen Christen*, 166–72; Jeffers, *Conflict at Rome*, 25–28; but cf. the more skeptical assessment of James Stevenson, ed., *A New Eusebius: Documents Illustrative of the History of the Church to A.D. 337* (London: SPCK, 1957), 8.

16. Jeffers, *Conflict at Rome*, esp. 90–120. For another interpretation of the *Shepherd* which finds less evidence for the economic cleavage proposed by Jeffers, cf. Carolyn Osiek, *Rich and Poor in the* Shepherd of Hermas, CBQMS 15 (Washington, D.C.: Catholic Biblical Association of America, 1983).

17. Jeffers, *Conflict at Rome*, 20–21.

18. Harry J. Leon, *The Jews of Ancient Rome* (Philadelphia: Jewish Publication Society, 1960), 167–94.

19. Lampe, *Die stadtrömichen Christen*, 301–45.

20. As Jeffers points out (*Conflict at Rome*, 42), "those of Aristobulus" and "of Narcissus who are in the Lord" (Rom 16:10–11) could refer to yet two more house churches in Rome.

21. Lampe traces the development of later heresies in Roman Christianity back to its geographical and social *Fraktionierung* ("fragmentation") (*Die stadtrömischen Christen*, 320–34).

22. Lampe, *Die stadtrömischen Christen*, 334–45; Brown, *Antioch and Rome*, 163–64. In this connection it is interesting to recall the absence, in the Second Gospel, of the tradition of Peter's recognition as the ecclesial stone and as recipient of the kingdom's keys (Matt 16:18–19). Of course, Mark may have been ignorant of this tradition, known to Matthew.

23. Suetonius's chronicle is brief: "Since the Jews constantly made disturbances at the instigation of Chrestus, [Claudius] expelled them from Rome . . ." (trans. J. C. Rolfe [LCL]). Although the identity of the instigator to whom Suetonius refers is uncertain, "Chrestus" was a fairly common variant spelling of "Christus." It is therefore possible, though not certain, that riots between Jews and Christians in Rome may have occasioned the Jewish expulsion in 49 (thus, Stevenson, *New Eusebius*, 1–2).

24. The translation is by John Jackson (LCL), with slight alterations.

25. See chapter 7.

26. Lampe, *Die stadtrömischen Christen*, 65–67.

27. Jeffers, *Conflict at Rome*, 17.

28. A notable work on this subject is Hans Lietzmann, *Petrus und Paulus in Rom*, 2d. ed. (Berlin: Töpelmann, 1927); see also Oscar Cullmann, *Peter: Disciple-Apostle-Martyr. A Historical and Theological Study*, trans. Floyd V. Filson (Philadelphia: Westminster, 1953), 89–112. Morton Smith, "The Report about Peter in I Clement V.4," *NTS* 7 (1960–61): 86–88, argues, to the contrary, that the tradition of Peter's Roman martyrdom was constructed from materials in Acts. All of the Roman traditions pertaining to Peter are judiciously appraised by Daniel William O'Connor, *Peter in Rome: The Literary, Liturgical, and Archaeological Evidence* (New York: Columbia University Press, 1969), whose basic thesis is summarized in an essay, "Peter in Rome: A Review and Position," in *Christianity, Judaism, and Other Greco-Roman Cults: Studies for Morton Smith at Sixty*, ed. Jacob Neusener (Leiden: E. J. Brill, 1975), pt. 2, 146–60.

29. Of this exceedingly complex history only the barest of summaries can be offered here. On the imperial convulsions of the period, consult Koester, *Introduction to the New Testament*, vol. 1: *History, Culture, and Religion of the Hellenistic Age* (Philadelphia, Berlin, and New York: Fortress / Walter de Gruyter, 1982), 311–17. The history of the first-century Jewish revolution against Rome is well chronicled in Emil Schürer, *The History of the Jewish People in the Age of Jesus Christ (175 B.C.–A.D. 135)*, ed. G. Vermes, F. Millar, P. Vermes, and M. Black, rev. ed. (Edinburgh: T & T Clark, 1973), 1:484–513.

30. For contrasting assessments of the kind and degree of Christian apologetic at work during the first century, cf. S. G. F. Brandon, *The Fall of Jerusalem and the Christian Church* (London: SPCK, 1951), with the various essays in *Jesus and the Politics of His Day*, ed. Ernst Bammel and C. F. D. Moule (Cambridge: Cambridge University Press, 1984). In the latter volume note especially G. W. H. Lampe, "A.D. 70 in Christian Reflection" (153–71).

31. Clarence L. Lee, "Social Unrest and Primitive Christianity," in *The Catacombs and the Colosseum: The Roman Empire as the Setting of Primitive Christianity*, ed. Stephen Benko and John J. O'Rourke (Valley Forge, Pa.: Judson, 1971), 121–38.

32. Brown (*Antioch and Rome*, 105–83) constructs an interesting argument for theological constancy and development in Roman Christianity from Paul to *1 Clement*, by way of 1 Peter and the Epistle to the Hebrews.

33. So also Gerhard Dautzenberg, "Zur Stellung des Markusevangeliums in den Geschichte der urchristlichen Theologie," *Kairos* 18 (1976): 282–91.

34. In addition, a Semitic idiom colors the Greek of Mark's Gospel. See James Hope Moulton, Wilbert Francis Howard, and Nigel Turner, *A Grammar of New Testament Greek*, 4 vols. (Edinburgh: T & T Clark, 1906–1963), 2/1:12–34 (N.B. 28); 4:11–25.

35. Given the frequent occurrence of Latin terms in the text—for example, *legiōn* (5:9); *spekoulatora* ("executioner" or "soldier of the guard" [6:27]); *denarius* (6:37, 14:5); *kodrantēs* ("penny" [12:42])—the Second Gospel appears also to have been written for a Gentile audience familiar with that

language. Scholarship both older and more recent has recognized that such "Latinisms" would have been intelligible to anyone in the empire with a knowledge of the language; they do not unequivocally point toward the Gospel's origin in Rome. See W. R. Ramsay, "On Mark xii.42," *ExpTim* 10 (1898–99): 232; Henry J. Cadbury, *The Making of Luke-Acts* (New York: Macmillan, 1927), 88–89.

36. The discrepant biblical reference in Mark 1:2 was noted by Jerome, as we saw in chapter 5.

37. Questions may also be raised about the accuracy of Mark's understanding of Jewish parties in the time of Jesus: thus, see Michael J. Cook, *Mark's Treatment of the Jewish Leaders*, NovTSup 51 (Leiden: E. J. Brill, 1978). The Second Gospel's stylized portrayal of Pharisees and other Jewish antagonists of Jesus is explored in Jack Dean Kingsbury, *Conflict in Mark: Jesus, Authorities, Disciples* (Minneapolis: Fortress, 1989), 63–88.

38. This point cannot be made to carry undue weight. The contemporaneous evidence is ambiguous, and some historians believe that a wife in first-century Palestine did have the right to initiate divorce: thus, Ernst Bammel, "Markus 10:1f und das jüdische Eherecht," *ZNW* 61 (1970): 95–101; Bernadette J. Brooten, "Konnten Frauen im alten Judentum die Scheidung betreiben? Überlegungen zu Mk 10,11–12 und 1 Kor 7,10–11," *EvT* 42 (1982): 65–80. Dissenting from this analysis are Eduard Schweizer, "Scheidungsrecht der jüdischen Frau? Weibliche Jünger Jesu?," *EvT* 42 (1982): 294–300; and Hans Weder, "Perspektive der Frauen?" *EvT* 43 (1983): 175–78. The issue remains controversial and unresolved.

39. For an interesting attempt to locate Mark 7 within the broader development of Jewish Christian reflection on the law, see James D. G. Dunn, "Jesus and Ritual Purity: A Study of the Tradition-History of Mark 7.15," in *Jesus, Paul and the Law: Studies in Mark and Galatians* (Louisville: Westminster, 1990), 37–60.

40. Elsewhere in Mark, Jesus is identified as "the Son of God" either by the narrator (1:1) or by supernatural beings, whether God (1:11, 9:7) or the demons (3:11, 5:7). The title is more obliquely associated with Jesus in the high priest's unbelieving question (14:61) and by Jesus himself in the parable of the vineyard (12:6).

41. The assumption of a fitful transition to a Christianity more Gentile than Jewish may partially account for Mark's mystifying challenge to Jesus' Davidic lineage (12:35–37), which tends to be presumed elsewhere in the New Testament (Matt 1:1–17; Luke 3:23–38; Rom 1:3; 2 Tim 2:8) and elsewhere even in Mark (10:47–48). As Morna Hooker suggests, for Mark the title, "Son of David," may have become christologically inadequate, "misleading in a Jewish context and meaningless in a Gentile one" (*The Gospel according to St. Mark*, BNTC [London: A & C Black, 1991], 292).

42. Thus, among others, see Edward Schweizer, *The Good News according to Mark* (Richmond: John Knox, 1970), 192–93, 206–7; Hugh Anderson, *The Gospel of Mark*, NCB (Grand Rapids, Mich., and London: Eerdmans/Mar-

shall, Morgan & Scott, 1976), 234, 246–47; Pesch, *Das Markusevangelium*, 2: 106–7, 133; Lührmann, *Das Markusevangelium*, 166, 171–72; Hooker, *St. Mark*, 228, 238–39.

43. See the discussion in David Rhoads and Donald Michie, *Mark as Story: An Introduction to the Narrative of a Gospel* (Philadelphia: Fortress, 1982), 129–36.

44. Careful exegetical study of the faithful but powerless characters in Mark is offered by Christopher D. Marshall, *Faith as a Theme in Mark's Narrative*, SNTSMS 64 (Cambridge: Cambridge University Press, 1989), 75–133. On Mark's favorable portrayal of women as disciples, see Elisabeth Schüssler Fiorenza, *In Memory of Her: A Feminist Theological Reconstruction of Christian Origins* (New York: Crossroad, 1983), 316–23.

45. In sociological perspective Wilhelm Wuellner probes *The Meaning of "Fishers of Men,"* NTL (Philadelphia: Westminster, 1967).

46. An illuminating analysis of the theme of family in Mark's description of discipleship is offered by John R. Donahue, *The Theology and Setting of Discipleship in the Gospel of Mark* (Milwaukee: Marquette University Press, 1983), esp. 31–51. Donahue's careful exegetical essay, "A Neglected Factor in the Theology of Mark" (*JBL* 101 [1982]: 563–94), highlights the Evangelist's conception of "the will of God," focusing on Mark 11–12.

47. It is hard for modern readers to hear the whisper of political protest in these terms. The Book of Daniel, for example, juxtaposes this world's ephemeral regimes with the indestructible kingdom of God (Dan 2:36–45; 4:2–3, 34–35; 7:13–14). "Good news" (*euangelion*) figures prominently in the rhetoric of a decree honoring Caesar Augustus (27 B.C.–A.D. 14), who, like other potentates of antiquity, was routinely accorded divine reverence.

48. William Wrede, *The Messianic Secret* (Cambridge and Greenwood, S.C.: James Clarke / Attic, 1971 [German original, 1901]), is the classic work on this topic, whose contours are explored in a volume edited by Christopher Tuckett, *The Messianic Secret*, IRT 1 (Philadelphia and London: Fortress / SPCK, 1983).

49. James Alan Wilde, "A Social Description of the Community Reflected in the Gospel of Mark" (Ph.D. diss., Drew University, 1974); Howard Clark Kee, *Community of the New Age: Studies in Mark's Gospel* (Philadelphia: Westminster, 1977; note esp. 77–105, 165–77); Joel Marcus, *The Mystery of the Kingdom of God*, SBLDS 90 (Atlanta: Scholars Press, 1986).

50. In my opinion S. G. F. Brandon's attempt to read Mark as a post-70 Roman apologia, sharply dissociating Christianity from Jewish nationalism, brackets out the Gospel's residual Jewish sympathies as well as its jaundiced view of the empire. Brandon's thesis is unfolded in *Jesus and the Zealots: A Study of the Political Factor in Primitive Christianity* (New York: Charles Scribner's Sons, 1967); its implications for interpreting Mark are summarized in "The Date of the Markan Gospel," *NTS* 7 (1961): 126–41. For a judicious critique, see Best, *Mark: The Gospel as Story*, 31–34.

51. Correlatively, in Mark one of Jesus' three predictions of the Son of

Man's suffering is framed in terms of a general betrayal "into human hands" (9:31; see also 8:31, 10:33–34).

52. In this connection one might ponder Gerd Theissen's intriguing proposal that Jesus' triumph over a demonic "legion" (a Roman regiment of about six thousand soldiers [Mark 5:1–20]) captures Jewish aspirations for expulsion of the forces of Roman occupation (*The Miracle Stories of the Early Christian Tradition*, ed. John Riches [Philadelphia: Fortress, 1983], 255).

53. Martin Hengel (*Studies in the Gospel of Mark*, 23) notes that Mark is the first New Testament writer to speak of Christians as being universally hated. As one might guess, I am generally sympathetic with Hengel's attempt to locate Mark 13 within the social and political climate of the mid-first century Rome (1–30, 117–38) while skeptical of the precision with which he believes the Gospel's final redaction can be dated (A.D. 69).

54. With Mark 13:12 one might compare John 9:22, 12:42, and 16:2, which no doubt also refer to painful divisions, later in the first century, among families and coreligionists over the claims of Christianity.

55. Mary Ann Tolbert's correlation of the disciples with the behavior described in Mark 4:16–17 seems to me more persuasive than her conclusion that Mark's last word on the disciples is one of "grieving failure" (*Sowing the Gospel: Mark's World in Literary-Historical Perspective* [Minneapolis: Fortress, 1989], 154–56, 195–230; quotation on 218). As I have tried to show in *The Disciples according to Mark: Markan Redaction in Current Debate*, JSNTSup 27 (Sheffield: Sheffield Academic Press, 1989), exactly what the reader is intended to conclude, from the Second Gospel, about the fortunes of the Twelve depends largely on one's overall interpretation of Markan theology.

56. Elliott, "Peter, Silvanus and Mark in I Peter and Acts," 253–57.

57. Additionally attractive for this theory is the fact that such a connection may thus be drawn without anachronistic appeal to Rome's ecclesiastical primacy, which supposedly lent credibility to a marginal document like Mark (among many others, see Alfred Loisy, *L'Évangile selon Marc* [Paris: Émile Nourry, 1912], 52; Bacon, *Is Mark a Roman Gospel?*, 39; Burnett Hillman Streeter, *The Four Gospels: A Study of Origins* [New York: Macmillan, 1925], 491; Cranfield, *Saint Mark*, 9). Although the church (or churches) in Rome may have enjoyed some renown among Christians as early as the first century (see Rom 1:8), the evidence for an acknowledged Roman primacy is slender until the third or fourth centuries (see James F. McCue, "Roman Primacy in the Second Century and the Problem of the Development of Dogma," *TS* 25 [1964]: 161–96). Not until much later, then, could the Second Gospel have so comfortably basked in the Roman church's reflected glory. Even more skeptical is Hans von Campenhausen (*The Formation of the Christian Bible* [Philadelphia: Fortress, 1972], 123), who doubts that each of the Gospels originally had its own territorial domain.

58. As argued by B. M. F. van Iersel, "The Gospel according to St. Mark— Written for a Persecuted Community?" *NTT* 34 (1980): 15–36.

59. With its heavily rural environment and location at a crossroads of

Christian traditions, southern Syria seems a likely provenance for Mark in the carefully reasoned judgments of Kee, *Community of the New Age*, 100–105; and Gerd Theissen, *The Gospels in Context: Social and Political History in the Synoptic Tradition*, trans. Linda M. Maloney (Minneapolis: Fortress, 1991), 236–49. Markan theology's ostensible Pauline sympathies suggest, to some scholars, a location of the Gospel in the region of that apostle's Hellenistic mission (Reginald H. Fuller, *A Critical Introduction to the New Testament* [London: Duckworth, 1971], 107; Helmut Koester, "*Gnomai Diaphorai:* The Origin and Nature of Diversification in the History of Early Christianity," in *Trajectories through Early Christianity*, ed. James M. Robinson and Helmut Koester [Philadelphia, Fortress, 1971], 114–57; Koester, *Introduction*, 2:166–67). Impressed by "the urgency Mark feels about the Jewish war," Marcus (*The Mystery of the Kingdom of God*, 10) is inclined to locate the Gospel in the East, probably in Syria, rather than in the West (Marcus, "The Jewish War and the *Sitz im Leben* of Mark," *JBL* 111 [1992]: 441–62). Though less sure of its precise location, Werner Georg Kümmel (*Introduction to the New Testament*, 17th rev. ed., trans. Howard Clark Kee [Nashville: Abingdon: 1973], 98) and Lührmann (*Das Markusevangelium*, 7) also consider an Eastern origin likely for Mark.

60. Thus, Marxsen: "Galilee, or the Sea of Galilee, has special significance for the primitive community of Mark's day. Hence, not only Jesus' activity is concentrated in this area; the communities as well are directed here; indeed, they come here" (*Mark the Evangelist: Studies on the Redaction-History of the Gospel*, trans. James Boyce et al [New York and Nashville: Abingdon, 1968], 64; cf. 54–116; see also Marxsen, *Introduction to the New Testament*, trans. G. Buswell [Philadelphia: Fortress, 1968], 143). Yet the certainty of this historical assessment seems somewhat shaken by Marxsen's own (arguably overstated) estimate of the theological symbolism of Galilee in Mark: "Where Jesus worked, there is Galilee" (*Mark the Evangelist*, 94–95). More recently, Werner H. Kelber has located Mark in Galilee, within the context of a larger theory of conflicting Christian traditions (*The Kingdom in Mark: A New Place and a New Time* [Philadelphia: Fortress, 1974]).

61. Among others, Schweizer, *The Good News according to Mark*, 25; Anderson, *The Gospel of Mark*, 26–29; Norman Perrin and Dennis Duling, *The New Testament: An Introduction: Proclamation and Paranesis, Myth and History*, 2d. ed. (New York: Harcourt Brace Jovanovich, 1982), 163; Hans Conzelmann and Andreas Lindemann, *Interpreting the New Testament: An Introduction to the Principles and Methods of N. T. Exegesis*, trans. Siegfried Schatzmann (Peabody, Mass.: Hendrickson, 1988), 219; Hooker, *St. Mark*, 7–8; Paul J. Achtemeier, "Mark, Gospel of," *ABD* 4 (1992): 543.

62. Bengt Holmberg, *Sociology and the New Testament: An Appraisal* (Minneapolis: Fortress, 1990), provides sympathetic criticism of this approach.

63. Dan O. Via, Jr., *The Ethics of Mark's Gospel—In the Middle of Time* (Philadelphia: Fortress, 1985), 71–76.

64. Norman R. Petersen, *Literary Criticism for New Testament Critics*,

GBSNTS (Philadelphia: Fortress, 1978), 38–40. Among recent analyses of Mark's social world Herman C. Waetjen's fascinating work, *A Reordering of Power: A Socio-Political Reading of Mark's Gospel* (Minneapolis: Fortress, 1989), has arguably stepped into this methodological quagmire; see my review of Waetjen's volume in *BTB* 21 (1991): 83–84.

65. José Ortega y Gasset, *The Dehumanization of Art and Notes on the Novel*, trans. Helene Weyl (Princeton: Princeton University Press, 1948), 10–11. I have slightly modified Weyl's translation.

66. See chapter 5. The principal patristic witnesses for Peter's activities in Antioch are cataloged by Glanville Downey in *A History of Antioch in Syria from Seleucus to the Arab Conquest* (Princeton: Princeton University Press, 1961), 583–86, which complements his treatment, in the same volume (272–316), of "The Christian Community at Antioch, from Apostolic Times to A.D. 284."

67. Thus, also E. A. Russell, "The Gospel of Mark: Pastoral Response to a Life or Death Situation? Some Reflections," *IBS* 7 (1983): 206–23. In his careful survey of *Petrine Controversies in Early Christianity* (207–8) Terence Smith shows that the earliest detectable allusions to Peter and Rome (1 Pet 5:13; 2 Pet 1:14) refer to the apostle's journey and martyrdom there.

68. See chapter 5.

69. Koester, *Introduction*, 2:223.

70. Very likely, Koester himself would disagree with my assessment, as he considers Mark's *Secret Gospel* to have been an earlier recension of what came to be edited and canonized as the Gospel according to Mark. Specifically, Koester conjectures that the canonical Second Gospel was actually a *third* edition of Mark—a somewhat elaborated version of a previously abbreviated form of the *Secret Gospel*, the most primitive of all Markan versions (*Ancient Christian Gospels*, 293–303). To consider this intriguing (to date, minority) hypothesis would carry us too far afield from our purposes. For an alternative assessment that points up the difficulty in discerning the direction of the derivations among canonical and noncanonical Gospels, see Frans Neirynck, "The Minor Agreements and Proto-Mark: A Response to H. Koester," *ETL* 67 (1991): 82–94.

71. Austin Farrer, *A Study in St Mark* (New York: Oxford University Press, 1952), 21. Farrer's next sentence speculates on an underlying motive for Papias's hypothesis, without exactly postulating the "something" that it was designed to explain: "The hypothesis supposes anyhow that the first Gospel in Greek to obtain authority in the Greek Churches was Mark's" (20–21).

Conclusion

Mark the Evangelist:
Some Reflections out of Season

From among several gossamer strands embedded in small patches of the New Testament, patristic authors plucked one, sometimes two, for weaving into a traditional miniature that characterized the composition of the anonymous Second Gospel. The effect of their portrayal has been, paradoxically, both ephemeral and enduring: for, while the personality of Mark has never preoccupied biblical interpreters, whether patristic or contemporary, that Gospel has ever since been personalized, by custom ancient and modern, as the one "according to Mark."

However deep or shallow its historical grounding, the attribution of the Second Gospel to Mark and the sustenance of that ascription across the centuries need never have happened. In a previous chapter we pondered the question of why patristic observers settled on Mark, among other possibilities, as an appropriate identification of that Gospel's author. Even so, one might wonder why the ancient church took the trouble to remember and to embellish a Markan personality, basted into stories about that Gospel's creation. Indeed, an even more fundamental question might be raised: Why bother with a human author at all? If the crucial factor were ultimately the legitimation of a religious text, why not simply impute to Mark's Gospel a divine origin, much as the Vedas are regarded in traditional Hinduism?

Considered as a dimension of the broader study of Christian religious phenomena, such questions are neither trivial nor easily answerable, whether one assumes of patristic traditions some basis in fact or dismisses their historical foundation altogether. More vexing still, the early fathers offer us little explicit guidance in addressing such questions, since they were understandably more occupied in practicing Christianity than in self-referentially abstracting its practical peculiarities.

251

PERSONIFICATION AND APOSTOLICITY

Theoretically, the formation of a rudimentary personality for Mark the Evangelist was likely one function of a larger process, by which the early church came to recognize Mark's Gospel as an apostolic document. The early fathers' reasoning probably moved in a circle. On the one hand, patristic figurations of the Second Evangelist helped the church to understand, and to appropriate as apostolic, the Gospel with which they associated Mark. On the other hand, the general shape and, to some degree, the motivations of that Gospel informed the fathers' personification of its putative Evangelist as an apostolic associate and interpreter. While this circular maneuver may have been informed by some extrinsic assumptions about apostolicity, the fathers probably arrived at their understanding of both Gospel and Evangelist as apostolic by virtue of that reflective process itself.

Typically, within the framework of Christian theology, discourse about apostolicity is not necessarily tantamount to the claim that an apostle actually authored a given religious text (like a Gospel or creed) or authorized a given religious practice (such as a ritual or form of ministry). Nor is apostolicity interchangeable with the concept of "catholicity," which usually refers to some general, if not universal, consensus on authentic Christian belief and practice. Apostolicity, rather, is essentially an expression of the church's hope for its own integrity across time. It refers to the actual or potential continuity of a normative Christian witness, extending from the earliest testimonies to Jesus through each successive Christian generation:[1] a constancy that persists among inevitably variable formulations, throughout history, of the meaning of Christian faith. Even as an individual Christian changes across the experience of a lifetime, yet remains a recognizably unified self, apostolicity embraces the church's quest for " 'a visible, historical community,' possessing an identity and yet developing in response to new demands and opportunities."[2] The formation of a Christian canon (those books accorded the status of scripture) and the emergence of an episcopate (the office and order of bishops) were institutional embodiments of the church's commitment to maintain and to perpetuate its practical and theological heritage, styled as "the faith of the apostles."[3]

With respect to Mark, an early but significant step was taken when the patristic church not only conceptually *aligned* the Second Gospel with the apostle Peter but also *distanced* the book's creation from the ministry of the earthly Jesus.[4] Although the rise of historical consciousness since the Enlightenment has helped us to appreciate some of its implications with a clarity and force that they could not have realized, Papias, Justin, Irenaeus, and their successors presumed, indeed theologically esteemed, an important insight: strictly speaking, the Second Gospel (like other Gospels) does not so much offer "the life of Jesus" as a *remembrance* of that life, a commemoration born of Christian faith.[5] Within that context it is surely no accident that a chain of reminiscence looms large in some of our earliest testimonies to Mark's proclamation of Jesus: thus, Justin's characterization of the Gospels as apostolic memoirs (e.g., *Apol.* 1.66.3; *Dial.* 105.1, 5, 6); thus, the unbroken sequence of memory that is recalled, backward, from Eusebius to Papias to John the Elder, from John to Mark to Peter (Eusebius, *H.E.* 3.39.14–15).

As decades, then centuries, passed after the creation of the Second Gospel, the traditions about its author eventually melded into an image with, as we have witnessed, a considerable degree of coherence. Naturally, the Second Evangelist was presumed to have been related to an acknowledged apostle; however, for the early church it was not *merely* that predication that rendered the Second Gospel apostolic. The figure of Mark itself acquired a discernible measure of definition and stability. Once a relationship was established between the Evangelist and Peter it persisted to the usual, though not complete, exclusion of other traditional options, even alternatives that existed elsewhere in the New Testament (Acts; the Pauline epistolary tradition). Moreover, the figure of Mark came to be elaborated in other, relatively consistent ways: thus, for example, the Evangelist's chastened authority and activity in Rome. Though neither historically implausible nor in every case subject to historical confirmation, these recurrent features (like Mark's association with Peter) manifest, as we have seen in part 3, an external coherence with the concerns of the Second Gospel and its general regard by the early church.[6] As such, the figure of Mark—his patristic personality, if you will—appears to have contributed a dimension to the broader interpretive framework within which the early church read the Second Gospel and heard its witness as continuous with Christ: that is, as apostolic.[7]

THE EVANGELISTS ON JESUS
AND THE FATHERS ON MARK:
SOME PROCEDURAL SIMILARITIES

The personification of Mark not only shaped the early church's acceptance of the Markan Gospel; that document appears to have influenced the manner in which the church personified the Evangelist. In support of this suggestion one might recall some general features, characteristic of the early fathers' *modus operandi* in their presentations of Mark, which surfaced in part 2 and were summarized in chapter 6. First, there is the notable *sketchiness* of that figure's patristic profile. On the teeming stage of Christian antiquity Mark is little more than a bit player. Second, our investigation has indicated a characteristic *treatment*, among the fathers, *of traditions about Mark*. At least through the fourth century patristic interpreters tended, in general, toward conservation of their traditional inheritance regarding the Evangelist, rather than *ad hoc*, much less capricious, fabrication of legendary novelties. There can be no doubt that particular presentations lean toward the improbable (Bishop Mark of Alexandria) or the fantastic (Mark, the self-mutilated Levitical priest). Yet, with a fair degree of confidence one can usually infer the bases for these portraits by Jerome and the Monarchian prologue, precisely because they preserve (with elaborations) recognizably stable aspects of "the patristic Mark." The variations on this common theme may bring to mind a third recurring factor that we have witnessed: be they conventional (as with Hippolytus) or venturesome (as with Clement), inevitably *the traditionists' own interests and biases* tend to color their presentations of Mark the Evangelist.

Little wonder that the Markan traditions of the early church moved along these lines: for, in compatible ways, traditions about Jesus were reconstituted in the Gospels themselves. (1) Although a minority demurs, most scholars regard Mark's Gospel as a conservation, to some degree, of antecedent traditions about Jesus.[8] That the bulk of the book was outrightly or largely concocted by the Second Evangelist is a highly remote possibility. The same observation manifestly holds for the other Synoptic Gospels: on the prevailing assumption that they adopted Mark as a source, we can actually measure the degree to which Matthew and Luke have been patterned after Mark. With its distinctive character the Fourth Gospel presents special problems of assessment in this regard; still, few scholars would deny that John, too, is the product of some conservation of earlier sources, however indeterminate their exact nature and use by the Fourth Evangelist may be.[9]

(2) On the other hand, as patristic interpreters like Clement and Augustine recognized,[10] the Evangelists more than merely replicated earlier sources. They purposefully, perhaps even ingeniously, adapted those traditions in the light of various historical and religious circumstances attending their Gospels' compositions. The later, canonical consequence of the Evangelists' creative enterprise was a common gospel, focused on Jesus, expressed in four different editions, each

with a distinguishable theological slant.[11] Earlier we conjured with the possibility that patristic personifications of Mark the Evangelist refract, if not reflect, something of the Second Gospel's theological shape.[12] The less speculative and more relevant point to be underscored here is that patristic interpreters filtered their renderings of the Evangelist Mark through the mesh of their own religious concerns, much as the authors of the Gospels did in their presentations of Jesus. Canonically and traditionally, the results are comparable: virtually as many different perspectives on Jesus as their are Evangelists; almost as many different perspectives on Mark as there are patristic observers.

(3) Quite clearly for the early church, however, the figure of Mark, or any Evangelist, was nowhere near as significant as that of the Christ whom they proclaimed. In a sense the fragmented sketches of Mark in patristic testimonies conform with the Second Gospel's complete lack of reference to its author. In another sense, of course, even a marginal curiosity about the Evangelists' personalities veers from the Gospels' own undeviating concentration on Jesus. Yet this slight shift of focus may be intelligible when viewed in the light of an even more profound influence that was probably exerted by the Second Gospel upon patristic musings on its Evangelist.

JESUS AND MARK AS BIOGRAPHICAL SUBJECTS

The similarities between the Gospels' presentation of Jesus and the fathers' presentation of the Evangelists are more than just formal; in a sense the motivations underlying those presentations were kindred. *Perhaps patristic figurations of the Evangelist Mark were religious by-products of the need, manifested by early Christians, to recall and to recast Jesus' activities.*

Neither I nor anyone would suggest that the ancient church accorded to the figure of Mark an esteem equal to that of Jesus. To the contrary, the significance of any Evangelist was measured against, and thus relativized by, the alleged author's presentation of Jesus and, specifically, that representation's fidelity to the church's emergent understanding of Jesus' lordship. Yet, from the middle of the first century onward, the Second Gospel's sheer existence proved to be no more sufficient for Christians than their sheer acceptance of Jesus as Lord: in both cases there appears to have been a religious pressure to construe apostolic testimony to Jesus, and to construe Jesus himself, within the landscape of time and space.[13] Although historical questions as such appear to have held for them little or no interest, early Christians were profoundly concerned about the situation of their faith within history, both Jesus' history and their own.[14] The principal literary precipitate of that concern was the creation of Gospels like Mark's, which eulogized and proclaimed, in faith, what God had done through Jesus of Nazareth.[15] A collateral literary offshoot of the same historical concern appears to have been the preservation of anecdotes about the authors of those Gospels and the circumstances under which those works came to be produced. This two-pronged interest in positioning both Jesus' and Mark's activities within a historical framework is clearly signaled by Papias, quoting the Elder John in the oldest of our patristic testimonies to the Second Evangelist: " 'Mark became Peter's interpreter and wrote accurately whatever he remembered, but not in order, of the things said or done by the Lord' " (Eusebius, *H.E.* 3.39.15).

A further analogy can be drawn when comparing early Christian portrayals of Jesus the Christ and Mark the Evangelist. In both cases the form adopted in the resulting literature was that of "classical popular biography": a sketch of a figure, perceived as historical, rendered for an edifying purpose.[16] Between the depictions of Jesus and of Mark there is, of course, a decided difference in degree: whereas the Markan Gospel is a coherent narrative, most of the patristic traditions about the Evangelist Mark are but narrative scraps. Yet the anecdotal quality of the fathers' rendition of Mark is not entirely unlike what form critics imagine to have been the mode of early Christian presentations of Jesus, prior to their congealment into any of the Gospels. Indeed, with such patristic testimonies as the Monarchian Gospel prologue and Jerome's *De viris illustribus* we can observe how many of those anecdotal snippets were being reformulated into biographical cameos of Mark. Viewed in this light, the maximal reconstruction with which this study was introduced—the slightly picaresque tale of the Evangelist John Mark, colleague of Paul and of Peter[17]—is one innocent, somewhat fanciful culmination of a religious impulse that is intelligible, scarcely reprehensible, and as old as Christianity itself.

Again, let us make no mistake: early Christians did *not* venerate the Evangelist as they revered Jesus. At issue, rather, is the church's inclination to personify Mark and to position that personality on the horizon of ecclesiastical events—a tendency reflective of, and perhaps indirectly stimulated by, the Gospels' own location of Jesus Christ within human history.[18]

To conclude: the fashioning of the figure of Mark as apostolic associate and interpreter was neither arbitrary, scattershot, nor purposeless.[19] Historically unverifiable and therefore debatable, yes, in many if not most respects. Yet to allow our historical preoccupations to dominate the early fathers is as anachronistic as their own procedure is sometimes branded by modern critics. Moreover, such reservations probably distract us from what their personifications of the Evangelist were arguably attempting to achieve, religiously and theologically. The figure of Mark was carefully crafted, one might say, as part of the "hermeneutical context" within which the Second Gospel was preserved, read, and interpreted by the early church as a faithful testimony to the significance of Jesus.[20] The "character" of the Evangelist helped to lend apostolicity to the Gospel, yet the Gospel's own character helped to lend apostolicity to the Evangelist's personification. Verification of this judgment lies in the church's own tradition: ultimately, the Evangelist Mark was canonized as Alexandria's bishop, and the Gospel according to Mark was canonized as scripture.

NOTES

1. Indeed, the early fathers tended to trace that line of continuity back to God, the source of all revelation, by way of Jesus Christ (see *1 Clem.* 42.2; Irenaeus, *Adv. Haer.* 5.1.1; Tertullian, *Prescription of Heretics* 32.6). See also the comments of Maurice Wiles, *The Making of Christian Doctrine: A Study in the Principles of Early Doctrinal Development* (Cambridge: Cambridge University Press, 1967), 45–46.

2. John Macquarrie, *Principles of Christian Theology*, 2d. ed. (New York: Charles Scribner's Sons, 1977), 411. My remarks on apostolicity are indebted to Macquarrie's general presentation (409–11).

3. On the criteria of apostolic continuity during the patristic period, consult Jaroslav Pelikan, *The Christian Tradition: A History of the Development of Doctrine*, vol. 1: *The Emergence of the Catholic Tradition (100–600)* (Chicago and London: University of Chicago Press, 1971), 108–20.

4. My suggestion of this bifocal character of apostolicity, embracing both proximity to and mediated distance from Jesus Christ, might be compared with John Knox's treatment of the subject in *Criticism and Faith* (New York and Nashville: Abingdon—Cokesbury, 1952), 68–70. In his interpretation of apostolicity, Knox emphasizes (one-sidedly, to my mind) "nearness to the normative event" (100).

5. Nils A. Dahl, "*Anamnesis*: Memory and Commemoration in the Early Church," in *Jesus in the Memory of the Early Church* (Minneapolis: Augsburg, 1976), 11–29.

6. On the interplay among scripture and tradition, publicly interpreted by the church, as criteria of apostolicity, see Pelikan, *Christian Tradition*, 115–16; John Norman Davidson Kelly, *Early Christian Doctrines*, rev. ed. (San Francisco: Harper & Row, 1978), 35–48.

7. As presented here, the concept of apostolicity may seem to some readers so artificially imposed upon ancient texts as to be, in principle, hermeneutically suspect. Yet we might bear in mind that scholars since the

nineteenth century have often viewed the New Testament through a similar lens, polished during the Enlightenment. Thus, when the Second Gospel was judged to be the earliest of the four, and was for that reason sometimes assumed (albeit fallaciously) to be the most historically reliable, then Mark finally emerged from the canon's penumbra to a position of equality, if not centrality, among the Gospels. For more detailed discussion, see Albert Schweitzer, *The Quest of the Historical Jesus: A Critical Study of Its Progress from Reimarus to Wrede*, trans. W. Montgomery (New York: Macmillan, 1968), esp. 121–36, 193–222.

8. Germane to this issue is the essay by Larry W. Hurtado, "The Gospel of Mark: Evolutionary or Revolutionary Document?" *JSNT* 40 (1990): 15–32, which critiques two recent proposals (by Werner Kelber and Burton Mack) for Mark's "revolutionary" creativity. See also Ernest Best, "Mark's Preservation of the Tradition," in *The Interpretation of Mark*, ed. William Telford, IRT 7 (Philadelphia and London: Fortress/SPCK, 1985), 119–33.

9. For judicious surveys of the problem, see Robert Kysar, *The Fourth Evangelist and His Gospel: An Examination of Contemporary Scholarship* (Minneapolis: Augsburg, 1976), 10–81; Kysar, "The Fourth Gospel: A Report on Recent Research," *ANRW* 2.25.3 (1985): 2389–2480, esp. 2391–2411.

10. See the discussions of these interpreters in chapters 4 and 5.

11. Thus, see Jack Dean Kingsbury, "The Gospel in Four Editions," and Robert Morgan, "The Hermeneutical Significance of Four Gospels," both in *Interpreting the Gospels*, ed. James Luther Mays (Philadelphia: Fortress, 1981), 27–40, 41–54. As we observed in chapter 3, this phenomenon was clearly recognized by Irenaeus (*Adv. Haer.* 3.11.8).

12. See chapter 7.

13. If Richard B. Hays is correct, a story about Jesus Christ, antedating the Gospels, may underlie Paul's nonnarrative theological formulations (*The Faith of Jesus Christ: An Investigation of the Narrative Substructure of Galatians 3:1–4:11*, SBLDS 56 [Chico, Calif.: Scholars Press, 1983], esp. 256–58).

14. The theological significance of history was inherited by Christians from ancient Judaism. See Gerhard von Rad, *Old Testament Theology* (New York: Harper & Row, 1965), esp. 2:99–125; Oscar Cullmann, *Salvation in History*, NTL (London: SCM, 1967).

15. Nor was this a Christian innovation. In substance and format Mark and other Christian Gospels resemble accounts of the lives of prophets like Elijah and Elisha (see 1 Kings 17–2 Kings 9) and of such Hellenistic philosophers as Apollonius of Tyana (see David R. Cartlidge and David L. Dungan, eds., *Documents for the Study of the Gospels* [Philadelphia: Fortress, 1980], 205–42).

16. The seminal investigations of the Gospels as ancient biographies were undertaken by Clyde Weber Votaw, *The Gospels and Contemporary Biographies in the Greco-Roman World*, FBBS 27 (Philadelphia: Fortress, 1970 [a collection of essays originally written in 1915]). A more recent, critically sympathetic assessment is offered by David E. Aune, *The New Testament in Its Literary Environment*, LEC 8 (Philadelphia: Westminster, 1987), 17–76.

17. See the introduction of the present study.

18. Such an assessment comports, I believe, with a more general judgment that has been tendered by some church historians: that in the patristic era scripture and tradition were typically considered as reciprocally interpretive, not polarized. See Ellen Flesseman-van Leer, *Tradition and Scripture in the Early Church* (Assen: Van Gorcum, 1954), 186–97; Kelly, *Early Christian Doctrines*, esp. 36, 48.

19. While according greater weight than I to the fathers' dependence on 1 Peter 5:13, Rudolph Pesch draws a similar conclusion in his essay, "Die Zuschreibung der Evangelien an apostolische Verfasser," *ZTK* 97 (1975); 56–71.

20. An Evangelist's figuration was, to be sure, only a small component of this process. On the larger framework within which the early church interpreted its scripture, with particular emphasis on Irenaeus's formulation of a "rule of faith," consult James L. Kugel and Rowan A. Greer, *Early Biblical Interpretation*, LEC 3 (Philadelphia: Westminster, 1986), 155–99.

Select Bibliography

PRIMARY SOURCES

The Acts of Barnabas. Translated by Alexander Walker. *ANF* 8 (1899): 493–96.

Alufi. *De Expositione Novi Testamenti*. *PL* 79 (1903): 1137–1424.

Die apokryphen Apostelgeschichte und Apostellegenden. Edited by Richard Adelbert Lipsius. Vol. 2, pt. 2. 1887. Reprint. Amsterdam: APA—Philo, 1976.

The Apostolic Fathers. Translated by Kirsopp Lake. 2 vols. LCL. Cambridge, Mass., and London: Harvard University Press/William Heinemann, 1912, 1913.

Augustine. *The Harmony of the Gospels*. Translated by S. D. F. Salmond. Edited, with notes, by M. B. Riddle. *NPNF* 6, 1st series (1980): 65–236.

Cassiodorus Senator. *An Introduction to Divine and Human Readings*. Edited and translated by Leslie Webber Jones. New York: W. W. Norton, 1946, 1969.

Cicero. *The Speeches: In Catilinam I–IV, Pro Murena, Pro Sulla, Pro Flacco*. Translated by Louis E. Lord. LCL. Cambridge, Mass., and London: Harvard University Press/William Heinemann, 1959.

Clement of Alexandria. *The Stromata, or Miscellanies, Fragments, Who Is the Rich Man that Shall Be Saved?* Translated by William Wilson. *ANF* 2 (1899): 299–568, 571–87, 591–605.

Constitutions of the Holy Apostles. *ANF* 7 (1899): 391–508.

Dio Cassius. *Dio's Roman History*. Translated by Earnest Cary, on the basis of the version of Herbert Baldwin Foster. 9 vols. LCL. Cambridge, Mass., and London: Harvard University Press/William Heinemann, 1954, 1955, 1961.

The Divine Liturgy of the Holy Apostle and Evangelist Mark, the Disciple of the Holy Peter. *ANF* 7 (1899): 551–60.

Documents for the Study of the Gospels. Edited by David R. Cartlidge and David L. Dungan. Philadelphia: Fortress, 1980.

Early Christian Fathers. Edited and translated by Cyril C. Richardson, Eugene R. Fairweather, Edward Rochie Hardy, and Massey Hamilton Shepherd. LCC 1. Philadelphia: Westminster, 1953.

Ephraem of Nisibis. *Éphrem de Nisibe: Commentaire de l'Évangile concordant ou Diatessaron*. Edited and translated by Louis Leloir. SC 121. Paris: Cerf, 1966.

Epiphanius. *The Panarion of Epiphanius of Salamis: Book I (Secs. 1–46)*. Edited and translated by Frank Williams. Nag Hammadi Studies 35. Leiden, New York, København, and Köln: E. J. Brill, 1987.

Eusebius. *Canones decem Harmoniae Evangeliorum. PG* 22 (1857): 1274–92.

———. *The Ecclesiastical History*. Translated by Kirsopp Lake, J. E. L. Oulton, and H. J. Lawlor. 2 vols. LCL. Cambridge, Mass., and London: Harvard University Press/William Heinemann, 1926, 1932.

Euthymius Zigabenes. *Expositio in Marcum. PG* 129 (1864): 756–852.

The Greek New Testament. Edited by Kurt Aland, Matthew Black, Carlo M. Martini, Bruce M. Metzger, and Allen Wikgren. 3d. ed. Stuttgart: Würtemberg Bible Society, for the United Bible Societies, 1975.

Gregory the Great. *De Expositione Veteris ac Novi Testamenti. PL* 79 (1903): 683–1136.

The HarperCollins Study Bible, New Revised Standard Version with the Apocryphal/Deuterocanonical Books. Edited by Wayne A. Meeks, Jouette M. Bassler, Werner E. Lemke, Susan Niditch, and Eileen M. Schuller. San Francisco: HarperCollins Publishers, 1993.

Herodotus. *Herodotus [Persian Wars]*. Translated by A. D. Godley. 4 vols. LCL. Cambridge, Mass., and London: Harvard University Press/William Heinemann, 1960, 1957, 1963, 1961.

Hippolytus. *Hippolytus: Refutatio Omnium Haeresium*. Edited by Miroslav Marcovich. Patristische Texte und Studien 25. Berlin and New York: Walter de Gruyter, 1986.

Homer. *The Iliad*. Translated by A. T. Murray. 2 vols. LCL. Cambridge, Mass., and London: Harvard University Press/William Heinemann, 1960, 1963.

———. *The Odyssey*. Translated by A. T. Murray. 2 vols. LCL. Cambridge, Mass., and London: Harvard University Press/William Heinemann, 1960.

Irenaeus. *Against Heresies. ANF* 1 (1885): 309–567.

Jerome. *The Homilies of Saint Jerome*. 2 vols. Translated by Marie Ligouri Ewald. The Fathers of the Church. Washington, D.C.: Catholic University of America Press, 1964, 1966.

———. *Letters and Select Works*. Translated by W. H. Fremantle. *NPNF 6*, 2d. series (1989).

———. *Saint Jérôme: Commentaire sur S. Matthieu*. Translated and introduced, with notes, by Émile Bonnard. Livres I–II. SC 242. Paris: Cerf, 1977.

———. *Saint Jérôme: Lettres*. Vol. 6. Edited by Jérôme Labourt. Collections des Universités de France. Paris: Société d'édition/"Les Belles Lettres," 1958.

———. *De viris illustribus*. Edited by E. C. Richardson. TU 14 (1896).

John Chrysostom. *Homilies on the Acts of the Apostles and the Epistle to the Romans*. Translated by J. Walker, J. Sheppard, H. Browne, J. B. Morris, and W. H. Simcox. Revised, with notes, by George B. Stevens. *NPNF* 11 (1989).

———. *Homilies on Galatians, Ephesians, Philippians, Colossians, Thessa-*

lonians, Timothy, Titus, and Philemon. Translated by G. Alexander, J. A. Broadus, and P. Schaff. *NPNF* 13 (1988).

———. *Homilies on the Gospel of Saint Matthew.* Translated by George Prevost. Revised, with notes, by M. B. Riddle. *NPNF* 10 (1986).

Josephus. *Jewish Antiquities.* Translated by H. St. J. Thackery, Ralph Marcus, and Louis H. Feldman. Completed and edited by Allen Wikgren. 7 vols. LCL. Cambridge, Mass., and London: Harvard University Press/William Heinemann, 1930, 1933, 1934, 1937, 1963, 1965.

———. *The Jewish War.* Translated by H. St. J. Thackery. 2 vols. LCL. Cambridge, Mass., and London: Harvard University Press/William Heinemann, 1927, 1928.

Justin Martyr. *First Apology, Dialogue with Trypho. ANF* 1 (1885): 159–87, 194–270.

Juvenal and Persius. *Juvenal and Persius [The Satires].* Translated by G. G. Ramsay. LCL. Cambridge, Mass., and London: Harvard University Press/ William Heinemann, 1961.

Lucian. *Lucian [How to Write History].* Translated by K. Kilburn. LCL. Cambridge, Mass., and London: Harvard University Press/William Heinemann, 1959.

The Mishnah. Translated, with introduction and explanatory notes, by Herbert Danby. Oxford: Oxford University Press, 1933.

The New English Bible with the Apocrypha: Oxford Study Edition. Edited by Samuel Sandmel, M. Jack Suggs, and Arnold J. Tkacik. New York: Oxford University Press, 1976.

A New Eusebius: Documents Illustrative of the History of the Church to A.D. 337. Edited by James Stevenson. London: SPCK, 1957.

The New Jerusalem Bible. Garden City, N.Y.: Doubleday, 1985.

New Testament Apocrypha. Vol. 1: *Gospels and Related Writings.* Vol. 2: *Writings Related to the Apostles, Apocalypses, and Related Subjects.* Edited by Wilhelm Schneemelcher. English translation edited by R. McL. Wilson. Cambridge, Philadelphia, and Louisville: James Clarke/Westminster/John Knox, 1965 (vol. 2), 1991 (vol. 1).

The Old Testament Pseudepigrapha. Vol. 1: *Apocalyptic Literature and Testaments.* Vol. 2: *Expansions of the "Old Testament" and Legends, Wisdom and Philosophical Literature, Prayers, Psalms, and Odes, Fragments of Lost Judeo-Hellenistic Works.* Edited by James H. Charlesworth. Garden City, N.Y.: Doubleday, 1983, 1985.

Origen. *De Principiis.* Translated by Frederick Crombie. *ANF* 4 (1890): 239–384.

The Other Gospels: Non-Canonical Gospel Texts. Edited by Ron Cameron. Philadelphia: Westminster, 1982.

Philo. *Philo.* Vol. 10: *The Embassy to Gaius.* Translated by F. H. Colson. LCL. Cambridge, Mass., and London: Harvard University Press/William Heinemann, 1962.

———. *Philo.* Vol. 9: *Every Good Man Is Free; On the Contemplative Life;*

On the Eternity of the World; Against Flaccus; Apology for the Jews; On Providence. Edited by F. H. Colson. LCL. Cambridge, Mass., and London: Harvard University Press/William Heinemann, 1960.

Plato. *Lysis, Symposium, Gorgias*. Translated by W. R. M. Lamb. LCL. Cambridge, Mass., and London: Harvard University Press/William Heinemann, 1961.

———. *The Statesman, Philebus, Ion*. Translated by Harold North Fowler and W. R. M. Lamb. LCL. Cambridge, Mass., and London: Harvard University Press/William Heinemann, 1962.

———. *Theaetetus, Sophist*. Translated by Harold North Fowler. LCL. Cambridge, Mass., and London: Harvard University Press/William Heinemann, 1961.

Septuaginta. Edited by Alfred Rahlfs. Stuttgart: Deutsche Bibelgesellschaft, 1935.

Suetonius. *Suetonius [The Lives of the Caesars]*. Translated by J. C. Rolfe. 2 vols. LCL. Cambridge, Mass., and London: Harvard University Press/William Heinemann, 1959, 1960.

Synopsis Quattuor Evangeliorum. 10th rev. ed. Edited by Kurt Aland. Stuttgart: Deutsche Bibelstiftung, 1976.

Tacitus. *The Histories, The Annals*. Translated by Clifford H. Moore and John Jackson. 4 vols. LCL. Cambridge, Mass., and London: Harvard University Press/William Heinemann, 1956, 1962, 1963.

Tertullian. *Adversus Marcionem*. Books 4 and 5. Translated by Ernest Evans. Oxford: Clarendon, 1972.

———. *The Prescription against Heretics*. Translated by Peter Holmes. *ANF* 3 (1899): 243–67.

Theophylact. *Enarratio in Evangelium Marci*. PG 123 (1864): 487–682.

Thucydides. *History of the Peloponnesian War*. Translated by Charles Forster Smith. 4 vols. LCL. Cambridge, Mass., and London: Harvard University Press/William Heinemann, 1956, 1958, 1959, 1958.

Venerable Bede. *Expositio in Evangelium S. Marci*. PL 92 (1862): 131–302.

Victorinus of Pettau. *Scholia in Apocalypsin Beati Joannis*. PL 5 (1844): 317–44.

Xenophon. *Scripta Minora*. Translated by E. C. Marchant. LCL. Cambridge, Mass., and London: Harvard University Press/William Heinemann, 1956.

SECONDARY SOURCES

Abramowski, Luise. "The 'Memoirs of the Apostles' in Justin." In *The Gospel and the Gospels*, edited by Peter Stuhlmacher. Translated by John Vriend, 323–35. Grand Rapids, Mich.: Eerdmans, 1991.

Achtemeier, Paul J. *The Inspiration of Scripture: Problems and Proposals*. Philadelphia: Westminster, 1980.

———. *Invitation to Mark: A Commentary on the Gospel of Mark with Complete Text from the Jerusalem Bible*. Garden City, N.Y.: Image Books/Doubleday, 1978.

———. *Mark*. 2d. rev. ed. PC. Philadelphia: Fortress, 1986.

————. "Mark, Gospel of." *ABD* 4 (1992): 541–57.

————. *The Quest for Unity in the New Testament Church: A Study in Paul and Acts*. Philadelphia: Fortress, 1987.

Ackroyd, P. R., and C. F. Evans, eds. *The Cambridge History of the Bible*. Vol. 1: *From the Beginnings to Jerome*. Cambridge: Cambridge University Press, 1970.

Allen, Willoughby Charles. *The Gospel according to Saint Mark with Introduction and Notes*. Oxford Church Bible Commentary. New York: Macmillan, 1915.

Allison, Dale C., Jr. "The Pauline Epistles and the Synoptic Gospels: The Pattern of the Parallels." *NTS* 28 (1982): 1–32.

Anderson, Hugh. *The Gospel of Mark*. NCB. Grand Rapids, Mich., and London: Eerdmans/Marshall, Morgan, & Scott, 1976.

Annand, Rupert. "Papias and the Four Gospels." *SJT* 9 (1956): 46–62.

Atiya, Aziz S. *History of Eastern Christianity*. Notre Dame, Ind.: University of Notre Dame Press, 1967.

Aune, David E. *The New Testament in Its Literary Environment*. LEC 8. Philadelphia: Westminster, 1987.

————, ed. *Greco-Roman Literature and the New Testament: Selected Forms and Genres*. SBLSBS 21. Atlanta: Scholars Press, 1988.

Babcock, William S., ed. *Paul and the Legacies of Paul*. Dallas: Southern Methodist University Press, 1990.

Bacon, Benjamin Wisner. "The Anti-Marcionite Prologue to John." *JBL* 49 (1930): 43–54.

————. *The Beginnings of the Gospel Story*. New Haven: Yale University Press, 1909.

————. *The Gospel of Mark: Its Composition and Date*. New Haven: Yale University Press, 1925.

————. *Is Mark a Roman Gospel?* HTS 7. Cambridge, Mass.: Harvard University Press, 1919.

————. "Papias." In *The New Schaff-Herzog Encyclopedia of Religious Knowledge*, edited by S. M. Jackson, 336–40. New York and London: Funk & Wagnalls, 1910.

Baker, D., ed. *The Materials, Sources and Methods of Ecclesiastical History*. Studies in Church History 11. Oxford: Basil Blackwell, 1975.

Bammel, Ernst. "Markus 10.1f und das jüdische Eherecht." *ZNW* 61 (1970): 95–101.

Bammel, Ernst, and C. F. D. Moule, eds. *Jesus and the Politics of His Day*. Cambridge: Cambridge University Press, 1984.

Barclay, William. "A Comparison of Paul's Missionary Preaching and Preaching to the Church." In *Apostolic History and the Gospel: Biblical and Historical Essays Presented to F. F. Bruce on His Sixtieth Birthday*, edited by W. Ward Gasque and Ralph P. Martin, 165–75. Grand Rapids, Mich.: Eerdmans, 1970.

Barnard, L. W. "Saint Stephen and Early Alexandrian Christianity." *NTS* 7 (1960): 31–45.

Barnes, Timothy David. *Tertullian: A Historical and Literary Study*. Oxford: Clarendon, 1971.

Barrett, C. K. *Freedom and Obligation: A Study of the Epistle to the Galatians*. Philadelphia: Westminster, 1985.

———. *The Pastoral Epistles in the New English Bible*. NClB. Oxford: Clarendon, 1963.

Bauckham, Richard J. *Jude, 2 Peter*. WBC 50. Waco, Tex.: Word Books, 1983.

Bauer, Walter. *Orthodoxy and Heresy in Earliest Christianity*. 2d. ed. Edited by Robert A. Kraft and Gerhard Krodel. Translated by a team from the Philadelphia Seminar on Christian Origins. Philadelphia: Fortress, 1971.

Beach, Curtis. *The Gospel of Mark: Its Making and Meaning*. New York: Harper & Brothers, 1959.

Beare, F. W. *The First Epistle of Peter: The Greek Text with Introduction and Notes*. 3d. rev. ed. Oxford: Basil Blackwell, 1970.

———. "Rome (Church)." *IDB* 4 (1962): 122–24.

Beavis, Mary Ann. *Mark's Audience: The Literary and Social Setting of Mark 4.11–12*. JSNTSup 33. Sheffield: Sheffield Academic Press, 1989.

Behm, Johannes. "*hermēneuō, k. t. l.*" *TDNT* 2 (1964): 661–66.

Bellinzoni, Arthur J. *The Sayings of Jesus in the Writings of Justin Martyr*. NovTSup 17. Leiden: E. J. Brill, 1967.

Benko, Stephen, and John J. O'Rourke, eds. *The Catacombs and the Colosseum: The Roman Empire as the Setting of Primitive Christianity*. Valley Forge, Pa.: Judson, 1971.

Best, Ernest. *1 Peter*. NCB. Grand Rapids, Mich., and London: Eerdmans/Marshall, Morgan & Scott, 1971.

———. "1 Peter and the Gospel Tradition." *NTS* 16 (1970): 95–113.

———. *Following Jesus: Discipleship in the Gospel of Mark*. JSNTSup 4. Sheffield: JSOT, 1981.

———. *Mark: The Gospel as Story*. Edinburgh: T & T Clark, 1983.

———. "Mark's Preservation of the Tradition." In *The Interpretation of Mark*, edited by William Telford, 119–33. IRT 7. Philadelphia and London: Fortress/SPCK, 1985.

———. "Peter in the Gospel according to Mark." *CBQ* 40 (1978): 547–48.

Betz, Hans Dieter, ed. *Christology and a Modern Pilgrimage: A Discussion with Norman Perrin*. Claremont, Calif.: New Testament Colloquium, 1971.

———. *Galatians: A Commentary on Paul's Letter to the Churches in Galatia*. Hermeneia. Philadelphia: Fortress, 1979.

Beyschlag, K. "Herkunft und Eigenart der Papiasfragmente." *Studia Patristica* (Berlin) 4 (1961): 268–80.

Black, C. Clifton. *The Disciples according to Mark: Markan Redaction in Current Debate*. JSNTSup 27. Sheffield: Sheffield Academic Press, 1989.

———. "An Oration at Olivet: Some Rhetorical Dimensions of Mark 13." In *Persuasive Artistry: Studies in New Testament Rhetoric in Honor of George A. Kennedy*, edited by Duane F. Watson, 66–92. JSNTSup 50. Sheffield: Sheffield Academic Press, 1991.

————. "The Quest of Mark the Redactor: Why Has It Been Pursued, and What Has It Taught Us?" *JSNT* 33 (1988): 19–39.

————. Review of Herman C. Waetjen, *A Reordering of Power: A Socio-Political Reading of Mark's Gospel*. *BTB* 21 (1991): 83–84.

Black, Matthew. "The Use of Rhetorical Terminology in Papias on Mark and Matthew." *JSNT* 37 (1989): 31–41.

Blaiklock, Edward Musgrave. *The Young Man Mark: Some Aspects of Mark and His Gospel*. Exeter: Paternoster, 1965.

Booth, Wayne C. *The Rhetoric of Fiction*. Chicago and London: University of Chicago Press, 1962.

Borg, Marcus J. *Jesus, A New Vision: Spirit, Culture, and the Life of Discipleship*. San Francisco: Harper & Row, 1987.

Bovon, François. "Foi chrétienne et religion populaire dans la première épître de Pierre." *ETL* 53 (1978): 25–41.

Bowman, John. *The Gospel of Mark: The New Christian Jewish Passover Haggadah*. Studia postbiblica 8. Leiden: E. J. Brill, 1965.

Brandenburger, Egon. *Markus 13 und die Apokalyptik*. FRLANT 134. Göttingen: Vandenhoeck & Ruprecht, 1984.

Brandon, S. G. F. "The Date of the Markan Gospel." *NTS* 7 (1961): 126–41.

————. *The Fall of Jerusalem and the Christian Church*. London: SPCK, 1951.

————. *Jesus and the Zealots: A Study of the Political Factor in Primitive Christianity*. New York: Charles Scribner's Sons, 1967.

Branscomb, B. Harvie. *The Gospel of Mark*. MNTC. London: Hodder & Stoughton, 1937.

Bromiley, Geoffrey W. et al., eds. *The International Standard Bible Encyclopedia*. Grand Rapids, Mich.: Eerdmans, 1986.

Brooten, Bernadette J. "Konnten Frauen im alten Judentum die Scheidung betreiben? Überlegungen zu Mk 10,11–12 und 1 Kor 7,10–11." *EvT* 42 (1982): 65–80.

Brown, Raymond E. *The Gospel according to John (i–xii)*. AB 29. Garden City, N.Y.: Doubleday, 1966.

Brown, Raymond E., and John P. Meier. *Antioch and Rome: New Testament Cradles of Catholic Christianity*. New York and Ramsey, N.J.: Paulist, 1983.

Brown, Raymond E., Karl P. Donfried, and John Reumann, eds. *Peter in the New Testament*. Minneapolis and New York: Augsburg/Paulist, 1973.

Brox, Norbert. *Der erste Petrusbrief*. EKKNT 21. Köln: Benzinger, 1979.

————. "Zur pseudepigraphischen Rahmung der ersten Petrusbriefs." *BZ* 19 (1975): 78–96.

Bruce, F. F. *The Acts of the Apostles: The Greek Text with Introduction and Commentary*. Grand Rapids, Mich.: Eerdmans, 1951.

————. *Commentary on the Book of the Acts*. NICNT. Grand Rapids, Mich.: Eerdmans, 1954.

————. *Stephen, James, and John: Studies in Early Non-Pauline Christianity*. Grand Rapids, Mich.: Eerdmans, 1979.

Bruns, J. Edgar. "The Confusion between John and John Mark in Antiquity." *Scripture* 17 (1965): 23–26.

———. "John Mark: A Riddle within the Johannine Enigma." *Scripture* 15 (1963): 88–92.

de Bruyne, Donatien. "Les plus anciens prologues Latines des Evangiles." *RBén* 40 (1928): 193–214.

Bultmann, Rudolf. *Existence and Faith: Shorter Writings of Rudolf Bultmann*. Translated and edited by Schubert M. Ogden. Cleveland and New York: Meridian/World, 1960.

———. "Die Frage nach dem messianischen Bewusstein und das Petrusbekenntnis." *ZNW* 19 (1919–20): 165–74.

———. *The History of the Synoptic Tradition*. Translated by John Marsh. New York: Harper & Row, 1963.

———. "Ignatius and Paul." In *Existence and Faith: Shorter Writings of Rudolf Bultmann*, edited and translated by Schubert M. Ogden, 257–77. Cleveland and New York: Meridian/World, 1960.

Burdon, Christopher. *Stumbling on God: Faith and Vision in Mark's Gospel*. Grand Rapids, Mich.: Eerdmans, 1990.

Burkill, T. Alec. "The Formation of St. Mark's Gospel." In his *New Light on the Earliest Gospel: Seven Markan Studies*, 180–264. Ithaca and London: Cornell University Press, 1972.

Cadbury, Henry Joel. *The Making of Luke-Acts*. New York: Macmillan, 1927.

von Campenhausen, Hans. *The Formation of the Christian Bible*. Philadelphia: Fortress, 1972.

Cannon, George E. *The Use of Traditional Materials in Colossians*. Macon, Ga.: Mercer University Press, 1983.

Carroll, Kenneth L. "The Creation of the Fourfold Gospel." *BJRL* 37 (1954–55): 68–77.

Case, Shirley Jackson. "John Mark." *ExpTim* 26 (1914–15): 372–76.

Cassidy, Richard J. *Society and Politics in the Acts of the Apostles*. Maryknoll, N.Y.: Orbis, 1987.

Chapman, John. *Notes on the Early History of the Vulgate Gospels*. Oxford: Clarendon, 1908.

Chase, F. H. "Mark (John)." In *Dictionary of the Bible*, edited by James Hastings, 3:245–46. Edinburgh: T & T Clark, 1909.

Chatman, Seymour. *Story and Discourse: Narrative Structure in Fiction and Film*. Ithaca and London: Cornell University Press, 1978.

Church, F. Forrester. "Rhetorical Structure and Design in Paul's Letter to Philemon." *HTR* 71 (1978): 17–33.

Colette (Sidonie-Gabrielle). *Oeuvres complètes de Colette de l'Académie Goncourt*. Vol. 11: *Mes Apprentissages, Bella-Vista, Chambre d'Hôtel, Julie de Carneilhan*. Paris: Le Fleuron, 1949.

Collins, John N. *Diakonia: Re-interpreting the Ancient Sources*. New York and Oxford: Oxford University Press, 1990.

Colson, F. H. "*Taxei* in Papias (The Gospels and the Rhetorical Schools)." *JTS* 14 (1912): 62–69.

Conzelmann, Hans. *Acts of the Apostles: A Commentary on the Acts of the*

Apostles. Edited by Eldon Jay Epp and Christopher R. Matthews. Translated by James Limburg, A. Thomas Kraabel, and Donald H. Juel. Hermeneia. Philadelphia: Fortress, 1987.

―――. *History of Primitive Christianity*. Translated by John E. Steely. Nashville: Abingdon, 1973. (*Geschichte des Urchristentums*. 4th ed. GNTNTD 5. Göttingen: Vandenhoeck & Ruprecht, 1978.)

Conzelmann, Hans, and Andreas Lindemann. *Interpreting the New Testament: An Introduction to the Principles and Methods of N. T. Exegesis*. Translated by Siegfried S. Schatzmann. Peabody, Mass.: Hendrickson, 1988.

Cook, Michael J. *Mark's Treatment of the Jewish Leaders*. NovTSup 51. Leiden: E. J. Brill, 1978.

Corley, Bruce C., ed. *Colloquy on New Testament Studies: A Time for Reappraisal and Fresh Approaches*. Macon, Ga.: Mercer University Press, 1983.

Coutts, J. "The Relationship of Ephesians and Colossians." *NTS* 4 (1957–58): 201–7.

Cranfield, C. E. B. *The Gospel according to Saint Mark*. CGTC. Cambridge: Cambridge University Press, 1959.

―――. "Mark, Gospel of." *IDB* 3 (1962): 267–77.

Cross, F. L. *1 Peter: A Paschal Liturgy*. London: Mowbray, 1954.

Cullmann, Oscar. *Peter: Disciple-Apostle-Martyr. A Historical and Theological Study*. Translated by Floyd V. Filson. Philadelphia: Westminster, 1953.

―――. "The Plurality of the Gospels as a Theological Problem in Antiquity." In *The Early Church: Studies in Early Christian History and Theology*, edited by A. J. B. Higgins, translated by Stanley Godman, 37–54. Philadelphia: Westminster, 1956.

―――. *Salvation in History*. Translated by Sidney G. Sowers and the editorial staff of the SCM Press. NTL. London: SCM, 1967.

Culpepper, R. Alan. *John, the Son of Zebedee: The Life of a Legend*. Studies on Personalities of the New Testament. Columbia: University of South Carolina Press, 1994.

―――. "Paul's Mission to the Gentile World: Acts 13–19." *RevExp* 71 (1974): 487–97.

Dahl, Nils A. "*Anamnesis:* Memory and Commemoration in the Early Church." In *Jesus in the Memory of the Early Church*, 11–29. Minneapolis: Augsburg, 1976.

Dautzenberg, Gerhard. "Zur Stellung des Markusevangeliums in den Geschichte der urchristlichen Theologie." *Kairos* 18 (1976): 282–91.

Davies, William David. *Invitation to the New Testament: A Guide to Its Main Witnesses*. Garden City, N.Y.: Doubleday/Anchor Books, 1969.

Davies, William David, and Dale C. Allison, Jr. *A Critical and Exegetical Commentary on the Gospel according to Saint Matthew*. Vol. 1. ICC. Edinburgh: T & T Clark, 1988.

Deeks, David G. "Papias Revisited." *ExpTim* 88 (1977): 296–301, 324–29.

Delclaux, A. "Deux Témoignages de Papias sur la Composition de Marc?" *NTS* 27 (1981): 401–11.

Dibelius, Martin. *From Tradition to Gospel*. Translated by Bertram Lee Woolf. New York: Charles Scribner's Sons, n.d.

———. "The Speeches in Acts and Ancient Historiography." In *Studies in the Acts of the Apostles*, translated by Heinrich Greeven, 138–85. New York and London: Charles Scribner's Sons/SCM, 1956.

Dibelius, Martin, and Hans Conzelmann. *The Pastoral Epistles: A Commentary on the Pastoral Epistles*. Edited by Helmut Koester. Translated by Philip Buttolph and Adela Yarbro. Hermeneia. Philadelphia: Fortress, 1972.

Dicharry, Warren. *Human Authors of the New Testament*. Vol. 1: *Mark, Matthew, and Luke*. Collegeville, Minn.: Liturgical, 1990.

Dix, Dom Gregory. *Jew and Greek: A Study in the Primitive Church*. Westminster: Dacre, 1953.

Dodd, Charles Harold. "The Framework of the Gospel Narratives." *ExpTim* 43 (1932): 396–400.

Donahue, John R. "A Neglected Factor in the Theology of Mark." *JBL* 101 (1982): 563–94.

———. *The Theology and Setting of Discipleship in the Gospel of Mark*. Milwaukee: Marquette University Press, 1983.

Donelson, Lewis R. *Pseudepigraphy and Ethical Argument in the Pastoral Epistles*. HUT 22. Tübingen: Mohr (Siebeck), 1986.

Downey, Glanville. *A History of Antioch in Syria from Seleucus to the Arab Conquest*. Princeton: Princeton University Press, 1961.

Dungan, David L. "The Purpose and Provenance of the Gospel of Mark according to the 'Two-Gospel' (Griesbach) Hypothesis." In *Colloquy on New Testament Studies: A Time for Reappraisal and Fresh Approaches*, edited by Bruce C. Corley, 133–56. Macon, Ga.: Mercer University Press, 1983.

Dunn, James D. G. "Jesus and Ritual Purity: A Study of the Tradition-History of Mark 7.15." In *Jesus, Paul and the Law: Studies in Mark and Galatians*, 37–60. Louisville: Westminster, 1990.

———. *Unity and Diversity in the New Testament: An Inquiry into the Character of Earliest Christianity*. London: SCM, 1977.

Edmundson, George. *The Church in Rome in the First Century: An Examination of Various Controverted Questions relating to Its History, Chronology, Literature and Traditions*. London: Longmans, Green, 1913.

Ehrhardt, Arnold. "The Gospels in the Muratorian Fragment." In *The Framework of the New Testament Stories*, 11–36. Cambridge, Mass.: Harvard University Press, 1964.

Eliot, Thomas Stearns. *The Sacred Wood: Essays on Poetry and Criticism*. The Fountain Library. London: Methuen, 1920.

Elliott, John H. "Backward and Forward 'In His Steps': Following Jesus from Rome to Raymond and Beyond. The Tradition, Redaction, and Reception of 1 Peter 2:18–25." In *Discipleship in the New Testament*, edited by Fernando F. Segovia, 184–209. Philadelphia: Fortress, 1985.

———. *A Home for the Homeless: A Sociological Exegesis of 1 Peter, Its Situation and Strategy*. Philadelphia: Fortress, 1981.

————. "Peter, Silvanus and Mark in 1 Peter and Acts: Sociological-Exegetical Perspectives on a Petrine Group in Rome." In *Wort in der Zeit. Neutestamentliche Studien: Festgabe für Karl Heinrich Rengstorf zum 75. Geburtstag,* edited by W. Haubeck and M. Bachmann, 250–67. Leiden: E. J. Brill, 1980.

————. "The Rehabilitation of an Exegetical Stepchild: 1 Peter in Recent Research." *JBL* 95 (1976): 243–54.

————. "The Roman Provenance of 1 Peter and the Gospel of Mark: A Response to David Dungan." In *Colloquy on New Testament Studies: A Time for Reappraisal and Fresh Approaches,* edited by Bruce C. Corley, 181–94. Macon, Ga.: Mercer University Press, 1983.

Ellis, E. Earle. "Gospels Criticism: A Perspective on the State of the Art." In *The Gospel and the Gospels,* edited by Peter Stuhlmacher, 26–52. Grand Rapids, Mich.: Eerdmans, 1991.

————. "Paul and His Co-Workers." *NTS* 17 (1971): 437–52.

Emden, Cecil S. "St. Mark's Debt to St. Peter." *CQR* 54 (1953): 61–71.

Epp, Eldon Jay, and George W. MacRae, eds. *The New Testament and Its Modern Interpreters.* Atlanta: Scholars Press, 1989.

Fander, Monika. *Die Stellung der Frau im Markusevangelium: Unter besonderer Berücksichtigung kultur- und religionsgeschichtlicher Hintergründe.* MTA 8. Altenberge: Telos, 1989.

Farkasfalvy, Denis. "The Presbyters' Witness on the Order of the Gospels as Reported by Clement of Alexandria." *CBQ* 54 (1992): 260–70.

————. "Theology of Scripture in St. Irenaeus." *RBén* 78 (1968): 319–33.

Farmer, William R. "Modern Developments of Griesbach's Hypothesis." *NTS* 23 (1976–77): 275–95.

————, ed. *New Synoptic Studies: The Cambridge Conference and Beyond.* Macon, Ga.: Mercer University Press, 1982.

Farrer, Austin M. *A Study in St Mark.* New York: Oxford University Press, 1952.

Feinmeier, Reinhard. "The Portrayal of Peter in the Synoptic Gospels." In Martin Hengel, *Studies in the Gospel of Mark,* translated by John Bowden, 59–63, 161–62. Philadelphia: Fortress, 1985.

Fenton, John C. "Paul and Mark." In *Studies in the Gospels: Essays in Memory of R. H. Lightfoot,* edited by D. E. Nineham, 89–112. Oxford: Basil Blackwell, 1957.

Fiorenza, Elisabeth Schüssler. *In Memory of Her: A Feminist Theological Reconstruction of Christian Origins.* New York: Crossroad, 1983.

Flesseman-van Leer, Ellen. *Tradition and Scripture in the Early Church.* Assen: Van Gorcum, 1954.

Foakes Jackson, F. J., and Kirsopp Lake. *The Beginnings of Christianity.* Part 1: *The Acts of the Apostles.* Vol. 2. London: Macmillan, 1922.

Francis, Fred O., and Wayne A. Meeks, eds. *Conflict at Colossae: A Problem in the Interpretation of Early Christianity Illustrated by Selected Modern Studies.* SBLSBS 4. N.p.: SBL, 1973.

272   Select Bibliography

Fuller, Reginald H. "Classics and the Gospels: The Seminar." In *The Relationships among the Gospels: An Interdisciplinary Dialogue,* edited by William O. Walker, Jr., 173–92. San Antonio, Tex.: Texas University Press, 1978.

———. *A Critical Introduction to the New Testament.* London: Duckworth, 1971.

Funk, Franz Xaver. *Die Apostolischen Konstitutionen: Eine Litterar-Historische Untersuchung.* 1891. Reprint. Frankfurt am Main: Minerva, 1970.

Gächter, P. "Die Dolmetscher der Apostel." *ZTK* 60 (1936): 161–87.

Gamble, Harry Y. *The New Testament Canon: Its Making and Meaning.* GBSNTS. Philadelphia: Fortress, 1985.

———. *The Textual History of the Letter to the Romans.* SD 42. Grand Rapids, Mich.: Eerdmans, 1977.

Gasque, W. Ward, and Ralph P. Martin, eds. *Apostolic History and the Gospel: Biblical and Historical Essays Presented to F. F. Bruce on His Sixtieth Birthday.* Grand Rapids, Mich.: Eerdmans, 1970.

Gerhardsson, Birger. *The Gospel Tradition.* Lund: Gleerup, 1986.

Gnilka, Joachim. *Das Evangelium nach Markus.* 2 vols. EKKNT 2/1–2. Zurich and Neukirchener Vluyn: Benzinger/Neukirchener, 1978, 1979.

———. *Der Kolosserbrief.* HTKNT 10. Freiburg: Herder, 1980.

Goppelt, Leonhard. *Der Erste Petrusbrief.* MeyerK 12/1. Göttingen: Vandenhoeck & Ruprecht, 1978.

Gore, Charles, Henry Leighton Goudge, and Alfred Guillaunu, eds. *A New Commentary on Holy Scripture, Including the Apocrypha.* Part 3. New York: Macmillan, 1928.

Gould, E. P. *A Critical and Exegetical Commentary on the Gospel according to St. Mark.* ICC. New York: Charles Scribner's Sons, 1896.

Grant, F. C. *The Earliest Gospel: Studies of the Evangelic Tradition at Its Point of Crystallization in Writing.* New York: Abingdon, 1943.

———. "The Gospel According to St. Mark: Introduction." *IB* 7 (1951): 629–47.

Grant, Robert M. *The Earliest Lives of Jesus.* New York: Harper & Brothers, 1961.

———. "Eusebius and His Church History." In *Understanding the Sacred Text: Essays in Honor of Morton S. Enslin on the Hebrew Bible and Christian Beginnings,* edited by John Reumann, 235–47. Valley Forge, Pa.: Judson, 1972.

———. *Eusebius as Church Historian.* Oxford: Clarendon, 1980.

———. "Morton Smith's Two Books." *ATR* 56 (1974): 58–65.

———. "The Oldest Gospel Prologues." *ATR* 23 (1941): 231–45.

———. "Papias and the Gospels." *ATR* 25 (1943): 218–22.

———. "Papias in Eusebius' *Church History.*" In *Mélanges d'histoire des religions offerts à Henri-Charles Peuch sous le patronage et avec le concours du Collège de France et de la section des sciences religieuses de l'École pratique des hautes études,* 209–13. Paris: Presses Universitaires de France, 1974.

Green, Henry A. "The Socio-Economic Background of Christianity in Egypt." In *The Roots of Egyptian Christianity,* edited by Birger A. Pearson and James E. Goehring, 100–113. SAC. Philadelphia: Fortress, 1986.

Green, William Scott. "What's in a Name?—The Problematic of Rabbinic 'Biography.' " In *Approaches to Judaism: Theory and Practice,* edited by William Scott Green, 77–96. BUJS 1. Missoula, Mont.: Scholars Press, 1978.

———, ed. *Approaches to Judaism: Theory and Practice.* BUJS 1. Missoula, Mont.: Scholars Press, 1978.

Gryson, Roger. "A propos du témoignage de Papias sur Matthieu: le sens du mot *LOGION* chez les Pères du second siècle." *ETL* 41 (1965): 530–47.

Guelich, Robert. "The Gospel Genre." In *The Gospel and the Gospels,* edited by Peter Stuhlmacher, 173–208. Grand Rapids, Mich.: Eerdmans, 1991.

———. *Mark 1–8:26.* WBC 34A. Dallas: Waco, 1989.

Gundry, Robert H. "Further Verba on Verba Christi in First Peter." *Bib* 55 (1974): 211–32.

———. " 'Verba Christi' in I Peter: Their Implications concerning the Authorship of I Peter and the Authenticity of the Gospel Tradition." *NTS* 13 (1967): 336–50.

Gunther, John J. "The Association of Mark and Barnabas with Egyptian Christianity (Parts I and II)." *EvQ* 54 (1982): 219–33; 55 (1983): 21–29.

Gustafsson, B. "Eusebius' Principles in Handling His Sources, as Found in His Church History, Books I–VII." *Studia Patristica* (Berlin) 4 (1961): 429–41.

Guthrie, Donald. *New Testament Introduction.* Downers Grove, Ill.: Inter-Varsity, 1970.

Gutwenger, Engelbert. "Papias: eine chronologische Studie." *ZKT* 69 (1947): 385–416.

Guy, Harold A. *The Origin of the Gospel of Mark.* London: Hodder & Stoughton, 1954.

Haefner, A. E. "The Bridge between Mark and Acts." *JBL* 77 (1958): 67–71.

Haenchen, Ernst. *The Acts of the Apostles: A Commentary.* Translated by Bernard Noble, Gerald Shinn, Hugh Anderson, and R. McL. Wilson. Philadelphia: Westminster, 1971.

Hagner, Donald A. "The Sayings of Jesus in the Apostolic Fathers and Justin Martyr." In *Gospel Perspectives: The Jesus Tradition outside the Gospels,* edited by David Wenham, 233–68. Sheffield: JSOT, 1984.

Hahneman, Geoffrey Mark. *The Muratorian Fragment and the Development of the Canon.* Oxford: Clarendon, 1992.

Hanson, Anthony Tyrrell. *The Pastoral Epistles.* NCB. Grand Rapids, Mich., and London: Eerdmans/Marshall, Morgan & Scott, 1982.

Hanson, R. P. C. *Allegory and Event: A Study of the Sources and Significance of Origen's Interpretation of Scripture.* London and Richmond, Va.: SCM/John Knox, 1959.

———. Review of Morton Smith, *Clement of Alexandria and a Secret Gospel of Mark. JTS* 25 (1974): 513–21.

von Harnack, Adolf. *The Expansion of Christianity in the First Three Centuries*. Vol. 2. Translated by James Moffatt. New York and London: G. P. Putnam's Sons/Williams & Norgate, 1905.

Harrison, P. N. *The Problem of the Pastoral Epistles*. London: Oxford University Press, 1921.

Harvey, W. J. *Character and Novel*. London: Chatto & Windus, 1965.

Hastings, James, ed. *Dictionary of the Bible*. Vol. 3. Edinburgh: T & T Clark, 1909.

Haubeck, W., and M. Bachmann, eds. *Wort in der Zeit. Neutestamentliche Studien: Festgabe für Karl Heinrich Rengstorf zum 75. Geburtstag*. Leiden: E. J. Brill, 1980.

Hays, Richard B. *The Faith of Jesus Christ: An Investigation of the Narrative Substructure of Galatians 3:1–4:11*. SBLDS 56. Chico, Calif.: Scholars Press, 1983.

Heard, Richard G. "The APOMNEMONEUMATA in Papias, Justin, and Irenaeus." *NTS* 1 (1954): 122–29.

———. "The Old Gospel Prologues." *JTS* 6 (1955): 1–16.

———. "Papias' Quotations from the New Testament." *NTS* 1 (1954–55): 130–34.

Hemer, Colin J. "The Address of 1 Peter." *ExpTim* 89 (1978): 239–43.

———. *The Book of Acts in the Setting of Hellenistic History*. WUNT 49. Tübingen: Mohr (Siebeck), 1989.

Hengel, Martin. *Acts and the History of Earliest Christianity*. Translated by John Bowden. Philadelphia: Fortress, 1980.

———. *Studies in the Gospel of Mark*. Translated by John Bowden. Philadelphia: Fortress, 1985.

———. "The Titles of the Gospels and the Gospel of Mark." In *Studies in the Gospel of Mark,* translated by John Bowden, 64–84. Philadelphia: Fortress, 1985.

Henry, Patrick, ed. *Schools of Thought in the Christian Tradition*. Philadelphia: Fortress, 1984.

Holmberg, Bengt. *Sociology and the New Testament: An Appraisal*. Minneapolis: Fortress, 1990.

Holmes, B. T. "Luke's Description of John Mark." *JBL* 54 (1935): 63–72.

Hooker, Morna D. *A Commentary on the Gospel according to St. Mark*. BNTC. London: A & C Black, 1991.

Houlden, J. L. *Paul's Letters from Prison: Philippians, Colossians, Philemon, and Ephesians*. WPC. Philadelphia: Westminster, 1977.

Howard, Wilbert Francis. "The Anti-Marcionite Prologues to the Gospels." *ExpTim* 47 (1935–36): 534–38.

Hunter, Archibald M. *The Gospel according to Saint Mark*. Torch Bible Commentaries. London: SCM, 1948.

Hunzinger, Claus-Hunno. "Babylon als Deckname für Röm und die Datierung des 1. Petrusbriefs." In *Gottes Wort und Gottes Land* (H.-W. Hertzberg *Festschrift*), edited by Henning Graf Reventlow, 67–77. Göttingen: Vandenhoeck & Ruprecht, 1965.

Hurtado, Larry W. "The Gospel of Mark: Evolutionary or Revolutionary Document?" *JSNT* 40 (1990): 15–32.

Hyldahl, Niels. "Hegesipps Hypomnemata." *ST* 14 (1960): 70–113.

van Iersel, B. M. F. "The Gospel according to St. Mark—Written for a Persecuted Community?" *NTT* 34 (1980): 15–36.

Jackson, S. M., ed. *The New Schaff-Herzog Encyclopedia of Religious Knowledge.* Vol. 8. New York and London: Funk & Wagnalls, 1910.

Jeffers, James S. *Conflict at Rome: Social Order and Hierarchy in Early Christianity.* Minneapolis: Fortress, 1991.

———. "Pluralism in Early Roman Christianity." *Fides et Historia* 22 (1990): 5–17.

Jefford, Clayton N. "Mark, John." *ABD* 4 (1992): 557–58.

Jervell, Jacob. "Zur Frage der Traditionsgrundlage der Apostelgeschichte." *ST* 16 (1963): 25–41.

Johnson, Luke Timothy. *The Literary Function of Possessions in Luke-Acts.* SBLDS 37. N.p.: Scholars Press, 1977.

———. *The Writings of the New Testament: An Interpretation.* Philadelphia: Fortress, 1986.

Jones, Edmund D. "Was Mark the Gardener of Gethsemane?" *ExpTim* 31 (1921–22): 403–4.

Judge, E. A. *The Social Pattern of the Christian Groups in the First Century.* London: Tyndale, 1960.

Kalin, Everett R. "Early Traditions about Mark's Gospel: Canonical Status Emerges, the Story Grows." *CurTM* 2 (1975): 332–41.

Kealy, Seán P. *Mark's Gospel: A History of Its Interpretation from the Beginning until 1979.* New York and Ramsey, N.J.: Paulist, 1982.

Keck, Leander E., and J. Louis Martyn, eds. *Studies in Luke-Acts.* Philadelphia: Fortress, 1980.

Kee, Howard Clark. *Community of the New Age: Studies in Mark's Gospel.* Philadelphia: Westminster, 1977.

———. *Good News to the Ends of the Earth: The Theology of Acts.* London and Philadelphia: SCM/Trinity Press International, 1990.

———. *Jesus in History: An Approach to the Study of the Gospels.* 2d. ed. New York: Harcourt Brace Jovanovich, 1977.

Kelber, Werner H. *The Kingdom in Mark: A New Place and a New Time.* Philadelphia: Fortress, 1974.

———. *The Oral and the Written Gospel: The Hermeneutics of Speaking and Writing in the Synoptic Tradition, Mark, Paul, and Q.* Philadelphia: Fortress, 1983.

Kelber, Werner H., Anitra Kolenkow, and Robin Scroggs. "Reflections on the Question: Was There a Pre-Markan Passion Narrative?" SBLSP 2 (1971): 503–85.

Kelly, John Norman Davidson. *A Commentary on the Epistles of Peter and Jude.* Thornapple Commentaries. 1969. Reprint. Grand Rapids, Mich.: Baker Book House, 1981.

———. *A Commentary on the Pastoral Epistles*. HNTC. New York: Harper & Row, 1963.

———. *Early Christian Doctrines*. Rev. ed. New York: Harper & Row, 1978.

———. *Jerome: His Life, Writings, and Controversies*. London: Duckworth, 1975.

Kelly, Joseph F. "The Patristic Biography of Mark," *Bible Today* 21 (1983): 39–44.

Kennedy, George A. *The Art of Rhetoric in the Roman World, 300 B.C.–A.D. 300*. Princeton: Princeton University Press, 1972.

———. "Classical and Christian Source Criticism." In *The Relationships among the Gospels: An Interdisciplinary Dialogue*, edited by William O. Walker, Jr., 125–56. San Antonio, Tex.: Trinity University Press, 1978.

———. *Greek Rhetoric under Christian Emperors*. Princeton: Princeton University Press, 1983.

Kingsbury, Jack Dean. *Conflict in Mark: Jesus, Authorities, Disciples*. Minneapolis: Fortress, 1989.

———. "The Gospel in Four Editions." In *Interpreting the Gospels*, edited by James Luther Mays, 27–40. Philadelphia: Fortress, 1981.

Kittel, Gerhard, et al. *"legō, k. t. l."* *TDNT* 4 (1967): 69–192.

Klijn, A. F. J. "Jewish Christianity in Egypt." In *The Roots of Egyptian Christianity*, edited by Birger A. Pearson and James E. Goehring, 161–75. SAC. Philadelphia: Fortress, 1986.

Knox, John. *Criticism and Faith*. New York and Nashville: Abingdon—Cokesbury, 1952.

———. *Philemon among the Letters of Paul*. London: Collins, 1960.

Knox, Wilfred Lawrence. *The Sources of the Synoptic Gospels*. Vol. 1: *St. Mark*. Cambridge: Cambridge University Press, 1952.

Körtner, Ulrich H. J. "Markus des Mitarbeiter des Petrus." *ZNW* 71 (1980): 160–73.

———. *Papias von Hierapolis: Ein Beitrag zur Geschichte des frühen Christentums*. FRLANT 133. Göttingen: Vandenhoeck & Ruprecht, 1983.

Koester, Helmut. *Ancient Christian Gospels: Their History and Development*. Philadelphia and London: Trinity Press International/SCM, 1990.

———. "Apocryphal and Canonical Gospels." *HTR* 73 (1980): 105–30.

———. *"Gnomai Diaphoroi:* The Origin and Nature of Diversification in the History of Early Christianity." In James M. Robinson and Helmut Koester, *Trajectories through Early Christianity*, 114–57. Philadelphia: Fortress, 1971.

———. *Introduction to the New Testament*. Vol. 1: *History, Culture, and Religion of the Hellenistic Age*. Vol. 2: *History and Literature of Early Christianity*. Philadelphia, Berlin, and New York: Fortress/Walter de Gruyter, 1982.

———. *Synoptische Überlieferung bei den apostolischen Vätern*. TU 65. Berlin: Akademie, 1957.

Krodel, Gerhard A. *Acts*. ACNT. Minneapolis: Augsburg, 1986.

de Kruijf, T. C. *De pastorale brieven*. Het Nieuwe Testament. Rosemond-Masseik: J. J. Romen, 1966.

Kümmel, Werner Georg. *Introduction to the New Testament*. 17th rev. ed. Translated by Howard Clark Kee. Nashville: Abingdon, 1973.

Kürzinger, Josef. "Die Aussage des Papias von Hierapolis zur literarischen Form des Markusevangeliums." *BZ* 21 (1977): 245–64.

———. "Irenäus und sein Zeugnis zur Sprache des Matthäusevangeliums." *NTS* 10 (1963): 108–15.

———. *Papias von Hierapolis und die Evangelien des Neuen Testaments: Gesammelte Aufsätze, Neuausgabe und Übersetzung der Fragmente, Kommentierte Bibliographie*. EM 4. Regensburg: Friedrich Pustet, 1983.

———. "Das Papiaszeugnis und die Erstgestalt des Matthäusevangeliums." *BZ* 4 (1960): 19–38.

Kugel, James L., and Rowan A. Greer. *Early Biblical Interpretation*. LEC 3. Philadelphia: Westminster, 1986.

Kuhn, Heinz-Wolfgang. *Ältere Sammlungen im Markusevangelium*. SUNT 8. Göttingen: Vandenhoeck & Ruprecht, 1971.

Kysar, Robert. *The Fourth Evangelist and His Gospel: An Examination of Contemporary Scholarship*. Minneapolis: Augsburg, 1976.

———. "The Fourth Gospel: A Report on Recent Research." *ANRW* 2.25.3 (1985): 2389–2480.

Lagrange, M.-J. *Évangile selon Saint Marc*. Études Bibliques. Paris: J. Gabalda, 1911.

Lampe, G. W. H. "A.D. 70 in Christian Reflection." In *Jesus and the Politics of His Day*, edited by Ernst Bammel and C. F. D. Moule, 153–71. Cambridge: Cambridge University Press, 1984.

Lampe, Peter. *Die stadtrömischen Christen in den ersten beiden Jahrhunderten: Untersuchungen zur Sozialgeschichte*. WUNT 18. Tübingen: Mohr (Siebeck), 1987.

Lancellotti, A. "La casa di Pietro a Cafarnao nei Vangeli sinottici: redazione e tradizione." *Antonianum* 58 (1983): 48–69.

Lane, William L. "From Historian to Theologian: Milestones in Markan Scholarship." *RevExp* 75 (1978): 601–17.

———. *The Gospel according to Mark*. NICNT. Grand Rapids, Mich.: Eerdmans, 1974.

La Piana, George. "Foreign Groups in Rome during the First Centuries of the Empire." *HTR* 20 (1927): 183–403.

———. "The Roman Church at the End of the Second Century." *HTR* 18 (1925): 201–77.

Lee, Clarence L. "Social Unrest and Primitive Christianity." In *The Catacombs and the Colosseum: The Roman Empire as the Setting of Primitive Christianity*, edited by Stephen Benko and John J. O'Rourke, 121–38. Valley Forge, Pa.: Judson, 1971.

Lee, G. M. "The Books and the Parchments (Studies in Texts: 2 Tim 4:13)." *Theology* 74 (1971): 168–69.

———. "Eusebius on St. Mark and the Beginnings of Christianity in Egypt." *Studia Patristica* (Berlin) 12 (1975): 422–31.

———. "Presbyters and Apostles." *ZNW* 62 (1971): 122.

Lemcio, Eugene E. *The Past of Jesus in the Gospels*. SNTSMS 68. Cambridge: Cambridge University Press, 1991.

Levin, Saul. "The Early History of Christianity, in Light of the 'Secret Gospel' of Mark." *ANRW* 2.25.6 (1988): 4270–92.

Lietzmann, Hans. *The Founding of the Church Universal: A History of the Early Church*. Vol. 2. New York: Charles Scribner's Sons, 1950.

———. *Petrus und Paulus in Rom*. 2d. ed. Berlin: Töpelmann, 1927.

Lightfoot, Joseph Barber. *St. Paul's Epistles to the Colossians and to Philemon*. 2d. ed. London: Macmillan, 1876.

Lightfoot, Robert Henry. *The Gospel Message of St. Mark*. Oxford: Clarendon, 1950.

———. *History and Interpretation in the Gospels*. London: Hodder & Stoughton, 1935.

Lincoln, Andrew T. "The Promise and the Failure: Mark 16:7, 8." *JBL* 108 (1989): 283–300.

Lindemann, Andreas. *Der Kolosserbrief*. ZB. Zurich: Theologischer, 1983.

———. *Paulus im ältesten Christentum: Das Bild des Apostels und die Rezeption der paulinischen Theologie in der frühchristlichen Literatur bis Marcion*. BHT 58. Tübingen: Mohr (Siebeck), 1979.

Linton, O. "Evidences of a Second-Century Revised Edition of St. Mark's Gospel." *NTS* 14 (1968): 321–55.

Lohse, Eduard. *Colossians and Philemon: A Commentary on the Epistles to the Colossians and to Philemon*. Edited by Helmut Koester. Translated by William R. Poehlmann and Robert J. Karris. Hermeneia. Philadelphia: Fortress, 1971.

Loisy, Alfred. *L'Évangile selon Marc*. Paris: Émile Nourry, 1912.

———. *Les Évangiles synoptiques*. Haute-Marne: Ceffonds, 1907.

———. *The Origins of the New Testament*. Translated by L. P. Jacks. London: George Allen & Unwin, 1950.

Lüdemann, Gerd. "Acts of the Apostles as a Historical Source." In *The Social World of Formative Christianity and Judaism: Essays in Tribute to Howard Clark Kee,* edited by Jacob Neusner, Peder Borgen, Ernest S. Frerichs, and Richard Horsley, 109–25. Philadelphia: Fortress, 1988.

———. *Early Christianity according to the Traditions in Acts: A Commentary*. Philadelphia: Fortress, 1989.

Lührmann, Dieter. *Das Markusevangelium*. HNT 3. Tübingen: Mohr (Siebeck), 1987.

McCue, James F. "Roman Primacy in the Second Century and the Problem of the Development of Dogma." *TS* 25 (1964): 161–96.

McDonald, H. Dermott. *Commentary on Colossians and Philemon*. Theta Books. Waco, Tex.: Word Books, 1980.

Mack, Burton L., and Vernon K. Robbins. *Patterns of Persuasion in the Gospels*. FFLF. Sonoma, Calif.: Polebridge, 1989.

Macquarrie, John. *Principles of Christian Theology.* 2d. ed. New York: Charles Scribner's Sons, 1977.

Malbon, Elizabeth Struthers. "Fallible Followers: Women and Men in the Gospel of Mark." *Sem* 28 (1983): 29–48.

Malherbe, Abraham J. *Ancient Epistolary Theorists.* SBLSBS 19. Atlanta: Scholars Press, 1988.

Mann, C. S. *Mark: A New Translation with Introduction and Commentary.* AB 27. Garden City, N.Y.: Doubleday, 1986.

Manson, T. W. "The Foundation of the Synoptic Tradition: The Gospel of Mark." In *Studies in the Gospels and Epistles,* edited by Matthew Black, 28–45. Philadelphia: Westminster, 1962.

Marcus, Joel. "The Jewish War and the *Sitz im Leben* of Mark." *JBL* 111 (1992): 441–62.

———. *The Mystery of the Kingdom of God.* SBLDS 90. Atlanta: Scholars Press, 1986.

Markus, R. A. "Church History and Early Church Historians." In *The Materials, Sources and Methods of Ecclesiastical History,* edited by D. Baker, 1–17. Studies in Church History 11. Oxford: Basil Blackwell, 1975.

Marshall, Christopher D. *Faith as a Theme in Mark's Narrative.* SNTSMS 64. Cambridge: Cambridge University Press, 1989.

Martin, Ralph P. *Colossians and Philemon.* NCB. London: Oliphants, 1974.

———. "John Mark." *ISBE* 3 (1986): 259–60.

———. *Mark: Evangelist and Theologian.* Grand Rapids, Mich.: Zondervan, 1972.

Martin, Wallace. *Recent Theories of Narrative.* Ithaca and London: Cornell University Press, 1986.

Marxsen, Willi. *Introduction to the New Testament.* Translated by G. Buswell. Philadelphia: Fortress, 1968.

———. *Mark the Evangelist: Studies on the Redaction-History of the Gospel.* Translated by James Boyce, Donald Juel, William Poehlmann, with Roy Harrisville. New York and Nashville: Abingdon, 1968.

Mays, James Luther, ed. *Interpreting the Gospels.* Philadelphia: Fortress, 1981.

Meade, David G. *Pseudonymity and Canon: An Investigation of the Relationship of Authorship and Authority in Jewish and Earliest Christian Tradition.* Grand Rapids, Mich.: Eerdmans, 1986.

Meeks, Wayne A. *The First Urban Christians: The Social World of the Apostle Paul.* New Haven and London: Yale University Press, 1983.

———. "*Hypomnēmata* from an Untamed Skeptic: A Response to George Kennedy." In *The Relationships among the Gospels: An Interdisciplinary Dialogue,* edited by William O. Walker, Jr., 157–72. San Antonio, Tex.: Trinity University Press, 1978.

Meeks, Wayne A., and Robert L. Wilken. *Jews and Christians in Antioch in the First Four Centuries of the Common Era.* SBLSBS 13. Missoula, Mont.: Scholars Press, 1978.

Mélanges d'histoire des religions offert à Henri-Charles Peuch sous le patronage et avec le concours du Collège de France et de la section des sciences religieuses de l'École pratique des hautes études. Paris: Presses Universitaires de France, 1974.

Metzger, Bruce M. *The Earliest Versions of the New Testament: Their Origin, Transmission, and Limitations.* Oxford: Clarendon, 1977.

———. *A Textual Commentary on the Greek New Testament.* N.p.: United Bible Societies, 1971.

Meye, Robert P. *Jesus and the Twelve: Discipleship and Revelation in Mark's Gospel.* Grand Rapids, Mich.: Eerdmans, 1968.

Meyer, Marvin W. "The Youth in the *Secret Gospel of Mark.*" *Sem* 49 (1990): 129–53.

Michaels, J. Ramsey. *I Peter.* WBC 49. Waco, Tex.: Word Books, 1988.

Moffatt, James. *An Introduction to the Literature of the New Testament.* ITL. Edinburgh and New York: T & T Clark / Charles Scribner's Sons, 1918, 1929.

Momigliano, Arnaldo. "Pagan and Christian Historiography in the Fourth Century A.D." In *The Conflict between Paganism and Christianity in the Fourth Century,* edited by Arnaldo Momigliano, 79–99. Oxford: Clarendon, 1963.

———, ed. *The Conflict between Paganism and Christianity in the Fourth Century.* Oxford: Clarendon, 1963.

Morgan, Robert. "The Hermeneutical Significance of Four Gospels." In *Interpreting the Gospels,* edited by James Luther Mays, 41–54. Philadelphia: Fortress, 1981.

Moule, C. F. D. *The Epistles of Paul the Apostle to the Colossians and to Philemon.* CGTC. Cambridge: Cambridge University Press, 1977.

———. "The Nature and Purpose of 1 Peter." *NTS* 3 (1956–57): 1–11.

Moule, C. F. D., and A. M. G. Stephenson. "R. G. Heard on Q and Mark." *NTS* 2 (1955): 114–18.

Moulton, James Hope, Wilbert Francis Howard, and Nigel Turner. *A Grammar of New Testament Greek.* 4 vols. Edinburgh: T & T Clark, 1906, 1919, 1929, 1963, 1976.

Müller, U. B. "Die christologische Absicht des Markusevangeliums und die Verklärungsgeschichte." *ZNW* 64 (1973): 159–93.

Mullins, T. Y. "Papias and Clement on Mark's Two Gospels." *VC* 30 (1976): 189–92.

———. "Papias on Mark's Gospel." *VC* 14 (1960): 216–24.

Munck, Johannes. "Presbyters and Disciples of the Lord in Papias." *HTR* 52 (1959): 223–43.

Neusner, Jacob. "Judaism within the Disciplines of Religious Studies: Perspectives on Graduate Education." *CSRBul* 14 (1983): 142–45.

———, ed. *Christianity, Judaism, and Other Greco-Roman Cults: Studies for Morton Smith at Sixty.* Pt. 2. Leiden: E. J. Brill, 1975.

———, Peder Borgen, Ernest S. Frerichs, and Richard Horsley, eds. *The*

Social World of Formative Christianity and Judaism: Essays in Tribute to Howard Clark Kee. Philadelphia: Fortress, 1988.

Nickle, Keith F. *The Synoptic Gospels, An Introduction: Conflict and Consensus*. Atlanta: John Knox, 1980.

Niederwimmer, Kurt. "Johannes Markus und die Frage nach dem Verfasser des zweiten Evangeliums." *ZNW* 58 (1967): 172–88.

Nielsen, Charles M. "Papias: Polemicist against Whom?" *TS* 35 (1974): 529–35.

———. "Polycarp and Marcion: A Note." *TS* 47 (1986): 297–99.

Nineham, Dennis Eric. "Eye-Witness Testimony and the Gospel Tradition. I, II, III." *JTS* n.s. 9 (1958): 13–25, 243–52; 11 (1960): 253–64.

———. *The Gospel of St. Mark*. PGC. Baltimore: Penguin, 1963.

———. "The Order of Events in St. Mark's Gospel–An Examination of Dr. Dodd's Hypothesis." In *Studies in the Gospels: Essays in Memory of R. H. Lightfoot*, edited by D. E. Nineham, 223–39. Oxford: Basil Blackwell, 1957.

———. ed. *Studies in the Gospels: Essays in Memory of R. H. Lightfoot*. Oxford: Basil Blackwell, 1957.

North, J. L. "MARKOS HO KOLOBODAKTYLOS: Hippolytus, *Elenchus*, VII.30." *JTS* 28 (1977): 498–507.

O'Brien, Peter. T. *Colossians and Philemon*. WBC 44. Waco, Tex.: Word Books, 1982.

O'Connor, Daniel William. *Peter in Rome: The Literary, Liturgical, and Archaeological Evidence*. New York: Columbia University Press, 1969.

———. "Peter in Rome: A Review and Position." In *Christianity, Judaism, and Other Greco-Roman Cults: Studies for Morton Smith at Sixty*, edited by Jacob Neusner, 2:146–60. Leiden: E. J. Brill, 1975.

Ortega y Gasset, José. *The Dehumanization of Art and Notes on the Novel*. Translated by Helene Weyl. Princeton: Princeton University Press, 1948.

Osborn, Eric Francis. *Justin Martyr*. BHT 47. Tübingen: Mohr (Siebeck), 1973.

Osiek, Carolyn. *Rich and Poor in the* Shepherd of Hermas. CBQMS 15. Washington, D.C.: Catholic Biblical Association of America, 1983.

Outler, Albert C. "The Gospel according to St. Mark." *PSTJ* 33 (1980): 3–9.

Papadopoulos, S. G. *"Hoi presbyteroi hai he paradosis tou Papias."* Deltion Biblikon Meleton 2 (1974): 218–29.

Parker, Pierson. "The Authorship of the Second Gospel." *PRS* 5 (1978): 4–9.

———. "John and John Mark." *JBL* 79 (1960): 97–110.

———. "Mark, Acts, and Galilean Christianity." *NTS* 16 (1970): 294–304.

Parsons, Mikeal C. *The Departure of Jesus in Luke-Acts: The Ascension Narratives in Context*. JSNTSup 21. Sheffield: JSOT, 1987.

Paul, G. J. *St. John's Gospel: A Commentary*. Madras: Christian Literature Society, 1965.

Peabody, David. "Augustine and the Augustinian Hypothesis: A Reexamination of Augustine's Thought in *De Consensu Evangelistarum*." In *New Synoptic Studies: The Cambridge Conference and Beyond*, edited by William R. Farmer, 37–64. Macon, Ga.: Mercer University Press, 1982.

Pearson, Birger A. "Earliest Christianity in Egypt: Some Observations." In *The Roots of Egyptian Christianity,* edited by Birger A. Pearson and James E. Goehring, 132–59. SAC. Philadelphia: Fortress, 1986.

———. "James, 1–2 Peter, Jude." In *The New Testament and Its Modern Interpreters,* edited by Eldon Jay Epp and George W. MacRae, 371–406. Atlanta: Scholars Press, 1989.

Pearson, Birger A., and James E. Goehring, eds. *The Roots of Egyptian Christianity.* SAC. Philadelphia: Fortress, 1986.

Pelikan, Jaroslav. *The Christian Tradition: A History of the Development of Doctrine.* Vol. 1: *The Emergence of the Catholic Tradition (100–600).* Chicago and London: University of Chicago Press, 1971.

Perkins, Pheme. *The Gnostic Dialogue: The Early Church and the Crisis of Gnosticism.* New York and Ramsey, N.J.: Paulist, 1980.

Perrin, Norman. *Rediscovering the Teaching of Jesus.* New York: Harper & Row, 1976.

———. "Towards an Interpretation of the Gospel of Mark." In *Christology and a Modern Pilgrimage: A Discussion with Norman Perrin,* edited by Hans Dieter Betz, 1–78. Claremont, Calif.: New Testament Colloquium, 1971.

Perrin, Norman, and Dennis Duling. *The New Testament: An Introduction: Proclamation and Paranesis, Myth and History.* 2d. ed. New York: Harcourt Brace Jovanovich, 1982.

Perumalil, A. C. "Are Not Papias and Irenaeus Competent to Report on the Gospels?" *ExpTim* 91 (1980): 332–37.

———. "Papias." *ExpTim* 85 (1974): 361–66.

Pesch, Rudolf. *Das Markusevangelium.* 2 vols. HTKNT. Freiburg: Herder, 1976, 1977.

———. "Die Zuschreibung der Evangelien an apostolische Verfasser." *ZTK* 97 (1975): 56–71.

Petersen, Norman R. *Literary Criticism for New Testament Critics.* GBSNTS. Philadelphia: Fortress, 1985.

———. *Rediscovering Paul: Philemon and the Sociology of Paul's Narrative World.* Philadelphia: Fortress, 1985.

Petersen, William L. "Tatian's *Diatessaron.*" In Helmut Koester, *Ancient Christian Gospels: Their History and Development,* 403–30. Philadelphia and London: Trinity Press International/SCM, 1990.

———. "Textual Evidence of Tatian's Dependence upon Justin's APOMNE-MONEUMATA." *NTS* 36 (1990): 512–34.

Phillips, J. B. *Peter's Portrait of Jesus: A Commentary on the Gospel of Mark and the Letters of Peter.* London: Collins & World, 1976.

Pokorný, Petr. "Das Markusevangelium: literarische und theologische Einleitung mit Forschungsbreicht." *ANRW* 2.25.3 (1985): 1969–2035.

Price, James L. *The New Testament: Its History and Theology.* New York and London: Macmillan/Collier, 1987.

Quasten, Johannes. *Patrology.* Vol. 1: *The Beginnings of Patristic Literature.*

Vol. 2: *The Ante-Nicene Literature after Irenaeus*. Utrecht-Antwerp and Westminster, Md.: Spectrum/Newman, 1953.

Quinn, Jerome D. "The Last Volume of Luke: The Relation of Luke-Acts to the Pastoral Epistles." In *Perspectives on Luke-Acts,* edited by Charles H. Talbert, 62–75. PRSSS 5. Danville and Edinburgh: Association of Baptist Professors of Religion/T & T Clark, 1978.

von Rad, Gerhard. *Old Testament Theology*. Vol. 2: *The Theology of Israel's Prophetic Traditions*. Translated by D. M. G. Stalker. New York: Harper & Row, 1965.

Ramsay, W. R. "On Mark xii.42." *ExpTim* 10 (1898–99): 232.

Rawlinson, A. E. J. *St Mark, with Introduction, Commentary, and Additional Notes*. WC. London: Methuen, 1925.

Regul, Jürgen. *Die antimarcionitischen Evangelienprologe*. Vetus Latina 6. Freiburg: Herder, 1969.

Reicke, Bo. *The Roots of the Synoptic Gospels*. Philadelphia: Fortress, n.d.

Rengstorf, K. H. *"hypēretēs, hypēreteō."* *TDNT* 8 (1972): 530–44.

Rensberger, David K. "As the Apostle Teaches: The Development of the Use of Paul's Letters in Second-Century Christianity." Ph.D. diss., Yale University, 1981.

Reumann, John, ed. *Understanding the Sacred Text: Essays in Honor of Morton S. Enslin on the Hebrew Bible and Christian Beginnings*. Valley Forge, Pa.: Judson, 1972.

Reventlow, Henning Graf, ed. *Gottes Wort und Gottes Land: Hans-Wilhelm Hertzberg zum 70. Geburtstag am 16. Januar 1965 dargebracht von Kollegen, Freuden und Schülern*. Göttingen: Vandenhoeck & Ruprecht, 1965.

Rhoads, David, and Donald Michie. *Mark as Story: An Introduction to the Narrative of a Gospel*. Philadelphia: Fortress, 1982.

Richards, Kent Harold, ed. *Society of Biblical Literature 1984 Seminar Papers*. Chico, Calif.: Scholars Press, 1984.

Rigaux, Béda. *The Testimony of St. Mark*. Chicago: Franciscan Herald, 1966.

Robbins, Vernon K. "The Chreia." In *Greco-Roman Literature and the New Testament: Selected Forms and Genres,* edited by David E. Aune, 1–23. SBLSBS 21. Atlanta: Scholars Press, 1988.

———. *Jesus the Teacher: A Socio-Rhetorical Interpretation of Mark*. Philadelphia: Fortress, 1984.

Robert, A., and A. Feuillet. *Introduction to the New Testament*. Translated by Patrick W. Skehan. New York: Desclée, 1965.

Roberts, Colin H. *Manuscript, Society and Belief in Early Christian Egypt*. The Schweich Lectures of the British Academy, 1977. London: British Academy/Oxford University Press, 1979.

Robinson, James M., and Helmut Koester. *Trajectories through Early Christianity*. Philadelphia: Fortress, 1971.

Robinson, John A. T. *Redating the New Testament*. Philadelphia: Westminster, 1976.

Rolston, Holmes. *Personalities around Paul: Men and Women Who Helped or Hindered the Apostle Paul*. 2d. ed. Richmond, Va.: John Knox, 1955.

Romaniuk, K. "Le Problème des Paulinismes dans l'Évangile de Marc." *NTS* 23 (1977): 266–74.

Russell, E. A. "The Gospel of Mark: Pastoral Response to a Life or Death Situation?" *IBS* 7 (1983): 206–23.

Sacks, Kenneth S. "Rhetorical Approaches to Greek History Writing in the Hellenistic Period." In *Society of Biblical Literature 1984 Seminar Papers,* edited by Kent Harold Richards, 123–33. Chico, Calif.: Scholars Press, 1984.

Sanders, E. P. *Jesus and Judaism.* Philadelphia: Fortress, 1985.

Sanders, E. P., and Margaret Davies. *Studying the Synoptic Gospels.* London and Philadelphia: SCM/Trinity Press International, 1989.

Schadewaldt, Wolfgang. "The Reliability of the Gospel Tradition." In Martin Hengel, *Studies in the Gospel of Mark,* translated by John Bowden, 89–113. Philadelphia: Fortress, 1985.

Schmid, Josef. *The Gospel according to Mark.* RNT. Edited by Alfred Wilkenhauser and Otto Kuss. Staten Island, N.Y.: Alba House/Mercie, 1968.

Schoedel, William R. "The Apostolic Fathers." In *The New Testament and Its Modern Interpreters,* edited by Eldon Jay Epp and George W. MacRae, 457–98. Atlanta: Scholars Press, 1989.

———. *The Apostolic Fathers.* Vol. 5: *Polycarp, Martyrdom of Polycarp, Fragments of Papias.* London: Thomas Nelson & Sons, 1967.

Schultze, Jürgen, and Leonhard Küppers. *Mark.* The Saints in Legend and Art. Recklinghausen: Aurel Bongers, 1966.

Schürer, Emil. *The History of the Jewish People in the Age of Jesus Christ (175 B.C.–A.D. 135).* Vol. 1. Rev. ed. Edited by Geza Vermes, Fergus Millar, Pamela Vermes, and Matthew Black. Edinburgh: T & T Clark, 1973.

Schweitzer, Albert. *The Quest of the Historical Jesus: A Critical Study of Its Progress from Reimarus to Wrede.* Translated by W. Montgomery. New York: Macmillan, 1968.

Schweizer, Eduard. "Concerning the Speeches in Acts." In *Studies in Luke-Acts,* edited by Leander E. Keck and J. Louis Martyn, 208–16. Philadelphia: Fortress, 1980.

———. *The Good News according to Mark.* Translated by Donald H. Madvig. Richmond, Va.: John Knox, 1970.

———. *The Letter to the Colossians: A Commentary.* Translated by Andrew Chester. Minneapolis: Augsburg, 1982.

———. "Scheidungsrecht der jüdischen Frau? Weibliche Jünger Jesu?" *EvT* 42 (1982): 294–300.

Scroggs, Robin. "The Sociological Interpretation of the New Testament: The Present State of Research." *NTS* 26 (1980): 164–79.

Segovia, Fernando F., ed. *Discipleship in the New Testament.* Philadelphia: Fortress, 1985.

Selwyn, E. G. *The First Epistle of St. Peter: The Greek Text with Introduction, Notes, and Essays.* 2d. ed. Thornapple Commentaries. 1946. Reprint. Grand Rapids, Mich.: Baker Book House, 1981.

Setzer, J. S. "A Fresh Look at Jesus' Eschatology and Christology in Mark's Petrine Stratum." *LQ* 24 (1972): 240–53.

Sider, Robert Dick. *Ancient Rhetoric and the Art of Tertullian.* Oxford: Oxford University Press, 1971.

———. "Literary Artifice and the Figure of Paul in the Writings of Tertullian." In *Paul and the Legacies of Paul,* edited by William S. Babcock, 99–120. Dallas: Southern Methodist University Press, 1990.

Siegert, Folker. "Unbeachtete Papiaszitate bei armenischen Schrifstellern." *NTS* 27 (1981): 605–14.

Smith, D. Moody. *John among the Gospels: The Relationship in Twentieth-Century Research.* Minneapolis: Fortress, 1992.

Smith, Jonathan Z. *Drudgery Divine: On the Comparison of Early Christianities and the Religions of Late Antiquity.* Chicago: University of Chicago Press, 1990.

Smith, Morton. *Clement of Alexandria and a Secret Gospel of Mark.* Cambridge, Mass.: Harvard University Press, 1973.

———. "Clement of Alexandria and Secret Mark: The Score at the End of the First Decade." *HTR* 75 (1982): 449–61.

———. *Jesus the Magician.* San Francisco: Harper & Row, 1978.

———. "The Report about Peter in I Clement V.4." *NTS* 7 (1960–61): 86–88.

———. *The Secret Gospel: The Discovery and Interpretation of the Secret Gospel according to Mark.* New York: Harper & Row, 1973.

Smith, Terence V. *Petrine Controversies in Early Christianity: Attitudes towards Peter in Christian Writings of the First Two Centuries.* WUNT 15. Tübingen: Mohr (Siebeck), 1985.

Sparks, H. F. D. "Jerome as Biblical Scholar." In *The Cambridge History of the Bible.* Vol. 1: *From the Beginnings to Jerome,* edited by P. R. Ackroyd and C. F. Evans, 510–41. Cambridge: Cambridge University Press, 1970.

von Spengel, Leonhard, ed. *Rhetores Graeci.* Vol. 2. Leipzig: Teubneri, 1853.

Spicq, C. "La Iᵃ Petri et le témoignage évangélique de saint Pierre." *ST* 20 (1966): 37–61.

Spivey, Robert A., and D. Moody Smith. *Anatomy of the New Testament: A Guide to Its Structure and Meaning.* 4th ed. New York: Macmillan, 1989.

St. Mark and the Coptic Church. Cairo: Coptic Orthodox Patriarchate, 1968.

Sternberg, Meir. *The Poetics of Biblical Narrative: Ideological Literature and the Drama of Reading.* Bloomington: Indiana University Press, 1985.

Stock, Augustine. *The Method and Message of Mark.* Wilmington, Del.: Michael Glazier, 1989.

Streeter, Burnett Hillman. *The Four Gospels: A Study of Origins.* New York: Macmillan, 1925.

———. *The Primitive Church, Studied with Special Reference to the Origins of the Christian Ministry.* New York: Macmillan, 1929.

Strode-Jackson, Myrtle. *Lives and Legends of Apostles and Evangelists.* London: Religious Tract Society, 1928.

Stuhlmacher, Peter, ed. *The Gospel and the Gospels.* Grand Rapids, Mich.: Eerdmans, 1991.

Sundberg, Albert C., Jr. "Canon Muratori: A Fourth-Century List." *HTR* 66 (1973): 1–41.

Swete, Henry Barclay. *The Gospel according to St Mark: The Greek Text with Introduction, Notes, and Indices.* 3d. ed. London: Macmillan, 1927.

Talbert, Charles H. *Literary Patterns, Theological Themes, and the Genre of Luke-Acts.* SBLMS 20. Chico, Calif.: SBL/Scholars Press, 1974.

———, ed. *Perspectives on Luke-Acts.* PRSSS 5. Danville and Edinburgh: Association of Baptist Professors of Religion/T & T Clark, 1978.

Tannehill, Robert C. "Israel in Luke-Acts: A Tragic Story." *JBL* 104 (1985): 69–85.

———. *The Narrative Unity of Luke-Acts.* 2 vols. Philadelphia and Minneapolis: Fortress, 1986, 1990.

Taylor, R. O. P. *The Groundwork of the Gospels, with Some Collected Papers.* Oxford: Basil Blackwell, 1946.

———. "The Ministry of Mark." *ExpTim* 54 (1942–43): 136–38.

Taylor, Vincent. *The Gospel according to St.Mark.* 2d. ed. Thornapple Commentaries. 1946. Reprint. Grand Rapids, Mich.: Baker Book House, 1981.

Telford, William. "Introduction: The Gospel of Mark." In *The Interpretation of Mark,* edited by William Telford, 1–41. IRT 7. Philadelphia and London: Fortress/SPCK, 1985.

———, ed. *The Interpretation of Mark.* IRT 7. Philadelphia and London: Fortress/SPCK, 1985.

Theissen, Gerd. *The Gospels in Context: Social and Political History in the Synoptic Tradition.* Translated by Linda M. Maloney. Minneapolis: Fortress, 1991.

———. *The Miracle Stories of the Early Christian Tradition.* Edited by John Riches. Translated by Francis McDonagh. Philadelphia: Fortress, 1983.

———. *Sociology of Early Palestinian Christianity.* Translated by John Bowden. Philadelphia: Fortress, 1978.

Tolbert, Mary Ann. *Sowing the Gospel: Mark's World in Literary-Historical Perspective.* Minneapolis: Fortress, 1989.

Trocmé, Étienne. "The Beginnings of Christian Historiography and the History of Early Christianity." *AusBR* 31 (1983): 1–13.

———. *The Formation of the Gospel according to Mark.* Translated by Pamela Gaughan. Philadelphia: Westminster, 1975.

Trummer, Peter. "'Mantel und Schriften' (2 Tim 4,13). Zur Interpretation einer persönlichen Notiz in den Pastoralbriefen." *BZ* 18 (1974): 193–207.

———. *Die Paulustradition der Pastoralbriefe.* BBET 8. Frankfurt am Main: Peter Lang, 1978.

Tuckett, Christopher. *Reading the New Testament: Methods of Interpretation.* Philadelphia: Westminster, 1987.

———, ed. *The Messianic Secret.* IRT 1. Philadelphia and London: Fortress/SPCK, 1983.

Turner, C. H. "The Gospel according to St. Mark." In *A New Commentary on Holy Scripture Including the Apocrypha,* edited by Charles Gore, Henry

Leighton Goudge, and Alfred Guillaunu, 3:42–124. New York: Macmillan, 1928.

———. "Marcan Usage: Notes, Critical and Exegetical, on the Second Gospel." *JTS* n.s. 26 (1925): 225–40.

Turner, H. E. W. "Modern Issues in Biblical Studies: The Tradition of Mark's Dependence on Peter." *ExpTim* 71 (1960): 260–63.

Tyson, Joseph B., ed. *Luke-Acts and the Jewish People: Eight Critical Perspectives.* Minneapolis: Augsburg, 1988.

van Unnik, W. C. "Peter, First Letter of." *IDB* 3 (1962): 758–66.

———. "Zur Papias-Notiz über Markus (Eusebius H. E. III 39,15)." *ZNW* 54 (1963): 276–77.

Vallée, Gérard. *A Study in Anti-Gnostic Polemics: Irenaeus, Hippolytus, and Epiphanius.* Studies in Christianity and Judaism 1. Waterloo, Ont.: Canadian Corporation for Studies in Religion/Wilfrid Laurier, 1981.

Via, Dan O., Jr. *The Ethics of Mark's Gospel—In the Middle of Time.* Philadelphia: Fortress, 1985.

Vielhauer, Philipp. "On the 'Paulinism' of Acts." In *Studies in Luke-Acts,* edited by Leander E. Keck and J. Louis Martyn, 33–50. Philadelphia: Fortress, 1980.

Volkmar, Gustav. *Die Religion Jesu.* Leipzig: Brockhaus, 1857.

Votaw, Clyde Weber. *The Gospels and Contemporary Biographies in the Greco-Roman World.* FBBS 27. Philadelphia: Fortress, 1970.

Waetjen, Herman C. *A Reordering of Power: A Socio-Political Reading of Mark's Gospel.* Minneapolis: Fortress, 1989.

Walker, William O., Jr., ed. *The Relationships among the Gospels: An Interdisciplinary Dialogue.* San Antonio, Tex.: Trinity University Press, 1978.

Walls, A. F. "Papias and the Oral Tradition." *VC* 21 (1967): 137–40.

Watson, Duane F., ed. *Persuasive Artistry: Studies in New Testament Rhetoric in Honor of George A. Kennedy.* JSNTSup 50. Sheffield: Sheffield Academic Press, 1991.

Weder, Hans. "Perspektive der Frauen?" *EvT* 43 (1983): 175–78.

Weeden, Theodore J., Sr. *Mark—Traditions in Conflict.* Philadelphia: Fortress, 1971.

Wells, C. B. *Royal Correspondence in the Hellenistic Period: A Study in Greek Epigraphy.* New Haven and Prague: Yale University Press/Kondakov Institute, 1934.

Wenham, David, ed. *Gospel Perspectives: The Jesus Tradition outside the Gospels.* Sheffield: JSOT, 1984.

Werner, Martin. *Der Einfluss paulinischer Theologie im Markusevangelium: eine Studie zur neutestamentlichen Theologie.* BZNW 1. Giessen: Töpelmann, 1923.

Wernle, P. *Die Synoptische Frage.* Freiburg: Mohr, 1899.

White, John L. "Ancient Greek Letters." In *Greco-Roman Literature and the New Testament: Selected Forms and Genres,* edited by David E. Aune, 88–105. SBLSBS 21. Atlanta: Scholars Press, 1988.

————. *Light from Ancient Letters*. FFNT. Philadelphia: Fortress, 1986.

Wicker, Brian. *The Story-Shaped World. Fiction and Metaphysics: Some Variations on a Theme*. London: Athlone, 1975.

Wilde, James Alan. "A Social Description of the Community Reflected in the Gospel of Mark." Ph.D. diss., Drew University, 1974.

Wiles, Maurice. *The Making of Christian Doctrine: A Study in the Principles of Early Doctrinal Development*. Cambridge: Cambridge University Press, 1967.

Wilken, Robert L. "Alexandria: A School for Training in Virtue." In *Schools of Thought in the Christian Tradition*, edited by Patrick Henry, 15–30. Philadelphia: Fortress, 1984.

————. *The Christians as the Romans Saw Them*. New Haven and London: Yale University Press, 1984.

Wills, Lawrence M. "The Depiction of the Jews in Acts." *JBL* 110 (1991): 631–54.

Wilson, S. G. *Luke and the Pastoral Epistles*. London: SPCK, 1979.

Woolf, Virginia. *The Common Reader*. New York: Harcourt, Brace & Company, 1925.

Wrede, William. *The Messianic Secret*. Translated by J. C. G. Greig. Library of Theological Translations. Cambridge and Greenwood, S.C.: James Clarke/Attic, 1971.

Wright, Arthur. "*Taxei* in Papias." *JTS* 14 (1913): 298–300.

Wuellner, Wilhelm. *The Meaning of "Fishers of Men."* NTL. Philadelphia: Westminster, 1967.

Yarbrough, R. W. "The Date of Papias: A Reassessment." *JETS* 26 (1983): 181–91.

Zahn, Theodor. *Introduction to the New Testament*. Vol. 2. Translated by M. W. Jacobus. Edinburgh: T & T Clark, 1909.

Index of Biblical and Ancient Sources

Index of Modern Authors

Index of Subjects

Abraham, 101, 214n4
Achaia, 70n35
Achaicus, 51
Acragas, 116
Acts of the Apostles, 5, 8–10, 13, 25–
44, 55, 58, 98, 116, 117, 152,
179n58, 197, 214, 253
historical questions raised by, 29,
38–39, 41, 43–44, 64–65, 179n58,
202–5
literary characteristics of, 28–30,
34–35, 37–38, 43, 45n9, 45n10,
48n56, 48n62, 64–65, 218n35
provenance of, 27
relationship to the Pastoral
Epistles, 73n63
relationship to the Pauline
Epistles, 73n63, 230
text-critical problems of, 45n11
theology of, 39–44, 48n59, 218n35
traditions underlying, 43–44, 45n9,
64, 218n36
Adamantius, 149–52, 153, 156, 158,
163, 175n34, 185, 187–89, 225
Aeschylus, 54
Africa (North), 226
Africanus, Julius, 179–80n64
Against Celsus (Origen), 222n69
Against Heresies (Irenaeus), 99, 120
Against Marcion (Tertullian), 125
Alexander (in the Gospel of Mark),
243n12
Alexander (in 2 Timothy), 58
Alexandria, 6, 85, 122, 137–49, 154–
56, 157, 158, 159, 160, 171n1,
171n3, 174n20, 174n26, 175n30,

175–76n34, 180n64, 181n87, 188,
190n4, 197, 238, 254, 257
Catechetical School at, 137, 145,
147, 171n4. *See also* Christianity
(early); Mark (Marcus)
Allegorical interpretation, 102, 137
Alogoi, 162, 164
Alulfus, 134n34
Ambrose, 131
Ambrosiaster, 243n11
Ampliatus, 226
Ananias, 48n57
Andrew, 81, 223n75
Andronicus, 226
Anepsios ("cousin"), 18n25, 54–55,
123
Annianus, 157, 160, 166, 168, 169,
181n86
"Anti-Marcionite" Gospel Prologue,
118–20, 121, 123, 124, 133n12,
136
date of, 132n8, 132n9, 133n13, 143,
146, 184–89, 199, 201, 213, 225
Antioch (Pisidian), 34
Antioch (Syrian), 2–3, 6, 9, 28, 29,
32, 34, 35, 37, 41, 47n44, 103n5,
131, 133n17, 149, 160, 175n31,
176n38, 219n41, 222n64, 250n66
Apocalypse, Johannine. *See*
Revelation to John, The
Apollonius of Tyana, 258n15
Apollos, 51, 60, 171n1, 175n30
Apomnēmoneumata
("reminiscences"), 94–96, 253
Apostolic Constitutions, 152–53, 156,
176n41, 185–87, 225

315

322   Index of Subjects

Mark (*continued*)
  associated with John the
    Evangelist, 126, 128–30, 187
  associated with Luke the
    Evangelist, 128–30
  associated with Matthew the
    Evangelist, 128–31, 136, 187, 189
  associated with Paul, 2–4, 9, 13,
    33–43, 47n44, 48n60, 50–60, 65,
    66–67, 68n16, 70n35, 72n63, 93,
    100, 116–17, 132n10, 132n11,
    136, 150–52, 153, 169, 178n51,
    185–88, 202, 209, 210, 217n30,
    256
  associated with Peter, 1–5, 9, 13,
    60–67, 71n50, 83, 87, 88, 89, 92,
    93, 94, 100, 102, 107n39, 107n49,
    112n93, 114, 117, 119—23, 126–
    27, 130, 132n10, 136, 138, 139,
    141–49, 154–55, 159–160, 162–
    64, 165–71, 173n14, 173n19,
    176n43, 177n46, 184–89, 190n6,
    196, 201–206, 209, 210–14,
    216n13, 217n22, 217n24, 219n43,
    224–25, 239–41, 242n4, 253, 256
  associated with the Gospel of
    Mark, 4–7, 11, 14, 90, 100–101,
    103n5, 117, 124–25, 136, 157,
    174n29, 175n30, 185, 189–90,
    197–201
  distinguished from the Gospel of
    Mark, 9–11, 90, 93, 185–86, 200
  historical problems concerning, 14,
    19n36, 21n59, 185, 256
  as John (in Acts), 1–3, 5, 21n60,
    26–44, 63, 65, 66–67, 133n12,
    147–48, 156, 160, 174n28,
    174n29, 178n49, 184, 185, 190n2,
    201–206, 214, 217n24, 219n43,
    256
  legends about the death and burial
    of, 133n18, 169, 175n30
  patristic depictions of, xiii, 11–14,
    77–79, 80, 88–94, 98, 99–102,
    114–31, 136–71, 182n92, 183–89,

    195–97, 210–14, 223n75, 223n76,
    224–41, 251–57
  possible feminine identity of,
    17n18
  rhetorical functions of literary
    references to, 25–26, 50, 52, 53–
    56, 58–59, 61–62, 66
  significance for considerations of
    early Christianity, 13, 15, 21n58,
    66–67, 183–84, 240, 251–57
  traditional assumptions
    concerning, 1–4, 7, 9, 22n62, 62–
    63
Mark, Acts of, 175n30
Mark, The Gospel of, 1, 3, 7, 58, 95,
    96, 97, 99, 100, 108n54, 174n20
  in association with Alexandria,
    154–56, 238
  in association with Gentiles. *See*
    Gentiles
  in association with Judaism. *See*
    Judaism
  in association with Rome, *See*
    Rome
  authorship of. *See* Mark (Marcus)
  in comparison to other Gospels, 2,
    5–6, 101–02, 112n90, 124,
    177n46, 213–14, 258n8. *See also
    Secret Gospel of Mark*
  in comparison with Pauline
    traditions, 5–6, 11, 14, 153, 208,
    220–21n55, 221n56, 249n59
  in comparison with Petrine
    traditions, 5–6, 8–9, 11, 14,
    18n27, 21n58, 63, 72n61, 89, 149,
    154–55, 157, 177n46, 178n55,
    206–09, 211–14, 217n27, 218n36,
    218n38, 219n45, 220n53, 220n54,
    222n65, 237–38
  disputed ending of, 16n13, 26–27,
    108n56, 118, 218n34
  historical problems raised by, 5, 8,
    18n22, 22n61, 201–06, 239, 241
  Latinisms in, 245–46n35
  literary characteristics of, 2, 3, 6,
    7, 8, 18n29, 19n40, 108n57, 155–